Volunteers of the Empire

Volunteers of the Empire

War, Identity, and Spanish Imperialism, 1855–1898

Fernando J. Padilla Angulo

BLOOMSBURY ACADEMIC
LONDON • NEW YORK • OXFORD • NEW DELHI • SYDNEY

BLOOMSBURY ACADEMIC
Bloomsbury Publishing Plc
50 Bedford Square, London, WC1B 3DP, UK
1385 Broadway, New York, NY 10018, USA
29 Earlsfort Terrace, Dublin 2, Ireland

BLOOMSBURY, BLOOMSBURY ACADEMIC and the Diana logo
are trademarks of Bloomsbury Publishing Plc

First published in Great Britain 2023
Paperback edition published 2024

Copyright © Fernando J. Padilla Angulo, 2023

Fernando J. Padilla Angulo has asserted his right under the Copyright,
Designs and Patents Act, 1988, to be identified as Author of this work.

For legal purposes the Acknowledgments on p. x constitute an
extension of this copyright page.

Cover image © Zappers' Squad of the Volunteers Battalion of Gibara, 1895–1898,
Spanish National Library, sig. 17-174-35.

All rights reserved. No part of this publication may be reproduced or transmitted
in any form or by any means, electronic or mechanical, including photocopying,
recording, or any information storage or retrieval system, without
prior permission in writing from the publishers.

Bloomsbury Publishing Plc does not have any control over, or responsibility for,
any third-party websites referred to or in this book. All internet addresses given
in this book were correct at the time of going to press. The author and publisher
regret any inconvenience caused if addresses have changed or sites have ceased
to exist, but can accept no responsibility for any such changes.

A catalogue record for this book is available from the British Library.

A catalog record for this book is available from the Library of Congress.

ISBN:	HB:	978-1-3502-8120-2
	PB:	978-1-3502-8123-3
	ePDF:	978-1-3502-8121-9
	eBook:	978-1-3502-8122-6

Typeset by Integra Software Services Pvt. Ltd.

To find out more about our authors and books visit www.bloomsbury.com
and sign up for our newsletters.

Contents

List of Plates		vi
Preface		viii
Acknowledgments		x
Author's Note		xi
1	Crossroads of Empires in the Antilles	1
2	A Reaction against Annexation	15
3	Saved by the Empire: Morocco, Santo Domingo, and Puerto Rico	29
4	Against the Revolution (1868–78)	43
5	Fighting the Revolution across the Atlantic	87
6	The Volunteers and the Reconstruction of Cuba	97
7	The Volunteers and the Emergence of Party Politics	107
8	The Volunteers and the Military Challenges of Peace	123
9	The Volunteers' Last Stand (1895–8)	143
10	The Volunteers in the Philippines	191
11	Dismantling the Volunteers	203
12	After the War	207
Sources Consulted		215
Index		239

Plates

Plate 1   Havana Volunteers. *La Ilustración de Madrid*, May 27, 1870, p. 8
Plate 2   Havana Volunteers. *La Ilustración de Madrid*, May 27, 1870, p. 9
Plate 3   Julián de Zulueta, one of Cuba's biggest landowners and slaveholders, as colonel of the 2nd Volunteer Battalion of Havana. José Joaquín Ribó, *Historia de los Voluntarios Cubanos*, vol. I, 1872, p. 622
Plate 4   Captain José Gener Batet, owner of the cigar brand "La Escepción", one of the responsibles of the murder of the eight medicine students on November 27, 1871. El Moro Muza, July 31, 1870, p. 1
Plate 5   Castillo de la Real Fuerza, in Havana, former seat of Cuba's Volunteer Subinspector General's Office. Taken by the author in 2015
Plate 6   Monument to the eight medicine students murdered on November 27, 1871, Havana, unveiled in 1890. Taken by the author in 2015
Plate 7   Officers of the 3rd Company, 1st Volunteer Battalion of Cárdenas (Matanzas), 1895. National Library of Spain, Sig. 17-174-62
Plate 8   Cuban Volunteers who fought on April 23, 1896 against a party of 400 rebels in Socarrás. Published by the magazine La Caricatura, Havana, on July 9, 1896. Spain, Ministry of Defence, AGMM, Iconography, Sig. F-05939
Plate 9   Patriotic Flag of the Volunteers Battalion of Holguín (Oriente). Museum of the City. Palace of the Captains Generals, Havana. Taken by the author in 2015
Plate 10 Volunteers of Dimas changing the guard at the Tejar Fort. Published by *La Caricatura*, Havana, on July 30, 1896. Signed by José Gómez de la Carrera on July 18, 1896. Spain, Ministry of Defence, AGMM, Iconography, Sig. F-05953
Plate 11 Staff of the Volunteer Battalion of Puerto Rico No. 1. Ángel Rivero Méndez, *Crónica de la Guerra Hispanoamericana en Puerto Rico*, 1922, p. 449

Plate 12 3rd Company, Loyal Volunteers' Battalion of Manila, taken by G. Sternberg, 1896. Spain, Ministry of Defence, AGMM, Iconography, Sig. F-09200

Plate 13 Officers of the Loyal Volunteers' Battalion of Manila taken by G. Sternberg, 1896. Spain, Ministry of Defence, AGMM, Iconography, Sig. F-09196

Plate 14 A Group of Macabebe Volunteers arriving to the port of Barcelona aboard the steamship *Alicante* on June 8, 1900. *La Ilustración Artística*, June 18, 1900, p. 402

Preface

This is the story of the men who volunteered in defense of the Spanish Empire over the second half of the nineteenth century. During the last decades of that century, thousands of civilians from metropolitan Spain and her territories of the overseas stepped up to join a militia which would become the single most important armed wing of Spanish Loyalism and the main auxiliary force to the regular army in Cuba, Puerto Rico, Santo Domingo, and the Philippines: the Volunteers. First created in Cuba in 1855 at a time when an invasion launched from the United States was a major threat, soon the Volunteers established a pattern which was replicated in territories where Spanish rule had to be imposed, such as Santo Domingo during the 1860s, but also defended, like in Puerto Rico and the Philippines.

For over forty years, essentially men of Spanish ancestry born either in the metropolitan territory—the *peninsulares*—or in the Antilles—the creoles—but also men of African descent and natives of the Philippines gathered under the old banner of Castile to take the last stands of a centuries-old dying empire in the Caribbean and the South China Sea. The role of the Volunteers to keep Cuba Spanish during the island's first war of independence in 1868–78 was essential. In Puerto Rico, they embodied the staunchest Spanish loyalism against any revolutionary attempt after 1868. In the aftermath of war, the Volunteers had a hard time trying to find their place in Spain's colonial policy in the Antilles. And yet, the Volunteers came to the fight's forefront during the last years of the nineteenth century, when Spain was at war against anticolonial nationalists and their allies, the soldiers and sailors of the United States in Cuba, Puerto Rico, and the Philippines. It ended badly for Spain, which lost all its overseas territories, known as *Ultramar*, reminder of its glorious old past, in 1898 at a time when other European powers were expanding their empires. The defeat was known in Spain and still is as the '98 Disaster, and popular memory remembers it as a disastrous war in which thousands of poor young men who could not afford to pay the economic exemption from the military service died out of tropical diseases rather than from enemy bullets in the jungles of Cuba and the Philippines. However, little is remembered about the Volunteers, part-time militiamen who were recruited locally and made up around a third of all the Spanish forces fighting in the Antilles and the Philippines during the wars for independence.

From sugar barons to humble peasants, from tobacco factory owners to cigar makers, from business tycoons to shopkeepers, from railway owners to coachmen, thousands of men donned the Volunteers' uniform in defense of the Spanish sovereignty in far-flung territories during the second half of the nineteenth century. Theirs was the story of the Spanish *Ultramar* during a tragically eventful period in the history of the Antilles, the Philippines, and Spain itself. World-renowned producers of Cuban rum and cigars, railway developers and sugar barons in Puerto Rico, business tycoons in the Philippines, and Spanish thinkers who would later end their lives violently during the Civil War were counted among their members. But most especially thousands of young men who left their place behind the counter or the cigar factory bench after their work shift to take up a rifle and perform unpaid military duties in the many forts, prisons, and military hospitals scattered throughout the main cities of Spain's *Ultramar*. In the fields, hardworking peasants switched the plow for the rifle and the machete to defend their town and land plot from harassing revolutionary armies and bandits. Service could be boring and monotonous during peacetime, but during wartime the Volunteers gallantly served side by side with the regular army, especially in the countryside, away from the relative safety of cities like Havana, San Juan, or Manila.

Galvanized by a staunch defense of Spanish sovereignty in far-flung territories, the fiery patriotism of the Volunteers served well during the wars but could also degenerate into hatred and gratuitous violence against groups of people they perceived as enemies of Spain. Poorly educated hardworking young men could easily fell prey to bigotry and inflammatory speeches against anyone perceived as a foe of Spain. The Havana of the late 1860s and early 1870s was a good witness of this, as we will see. The execution of eight innocent university students at the hands of a group of fanaticized militiamen in Havana in 1871 has been ever since regarded by many as the landmark in the Volunteers' history and the epitome of Spanish colonial rule. And yet, the history of the Volunteers reveals a much more complex past, which impels us to reconsider the nature of the struggle for independence in the Spanish colonies, especially in Cuba.

Written only twelve years after the end of the last war for independence (1895–8), when the country was still licking its wounds, in 1910 a local journalist wrote a piece in Havana's *Diario de la Marina*, the most widely read newspaper in Cuba back then, that Spaniards alone were not to blame for the atrocities that might have been committed before 1898. After all, he honestly recalled, after thirty years of struggling for independence, by the time the war started, half the Volunteers and two-thirds of the Guerrillas—another militia—were Cubans.[1] Something very similar can be said about Puerto Rico's Volunteers, while many natives of the Philippines joined Volunteers units during its war for independence. In line with what a Cuban journalist wrote over a century ago, this book reveals that anticolonial wars in the Spanish Empire during the second half of the nineteenth century were essentially civil wars, during which the Volunteers played an essential role.

In Spain, the history of these men remains essentially forgotten. In Puerto Rico, the events around 1898 are basically understood as the brief war which caused the change of colonial ruler. In Cuba and the Philippines, their wars for independence are essentially remembered and celebrated as fights for freedom in which the people summoned under the flag of freedom against the old Spanish colonial yoke, often concealing the fact that thousands of Cubans and Filipinos stood loyal to Spain and fought against the very independence ideal in the Volunteer units. In Spain as well as in the territories lost in 1898, the history of the Volunteers remains largely untold and forgotten. This book aims at telling their story.

---

[1] The journalist was Mariano Aramburu. *Diario de la Marina*, 26-03-1910, p. 2.

Acknowledgments

Writing this book has been a long personal journey of which you, the reader, see the final result. I thank you for your interest in reading this history. I hope you like it and find it interesting. For me, working on this story has been an adventure during which I have been fortunate enough to count on the help of many people.

First of all, I am thankful to my parents. Without their endless love and support nothing of this would have been possible. And to my sister, who inspired me to follow her steps and venture into the fascinating experience of making a PhD. I am hugely indebted to Andrea, for the sincere love, endless generosity, and immense patience I undeservedly receive from her. I am also thankful to my uncle and friend Miguel, for his generosity, for the many chess games, and for the long cigar and pipe smokes. I can't forget to thank my friends Jorge (we miss you), Rosa María, and Osvaldo, examples of kindness and dignity. Also, I must mention Ana Margarita and Jorge, for becoming my family in Havana.

This book has a life of its own, but it is the offspring of the doctoral thesis I defended in 2018. I owe much of this success to my supervisors Paco Romero, Matthew Brown, and Kristofer Allerfeldt. As well, I am hugely indebted to my editor at Bloomsbury, Maddie Holder, who has believed in this project from the very beginning, and to Abigail Lane and Megan Harris, for their valuable assistance. I would also like to thank the manuscript reviewers, who have definitely contributed to make it a better book.

I would also like to thank Gerardo Arriaga, Bárbara Castillo, Aggelis Zarokostas, Joan-Xavier Quintana, Alessandro Bonvini, and Alberto Martí for the many enriching conversations, but above all for honoring me with their friendship. I am also thankful to Francisco Javier Navarro, Matthew Ehrlich, Luis Sorando, and Fernando Camareno for providing me with some insightful data.

I'd like to acknowledge the useful assistance of the staff of the many archives and libraries I have visited, but I would like to specially mention Captain Pacheco of the Military General Archive in Madrid. His generosity is rarely seen.

Last but not least, to the descendants of Volunteers who have generously shared stories, letters, and pictures with me. In this regard, I would like to especially mention my friends Osvaldo Betancourt, Lindy Usera, Lluís Riudor, and Antonio Moreno.

To me memory of their forefathers and their colleagues, who fought, lost, and have been much forgotten. Perhaps this book will humbly help to retrieve some of their fascinating stories.

Author's Note

Language considerations have been taken into account in order to make the text friendlier to the English-speaking reader. Concepts have been adapted. For instance, the head of the Spanish Government was known as president of the Council of Ministers during the nineteenth century and a good deal of the twentieth. Here, instead, we are using *prime minister* or simply *premier*. Similarly, the Ministry of the Overseas, which dealt with the administration of Cuba, Puerto Rico, and the Philippines between 1863 and 1899, has been renamed here as Ministry of the Colonies.

As to place names, the versions used in the nineteenth century are preferred to the current ones, in order to avoid an unnecessary anachronism. Thus, Puerto Príncipe is used instead of Camagüey, and Fernando Poo instead of Bioko, for instance. For the same reasons, when referring to the original inhabitants of the Maghrib, Berber is used instead of Amazigh, which may sound anachronistic in a nineteenth-century history. More importantly, Berber is still used without negative connotations by many Berbers, or Imazighen, themselves.

When it comes to namesakes, we have opted for the version which appears in original documents with the exception of monarchs, which have been translated into English. Hence, *Fernando VII* and *Isabel II* appear as Ferdinand VII and Isabella II, among others.

1

Crossroads of Empires in the Antilles

The use of armed civilians in auxiliary forces in support of the regular army has been a common practice in European warfare for centuries. In the Middle Ages, the king, noblemen, or towns of the Crown of Castile could raise *mesnadas* to temporarily fight during the Reconquista against the Moors or neighboring Christian kingdoms. During the sixteenth and seventeenth centuries, a series of local militias were used to keep peace in the Iberian Peninsula while the Tercios' professional soldiers and the navy coped with the many global military needs of the Habsburg's Spanish Monarchy in Europe, America, Africa, and Asia. As Spanish power declined in Europe, reaching a bottom line with the War of the Spanish Succession, the militias entered a state of nearly dereliction until 1734, during the reign of Philip V of the House of Bourbon, when a Royal Decree created the Provincial Militias. These were to become the backbone of the military institution in Spain, with the French-inspired regiment as the basic unit and a recruit system which combined volunteering and conscription whenever forcible service was necessary to fill the ranks. The basic aim was to provide security to the homeland with the Provincial Militias while the regular army was used to rebuild Spanish power in Europe and to keep the vast imperial dominions under control.[1]

A very similar system of militias combining volunteers and conscripts was established in Spanish America after 1762, the annus horribilis during which the British occupied for one year Havana and Manila in the context of the Seven Years' War. Paying for a regular army to protect the vast Spanish territories in the Americas from the many contenders that coveted them—British, French, Dutch, Portuguese—would have been simply unbearable to the beleaguered treasury of the Bourbons. Instead, a system of so-called *Milicias Disciplinadas* (Disciplined Militias) was first created in Cuba in 1763 and later expanded to the continent, from the viceroyalty of the New Spain to the River Plate.[2] The aim was that America should provide men and money for its defense. Their members received a stipend and depended on volunteering but

---

[1] Fernando Puell de la Villa. *Historia del Ejército en España*. Madrid: Alianza Editorial, 2017 (1st ed. 2000) pp. 35–47.
[2] Juan Marchena Fernández. *Ejército y milicias en el mundo colonial americano*. Madrid: Editorial MAPFRE, 1992, pp. 190–210; Allan J. Kuethe. "Las Milicias Disciplinadas en América," in Allan J. Kuethe & Juan Marchena Fernández (eds.). *Soldados del Rey: el ejército borbónico en América colonial en vísperas de la independencia*. Castellón de La Plana: Publicacions de la Universitat Jaume I, 2005, pp. 101–26.

resorted to compulsory recruiting when the ranks were not filled. This made them a bit unpopular in some areas but represented a huge leverage power for local American elites. These Disciplined Militias also provided a mechanism of power and social promotion to "American Spaniards," the creoles, at a time when the Bourbon reforms were intensely centralizing power in the Spanish Monarchy and mostly appointing *peninsulares* in key positions, deemed more loyal to the Crown. Essentially staffed by creoles, these militias became the backbone of the defense of Spanish America during the eighteenth and early nineteenth centuries, until many of its units embraced the revolutionary cause during the wars for independence, while others remained loyal to the Crown. Some of their officers, such as Simón Bolívar, José de San Martín, or Bernardo O'Higgins, would become leaders of the independence struggle in Venezuela, Argentina, and Chile.[3] They are just the most conspicuous examples out of many. This instilled a deep distrust among many *peninsulares* in the military and politics toward creoles, even though the Spanish Royalist Army in the Americas was overwhelmingly staffed by natives of the land.[4]

In Europe, the French invasion of Spain in 1808 was to turn the whole edifice of the monarchy upside down, including the army and the main political institutions. The bloody six-year war that ensued needed a new type of combatant for the irregular kind of war the Spanish people were forced to wage. While the Provincial Militias did not disappear, they tended to merge into regular army units, whereas new units of purely volunteer forces began to be established in Spain's main towns. After the Spanish victory at Bailén in July 1808, the French counterattack nearly dismantled the regular army. As the Anglo-Portuguese forces of the Duke of Wellington entered Spain and the regular military was trying to rebuild itself, a November 18, 1808, decree by the patriotic Junta Suprema Central created the *Milicias Honradas* (Honorable Militias) to keep public order in the cities. These were entirely staffed by volunteers who would become part-time law enforcement agents and eventual soldiers. In Cádiz, the bulwark against the French invader where Spanish free institutions had settled by the end of 1808, a sort of parallel army was created. Infantry and artillery units such as the *Voluntarios Tiradores*, the *Artilleros Voluntarios Distinguidos de Línea*, or the *Voluntarios Distinguidos Ligeros de Cazadores*, among others, were raised to keep public order and to contribute to the military efforts to defend the city. Merchants played a crucial role in establishing these forces, for they funded the companies' uniforms and weapons and often staffed the officers' ranks, while many of their employees filled the rank and file.[5]

While these volunteers were not properly military trained and were not famous for abiding to a strict discipline, they were useful as auxiliary forces and were almost costless for the extremely stressed Spanish treasury. Soon the system was implemented in the Americas, where the authorities needed units to keep order in the cities and to

---

[3] Juan José Benavides Martínez. *De milicianos del Rey a soldados mexicanos. Milicias y sociedad en San Luis Potosí (1767–1824)*. Madrid: CSIC, 2014, pp. 361–77.

[4] Julio Albi de la Cuesta. *Banderas olvidadas. El Ejército español en las guerras de Emancipación de América*. Madrid: Desperta Ferro Ediciones, 2019, pp. 21–38.

[5] Helios González de la Flor. *Los Voluntarios de Cádiz (1808–1814)*. Cádiz: Servicio de Publicaciones de la Universidad de Cádiz, 2018, pp. 111–48.

reinforce the defense as many Disciplined Militias had now defected to the cause of independence. In the New Spain, the influential merchants of Mexico City created the Volunteers of Ferdinand VII in the autumn of 1808, while similar units were raised in other major towns of the viceroyalty, and later in Peru, the New Granada, and the River Plate.[6] Their aim was the same as their colleague units in the Peninsula: to provide security in the cities and perform auxiliary duties to the regular army whenever and wherever necessary. Uniforms and weapons were also to be provided by affluent traders, among whom there were many *peninsulares*, who would also be appointed officers while their employees, peasants and other laborers, filled the rank and file.[7] For instance, in Orizaba, a prosperous town in the road between Mexico City and the port of Veracruz, a *Compañía de Patriotas Voluntarios Distinguidos del Sr. D. Fernando VII* was raised in November 1810. Among its 154 members, 115 were employed in the commerce and 33 were laborers, while 77 of them were *peninsulares*, 74 Mexican, and 3 Cuban.[8] The presence of *peninsulares* was disproportionately high considering they only represented a minority in the New Spain, but they controlled a good deal of the commercial flux between both sides of the Atlantic and tended to enjoy a privileged social position in the administration and the economy. They, along with royalist creoles, had much to lose from the end of Spanish rule in the Americas.

Following the Spanish defeat by 1825, sealed by the battle of Ayacucho, these volunteer units were dismantled, but thousands of royalists settled in Cuba and Puerto Rico, taking their ideas and practices with them.[9] The Disciplined Militias continued to exist in both islands, but the defection of many of their colleague units during the wars in the continent made them suspicious at the very least. The idea of creating a new unit with a stronger presence of *peninsulares* was mulled by the authorities. For instance, due to the political crisis triggered by the proclamation of the 1812 Spanish Constitution in Santiago de Cuba by the local governor in 1836, Captain General Miguel Tacón (1834–8) began to recruit a militia of 1,500 men from among the most loyalist elements of Havana's commercial elite: the *Batallón de Voluntarios Distinguidos del Comercio*. Among them, a young Julián de Zulueta, who would become one of Cuba's richest men. Unlike volunteer units in Spanish America during the wars for independence, creoles were entirely excluded from this militia, probably stemming from the ingrained and open distrust of Tacón toward them. Subverting the traditional autonomy enjoyed by the Cuban elite in relation to affairs in the island, Tacón appointed *peninsulares* in key positions and excluded creoles from his closest circle of advisers and associates. This was one of the reasons parts of the Cuban elite played with the idea of joining the American Union in the following years, and this was

---

[6] J. F. Heredia. *Memorias del regente Heredia (de las Reales Audiencias de Caracas y México)*. Madrid: Editorial América, 1916, p. 282; Andrés García Camba. *Memorias del general García Camba para la historia de las armas españolas en el Perú, 1809–1821*. Madrid: Editorial América, 1916, p. 479.

[7] Jesús Ruiz de Gordejuela Urquijo. "Los Voluntarios de Fernando VII de Ciudad de México. ¿Baluarte de la capital y confianza del reino?." *Revista de Indias*, 2014, vol. LXXIV, No. 262, pp. 751–82.

[8] AGN, Operaciones de Guerra, vol. 879, exp. 11, fs. 34–41.

[9] Pérez, Jr. *Cuba. Between Reform & Revolution*. Oxford and New York: Oxford University Press, 1995 (first published in 1988), pp. 95–6.

something De la Concha was willing to redress. In this line, the Volunteers represented a new institution to engage anew the "Spaniards of both hemispheres," creoles as well as *peninsulares*, in the defense of the island. This new militia was only organized on paper, for it was given neither weapons nor uniforms as it was dissolved by mid-1837 as the situation in Santiago de Cuba was rapidly controlled.[10]

During the central decades of the nineteenth century, the Spanish Antilles were at the center of an empires' crossroads. Spain, which had lost its vast continental empire in the Americas in the 1820s, clung to Cuba and Puerto Rico as firmly as the United States coveted them. Possessing both islands, but especially Cuba, was a source of prestige, of financial revenue due to the sugar boom, and of a geopolitical advantage due to their strategic position as the keys to the Caribbean Sea. Which nation, Spain or the United States, was to possess Cuba was the very issue that dominated Spanish Antillean politics during the nineteenth century. Yet other phenomena were reshaping the destinies of Cuba.

Between the 1820s and the 1860s metropolitan Spain was determined to make Cuba even more Spanish, especially regarding its population, political system, and economic structures. This process had already begun because of the wars for independence which took place after the 1810s from New Spain to the River Plate, which made Cuba, alongside Puerto Rico, a haven for thousands of Spanish American royalists, but the scale of the changes which occurred during the central decades of the century was unparalleled in the island's history. The power of the Cuban elite of old Spanish families long established in the island which had emerged on slave work and sugar profit since the economic boom of the late eighteenth century and mid-nineteenth century began to be challenged by a thriving elite of *peninsulares* which intermarried with old and prestigious Cuban lineages that had not taken part in the sugar boom. Beyond the highest echelons of society, the arrival of thousands of migrants from Galicia, Asturias, Catalonia, and the Canary Islands rapidly and intensely altered the human landscape of human cities and even the countryside, taking jobs that had traditionally employed free Cubans of African descent.[11]

The making of a true Cuban sugar aristocracy was built on the collapse of the elite of Saint-Domingue after the Haitian Revolution (1791–1804), during which the enslaved Africans massacred and expelled their former rulers from the French colony.[12] Hundreds of families from Saint-Domingue settled in Cuba with their slaves and know-how, making the Spanish island the world's main sugar producer.[13] The Haitian Revolution was opportunity for Cuba but also an admonition of the dangers

---

[10] Nicomedes Pastor Díaz & Francisco de Cárdenas. *Galería de españoles célebres contemporáneos, ó biografías y retratos de todos los personajes distinguidos de nuestros días en las ciencias, en la política, en las armas, en las letras y en las artes*, vol. III. Madrid: Boix, Editor, 1843, p. 44.

[11] Manuel Moreno Fraginals. *Cuba/España, España/Cuba. Historia común*. Barcelona: Crítica, 1995, pp. 220–31; Pérez, Jr. *Cuba. Between Reform & Revolution*, pp. 70–103.

[12] Julio Le Riverend. *Historia económica de Cuba*. Barcelona: Ariel, 1972, pp. 147–57; Manuel Moreno Fraginals. *El ingenio. Complejo económico social cubano del azúcar*. Barcelona: Crítica, 2001 (first published in Havana, Editorial de Ciencias Sociales, 1964, 3 vols.), pp. 27–86; *Cuba/España*, pp. 145–56.

[13] Manuel Barcia. "'Un coloso sobre la arena': definiendo el camino hacia la plantación esclavista en Cuba, 1792–1825." *Revista de Indias*, 2011, vol. LXXI, No. 251, pp. 53–76.

associated with slavery and the dangers of a big and potentially rebellious enslaved population.[14] Yet Spanish rule could potentially cope with both issues. Spain allowed the slave trade even after legally abolishing it in 1820 due to British mounting pressure, provided the military presence to keep the enslaved population under control, and ended its monopoly on the Cuban economy in 1818, allowing a flourishing trade with the United States, Cuba's nearest and biggest market.[15] This reinforced a strong sense of loyalty of the Cuban elite toward the Spanish Crown, which spared the island from the hardships of the wars for independence that swept over Spanish America during the first quarter of the century.[16]

The establishment of the liberal regime in Spain after the 1830s, with its more centralized power structure and a generalized distrust toward creoles among the metropolitan ruling elite, was to alter the power equilibrium in Cuba. A new elite of merchants, mostly *peninsulares* and allied with old powerful Cuban families that had not benefited from the sugar boom and with royalists refugees from continental Spanish America, succeeded the landowning sugar barons as the true rulers of Cuba.[17] Their commitment to the cause of national integrity between metropolitan Spain and the Spanish overseas territories earned them the label of *integristas*, which was later applied to any staunch supporter of Spanish national unity, either peninsular or creole.

The position of the *integristas* was strengthened by the continuous influx of migrants from metropolitan Spain to Cuba, which mostly settled in the cities and found employment in the commercial sector, but also in a series of relatively skilled jobs such as coachman, stevedore, bricklayer, and cigar maker, which had traditionally employed free blacks and mulattoes. Thus, in a matter of decades, the labor force of places like Havana, Matanzas, or Santiago de Cuba became dominated by *peninsulares*, and hence more Spanish.[18]

---

[14] Ada Ferrer. "Noticias de Haití en Cuba." *Revista de Indias*, 2003, vol. LXIII, No. 229, pp. 675–94; *Freedom's Mirror. Cuba and Haiti in the Age of Revolution*. Cambridge: Cambridge University Press, 2014, pp. 189–235; Carrie Gibson. "'There is no doubt that we are under threat by the Negroes of Santo Domingo': The Spectre of Haiti in the Spanish Caribbean in the 1820s," in Matthew Brown & Gabriel Paquette (eds.). *Connections after Colonialism. Europe and Latin America in the 1820s*. Tuscaloosa: The University of Alabama Press, 2013, pp. 223–35.

[15] Christopher Schmidt-Nowara. "Bartolomé de las Casas and the Slave Trade to Cuba circa 1820s," in Brown & Paquette. *Connections after Colonialism*, pp. 236–49. For the activities of the illegal slave trade merchants see Martín Rodrigo y Alharilla. "Spanish Merchants and the Slave Trade: From Legality to Illegality, 1814–1870," in Josep M. Fradera & Christopher Schmidt-Nowara (eds.). *Slavery and Antislavery in Spain's Atlantic Empire*. New York and Oxford: Berghahn, 2013, pp. 176–99.

[16] Hugh Thomas. *Cuba. La lucha por la libertad*. Barcelona: Debolsillo, 2011 (first published as *Cuba. The Pursuit of Freedom*. London: Pan Macmillan, 1971), pp. 93–110.

[17] Ángel Bahamonde & José G. Cayuela. *Hacer las Américas. Las elites coloniales en el siglo XIX*. Madrid: Alianza Editorial, 1992, pp. 15–52; Martín Rodrigo y Alharilla. "Hacendados versus comerciantes. Negocios y práctica política en el integrismo cubano," in Francisco Morales Padrón (coord.). *III Coloquio de Historia Canario-Americana; VIII Congreso Internacional de Historia de América (AEA v*. Las Palmas de Gran Canaria: Cabildo de Gran Canaria, 2000, pp. 647–63.

[18] Joan Casanovas. *Bread, or Bullets! Urban Labor and Spanish Colonialism in Cuba, 1858-1898*. Pittsburgh: University of Pittsburgh Press, 1998, pp. 15–42; Rosario Márquez Macías. "La Habana en el siglo XIX. Una visión a través de la emigración." *Ubi Sunt? Revista de Historia*, 2008, No. 23, pp. 13–21.

By the second third of the century, the *peninsulares* dominated the trading sector in Cuba. They distributed the Cuban exports and controlled the imports. More importantly, since Cuba lacked a modern banking system, big traders often became moneylenders for sugar mill owners who wished to buy more land, enslaved workforce, or new machinery, and who often happened to be Cuban. The abusive interest rates and the high costs of modernizing and increasing sugar production often ended up in the sugar mills being seized by these merchants, becoming sugar barons in their turn. The often-humble social background of these self-made men was soon forgotten through marriage within Cuban families who owned land, prestige, and political influence.

This was the case, for instance, of Julián Zulueta y Amondo, the biggest slaveowner and sugar producer of mid-nineteenth-century Cuba. A native of the Basque province of Álava, Zulueta settled in Cuba in 1832 at the age of 18 to work for his uncle, amassing a fortune by inheriting his uncle's business, through illegal slave trade and a staunch commitment to the cause of Spanish unity. He joined several militias during the 1830s, being appointed colonel of a Havana Volunteer battalion in 1866. He was mayor of Havana between 1864 and 1876 and was bestowed Marquis of Álava in 1875 due to his services to Spain.[19] Another significant example was José Eugenio Moré de la Bastida, a royalist who arrived in Cuba as a refugee in 1820 fleeing from his native New Granada, present-day Colombia. He settled with his family after being expelled by the revolutionary government following the independence of his native land. Starting as a hardware owner, Moré developed an impressive career as merchant, sugar mill owner, and railway developer. A long-standing officer of several Volunteer battalions in Havana, the Crown bestowed him Count of Casa Moré in 1879, and was appointed president of the Cuban landowners' association, the *Círculo de Hacendados*, and leader of the main *integrista* political party, the Constitutional Union, until his death in 1890.[20]

The ascendancy of the *integrista* elite into being Cuba's dominant group became even more evident during the term as the island's governor of Miguel Tacón. Politically considered a liberal, Tacón was a peninsular soldier who had fought long years in New Granada and Venezuela during the war for independence, growing a profound distrust toward creoles. Contrary to the governors of Cuba who preceded him, Tacón had no interest in keeping the delicate equilibrium between the Crown and the local elite. Instead, he explicitly excluded the sugar Cuban elite from spheres of influence, relying instead on a group of *integristas* who were mostly *peninsulares*.[21] The establishment of a liberal regime in Spain after 1834 only exacerbated this marginalization of the local

---

[19] AGMS, leg. Z-267; AS, ES.28079.HIS-0009-09.
[20] Villa. *Álbum biográfico*, pp. 14–18; *Gaceta de Madrid*, No. 105, 15-04-1879; *La Ilustración española y americana*, 15-11-1890, p. 291; AHN, Ultramar, 4740, exp. 67; Leida Fernández Prieto. *Espacio de poder, ciencia y cultura en Cuba: el Círculo de Hacendados, 1878–1917*. Madrid: CSIC/Universidad de Sevilla/Diputación de Sevilla, 2008, p. 54; Ángel Bahamonde & José G. Cayuela. "La creación de nobleza en Cuba durante el siglo XIX." *Historia Social*, Autumn 1991, No. 11, pp. 56–82.
[21] Thomas. *Cuba*, pp. 130–3; María José Vilar. "Un cartagenero para Ultramar: Miguel Tacón y el modelo autoritario de la transición del Antiguo Régimen al liberalismo en Cuba (1834–1838)." *Anales de Historia Contemporánea*, 2000, No. 16, pp. 239–78.

oligarchy. Due to the incompatibility between institutional slavery in the Antilles and a liberal system in metropolitan Spain, where slavery had been abolished in 1811, the new regime decided to exclude Cuba and Puerto Rico from the Spanish laws in force in the metropolitan territory. Since the days of the conquest in early sixteenth century, the political units comprising Spanish America were considered members of the Crown of Castile, not mere colonies. This inclusion was ingrained in Spanish political tradition. Even during the first steps of the liberal regime in Spain during the war against France in 1808-14, the American territories, and even the Philippines, had sent representatives to the parliament gathered in Cádiz and kept having their own voice until 1836. That very year, the elected representatives of Cuba and Puerto Rico were not allowed to take their seat in the Spanish parliament.[22] The new Constitution passed in 1837 declared that both islands should be ruled by "special laws," which nevertheless were never passed. The legal corpus of the Antilles essentially remained the set of laws known as Laws of the Indies, or *Leyes de Indias*, mostly unaltered since the last compilation of 1680. Captains generals, the military title bestowed to the governors of Cuba and Puerto Rico, became he *ultima ratio regis*, especially after they were granted discretionary powers by the Crown in 1825.[23] Thus, Cuba and Puerto Rico, though legally members of the Spanish Nation, even though their free inhabitants were legally Spaniards, were rather ruled as mere colonies.

Yet this exclusion might even have been taken as an advantage by the elites in Cuba. The *integristas* preferred that captains generals keep their extraordinary powers as a firewall against reforms, whereas the creole reformist sugar aristocracy hoped that this exclusion might open the door to a sort of autonomy and the guarantee that the abolition of slavery in the Peninsula would not apply in the Antilles.[24] The fact is that said "special laws" were not even discussed in Madrid, and the policy of excluding creole sugar barons from spheres of power was continued by Tacón's successors, widening the gap between them and the Crown. Distrust toward creoles also had that *peninsulares* were overrepresented in the island's administration. In 1844, a visitor from the United States considered that "The native of Cuba [...] sees himself almost entirely excluded from all offices under government, the army, and the church, and regards with no favourable eye

---

[22] Josep M. Fradera. *Gobernar colonias*. Barcelona: Ediciones Península, 1999, pp. 71-93; "Include and Rule: The Limits of Colonial Policy, 1810-1837," in Brown & Paquette. *Connections after Colonialism*, pp. 64-86; *La Nación Imperial. Derechos, representación y ciudadanía en los imperios de Gran Bretaña, Francia, España y Estados Unidos (1750-1918)*, vol. I. Barcelona: Edhasa, 2015, pp. 751-848.

[23] M.ª Paz Alonso Romero. *Cuba en la España liberal (1837-1898)*. Madrid: Centro de Estudios Políticos y Constitucionales, 2002, pp. 17-22; Javier Alvarado Planas. *La Administración Colonial española en el siglo XIX*. Madrid: Centro de Estudios Políticos y Constitucionales, 2013, pp. 13-40; Josep M. Fradera. *Colonias para después de un imperio*. Barcelona: Edicions Bellaterra, 2005, pp. 220-52.

[24] José A. Piqueras Arenas. *Sociedad civil y poder en Cuba. Colonia y poscolonia*. Madrid: Siglo XXI de España Editores, 2005, pp. 80-92; José G. Cayuela Fernández. "Los capitanes generales de Cuba: élites coloniales y élites metropolitanas (1823-1898)." *Historia contemporánea*, 1996, No. 13-14, pp. 197-222.

those who are thus sent to mend their fortunes at his expense."[25] To many, it felt as if there was "no place for Cubans in Cuba."[26] And yet, the island remained loyal to Spain.

Cuba had been part of the Spanish world since the early sixteenth century, and its free inhabitants, roughly half of the population, were of Spanish ancestry, but the keystone supporting the entire edifice binding Spain and Cuba was not loyalty, but slavery. Yet its very survival was precarious due to mounting pressure from Britain to abolish it. Since 1820, the transatlantic slave trade, not slavery itself, was illegal in the Spanish Antilles. Following the formal abolition of slavery in the British Empire in 1833, the Royal Navy repressed the illicit slave trade between Africa and the Americas, which could have put the Cuban sugar industry in danger.[27] British consular agents in Havana actively promoted the abolitionist ideal, and purportedly conspired for a general slave revolt in 1843–4.[28] Although the uprising never took place, the fear that Spain might not be able to resist the British abolitionist pressure was real and well grounded. In 1845 the Spanish Parliament passed a law aimed at repressing the illegal slave trade which forced slaveowners to keep an up-to-date census of their human property, thus making enslaved workers illegally imported from Africa very difficult to hide. Despite this, the Spanish authorities in Havana continued to tolerate the arrival of enslaved Africans, thus perpetuating tensions with the British Government.[29]

Being excluded from power, and fearing that slavery might come to its end, the reformist Cuban sugar oligarchy began to look for alternatives that could guarantee both slavery and political participation outside the Spanish Monarchy. The United States, with its contradictory, yet apparently successful, combination of democracy with enslaved laborers, where state elites enjoyed a great leverage power against the federal government, seemed the most obvious model to follow. Being so close to Cuban shores and so important to its economy, the sugar elite hoped to make the American Union not only a business partner but also their political master. Ending Spanish sovereignty in Cuba and annexing the island as a new member of the United States was the way forward.

The Annexationist Momentum

The idea of annexing Cuba into the United States was as a somehow desperate attempt to perpetuate slavery, which had become a "peculiar institution" in retreat, in the words of the South Carolinian political thinker John C. Calhoun. In the Americas, only a few

---

[25] John George F. Wurdermann. *Notes on Cuba*. Boston: James Munroe and Company, 1844, pp. 196-9, quoted in Louis A. Pérez, Jr. (ed.). *Slaves, Sugar, & Colonial Society. Travel accounts of Cuba, 1801–1899*. Wilmington: Scholarly Resources Inc., 1992, p. 228.

[26] Pérez, Jr. *Cuba. Between Reform & Revolution*, p. 98.

[27] David Murray. *Odious Commerce. Britain, Spain and the Abolition of the Slave Trade*. Cambridge: Cambridge University Press, 1980, pp. 72–91.

[28] Michele Reid-Vázquez. *The Year of the Lash. Free People of Color in Cuba and the Nineteenth-Century Atlantic World*. Athens and London: The University of Georgia Press, 2011, pp. 42–67; Murray. *Odious Commerce*, pp. 133–80.

[29] Franklin W. Knight. *Slave Society in Cuba during the Nineteenth Century*. Madison: The University of Wisconsin Press, 1970, pp. 137–53.

countries remained slaveholding bulwarks. Elsewhere in the Caribbean region, slavery had been abolished in the colonies of Britain (1833) and France (1848), as well as in the republics of Colombia (1851) and Venezuela (1854). By the end of the 1850s, slavery in the Americas only existed in the Spanish territories of Cuba and Puerto Rico, Brazil, the Dutch colonies, and the United States.[30]

Though desperate, annexing Cuba to the American Union to keep slavery was a logical move. The United States had been expanding its territory almost since its very inception and certainly the southern states would be more than happy to count with a new slaveholding ally. The American Union incorporated Louisiana from France in 1803, Florida from Spain in 1819, had just conquered the immense northern half of Mexico after the 1846–8 war, and was expanding continuously westward to the Pacific Ocean.[31] As for Cuba, it had always been coveted by the ruling elite in Washington DC due to the island's key position in the Caribbean. In 1809, President Thomas Jefferson famously summed up this interest by stating that Cuba "can gravitate only towards the North American Union which by the same law of nature cannot cast her off its bosom."[32]

Though logical a move, annexing Cuba to the United States to save slavery was also a risky move and a source of major political troubles. The very existence of slavery had proven an unsolvable problem that confronted northern and southern US states throughout the country's process of territorial expansion. Every new land acquisition by the Union opened intense debate about the status of slavery in the new territory. During the 1850s North and South were only able to reach a series of feeble compromises. The dispute over the status of slavery in the newly acquired territories taken from Mexico in 1848 led to the Compromise of 1850, which, among other considerations, stated that the implementation of slavery was to be decided by popular vote in each new territory. The failure of this compromise became evident after the Nebraska-Kansas Act (1854), when pro-slavery and abolitionist settlers engaged in a quasi-civil war within these two territories, known as "Bleeding Kansas" (1854–61). Such a fragile equilibrium proved unsustainable when the southern states began to secede from the Union in December 1860 to protect slavery as a response to the Republican victory in the presidential elections of the month earlier, pushing the North to take up arms to protect the union under the command of the newly elected President Abraham Lincoln. This was the very cause of the American Civil War (1861–5).[33]

---

[30] Jeremy Black. *Slavery. A New Global History*. London: Constable & Robinson, 2011, pp. 192–229.
[31] Ramiro Guerra y Sánchez. *La expansión territorial de los Estados Unidos a expensas de España y de los países hispanoamericanos*. Havana: Editorial Nacional de Cuba, 1935, pp. 182–281; Luis Martínez-Fernández. *Town Between Empires. Economy, Society, and Patterns of Political Thought in the Hispanic Caribbean, 1840–1878*. Athens & London: The University of Georgia Press, 1994, pp. 11–57.
[32] José Ignacio Rodríguez. *Estudio histórico sobre el origen, desenvolvimiento y manifestaciones prácticas de la idea de la anexión de la isla de Cuba á los Estados Unidos de América*. Havana: Imprenta La Propaganda Literaria, 1900, pp. 50–63.
[33] Bruce Catton. *The Civil War*. Boston and New York: Mariner Books, 2004; James M. McPherson. *Battle Cry of Freedom. The American Civil War*. London: Penguin Books/Oxford University Press, 2013, pp. 47–202.

Twenty years before this war, fate was not sealed. Cuban annexationists began to approach the United States in 1847. This very year, a group of sugar barons led by Miguel de Aldama, the wealthy son of a *peninsular*, created the Club de La Habana to provide the annexation movement a coordinating platform. In New York and New Orleans, a Junta Cubana was created to look for allies and funds. The cause of annexing of Cuba was positively received by some sectors both North and South. Southerners considered it an opportunity to strengthen the pro-slavery front against abolitionist North. Northerners saw the annexation of Cuba as chance to make the island a captive market for their industrial products without the heavy Spanish tariffs. The annexationist discourse could potentially find fertile ground in the United States, where the Monroe Doctrine's "America for the Americans" fueled its self-perceived vision as the guarantor of American independence from Old Europe.[34] So fertile was the ground that the Cuban annexationist lobbyists reached President James K. Polk (1845–1849), who offered the Spanish Government to buy Cuba for $100 million on behalf of the Club de La Habana in 1848, which promised the American Treasury to provide the funds beforehand.[35]

Spain firmly refused to sell off part of its national territory which was also its Crown's jewel. A peaceful transaction was clearly not an option the Spaniards would consider. This was a turning point. Although the annexation did enjoy relevant support, the US Government was not willing to embark on a military operation against a nation with which it had peaceful relations, especially when Britain and France were against changing the status quo in the Caribbean. Both London and Paris had many interests in the Caribbean and preferred to keep Cuba under the weak control of Spain than in the powerful hands of the United States.[36]

All the geopolitical considerations seemed not to worry Cuban annexationists, who were determined to launch an expedition against the Spanish sovereignty in the island, even in precarious circumstances. As their efforts to find a suitable US Army officer to lead the expedition were fruitless, the Club de La Habana offered the job to Narciso López, a former general in the Spanish Army openly discontent with the Spanish Government. A native of Venezuela, López fought for Spain against the armies of Simón Bolívar and pursued a military career in the Spanish Army. He sided with the liberals against the advocates of the traditional monarchy during the First Carlist War (1833–40), and in reward he was appointed governor of Trinidad de Cuba in 1840, where he married into a wealthy sugar-producing family known for supporting the

---

[34] Jay Sexton. *Empire and Nation in Nineteenth-Century America*. New York: Hill and Wang, 2011, pp. 85–122. Also see Walter Johnson. *River of Dark Dreams. Slavery and Empire in the Cotton Kingdom*. Cambridge & London: Harvard University Press, 2013; Matthew Karp. *This Vast Southern Empire. Slaveholders at the Helm of American Foreign Policy*. Cambridge & London: Harvard University Press, 2016.

[35] Tom Chaffin. *Fatal Glory. Narciso López and the First Clandestine U.S. War against Cuba*. Charlottesville and London: University Press of Virginia, 1996, pp. 11–15.

[36] Ibid., pp. 44–72.

annexation. Beware of the political leaning of his in-laws, Captain General Leopoldo O'Donnell (1841–6) dismissed López from his office in 1843, turning him into an enemy of Spain's presence in Cuba.[37]

The annexationists had secured funds in the United States and had found a military leader but lacked any substantial popular support in Cuba for such a radical move. Twice, in May 1850 and August 1851, López headed two failed expeditions which garnered no support from Cubans. It made evident that the idea of annexing the island to the United States had barely permeated into the Cuban population beyond the small circle of sugar barons summoned by the Club de La Habana. In fact, there were barely any Cubans in the expeditionary force commanded by Narciso López. Most of his mercenaries were citizens of the United States, as well as German and Hungarian veterans of the 1848 liberal uprisings in Europe.[38] The whole idea of rising an enthusiastic Cuban population in favor of annexing the island into the American Union ending centuries-old ties with Spain was but a pie in the sky. The invasions of 1850 and 1851, however, did spur some sort of popular armed participation, but in support of keeping Cuba Spanish.

The Noble Neighbors

Just as happened in continental America during the 1810s and 1820s, armed civilians were mobilized to defend the old banner of Castile when Narciso López launched his two expeditions in 1850 and 1851. They backfired. Rather than spurring a popular revolt against Spanish rule, the two expeditions triggered the rebirth of a militant loyalism which was to mark a good deal of the island's history. Imitating the attitude of patriots in Cádiz and Mexico City a few decades earlier, the *integrista* elite mobilized resources for the creation of a militia to defend their interests and Spain's rule in Cuba, in opposition to the reformist sugar barons who backed López's attempts.

The idea of creating a militia was incepted as Narciso López's men landed in the town of Cárdenas, 150 km east to Havana, and ransacked it on May 19, 1850. Captain General Federico Roncali ordered that two army battalions be sent from Havana to kick them out.[39] Fearing that the expedition might get hold of some territory, and willing to declare their commitment to the Spanish cause, around 13,000 *integristas* demonstrated before the captain general's palace in Havana asking him permission to create a militia in order to keep the city under control while the two regular battalions fought in Cárdenas.[40] Following the example of what had been done in America and the Peninsula, affluent *integristas* would provide uniforms, weapons, and officers, while their employees and other petty laborers filled the ranks.[41]

---

[37] Herminio Portell Vilá. *Narciso López y su época*, vol. I. Havana: Cultural, 1930, pp. 142–54.
[38] Portell Vilá. *Narciso López y su época*, vol. III, pp. 483–95.
[39] Herminio Portell Vilá. *Historia de Cárdenas (edición del centenario)*. Havana: Talleres Gráficos "Cuba Intelectual," 1928, pp. 97–126.
[40] Jacobo de la Pezuela. *Crónica de las Antillas*. Madrid: Rubio, Grilo y Vitturi, 1871, p. 116.
[41] Portell Vilá. *Narciso López y su época*, vol. II, pp. 390–1.

Thus, in need of men to defend the island, on May 21, 1850, the captain general agreed to officially create the *Milicia Voluntaria de Nobles Vecinos* (Volunteer Militia of Noble Neighbors).[42] Four infantry battalions were raised in Havana. The first battalion was commanded by the Count of Fernandina, a Cuban; the second by the *peninsular* Jacinto Larrínaga; the third by the Cuban Count of San Esteban de Cañongo; and the fourth by Manuel Izquierdo Villavicencio, a *peninsular*.[43] This reversed the policy of excluding creoles from the military and sent a powerful message that all *integristas*, either *peninsulares* or Cuban, were to defend the Spanish cause in the island. The example was followed in other cities. Soon, Trinidad, Matanzas, Puerto Príncipe, and Cienfuegos counted with one battalion each, while Cárdenas raised two companies, and Santiago de Cuba, Manzanillo, and Pinar del Río one each.[44]

The creation of Noble Neighbors units across the island, even in areas where the presence of *peninsulares* was rather scant, implied that part of the Cuban society stood loyal to Spain. Despite this, sticking to his prejudices, Captain General Roncali profoundly distrusted the Cubans. Shortly after the creation of the Noble Neighbors, he wrote to the Ministry of War, in Madrid, asking for permission to create a militia of 30,000 men with which to reinforce the island's defenses, yet made up of "only *peninsulares*, for I do not trust in handing over weapons to the natives."[45] Using the very term "natives," especially in a formal correspondence, was pretty derogatory for Cubans, taking into account that they—except for the enslaved population—were Spanish subjects in equal terms with their fellow countrymen in the Peninsula, at least in theory. Back then, "native" might have been a term used to refer to non-Spanish peoples in the Philippines or the Gulf of Guinea, but not to Spanish subjects, and citizens, of the Antilles. Though Narciso López had found no explicit popular support among Cubans, Roncali probably feared that many of them had supported him silently.

Beyond the disputed loyalty of the Cubans, Roncali also feared the dangers of arming working-class *peninsulares*. The growing importance of the labor organization in Havana, fed by the constant influx of migrants from metropolitan Spain, could have found an influence in the lower ranks of the Noble Neighbors. In case of a clash of interest between the authorities and the workers, the latter could direct their weapons against the former. Thus, despite the threat of a new annexationist attempt against Cuba not having disappeared, the captain general decreed the dissolution of the Noble Neighbors on September 24, 1850.[46]

The fact that the Noble Neighbors was dissolved because of the captain general's distrust rather than of the theoretical likeliness of a new annexationist attempt was confirmed in the summer of 1851. In July, two landowners and officers of the

---

[42] *Gaceta de La Habana*, 21-05-1850, p. 1.
[43] *Diario de la Marina*, 21-05-1850, p. 1.
[44] G., M. & M-C. *Novísimo Reglamento del Instituto de Voluntarios de la Isla de Cuba*, p. VI; Marilú Uralde Cancio. *Voluntarios de Cuba española (1850–1868)*. Havana: Editorial de Ciencias Sociales, 2011, p. 23.
[45] Antonio Pirala. *Anales de la Guerra de Cuba*. Madrid: Felipe González Rojas Editor, 1895, vol. I, p. 78.
[46] *Gaceta de La Habana*, 24-09-1850, p. 1; *La Nación*, 29-10-1850, p. 2.

Disciplined Militias, José Isidoro Armenteros and Joaquín de Agüero, took up arms in two ill-coordinated uprisings in Trinidad and Puerto Príncipe, respectively. This was followed by the landing of Narciso López with 600 mercenaries at Bahía Honda, a town 60 km west to Havana, on 12 August.[47] The annexationists had clearly worked on widening their support network in Cuba, coordinating an uprising within the island and an expedition launched from the United States.

On this occasion, Captain General José Gutiérrez de la Concha Irigoyen (1850–2) called the Noble Neighbors again, for he could only count on a tiny regular army garrison, perhaps not enough to fight a combined uprising by land and sea. The Noble Neighbors played a crucial role in crushing the expedition. The battalion of Pinar del Río collaborated alongside the regular army in defeating the expeditionary force in late August 1851, in what was the first armed action of the Noble Neighbors.[48] This led to the capture of López and some other leaders of the expedition, who were executed in Havana on September 1, 1851.

Unlike his predecessors, Gutiérrez de la Concha, a creole from the River Plate, trusted the Cubans and the participation of civilians in the defense. He had trusted the Noble Neighbors' battalion in Pinar del Río, overwhelmingly staffed by *guajiros*, as Cuban peasants are popularly called, for military operations. On the day before the execution of Narciso López, Gutiérrez de la Concha gave a speech in which he praised the participation of the Noble Neighbors in repelling the expedition, and acknowledging the role played by the *guajiros* of the Pinar del Río battalion.[49] Aware of the convenience of counting with the *integristas*, Gutiérrez de la Concha aimed to make the Noble Neighbours a permanent element of the Spanish defensive system in Cuba within a wider set of military reforms for the island.[50] This went in line with the captain general's aim at alleviating the pressure on the island's treasury. Gutiérrez de la Concha planned to establish a smaller yet better equipped regular army and navy, aided by local militias and public order forces. Consequently, he established the first units of the Civil Guard in Cuba in 1851, the rural police force which had been created in the Peninsula seven years earlier.[51] He also created the *Milicias de Color* (Colored Militias) which would enlist free Cubans of African descent, thus retrieving a long tradition of blacks serving in the Spanish military in the Americas which dated back to the very early days of the conquest. This reversed the banning of blacks in the military which followed the uncovering in 1844 of the conspiracy of "La Escalera," a plot in which thousands of enslaved Africans were allegedly going to stage a Haiti-inspired revolution in Cuba.[52]

---

[47] AHN, Ultramar, 4645, exp. 9; Portell Vilá. *Narciso López y su época*, vol. III, pp. 378–435.
[48] ANRC, Asuntos Políticos, leg. 222, sig. 121.
[49] AHN, Ultramar, exp. 58, *Gaceta Extraordinaria de La Habana*, 31-08-1851, p. 1.
[50] José G. Cayuela Fernández. *Bahía de Ultramar. España y Cuba en el siglo XIX. El control de las relaciones coloniales*. Madrid: Siglo XXI de España Editores, 1993, pp. 139–52.
[51] François Godicheau. "La Guardia Civil en Cuba, del control del territorio a la guerra permanente (1851–1898)." *Nuevo Mundo Mundos Nuevos*, 2014 (online): https://nuevomundo.revues.org/67109.
[52] Herbert Klein. "The Colored Militia of Cuba: 1568–1868." *Caribbean Studies*, 1966, vol. 6, No. 2, pp. 17–27; María del Carmen Barcia Zequeira. "Los batallones de pardos y morenos en Cuba (1600–1868)." *Anales de Desclasificación*, 2004, vol. 1, No. 2, pp. 1–16.

The troubled waters of Spanish politics had Gutiérrez de la Concha called back to the Peninsula in 1852 and replaced in by other governors who were much less willing to compromise with the interests of the *integrista* elite, meaning the slave trade. The ruling Moderate Party, the conservative wing of Spanish liberalism, defended strong powers for the Monarch, restricted political rights, a centralized State, and free trade. The new cabinet which assumed power in 1852 was determined to tighten the restrictions over the illegal trade due to British pressure, and to reinforce the state capacities in order not to depend on the local elite. The new governors, Valentín Cañedo (1852–3) and Juan de la Pezuela (1853–4), not only tried to effectively end the illicit slave trade but also to dissolve the Noble Neighbors, for they deeply distrusted the existence of a militia of armed civilians that were not constrained by military discipline.[53]

Nonetheless, in a context where the annexationist threat still was to be taken into account, the new Spanish authorities finally decided not to decree the dissolution of the Noble Neighbors. Instead, they were left to wither, not allowing for the recruitment of new members, and barely letting them carry out military exercises. The experiences of 1850 and 1851, however, had planted the seeds of a militant *integrismo* which would reappear whenever the situation would be ripe.

---

[53] M. Estorch. *Apuntes para la historia sobre la administración del Marqués de la Pezuela en la isla de Cuba, desde el 3 de diciembre de 1853 hasta 21 de setiembre de 1854.* Madrid: Imprenta de Manuel Galiano, 1856, pp. 20–9; Uralde Cancio. Voluntarios de Cuba española, pp. 34–7.

2

A Reaction against Annexation

On February 6, 1855, the people of Havana were shocked by knowing through the newspapers that Ramón Pintó, a cultural promoter, art critic, and journalist, known to be a friend of Captain General Gutiérrez de la Concha—who had been called back to Havana in September 1854—had been arrested for allegedly conspiring to end Spanish sovereignty with unclear ends, possibly to proclaim an independent republic in Cuba, probably to make it another state of the United States. In any case, it was another attempt against Spain's centuries-old presence in the island, and it represented a serious threat for the importance of some of the people and institutions involved.

Born in Barcelona in 1803, Ramón Pintó had settled in Cuba in 1823, escaping from the purges carried out against liberals by the restored absolutist monarchy of Ferdinand VII. As many other young Spaniards imbued with revolutionary ideals, Pintó joined the National Militia, engaging in combat on several occasions, including the final defeat of the liberals against the Duke of Angoulême's invading army at the battle of Trocadero. After over three decades in Cuba, Pintó enjoyed the liberals' triumph in Spain and developed a successful career in Havana. In 1844, he co-founded the *Diario de la Marina*, Cuba's most widely read newspaper, and established the *Liceo Artístico y Literario*, a hotspot for sectors of a Cuban bourgeoisie which dreamt of gaining more political power and securing their social and economic interest under the aegis of the United States, rather than to Spain, a country from where virtually all of them could trace their roots, but which they saw as decadent and riddled by internecine and endless wars.

Rumors in Havana insisted that the arrest of Pintó may be related to an expedition that was about to be launched in the United States. On February 9, 1855, the *Diario de la Marina* published an article stating that around 2,500 men were waiting in different points of the American South ready to embark for Cuba. The detention of Pintó was a major setback for the purported plan, but he was not alone. New findings on the conspiracy were the most worrying for the Spanish authorities and loyalist population. According to official reports, no less than 1,400 men were prepared to seize key infrastructures of the island following Pintó's orders, who also relied on the financial support of the *Caja de Ahorros*, the island's first savings bank, on which

Cuban planters often relied for financial backing to avoid peninsular money lenders. The very elite which had supported the attempts by Narciso López only four years earlier was apparently testing its luck anew.[1]

Fear in Havana was probably overestimating the real prospects of a full-scale invasion coming from the north of the Straits of Florida, but there were good reasons to be prepared for some intervention. The echoes of the Ostend Manifesto were still heard on both shores of the Straits of Florida. The United States had never concealed its appetite for Cuba as a new market for its products, and as a key point for controlling the Gulf of Mexico. According to the information sent to the governor's palace in Havana by Spanish informants in New Orleans, John A. Quitman was the leader of the military expedition. Twice a brief governor of Mississippi, Quitman was a Southern Democrat committed to the cause of expanding the influence of the United States in the Americas, hand in hand with slavery. He had commanded men in the field as a US Army officer during the war against Mexico a few years earlier and had been involved in at least three attempts at invading Cuba to incorporate it as a new slaveholding state. But it was the very issue of slavery, deeply ingrained in the American heated political debate at that time, the factor which thwarted the expedition. President Franklin Pierce, a Northern Democrat, feared that adding a new slavery state would deepen the widening gap between North and South. Compromise between the two factions seemed more and more difficult over time as the country was still trying to come to terms with the delicate equilibrium set by the recent Compromise of 1850 and the Kansas-Nebraska Act of 1854. Unwilling to risk this weak architecture of agreement, President Pierce ordered Quitman to call the invasion off. Though the link between Pintó and Quitman was never officially proved, it seems rather likely that the two were involved in the same adventure to free Cuba from Spanish rule. With the leader of the uprising in the island in prison, the expedition from US shores had necessarily to be postponed.

Amid this tense situation, on February 12, 1855, Captain General Gutiérrez de la Concha issued a decree at the *Gaceta de La Habana*, the Spanish authorities' bulletin in Cuba, declaring the state of siege all over Cuba, the naval blockade of all its long and intricate coast, and calling for all male Spaniards "of both hemispheres" between the ages of 18 and 50 to step up and form a militia of volunteers in defense of Spain's rights in Cuba. These Volunteers were to be organized in infantry and cavalry units, following the military organization of companies, battalions, and regiments or squadrons, assembling a force ready to fight side by side with the regular army. According to the decree, rapidly circulated across the island through the *Gaceta*, local newspapers, and a dense wire network, Cuba was facing no less than an imminent military invasion by a force that was waiting in the United States for instructions to set sail for Havana.[2]

The threat of rebellion was old and well known for supporters of Spanish sovereignty in Cuba. They had recently served in the Noble Neighbors which so brilliantly had aided to quash the 1851 invasion of Narciso López. Involving civilians

---

[1] Vicenç Bernades. *Ramon Pintó. Una conspiració a la Cuba colonial.* Barcelona: Edicions La Paraula Viva, 1975, pp. 157–69.

[2] *Gaceta de La Habana*, 12-02-1855, p. 1.

in the defense of Cuba was precisely one of the aims of the military reforms Gutiérrez de la Concha wanted to implement. The regular army in Cuba could only count on 16,000 soldiers, of whom just around 7,000 were ready for action, as the rest laid in military hospitals due to tropical diseases, the eternal burden of the Spanish Army in the warm climate of the Antilles. Hence, the involvement of civilians in the defense of the island was more than welcomed; it was necessary. As well, Gutiérrez de la Concha was not willing to risk a second expulsion from America. He was born in 1809 in Córdoba de Tucumán, in the Viceroyalty of the River Plate, to a peninsular officer of the Royalist Army and a creole mother. Following his father's execution at the hands of the revolutionaries in 1810, Gutiérrez de la Concha had to leave his native land at the age of five with his family in 1814 and settle in Spain, where he developed a brilliant military career.[3]

With the will of the captain general and fresh memories of the recent experience against Narciso López, the response to the call to the February 12, 1855 decree creating the Volunteers was massive. The day after its publication, five recruiting stations were established in Havana, one per district: in the City Hall, the Customs House, the Jesuits-run Belen School, the Tacón Theatre, and the police station of Cerro, which comprised some of the most populous quarters of the city around the harbor.

The will to participate in the defense of Spanish sovereignty also united former foes under the same banner. So much so, a delegation of veterans of the First Carlist War (1833–1840), both *carlistas* and liberals, alongside a group of youngsters, offered the Captaincy General to create a corps of mobilized Volunteers who would join the army in the battlefield should the feared invasion land in Cuba. Having been granted permit by the authorities, this group opened its own recruiting station at the *Nobleza Vascongada*, a tavern located in Havana's *Plaza Vieja* that was staffed and frequented by *peninsulares*.[4]

A wide segment of Cuba's population was not considered for the creation of the Volunteers. People of African descent, free or enslaved, were simply not considered for the task. Gutiérrez de la Concha was trying to revive the colored militias that had been disbanded ten years before after "La Escalera" affair in 1844. But regarding the Volunteers, he was not willing to integrate them, for he aimed at creating a militia of purely Spanish elements, in the understanding that this included men from "both hemispheres." By using this formula, first coined by the Constitution of 1812, the captain general implied that only Spanish citizens could join the militia. And this meant that the Volunteers welcomed *peninsulares* as well as creoles. Another sector of Cuban society marginalized itself from the creation of the Volunteers, but for political reasons. Wide sectors of the island's bourgeoisie, including many in the middle class and university students, who still flirted with the idea of joining the United States as a better prospect for Cuba's future, resented the creation of the Volunteers, for this militia represented two things they deeply resented: Spain's rule

---

[3] Olivero, Sandra Fabiana. "José Gutiérrez de la Concha," in *Real Academia de la Historia, Diccionario Biográfico electrónico* (online): https://dbe.rah.es/biografias/108537/jose-gutierrez-de-la-concha).
[4] *Diario de la Marina*, 15-02-1855, p. 1.

and the emergence of *peninsulares* in Cuban life. But not all Cubans thought alike, and some of them felt compelled by the defense of Spanish sovereignty in the island alongside the *peninsulares*.

Soon, the ranks were filled, and in a matter of days, Havana counted with four infantry battalions of Volunteers of six companies each. The call for creating volunteer units was heard across the island. In a matter of weeks, most of Cuba's big towns had formed their own battalion, such as Matanzas, Santa Clara, and Santiago de Cuba. But small towns took part in the movement too. In Vuelta Abajo, in the westernmost tip of the island, home to the finest tobacco fields in the world, several infantry and cavalry volunteer units were raised to protect its rugged coastline, too close to the United States not to consider the still alarming prospect of an invasion. East to Havana, in the vast plains around Matanzas, home to hundreds of sugar mills worked by thousands of enslaved Black people who produced tons of sugar, the backbone of Cuban economy, numerous cavalry squadrons and infantry companies were created, for a slave rebellion was always a possibility to be feared in times of trouble.

The Volunteers became a cross-class militia in which the social hierarchy of Cuba's whites was somehow reflected, and whose motivations for joining it were a mix of patriotism, vested interests, social reputation, and hopes of climbing the social ladder. The men in command were a mix of prominent Cubans and *peninsulares* of proven loyalty to the Crown and many interests to protect. In Havana, José María Morales, a Cuban sugar planter, assumed command of the 1st Battalion; the 2nd was given to Salvador Samá, a Catalan businessman who took part in the slave trade and used the benefits to heavily invest in Havana's Marianao neighboring municipality; the 3rd to the Count of San Esteban de Cañongo, a Cuban aristocrat belonging to a family long involved in serving the Crown as politicians and soldiers; and the 4th to Manuel Ramos Izquierdo, a former councilor of Havana.[5] Outside of Havana, men of similar background took command of the local volunteer units. For instance, in Santa Clara, an affluent Cuban landowner, Pedro Nolasco González-Abreu, created a cavalry squadron, perhaps against the opinion of his young daughter, Marta, who would later became a philanthropist who devoted much of her wealth to the cause of Cuban independence.[6] The message was clear: the many vested interests, shared by *peninsulares* and many Cubans who still identified with the Mother Country, who had found their place in society under Spanish sovereignty, were to be protected through a direct participation in the defense of the island.

Once officers had been appointed, the ranks now had to be filled with men of proven loyalty to Spain and the Crown. Below the leading officers, the ranks of second lieutenant, first lieutenant, and captain were often trusted to middle-class business owners who often run shops or small- to mid-size companies, but in some cases were people who had succeeded in business. Men like José Eugenio Moré, captain of a company in Havana's 1st Battalion. Moré was born in 1807 in Santa Marta, in the viceroyalty of the New Granada, later Colombia, to an affluent family that lost everything due to their loyalty to Spain during the war for independence. After settling

---

[5] Ibid., p. 2.
[6] BNC, CM Abreu, No. 91, 94 & 324.

penniless in Cuba in 1820, Moré started to build its way up as a shopkeeper in Santiago de Cuba, and later became business partner with *peninsulares* in the hardware sector and the sugar industry, which later allowed him to establish a trading company in Sagua la Grande, promote the construction of its first railway, and settle in Havana to hobnob with the island's elite to better promote his many interests. Outside the capital, the connection between trade and the Volunteers was also evident. In the eastern tip of the island, in Santiago de Cuba, a Catalan lingerie shop owner from Sitges, in his early forties, who had arrived a teenager to the city in 1828 and was beginning to experiment with rum production, was appointed officer of the local battalion. He was Facundo Bacardí, who would create the world-famous rum company a few years later.[7]

Almost replicating the social hierarchy of Cuba's whites, often following a company's structure of owner-manager-employee, below the commanding men, there were thousands of commanded men who were the backbone of the Volunteers. In the cities, most of the rank and file was filled by hard working-class *peninsulares*, who were flocking to the island, taking the jobs middle-class Cubans were not willing to take, and displacing free Blacks and mulattos from activities they had dominated up until recently. Mostly coming from regions in northern Spain, most notably Galicia and Asturias, but also from Catalonia and the Canary Islands, these men commonly arrived in Cuba as teenagers, often following relatives and friends who provided them with a job and a place to stay, usually not much better than a pallet in the backroom. They were found behind the shop counters in most cities, but also in tobacco factories, and as coachmen, bakers, barbers, and waitress in the taverns, often displacing people of African descent who had found in these activities a way of living after slavery, and thus saw the newcomers resentfully. These young *peninsulares* were the most thriving community of Havana, willing to fight their way up in a highly hierarchical society, and they were growing fast. By the late 1850s, around 17 percent of Havana's 145,000 inhabitants were *peninsulares*. Among this milieu came most of rank-and-file Volunteers. Men like Saturnino Martínez, an Asturian who settled in the city in 1850 at the age of 13, found a job as *torcedor* (cigar maker) through a friend at the renowned Partagás tobacco factory, and over the years became the leader of the local labor movement, and created the first trade union in Cuban history.

Men from all backgrounds, from the humble *peninsular* migrant to the shop owner and the business tycoon, from the Cuban *guajiro* to the wealthy landowner, soon filled up companies, squadrons, and battalions of Volunteers, who had to be provided with weapons. The Captaincy General ordered that infantry units be armed with a rifle, a bayonet, and a cartridge belt, while cavalrymen were given a sabre, a spear, a carbine, and a pistol or a machete, the long knife commonly used in the tropics. The hurry with which the units were created, and the precarious financial state of Cuba's military budget, often implied that Volunteer commanding officers had to afford the purchase of weapons for their men. For instance, the major of the local cavalry squadron of Guamutas, a town located in the sugar heartland around Matanzas, was granted permit by the captain general to purchase fifty Sharp carbines from the United States,

---

[7] AGMS, leg. B-585, exp. 30.

the potential enemy of Spain for Cuba, but also home to some of the finest firearms of the day which were conquering the Wild West. Due to its proximity, weapons could arrive from the United States much faster than they would from Spain, and quickness was important for men who were trying to create a militia in an area like Guamutas, surrounded by thousands of enslaved people prone to rebel in case of turmoil.

Buying weapons from factories in the Peninsula meant much longer delivery times. Only crossing the Atlantic took two weeks. But Volunteers in cities like Havana or Cienfuegos, relatively far from the countryside and the prospects of a slave revolt, could allow themselves to wait for longer and usually purchased weapons in the Mother Country. For instance, a company captain in Havana bought 150 rifles from the renowned arms factory of Placencia de las Armas, in Guipúzcoa, which had been making weapons since the sixteenth century with good Basque iron.[8] Similarly, buying uniforms for the rank and file was also paid for by officers, who provided their men white trousers, a stripped dark shirt, and a straw hat with a red and yellow cockade with the colors of the Spanish flag.

Events rapidly unfolded in Cuba for the Volunteers. In just a matter of weeks, thousands of Volunteers were donning the uniform and carrying a weapon in their hands, being able to drill and form paramilitary units of infantrymen in the cities and cavalrymen in the countryside. By mid-March, only a month and a half after their official creation, the volunteer units could gather around 20,000 men throughout the island, thus outnumbering the 16,000-strong regular army. Due to their impressive numbers, the Volunteers soon became a social phenomenon to be reckoned with. Their numbers made them a strong asset for Spain's cause in Cuba, but the lack of military discipline combined with a lack of social cohesion made them a potentially volatile force. Beyond a staunch defense of Spanish sovereignty, there were few other elements that bounded this militia together. Industrial tycoons, company owners, overseers, and working-class *peninsulares* had not much of a well-defined political agenda in common. In the countryside, the mostly-*guajiros* Volunteers were essentially unaffected from such divisions, but in Havana tensions would soon run high.

As fear of an invasion still loomed on the horizon, thousands of men joined the new militia and were given weapons and a basic military training. Meanwhile the case against Ramón Pintó continued at the courts. Animosity against him grew strong, especially among the rank-and-file Volunteers, who were mostly young scarcely educated men who had just been provided with a rifle and a uniform and were eager to prove their patriotism. Pintó, an educated liberal, a Spaniard who was allegedly plotting against Spain, was a traitor before their eyes. Thus, they insisted that the man must be executed.[9]

The fate of Pintó was in the hands of the authorities, which seemed not very prone to yield to the Volunteers' demands. Apparently, Gutiérrez de la Concha was mulling the idea of honoring his old friendship with Pintó with trying to sort out a way for the

---

[8] *Cuerpos de Voluntarios de la Isla de Cuba. Escalafón General de señores jefes, oficiales y sargentos por el orden de antigüedad a 1 de enero de 1860.* Havana: Imprenta del Gobierno y Capitanía General, 1860, pp. 7–8.

[9] Bernades. *Ramon Pintó*, pp. 125–32.

latter to come out of the process alive. The reasons are not entirely clear, but it is not far-fetched to infer that the captain general used his power to influence the military court hearing the case, for Pintó and the other individuals arrested in the case were acquitted of charges of sedition in the first instance on grounds of lack of evidence.

The acquittal outraged the Volunteers, who felt that the authorities which had them flocking to the banner of Spain and the Queen were now committing treason by letting Pintó and his colleagues go unpunished. Anger can be a powerful weapon for armed men with a clear goal, even if it clashes with the authorities they were supposedly defending. In comparison to regular soldiers, the Volunteers lacked discipline and military training, which in combination with their enthusiasm could easily turn into unruliness. As well, the Volunteers were aware that they greatly outnumbered the garrison of scarcely motivated and scantly paid conscripts sent from the Peninsula to serve their military service, who were to protect the authorities in case of conflict.

Complaints against the captain general and Pintó's acquittal, and rumors of direct action, soon circulated throughout the many popular cafés and taverns of Havana which were frequented by the Volunteers. The rumors could be heard louder, as the anger among these men intensified. The Volunteers began to perform informal military parades in front of the court hearing Pintó's case in a tour de force against the authorities, and meetings were held which scarcely concealed plans of sedition. During one such meeting held at a café in Havana, a Volunteer captain, disregarding the most basic rules of military discipline, boasted out loud that his comrades-in-arms would kill Pintó with "their own hands" should the captain general spare his life.[10] As the Volunteers became more aware of their coercive power, plans to subvert order were discussed more openly, thus posing an open threat to Gutiérrez de la Concha's authority.

Only being able to count on a tiny garrison of regular soldiers, the captain general had to choose between trying to impose his authority at the risk of sparking a most likely rebellion in Havana among the Volunteers, or appeasing them by meeting their demands, at the cost of undermining his position. He chose to compromise his authority and ordered that the case against Pintó be reviewed in a second trial, thus yielding to the pressures. On this occasion, on March 10 a new military court with new members heard the case. Rather than appeasing the Volunteers, this encouraged their demands for blood. During a military parade before Gutiérrez de la Concha at Havana's Campo de Marte on March 14, the Volunteers insistently shouted, "death to the traitors!" making clear that they would not tolerate a second acquittal. Thus, as expected, after a quick trial Pintó was sentenced to death.[11]

On March 22, 1855, Ramón Pintó appeared in black on the esplanade in front of La Punta fortress, to be executed by strangulation, which was the means sanctioned for civilians by the Penal Law of 1848. The execution was witnessed by thousands of

---

[10] Justo Zaragoza. *Las insurrecciones de Cuba. Apuntes para la historia política de esta isla en el presente siglo*, vol. II. Madrid: Imprenta de Manuel G. Hernández, 1873, p. 673.

[11] Antonio de las Barras y Prado. *La Habana a mediados del siglo XIX*. Madrid: Imprenta de la Ciudad Lineal, 1926, p. 31.

habaneros who gathered around the old fortress, and who could also see that alongside regular soldiers and members of the Civil Guard; walking Pintó to the scaffold where the executioner had already set the *garrote*, there was a squad of Volunteers.[12] They were, or at least the most radical elements among them, the true victors of that truculent scene. The death of Pintó symbolized the victory of the Volunteers, for in just two months since their creation, they had been able to impose their will upon the captain general, who represented the authority of the Spanish Crown in the island.

What to Do with the Volunteers?

Despite the political victory of the Volunteers over the captain general in the Pintó affair, the fact that they had contravened the authorities' will made their future look uncertain. The reasons to keep the militia as a permanent element of Cuba's defensive system were, at least, dubious, but could not completely be dispensed with. The Spanish Government could not be content with the captain general's authority being undermined by the Volunteers, but it could neither look away from the international scenario and the need to reinforce Cuba's defenses. The Volunteers had been created *ex professo* to defend the island from an invasion, and though it was not coming, the US interest in Cuba was not to go away. It had not since the establishment of the American Union, whose interest in expanding its influence south of the border with Mexico was still alive and kicking. Britain and France, which had strong interests in the Gulf of Mexico and the Caribbean, were busy fighting the Russians in Crimea alongside the Ottomans since 1853, thus making it more affordable for expansionists in the United States to try their chances. For instance, those were the years of William Walker's disastrous adventures in Mexico and Nicaragua, among others. Yet, against the expansionist thrust southward, the nearly impossible equilibrium in US politics between North and South upon the issue of slavery functioned as a brake for such projects. After all, the expansion of slavery was a major force behind most of these adventures in the continent. Such an explosive material was only to be dealt with extreme care by American politicians, as President Pierce had shown by ordering Quitman to cancel the expedition.

Aware of the international dimension of the Cuban status quo, Gutiérrez de la Concha had to deal with the Volunteers as a strong new element in the local scenario. He could have tried to reinforce his authority over a militia that had imposed upon him the execution of an old friend. For instance, by asking the Ministry of the War for more troops, thus making the Volunteers unnecessary and dispensable with, just as had happened after the invasions of 1850 and 1851 by Narciso López. But this was hardly an option, for Spain, suffering from an almost endemic instability, was in no position to send thousands of soldiers across the Atlantic. Since a military coup had brought them to power in July 1854, a feeble coalition of progressives and liberals, headed respectively by Generals Baldomero Espartero, the premier, and Leopoldo

---

[12] Bernades. *Ramón Pintó*, p. 146.

O'Donnell, minister of War, was dealing with more urgent problems for the Spanish ruling class. Among them, opening Spanish economy to foreign investment, which caused much unrest among the Catalan industrial bourgeoisie. With its many strong interests in the Antilles, it firmly advocated for a protectionist policy. All in all, 1855 was not an uneventful year for Spain. In addition to a terrific cholera outburst, Spain's first labor violent strikes had rocked Barcelona, and much discontent was found among peasants for the selling of municipal-owned agricultural land sanctioned by the Madoz Law, which ended up enlarging latifundia in rural Spain. Thus, reinforcing Cuba's garrison was not even in the political agenda. Gutiérrez de la Concha had to deal with the Volunteers.

One of the main tasks the captain general had been charged with was to make the defense of the island less of a burden for the beleaguered Spanish treasury. Cuba ought to be supported with its own means. Since the French invasion of 1808, followed by the collapse of Spanish power in America during the 1820s and a series of civil wars and intermittent military coups, Spain had fallen prey to an almost permanent instability. Unable to count on the American silver and gold revenues and lacking a powerful industry, the Spanish treasury had been bordering on bankruptcy for the most part of the century. Not even the sugar boom was able to cover on all the needs of the Spanish administration in Cuba.

Taking this into account, Gutiérrez de la Concha had good reasons for quickly forgetting the Pintó affair and being pragmatic regarding the Volunteers. They quickly grew into a formidable force. On April 30, 1855, only two months and a half after the establishment of the first companies and battalions, no less than 24,000 Volunteers coming from all parts of Cuba paraded before the captain general in Havana in a true demonstration of power.[13] Though they were somehow unruly, keeping this militia of men who afforded their own uniforms and weapons and costed the treasury virtually peanuts was consistent with his plans to reform Cuba's military system.

The biggest challenge was to engage creoles in the defense of Spanish sovereignty in Cuba, after years of frictions. To reintegrate the local elite into the system was a wise and necessary move for the island's stability. The annexationist ideals did not entirely fade away, but the failure of Pintó's plot had been but another defeat for the cause of making Cuba a new star in flag of the United States. The desire might remain, but turning it into a reality had proved, once again, impossible. Thus, a compromise between the Cuban annexationist elite and the Spanish authorities was necessary for both sides. For the time being, Cuba would stay under Spanish sovereignty, but the captain general knew it was necessary to implement policies that made the creole elite feel they had a stake in it.

Since the exclusion of Cuban representatives from the Spanish Parliament in 1837, local politics could not be articulated through political parties and a local assembly. Instead, an oligarchic system in which the captain general was the last interpreter of the interest of the Nation in Cuba prevailed. The ways to integrate the Cuban elite back

---

[13] Luis Otero Pimentel. *Memoria sobre los Voluntarios de la isla de Cuba. Consideraciones relativas a su pasad, su presente y su porvenir*. Havana: La Propaganda Literaria, 1876, p. 10.

into the system revolved around granting public contracts and appointments in key positions and continuing to turn a blind eye to the illegal slave trade, resisting British pressures to end it. But below the elite, ordinary creoles, from liberal professionals to employees, could be integrated through their direct involvement in the military defense of Spanish Cuba.

On June 20, 1855, Gutiérrez de la Concha wrote a report to the minister of War, Leopoldo O'Donnell, himself former governor of Cuba, stating that the island would need an army of 40,000 men to successfully counter an invasion launched from the United States.[14] The problem was that the Cuban treasury had no means to afford it. But the island could count on the Volunteers. And with them, Gutiérrez de la Concha wrote in the report, he also intended to address one of the major issues which endangered stability in the island: the widening gap between creoles and *peninsulares*. A creole who had lost his father and his native land due to the war of independence in South America, Gutiérrez de la Concha, just as many other contemporary Spaniards, was aware of the perils of division among "Spaniards of both hemispheres." The issue was hardly avoidable in any colonial society, but in Cuba the problem was especially acute since the days of Captain General Miguel Tacón.

In this context, the Volunteers seemed a militia especially fit for engaging Cubans and *peninsulares* in a military institution anew. This is one of the main reasons alleged by the captain general to convince the Spanish Government of making the Volunteers a permanent element of the defensive system.[15] Contrary to the Disciplined Militias, the Volunteers had been recently created under the supervision of the authorities with a strong participation of *peninsulares*, especially in the cities and among the rank and file, but favored the participation of Cubans, who could thus feel they had a stake in the defense of Spanish sovereignty in the island. Beyond this, the captain general argued that their uniforms and arms were provided by themselves or their officers, thus not representing any burden to the treasury. The many advantages allowed the Volunteers to stay and, on April 24, 1856, shortly over a year after their creation, their first *Reglamento*, or military regulations, were published by the Captaincy General's official print. In the first article of its first chapter, the raison d'être of the Volunteers is clearly stated: "the main object the Volunteer Battalions have been created for, and the main obligation of their members, is to maintain the order and public tranquillity of the towns: the armed defence of the rights of the Mother Country and our queen *Doña* Isabella II with one's life if necessary."[16]

The *reglamento* set the basic rules for the organization and military instruction of the Volunteers. It stated that "Spaniards from both hemispheres" between the ages of 18 and 50 with "a proper behaviour" could join the militia, which was to have infantry and cavalry units. Breaking from the Disciplines Militias and stating so neatly their very purpose of standing for Spain was a way to filter the loyalty of new members,

---

[14] AGMM, Ultramar, Capitanía General de Cuba, caja 2634, carpeta 72-3, subcarpeta 72-3-1.
[15] AHN, Ultramar, 4669, exp. 57.
[16] *Reglamento para los cuerpos de Voluntarios de la Isla de Cuba*, cap. I, art. 1.

for people discontented with Spanish rule would hardly join such a unit. As to the military instruction, the *reglamento* stated that the Volunteers were to receive basic military training during holidays between November and February, thus coinciding with the *zafra*, the period of lowest activity in Cuban economy, when sugarcane was harvested, and its juice turned into sugar in the mills across the island. As to structure of command, the *segundo cabo*—the captain general's second-in-command—was instituted as general subinspector of the Volunteers. His role was rather as a general coordinator, while direct command was bestowed upon the units' officers. There were many aspects not contemplated by a very basic set of rules, but although vague, the *reglamento* of 1856 marked the consolidation of the Volunteers as a permanent element of the Spanish defensive system in Cuba.

Joining the Volunteers granted some social prestige and was a proof of loyalty to Spain in times when its sovereignty was challenged. In the cities, laborers, specially *peninsulares*, found pride in donning the uniforms and in carrying a weapon in military parades; shop and factory owners could also display their pride and loyalty by commanding men who often happened to be their employees. As to the local elite, joining the Volunteers was also a sign of commitment to the Spanish cause, a measure to distance oneself from "annexationists," and a way to establish good relations with political power.

More than a year after their creation, it seemed that the Volunteers had come to stay. The main raison d'être that had led to their inception, an annexationist attempt, had gone away, at least temporarily. And yet, new companies were created across Cuba, and men who joined the militia were given uniforms, arms, and a basic military training. The authorities saw the Volunteers as a necessary asset in an island placed at the crossroads between the declining power of Spain and the expansionism of the United States. However, there were voices who disagreed with establishing the Volunteers as a permanent element of the Spanish military in Cuba, and not because they reinforced the status quo, but precisely because they might endanger it.

Some of these voices even came from the Spanish loyalist milieu. For example, Dionisio Alcalá Galiano, the director of the *Diario de la Marina* and himself a Volunteer officer. He was born in 1811 in Cádiz, the grandson of the homonymous brigadier who is considered a Spanish national hero after he was killed during the battle of Trafalgar fighting Nelson's fleet. His father, Antonio, was a liberal politician who walked the path from radical liberalism to conservatism as the liberal principles embraced by the generation who fought against Napoleon and gave birth to the Constitution of 1812 degenerated into chaos and plunged Spain into a permanent anarchy. After the defeat of radical liberalism at the hands of another French invading army in 1823, when the Duke of Angoulême's Hundred Thousand Sons of Saint Louis came to the rescue of Ferdinand VII and the old monarchy, Antonio Alcalá Galiano went into exile in France and Britain for a decade. During those years, he tamed his idealistic liberalism by witnessing the benefits of a strong parliamentary system based on moderate liberal principles. After returning to Spain in the 1830s, he joined the conservative banner which aspired to keep the liberal revolution by moderating it. With such a background, Dionisio Alcalá Galiano was especially worried by the fact that a strong militia of Volunteers might hijack the real political power in Cuba from the hands of the captain general. The outcome of the Pintó affair was a fair reminder that the will of the militiaman's boot could prevail over the official seat of power.

In a book published in 1859, Alcalá Galiano recognized that the Volunteers could only be positive for Cuba under certain circumstances. He considered that they had the elements which could make them a good military reserve. The Volunteers were mostly commanded by propertied and well-respected officers, men like Julán de Zulueta and the Count of Casa Moré, who naturally shied away from revolutionary temptations which could subvert social order and could thus use their prestige and power to instill their ideals to their subordinates. He also considered a social benefit the fact that men of African descent were not allowed into the Volunteers. From his viewpoint, their exclusion prevented Blacks and mulattos from allying with poor white Volunteers, who underwent different degrees of discrimination but who could share a similar social unrest. As well, by not allowing them in, young Blacks and mulattoes had no easy access to weapons and military training. Only the Colored Militias, subject to a tighter control under the command of army officers, let them open doors to military life.

Against the advantages he saw from the Volunteers, Alcalá Galiano's main concern was that keeping them as a permanent militia was a dangerous way of arming commoners. Probably having in mind his father's experience, and the recent example of Spain, where politically driven militias made political stability nothing but wishful thinking, Alcalá Galiano greatly distrusted armed civilians. He considered that any conservative and moderate liberal should be worried about this, for citizens must be taught how to respect law and order, not how to shoot a rifle. Only soldiers and members of public order forces should enjoy the monopole of violence. Otherwise, the use of violence to impose a political agenda was too tempting. Beyond this main concern, Alcalá Galiano was also aware that the enthusiasm was fading away from among the Volunteers. Their numbers were dwindling as the threat of an invasion was dissipating, and the unpaid military duties they were subject to, such as guarding military hospitals, prisons, or forts, became more of a burden for their employers, who had to dispense with some of their workers several days a month.[17] Down from the nearly 24,000 members reported in 1856, in just three years their numbers had dropped to little less than 12,000.[18]

The fact is that beyond their usual duties, during peacetime the Volunteers could do little more than take part in military parades, maneuvers, or patriotic and religious events. For instance, in February 1857, men from all the Havana Volunteer units partook alongside the army in the military exercises which took place at and around El Príncipe Castle in the outskirts of the city, which gathered 7,000 men overseen by the captain general.[19] A year later, in April 1858, the Volunteers also participated in the long celebrations for the birth of Alphonse, who was proclaimed Prince of Asturias,

---

[17] Dionisio Alcalá Galiano. *Cuba en 1858*. Madrid: Imprenta de Beltrán y Viñas, 1859, pp. 132–4.
[18] *Cuerpos de Voluntarios de la Isla de Cuba. Escalafón General de señores jefes, oficiales y sargentos por el orden de antigüedad en 1º de enero de 1860*. Havana: Imprenta del Gobierno y Capitanía General, 1860, p. 14.
[19] *Gaceta de Madrid*, 13-03-1857, p. 4.

heir to the throne. He was the Queen's first son, after four daughters. The celebrations unfolded over weeks in all Spanish territories, and Havana's authorities did not miss the opportunity to show their allegiance to the Bourbons as one of the monarchy's main cities. Between April 4 and 12, 1858, the city of Havana organized banquets, public shows, bullfights, theater plays, military parades, and maneuvers. On the 6th, the Volunteers, alongside cadets of Havana's Military Academy, took part in a military show during which they stormed the Monserrate bastion of the old wall. After an intense shooting with blanks, the Volunteers used ladders and ropes to climb the bastion, illuminated by flare letters which read "Long Live the Queen! Long Live the Prince of Asturias!" as they reached the top.[20] Outside Havana, the Volunteers took part in similar performances. For instance, the visit of the captain general was a major event for a city like Puerto Príncipe, a major cattle center and home to some affluent families who had been involved in the annexationist movement. In February 1856, the local Volunteer battalion and the army garrison paraded in front of Gutiérrez de La Concha, who invited its officers to the banquet and ball, which was attended by no less than 2,000 people of the city's finest society.[21]

Religion was another sphere of public life that did not escape from the Volunteers' activities, imitating the relationship between Spanish regular military units with their saint patrons and their participation in processions and other sacred feasts. Our Lady of El Cobre was one of the most revered holy figures of Cuba, especially among creoles who regarded her as their virgin protector. It was also the patroness of the 4th Volunteer Battalion of Havana, headed by a Cuban *hacendado*, the colonel Count of Casa Calderón, who ordered hundreds of images of Our Lady of El Cobre to celebrate her day on September 8, 1861.[22]

Public demonstrations of patriotism were also commonplace for the Volunteers during the years following their inception. During January and February 1859, volunteer units all over the island published open letters to the Queen upholding their commitment to the defense of the cause of Spain in the Antilles against the expansionist interest of the United States. During the annual message he addressed to members of the Senate and the Congress on December 6, 1858, President James Buchanan, a Pennsylvania Democrat who staunchly opposed the abolition of slavery, blatantly declared that the presence of Spain in Cuba, an island which "commands the mouth of the Mississippi," was a permanent source of annoyance to the American Union.[23]

The northern neighbor still coveted the dominion of Cuba, but prospects of an invasion seemed less likely for the time being. Despite the many tensions existing between the United States and Spain in relation to Cuba, these rarely escalated beyond the realms of diplomacy, for the days of annexationist invasions and filibuster adventures were, though fresh memories, essentially gone. The sovereignty of Spain in Cuba may have been annoying, but the situation was not yet ripe for an outright assault

---

[20] *Gaceta de Madrid*, 25-05-1858, p. 2.
[21] *Gaceta de Madrid*, 02-04-1856, p. 4.
[22] *Antón Perulero*, 15-09-1861, p. 8.
[23] *Gaceta de Madrid*, 15-02-1859, pp. 1–2.

against it. In this context, the Volunteers were of little use, other than taking part in events organized by the authorities or showing public demonstrations of patriotism. They were present at the most important ones, but by the end of 1858 the captain general was still asking the Ministry of War in Madrid whether the militia was to be kept at all.[24]

In such a state of patriotic lethargy the Volunteers had become a sort of decorative armed force whose real purpose was difficult to understand, if not to justify. The doubts of Spain's main authority in the island over their continuity put them to the brink of dissolution, but a series of events taking place in a Spanish enclave in northern Africa came to save them from a likely fate.

[24] AHN, Ultramar, 4669, Exp.57.

3

Saved by the Empire: Morocco, Santo Domingo, and Puerto Rico

On August 10, 1859, a group of twelve men from the Anyera clan attacked a military post the Spanish Army was building around Ceuta, destroying the Spanish coat of arms carved in stone which delimited the Kingdom of Spain from the Sultanate of Morocco. Ceuta was an enclave conquered by the Portuguese in 1415 which came under the rule of the Habsburgs with the Iberian Union in 1580. It chose to stay with the Spanish Monarchy in 1640 when its inhabitants remained loyal to Philip IV when the Duke of Braganza, proclaimed king of Portugal, broke the dynastic union with Castile. Out of the old network of over a dozen outposts which ran along the northern African coast from Larache to Tripoli, by the nineteenth century Spain retained Ceuta, Melilla, and a few islets a stone's throw from the Moroccan coast. These enclaves were frequently attacked by small parties of neighboring Berber clans, which went mostly unpunished due to the tiny Spanish garrisons and the weak control Moroccan authorities really had in the north.

Historically, the sultans of Morocco allowed such attacks to take place without formally organizing them as an indirect way of pressing Spain for trading or diplomatic reasons, or to relieve internal tensions without starting a war. The attacks were usually followed by some limited military response by Spain, and negotiations between the authorities of both countries, which often ended up with a few hangings of Berber clansmen, some form of economic compensation, and new diplomatic and trading agreements.

In 1859, however, the attack provided the casus belli to the Spanish Government, eager to launch a punitive campaign. An external threat would ideally foster national unity and restore some of the country's lost prestige in a time of European expansionism. For over a year, Spain had been ruled by the Liberal Union, a party of moderate liberals headed by General Leopoldo O'Donnell. O'Donnell was the strong man of Spanish politics of the day, having been appointed prime minister and minister of War by the Queen in June 1858. With a country still prey to lingering political divisions between liberals and *carlistas*, who had fought two civil wars in two decades for the restoration of the traditional monarchy, divided also between conservatives and progressives, with an army prone to meddle into politics, the Liberal Union cabinet saw in Morocco an opportunity to healing Spain's many open wounds.

Enticing a war against a foreign enemy seeking to enhance unity at home while trying to restore some international prestige became a staple policy of Spanish Government in the 1860s. Before intervening in Morocco, Spain deployed a few thousand Filipino soldiers to fight alongside the French in the Cochinchina Campaign (1858–62), reintegrated the Dominican Republic as an overseas territory (1861–5), joined forces with the French and the British against Mexico in 1861 for unpaid foreign debt, and occupied a few guano-producing Peruvian islands seeking to receive compensation for the independence wars of the 1820s which led to the Chincha Islands War against Peru, Chile, Ecuador, and Bolivia (1865–6). But the most popular of these campaigns was undoubtedly against an old enemy: Morocco.

All offers from Morocco to try to avoid war went unheard in Madrid, which was able to sneak its way around the reluctance of Britain and France for a Spanish intervention in northern Africa. Spain had no material means for attaining major territorial gains in Africa, but a military adventure could alter the status quo in the region. Ceuta was right across Gibraltar, a vital step in the British passage to India and a geopolitical key point for the British Empire. As for the French, they had been considering expanding westward from their Algerian basin at least since their war with Morocco in 1844. Being aware that London and Paris would not support the campaign, but neither prevent it from happening, for Spanish diplomacy insisted that no major territorial expansion was sought, O'Donnell had the Spanish Parliament declare war on Morocco on October 22, 1859.

The African war sparked a wave of patriotic enthusiasm in Spain and its overseas territories unseen since the days of the war against Napoleon's invasion. Political parties, the press, and the Church supported the war almost unanimously, and provincial authorities in Catalonia and the Basque Country organized volunteer battalions to fight in Morocco. Veterans of both sides of the Carlist wars of 1833–40 and 1846–9 joined together, in a powerful symbol which implied that this war might heal old wounds. Cities and towns performed popular parades, hundreds of songs and poems were composed, and an army of painters got ready to accompany the soldiers to Morocco and depict a war against an old enemy they deemed exotic. Echoing the popular belief that her foremother Isabella of Castille had pawned her jewels to finance Columbus' first voyage in 1492, Isabella II did alike with hers to finance the military effort as a patriotic gesture.[1] Fundraising for the campaign was organized in most Spanish major cities, including Havana, San Juan de Puerto Rico, and Manila. According to Nicolás Estévanez, an army officer who fought in Africa, "nothing was more popular in Spain than the war against the Moors."[2]

Amidst this euphoric context, an army of 55,000 crossed the Strait of Gibraltar between November and December 1859 seeking to punish Morocco. It was headed by Leopoldo O'Donnell himself and was composed of three army corps commanded by Generals Antonio Ros de Olano, Rafael de Echagüe, and Juan Prim, a former captain general of Puerto Rico who would owe much of his rising star in Spanish politics to his

---

[1] Tomás García Figueres. *Marruecos (la acción de España en el norte de África)*. Madrid: Ediciones Fe, 1941, p. 76.
[2] Nicolás Estévanez. *Mis memorias*. Madrid: Tebas, 1975 (first published in 1899), p. 48.

performance in this war. The army was mostly made up of conscripts forced to serve an eight-year-long military service, one of the longest in Europe. They soon fell prey to terrible weather, a muddy terrain, and a cholera pandemic which would end up affecting around two thirds of the expeditionary forces. But the tide turned in January 1860, with the Spanish victory at the battle of Castillejos, nearby Ceuta, on New Year's Day. This was celebrated across Spain and her colonies.

According to *La América*, "each one of our army's victories is celebrated in the ever-faithful island of Cuba with demonstrations of immense joy."[3] This magazine had been created a few years earlier in Madrid by a group of Cuban reformists who considered that this war might provide a fruitful ground for reconciliation between the creole bourgeoisie and the Crown. After the annexationist movement's incapacity to bring any positive results, the powerful island's elite realized that cooperation with the Crown, not rupture, was the way forward for Cuba. The Crown, on its turn, acknowledged that they could not rule the island against its elite, thus advocating for rapprochement as the best way to secure Spanish sovereignty in Cuba.

Due to the absence of party politics in Cuba, for the overseas territories had been excluded from Spain's constitutional regime 1837, the political system in the island was based on a delicate equilibrium of influence which was lost and gained through gestures and commitment. Contributing financially to the war effort was an evident way of showing support for reconciliation, and many in the island did so, including convinced liberals who had flirted with the annexationist ideal. Among them a lawyer from Bayamo, an old town in the east of Cuba, Carlos Manuel de Céspedes, who befriended General Prim during his university days in Barcelona in the early 1840s and who would lead the first war of Cuban independence against Spain in 1868, contributed with a 4 percent of his income for supporting a soldier fighting in Morocco.[4]

Across the political spectrum, loyalists also mobilized in support of the Spanish military effort in Morocco. The Volunteers were carried away by the patriotic enthusiasm sparked by the war. A neat commitment with Spain's cause in Africa might also help them consolidate as a part of Cuba's defensive system. Direct participation in the fighting was out of question for a militia of civilians who depended on their regular jobs and only had basic military training, however they could contribute otherwise, such as with financial help. All their units across Cuba fundraised money, contributing over 273,000 pesos during the war.[5] The war against Morocco seems to have been very popular among a good deal of the nearly 12,000 Volunteers registered in 1860.[6] Donations ranged from 4 pesos monthly given by Tomás Abreu, a caporal in Santiago de Cuba, to the 37,000 collected by Havana's four infantry battalions. Major Cosme de la Torriente, the Cuban commander of Matanza's battalion, managed to collect over 5,000 pesos from among his men.[7]

---

[3] *La América*, 08-02-1860, p. 4.
[4] *La América*, 24-01-1860, p. 16.
[5] Elías Martínez Nubla. *Los voluntarios de Ultramar. El Libro Azul. Apuntes para la Historia*. Madrid: Imprenta del Fomento Naval, 1903, p. 38.
[6] *Cuerpos de Voluntarios de la Isla de Cuba*, p. 13.
[7] *La América*, 24-01-1860, pp. 12–16.

Funds submitted by individuals as well as by entire units, from Havana, Matanzas, and Santiago, but also from small towns, proved the morale and esprit de corps of the Volunteers, who had other ways to show their patriotism. Among other events, the battalions of the capital organized a masquerade at Havana's impressive Tacón Theatre, which included a popular raffle for the men serving in Africa.[8] Bullfighting, which was the most popular entertainment among Spaniards alongside theater, was not left out of the array of events organized by the Volunteers to support the war. Indeed, Havana's arena was visited by bullfighters during the so-called American season, which lasted during winter months, when climate in mainland Spain was too harsh for the *corridas*. Bullfighting was widely popular in countries like Mexico, Peru, and Colombia, but in Cuba it had political connotations. Whereas it was mostly popular among *peninsulares* and loyalist creoles, many Cubans usually preferred other shows, like baseball, which represented modernity and the influence of the United States.[9] Thus, organizing a bullfight in Havana to fundraise money for Spanish soldiers was an evident patriotic affirmative action. The Volunteers not only organized the event, but they also decorated the arena and its surrounding streets with Spanish flags and kept public order instead of the police during the *corrida*.[10]

Far from Havana, across the Atlantic, events unfolded rapidly in Morocco. The occupation of Tetuan, a major northern Moroccan town in early February 1860, was followed by the Spanish victory at Wad-Ras on March 23, 1860, which left the troops by O'Donnell at the gates of Tangiers, a major port and one of the gates of the Strait of Gibraltar. Fearing to lose the city and the throne with it, Sultan Muhammad V offered Spain a peace that was signed just a month after the battle of War Ras. With British and French diplomacy intensely working to impede any major territorial changes, Spain gained very little at a cost of between 4,000 and 7,000 deaths, and around 20,000 casualties, mostly by cholera, which ended filling military hospitals in Ceuta, Cádiz, and Málaga.[11] The country was granted economic compensation and trade rights by Morocco, the right to take a small territory at the gates of the Saharan desert—Ifni— where a tiny Spanish fort, Santa Cruz de la Mar Pequeña, had supposedly existed between the late fifteenth and the early sixteenth centuries, a moderate border expansion of the enclaves of Ceuta and Melilla, and two guns which were melted into two bronze lions that flank the entrance of the Spanish Congress of Deputies in Madrid to this day. The city of Tetuan, home to a large community of the descendants of the Muslims and Jews who were expelled from Spain between the fifteenth and seventeenth centuries, was to be occupied by Spanish soldiers for as long as the compensation was not entirely paid. This occupation allowed the reunion after centuries of Spanish soldiers and diplomats with the local Spanish-speaking Sephardic Jews, the arrival of dozens of painters attracted by Moroccan exoticism, such as Mariano Fortuny, and the introduction for

---

[8] ANRC, Asuntos Políticos, leg. 53, exp. 1.
[9] Louis A. Pérez, Jr. "Between Baseball and Bullfighting: The Quest for Nationality in Cuba, 1868-1898." *The Journal of American History*, 1994, vol. 81, No. 2, p. 505.
[10] *Boletín de loterías y de toros*, 23-08-1860, p. 2.
[11] Joan Serrallonga Urquidi. "La Guerra de África y el cólera (1859-60)." *Hispania*, 1998, vol. LVIII, No. 198, pp. 233-60.

the first time in Morocco of a printing press, brought by the writer Pedro Antonio de Alarcón, which was able to print in Spanish and Arabic. It was used to edit the first newspaper in Moroccan history: *El Eco de Tetuán*.

Cuba was too distant from Morocco, and the war had been too short for any need of a direct military participation of the island's garrison. Only thirty-six men from Cuba had crossed the Atlantic to join the troops fighting in Africa.[12] As to the Volunteers, sending them to Africa was simply not an option for the military authorities, due to their very nature of being a civilians' militia with scant military training. However, as the presence of Spanish soldiers in northern Morocco continued until securing the full compensation's payment—completed in 1862, the Volunteers provided an example which some members of the administration thought fit for defending Spain's rights in Africa. In September 1860, almost half a year after the end of the war, Martín de Arredondo y Olea, a native of Trinidad de Cuba and honorary secretary of the Queen, sent a report to the Ministry of War suggesting the creation of a battalion of Cuban Blacks and mulattoes following the example of Havana's Volunteers. Arredondo thought these men fit for garrisoning Spanish-occupied cities in Morocco. No cultural or racial ties linked Cubans of African descent with northern Morocco's Arabs and Berbers, so it is not clear why Arredondo considered these men especially fit for the northern African scenario. What he really wanted was to reaffirm Cuba's clear support for Spanish military adventures, for sending such a battalion of black volunteers as he suggested would have been a "Cuban contribution to the glory of the Nation."[13]

No battalion of Black volunteers was ever organized and dispatched to Africa, probably because their participation was not really needed. However, the report was symptomatic of the reputation earned by the Volunteers. The fact that they appear as an example to be followed in an official report sent by a Queen's secretary to the Ministry of War means that they were holding ground as a permanent element of the Spanish defensive system in Cuba in the mind of leading advisers to the administration. Due to their characteristics, the existing Volunteer battalions were not sent to Morocco to take part in the fighting, but the war had given them the opportunity to show their commitment to the Spanish cause by contributing financially to the cause, thus helping to consolidate their position in Cuba.

Also, resulting from the war, giving financial support to causes they deemed patriotic became a common practice for the Volunteers. For instance, they donated 10,000 pesos for the creation of barracks for invalid soldiers in Havana and collected around 28,000 for the reconstruction of Manila after the earthquake that caused severe damage to the city in June 1863.[14] These displays of solidarity toward disabled soldiers in Cuba or victims of a natural disaster in the Philippines were a way of showing support for the idea of Spanish national integrity between the Peninsula and its overseas

---

[12] ANRC, Reales Decretos y Ordenanzas, leg. 216, exp. 237.
[13] ANRC, Asuntos Políticos, leg. 53, exp. 1; David Sartorius. *Ever Faithful. Race, Loyalty, and the Ends of Empire in Spanish Cuba*. Durham and London: Duke University Press, 2013, p. 91.
[14] Martínez Nubla. *Los Voluntarios de Ultramar*, p. 38. For the Manila earthquake, see Susana María Ramírez Martín. *El terremoto de Manila de 1863: medidas políticas y económicas*. Madrid: CSIC, 2006.

territories. This reinforced the idea of the Volunteers as a militia undoubtedly loyal to the authorities and the Crown, but a major political change in a nearby Caribbean Island provided a new opportunity for the Volunteers to consolidate as a permanent element in Cuba and abroad.

War in Santo Domingo

In 1861, the Dominican Republic, commonly known as Santo Domingo at the time, returned to Spain's sovereignty forty years after the last Spanish soldiers left the country. Going against the trend of history and the political culture of the last half a century of independence in the Americas, the Dominican Parliament passed a law reintegrating the country with its old colonizer. It was the only case in which an independent nation revoked voluntarily its sovereignty in favor of the old ruler. It was the result of a particular context of weaknesses and opportunities.[15]

Santo Domingo, in the island of Hispaniola, where the Spaniards had begun their expansion in the Americas from 1492 onward, was a territory where their rule had been more loosely felt at the turn of the eighteenth and nineteenth centuries. Since the country was formally ceded to revolutionary France in 1795 following the Spanish defeat in the War of the Pyrenees (1793–5), Santo Domingo had fallen prey to anarchy and foreign invasion, being unable to build a strong sense of national independence, let alone a set of stable institutions. Santo Domingo was a country in turmoil in an island on fire, for neighboring Haiti underwent its own long and bloody revolutionary process between 1791 and 1804 which would echo across the region for most of the nineteenth century. The country had been exchanged back and forth between Spain and France until 1822, when the invasion by Haiti put an end to a short-lived republic and decades of instability. For twenty years, the Dominican elite grew a deep sentiment of resentment for being ruled by a foreign nation which did not even speak Spanish and was overwhelmingly made up of former enslaved people who had rebelled against their masters. Most of Dominicans shared with Haitians a common African ancestry, but the Dominican elite was mostly made up of families of Spanish descent who generally despised the African roots of their neighbors and rulers.

After two decades of Haitian misrule and accumulated resentment, a group of nine Dominican nationalists gathered around *La Trinitaria*, a secret society founded and headed by Juan Pablo Duarte. The Dominican Republic was proclaimed and gained its independence after a short war in 1844.[16] Stability did not come along with independence, and the country seemed unable to overcome profound political divisions and the ever-present threat of a Haitian invasion which led to endless cabinets, military coups, and clashes with the neighbor. Coming under the protection of another nation began to be regarded as a viable option out of anarchy. Seeking a protector greatly

---

[15] Luis de la Gándara y Navarro. *Anexión y guerra de Santo Domingo*, vol. I. Madrid: Imp. de "El Correo Militar," 1884, pp. 13–75.

[16] Martínez-Fernández. *Torn Between Empires*, pp. 141–9.

divided the Dominican ruling class, for it threatened national sovereignty. Widely speaking, the merchants of Santo Domingo and the cattle ranchers of its hinterland favored closer ties with Spain for its cultural similarities, conservative values, and the possibility of integrating into a wider space of commercial and cultural exchanges with the rest of the Spanish Antilles. Their political leader was a soldier and former *trinitario*, Pedro Santana. Opposing them were the tobacco and mahogany producers of the interior region of Cibao, the most dynamic area of the country, who favored the union with the United States for the greater economic opportunities represented by a huge market. This faction was headed by another *trinitario* and soldier, Buenaventura Báez. Both parties alternated in power and knocked at several doors at the same time.[17]

Britain and France were unlikely candidates for they had repeatedly shown resistance to any major territorial changes in the Caribbean. The Dominican diplomacy tested the US waters in the mid-1850s with some degree of acceptance, in a context where the idea of gaining territory in the Caribbean was having its momentum in the country. But concerns of political division and the fear of an influx of people of African descent into the United States, similar to the ones in 1855 regarding Cuba, thwarted the project. By 1860, when Abraham Lincoln was elected president and North and South were on a rapid collision course, the United States appeared no longer a viable candidate. With the southern states seceding in cascade since November 1860 and the start of the Civil War in April 1861, the bid for Santo Domingo was over, at least for as long as the war lasted.

The events in the United States greatly benefited the chances of the other nation coveting the dominion of Santo Domingo: Spain. At least since the 1850s, the Spanish diplomacy had been very active in the former colony, trying to make the Dominican elite lean toward the old ruler. For instance, in a daring move in 1856 the consul in Santo Domingo registered all Dominicans born before 1821, when the country became independent, as Spanish citizens. By retrieving their old status, virtually most of the Dominican population was turned into subjects to a foreign nation. This widened the gap between supporters of the Spanish option and those disposed toward the United States. Returning to the direct rule of the old mother country was the option defended by part of the Dominican elite as the solution for the chronic instability of the country and to the threat of Haitian expansionism.[18]

Despite deep divisions caused by the issue, Pedro Santana, who had been president of the Dominican Republic since 1858, managed to earn support from the Parliament, which passed a law declaring the country reintegrated into the Spanish Monarchy on March 18, 1861. This was accepted with little surprise, but also little excitement, by the Spanish Crown, which was aware that the major change in the status quo of the Caribbean since Haiti's independence in 1804 was likely to cause turmoil in the island

---

[17] Cristóbal Robles Muñoz. *Paz en Santo Domingo (1854-1865). El fracaso de la anexión a España.* Madrid: CSIC, 1987, pp. 45-61.

[18] Luis Alfonso Escolano Jiménez. "El comienzo de las relaciones diplomáticas entre España y la República Dominicana en 1855." *Revista Complutense de Historia de América*, 2011, vol. 37, pp. 277-99; Inarejos Muñoz. *Intervenciones coloniales y nacionalismo español. La política exterior de la Unión Liberal y sus vínculos con la Francia de Napoleón III (1856-1868).* Madrid: Sílex, 2007, pp. 63-74.

and abroad. Nevertheless, before a fait accompli provoked by its diplomacy, the Crown and the Government accepted the Dominican petition to reincorporate the country. Pedro Santana ceased to be president of the Dominican Republic and became captain general of Santo Domingo. In theory, the country became another Captaincy General on equal terms with Cuba and Puerto Rico, but in fact it was to be monitored from Havana. Before the likely prospects of fierce opposition to the reintegration by the sectors of the Dominican ruling class which favored tutelage by the United States, or simply wanted to keep the country independent, the Spanish Government considered that the Cuban administration was much more fit to handle the situation than a Dominican elite which had fared poorly in ruling their own country. The Spanish authorities were aware that Santana and the merchants of Santo Domingo's capital city were far from representing most of the Dominican population. Fifty years of fighting for independence had created a strong national sentiment among a good deal of a people who would not easily give away a sovereignty they had long fought for.

Opposition to the reincorporation was to be expected, and indeed it took place from the very beginning. This proved decisive for the history of the Volunteers. Even before the so-called Restoration War began in August 1863, Dominicans who opposed the reintegration into Spain gathered around Buenaventura Báez and staged a low-scale guerrilla war from the very beginning of the operation. On February 24, 1861, weeks before the Dominican Parliament passed the law giving up its sovereignty, a group of Dominicans who opposed re-annexation attacked the country's second most important city, Santiago de los Caballeros. According to the Madrid newspaper *La Discusión*, the reincorporation was born among "members of the Royal Audience, government officials, merchants, employees, and neighbors of that city [Santo Domingo]."[19] In June 1861, only a month after the Spanish began to disembark in Santo Domingo, Dominican patriots launched an attack from their Haitian haven against the neighboring town of Las Matas de Farfán. The attack created great concern about the frailty of Spain's position in the island among the community of Dominicans and Spaniards who supported the reintegration.[20] Much was at stake, and these men were not entirely confident in the local authority's capacity to manage the situation. Thus, a group of them, mostly merchants and civil servants, only days after the attack asked Cuba's captain general Francisco Serrano (1859–62) permission to create two companies of Volunteers to reinforce the capital's garrison. Many of these men had recently settled in Santo Domingo from Cuba. Alongside the first troops, hundreds of civil servants with experience in the Antilles flocked to Santo Domingo to rebuild Spanish sovereignty in the country. Thus, they were men who had become familiar with the Volunteers in Cuba and knew that, in case of need, arming civilians would be a quick way to reinforce of securing Spain's rights and their position. As Serrano had no authority to create military units, he escalated the request sent to him to the Ministry of War in Madrid, which approved it on July 26, 1861.[21] The approval was

---

[19] *La Discusión*, 07-04-1863, p. 2.
[20] Frank Moya Pons. *The Dominican Republic. A National History*. Princeton: Markus Wiener Publishers, 2010 (first published in 1998), pp. 185–99.
[21] AGMM, Ministerio de la Guerra, sig. 5664.9.

only partial, however, as no units were created in Santo Domingo's capital. Instead, a section was organized in Santiago de los Caballeros, for it was close to Haiti, where droves of patriots had found shelter, and hence was more prone to be attacked again.[22]

Officially, Spain only faced minor skirmishes in Santo Domingo, but the authorities knew of its frail position and could hardly disregard the pressure from the community of Spaniards and their Dominican allies to take firmer action. A series of attacks against Spanish positions revealed the authority's frail holding of the ground, thus putting themselves at risk in case of a major uprising. It was evident that the first enthusiasm the reincorporation might had raised soon faded away amid proof that Spain was in no condition to build an administration and a military structure anew in Santo Domingo. Anti-Spanish sentiments ran high among a great deal of the local population. Calls to join the Spanish cause were not popular. Apart from the proposed Volunteer force, only a few hundred men answered the call to join the *Cuerpo de Reservas*, or Dominican Reserves, an auxiliary force to the Spanish regular army mostly composed of Dominican Army veterans who distrusted the local ruling elite's capacity to stabilize the country. One of these men was Sergeant Máximo Gómez, whose trust in Spain was soon diluted to the point that he played a major role in the Cuban struggles for independence in the following years.

Amid this context, on March 2, 1863, Felipe Ribero y Lemoyne (1862–3), who had recently replaced Santana as captain general of Santo Domingo, officially called for the creation of a Volunteer battalion in the capital city following the Cuban model. Members of the Spanish administration and merchants were the bedrock of the project. According to the report sent by Ribero to the Ministry of War on May 17, 1863, the twenty-two officers of the future battalion were ten civil servants, five merchants, five owners, and one officer from the Dominican Reserves.[23] This meant that, for the first time, the Volunteers organized in Havana in 1855 served as a blueprint to be used by Spain in a colonial campaign outside the island. The idea had been considered during the war in Morocco, but Santo Domingo was the first place where the volunteer model was implemented outside Cuba. A major recruiting problem for organizing volunteer units in Santo Domingo was the initial lack of Spaniards. The country had only been recently reincorporated into Spain, and the Dominicans who had retrieved the Spanish citizenship thanks to the consul back in 1856 were for the most part men over their forties, not much fit for military service below the senior officer positions. Certainly, the number of Spaniards in Santo Domingo had been growing since the 1850s. By 1861, there were around 2,000, excluding the ones who benefited from the 1856 register, and some of them had established firms which controlled much of the tobacco and mahogany commerce in the capital and its hinterland.[24] Alongside this group, the

---

[22] AGMM, Ministerio de la Guerra, sig. 5664.4.
[23] AGMM, Ministerio de la Guerra, sig. 5664.5.
[24] Serulle Ramia, José & Boin, Jacqueline. "Evolución económica de la República Dominicana, 1844–1930," in Moya Pons, Frank (ed.). *Historia de la República Dominicana*. Madrid: CSIC / Academia Dominicana de la Historia / Ediciones Doce Calles, 2010, p. 150; Luis Alfonso Escolano Jiménez. *La rivalidad internacional por la República Dominicana y el complejo procesal de su anexión a España (1858-1865)*. Santo Domingo: Archivo General de la Nación, 2013, pp. 243–62; Robles Muñoz. *Paz en Santo Domingo*, pp. 9–22.

solution to the lack of men came from the civil servants who had settled in the country following the troops. As Cuba's captain general reported to Madrid, members of the recently established justice branch joined the two volunteer companies nearly in toto, alongside some prominent Dominican merchants who had retrieved their Spanish citizenship after 1856 and who would hold top positions.[25]

Little is known of the military activity of Santo Domingo's Volunteers. Military reports sent to the Ministry of War from Havana barely mention them, which suggests that they were never activated outside of the city, where most of the military action took place. José de la Gándara y Navarro (1864–5), the last Spanish captain general of Santo Domingo who was charged with putting an end to the reintegration, did not mention the Volunteers even once in *Anexión y guerra de Santo Domingo*, published in 1884, his two-volume detailed account of the war between Spanish soldiers and Dominican nationalists between August 1863 and May 1865. Hence, it is much likely that the Volunteers of Santo Domingo were dismantled during the withdrawal of Spanish troops which took place between May and July of 1865, if not before.

Establishing volunteer units in Santo Domingo might have been an unsuccessful short-lived experiment with no clear military use, but the war in Hispaniola helped their colleagues in Cuba to reaffirm their role within the Spanish defensive system. Certainly, the Dominican war was not as popular as the war in Morocco. Rather than supporting military expeditions for the sake of Spain's prestige, Cuba's captain generals Francisco Serrano (1859–62) and Domingo Dulce (1862–6) were two liberal soldiers who regarded collaboration with the Cuban reformist elite as the best way to secure Spanish sovereignty in the island. Both captain generals, but especially Dulce, allowed creole reformists to openly disseminate their ideas through publications and newspapers, most notably *El Siglo*. This gave shape to a sort of organized reformist party which pushed the Spanish Government to call for a *Junta de Información* in 1865–7, aimed at providing a platform for discussion between the authorities in Madrid and elected representatives of Cuba and Puerto Rico.[26] In this context, the authorities opted not to engage excessively in promoting events to support the war against Dominican nationalists. Fighting a distant Muslim army had garnered much popular support, but the implications of waging a war against a society so similar in language, culture, and society could cause much unrest in the island.

Outside the island, the US factor was also to be considered as a likely source of troubles for Spain in Cuba stemming from the war in Santo Domingo. As the Union Army steadily advanced in a series of victories against the Confederacy during 1864 and 1865 and the Southern resistance was not tenable for much longer, the most likely scenario was that the United States would revive its interests in the Caribbean. Spanish sovereignty over the three major Antilles of Cuba, Santo Domingo, and Puerto Rico was simply not compatible with US interests and the Monroe Doctrine.[27] Hence,

---

[25] Robles Muñoz. *Paz en Santo Domingo*, pp. 127–63.
[26] María Dolores Domingo Acebrón. "La Junta de Información en Madrid para las reformas en las Antillas, 1866." *Hispania*, 2002, vol. LXII/1, No. 210, pp. 141–66.
[27] Martínez-Fernández. *Torn Between Empires*, pp. 161–70.

this was another source of potential trouble for Spain in the Antilles. If the financial contribution can be taken as a measure to determine the Volunteers' support for this war, the fact that they donated less than 30,000 pesos for the Dominican campaign is quite telling (whereas they had contributed *c.* 275,000 for the Moroccan war).[28]

Despite this, and although the outcome of the war in Santo Domingo was a setback for Spain's imperial aspirations to a stronger presence in the Caribbean, the Volunteers did contribute to the war effort, which helped to consolidate them as a permanent element of the Spanish defensive system in Cuba. In fact, just as had been considered during the war against Morocco, there were plans to send Volunteers to fight in Santo Domingo. In April 1864, Baudilio Vila, who was an officer in a Havana's Volunteer battalion, sent a report to the Ministry of War while military operations were still ongoing in Santo Domingo. Vila suggested recruiting men from among the already existing Volunteer units to create a 600-strong Prince of Asturias Volunteer Battalion and send it from Cuba to Santo Domingo under his direct command. He claimed some military experience as a former member of the radical liberal National Militia uprising against the Moderate Party government that took place in Barcelona between August and November 1843.[29]

Another way the Volunteers contributed to the military effort in Santo Domingo was through logistics. Due to its proximity to Hispaniola, Santiago de Cuba became a platform used to send and receive troops and goods to and from Santo Domingo.[30] This allowed the local Volunteers to claim their role in the Spanish defensive system. Since most of the local army garrison had left for Santo Domingo, the Volunteers assumed its tasks during the duration of the war, as well as organized a structure of support for the men fighting in Santo Domingo. This included sending spirits and cigars, but more importantly, the transport of sick soldiers returning from Santo Domingo to the military hospitals of Santiago de Cuba. This task was extremely dangerous, due to the infectious nature of the tropical diseases present. A group of 65 men, out of the 1,400 Santiago de Cuba Volunteers, was selected to carry out the transportation.[31] In total, it is estimated that the Santiago de Cuba Volunteers transported more than 10,000 men between August 1863 and July 1865.[32]

The efforts of the Volunteers were praised by the authorities, earning the recognition of the Crown. Their contribution helped their consolidation as a permanent militia in Cuba. In fact, Captain General Dulce informed the Ministry of War about the Santiago de Cuba Volunteers' efforts. He advised that giving some official recognition to their contribution would raise their morale and would help to consolidate their role in Cuba. As a result, twenty-three of the Volunteers were awarded military decorations by the

---

[28] Martínez Nubla. *Los Voluntarios de Ultramar*, p. 38.
[29] AGMM, Ministerio de la Guerra, "Propuesta de creación de un Batallón de Voluntarios en Cuba para Santo Domingo (1864)," sig. 5664.6; AHN, Ultramar, 4366, exp. 8. For an overview of the National Militia, see Juan Sisinio Pérez Garzón. "La Milicia Nacional," in VVAA. *Sagasta y el liberalismo español*. Madrid: Fundación BBVA, 2000, pp. 137–48.
[30] José de la Gándara. *Anexión y guerra de Santo Domingo*, vol. II, pp. 200–28.
[31] AGMM, Ministerio de la Guerra, sig. 5636.25.
[32] AHN, Ultramar, 4717, exp. 1.

Crown in December 1865, seven months after the end of the war.[33] After that war, the Volunteers had clearly consolidated their role thanks to the recognition of the Spanish authorities in Havana and Madrid of their efforts during the war.

Volunteers in Puerto Rico

One of the effects of the war in Santo Domingo was the creation of a Volunteer battalion in San Juan, Puerto Rico's capital, on December 23, 1864, following the model of their colleagues in Cuba. The idea to emulate the Cuban Volunteers was suggested by the Puerto Rican sugar baron José Ramón Fernández to Captain General Félix María de Messina (1862–5). Fernández was the most prominent figure of the commercial elite— mostly made up of *peninsulares*—who dominated San Juan. They recruited around 500 of their employees, and gave them uniforms and weapons, creating Puerto Rico's first Volunteer Battalion. Following the Cuban model, the promoters of the battalion also became its first officers. José Ramón Fernández was appointed its colonel.[34] The official reason for creating the Volunteers was the fact that half of Puerto Rico's Army garrison was fighting in Santo Domingo. Thus, the Volunteers were supposed to replace these men during the war.[35]

Puerto Rico's Volunteers were linked to the imperial projection of Spain from their very inception. The island was a fertile ground for the Spanish imperial discourse that considered the Peninsula and the Antilles as members of the Spanish Nation. The organization of a local Volunteer battalion was also a result of the ascent of the elite of merchants and landowners, mostly made up of *peninsulares*, which dominated the island's economy by the mid-nineteenth century. Certainly, there was never a mass migration from Spain to Puerto Rico, but the tiny community of *peninsulares* came to dominate the local credit and commerce at the expense of the declining landowning creole elite. In a way, the Volunteers represented the rising power and stronger position of the *peninsulares* who had been expressed their patriotism in the last few years.[36] During Spain's war in Morocco the very elite or merchants that would later create the Volunteers coordinated alongside the Captaincy General a donation of 360,000 pesos for the Spanish soldiers fighting in Africa.[37]

The creation of the Volunteers also sent a powerful political message. The elite of *peninsulares* and their closest Puerto Rican allies would use their loyalty to the Spanish authorities to defend their privileged status within society. To a certain extent, José

---

[33] AHN, Ultramar, 4697, exp. 43.
[34] González Cuevas. ¿*Defendiendo el honor? La institución de voluntarios en Puerto Rico durante la guerra hispanoamericana*. San Juan: Ediciones Puerto, 2014, pp. 59–64.
[35] Rafael Rosado y Brincau. *Bosquejo histórico de la institución de Voluntarios en Puerto-Rico*. San Juan: Imprenta de la Capitanía General, 1888, pp. 11–12.
[36] Astrid Cubano Iguina. *El hilo en el laberinto. Claves de la lucha política en Puerto Rico (siglo XIX)*. San Juan: Ediciones Huracán, 1990, pp. 49–74.
[37] AGPR, Gobernadores Españoles, caja 60; *Gaceta de Puerto Rico*, 05-01-1860; Herminio Flores Onofre. *Donaciones y voluntarios a las guerras de Marruecos durante la segunda mitad del siglo XIX*. MA Thesis, #260. San Juan: Centro de Estudios Avanzados de Puerto Rico y el Caribe, 2008, p. 101.

Ramón Fernández and his colleagues began to promote the idea that the Volunteers were also necessary to defend Spanish authority, since there were groups of creoles that might conspire against Spain. Due to the emergence of the merchant elite of *peninsulares* and the decline of the creole landowners, there was certainly some discontent toward the way Spain ruled Puerto Rico among the propertied and educated circles. These groups had never conspired against Spanish sovereignty, and there was no serious plot to oust Spain by 1864. In Puerto Rico, there had never been an annexationist or nationalist movement aimed at severing ties with Spain. On this island, the main political aspiration of wide echelons of creole society was to have better conditions under Spanish rule. Despite this, the elite of *peninsulares* exploited the tiniest expression of discontent with the Spanish authorities to justify the creation of a militia of armed loyalists.

Only a tiny minority of Puerto Ricans openly advocated for the independence of the island.[38] The two leading voices of the nationalist movement were Ramón Emeterio Betances and Segundo Ruiz Belvis. Betances, son of a Dominican landowner established in Puerto Rico, studied medicine at the University of Paris and advocated for the complete abolition of slavery. Belvis, son of a well-to-do family of creole landowners, was a lawyer educated in the Peninsula and a member of the City Council of Mayagüez, the main city of Puerto Rico's west coast.[39] During the second half of 1864, they circulated a manifesto calling all the *peninsulares* living on the island "scum" and "thieves." Considering that the army garrison in Puerto Rico had sent almost half its personnel to Santo Domingo, the manifesto urged the islanders to start an uprising against Spain, for "there are no soldiers in the island […] and a *jíbaro* and his machete are worth twenty Spaniards."[40] This was an incitement for Puerto Rican peasants, popularly known as *jíbaros*, to rise up against Spain.

The reality was, however, that no one answered the call, and peace in Puerto Rico remained unperturbed. Nonetheless, rumors of an imminent uprising reached San Juan and were exaggerated by the elite of *peninsulares*. They even falsely accused a Puerto Rican officer serving in the Spanish Army, Luis Padial y Vizcarrondo, of preparing an armed uprising for the mere fact of having expressed publicly some disagreement with the way the authorities ruled the island.[41] Padial was expelled from the island by the captain general despite the accusation being unfounded. Finally, the Volunteer Battalion was created on December 23, 1864.[42]

Not really believing in the likelihood of an uprising, the captain general and the *peninsular* merchants based in San Juan used the Betances and Belvis manifesto,

---

[38] Luis González Vales. "The Challenge to Colonialism," in Arturo Morales Carrión (ed.). *Puerto Rico. A Political and Cultural History*. New York and Nashville: W. W. Norton & Company/American Association for State and Local History, 1983, pp. 108–25.

[39] Salvador Brau. *Historia de Puerto Rico*. San Juan: Editorial Coquí, 1966 (first published in New York: Appleton & Company, 1904), pp. 258–60.

[40] Lidio Cruz Monclova. *Historia de Puerto Rico (siglo XIX)*, t. III, vol. I. Río Piedras: Ediciones Universitarias, 1962, pp. 367–8; Francisco A. Scarano. *Puerto Rico. Cinco siglos de Historia*. Bogotá: McGraw-Hill Interamericana, 1993, pp. 431–3.

[41] AHN, Ultramar, 1134, exp. 50; Brau. *Historia de Puerto Rico*, pp. 259–60.

[42] Rosado y Brincau. *Bosquejo Histórico*, p. 12.

and the rumors accusing Luis Padial of conspiring against Spain, as an excuse to tighten their control over the island. Peace in Puerto Rico was not threatened by any nationalist conspiracy. On a report sent to the Ministry of War on August 31, 1865, Captain General Messina wrote that he had stopped the organization of the Volunteers for "peace was secured, and they were not necessary."[43]

The Volunteers were left almost inactive since the Spanish troops returned from Santo Domingo to Puerto Rico in May 1865, after Spain had relinquished its sovereignty over that country.[44] The only known activity of the Volunteers during the war was to send 3,000 pesos, shoes, and clothing to the soldiers fighting on the neighboring island.[45] After 1865 the alliance between the captain general and the elite of *peninsulares* that created the Volunteers exerted an oppressive control over Puerto Rico. Consequently, some members of the Puerto Rican landowning elite began to conspire against Spanish rule, which would crystalize into the uprising of September 1868, as we will see.

---

[43] AHN, Ultramar, 5457, exp. 23.
[44] González Cuevas. *¿Defendiendo el honor?*, pp. 64–5.
[45] AGMM, Documentación de Puerto Rico, sig. 5169.2 & 5169.4.

4

Against the Revolution (1868–78)

In the autumn of 1868, the whole edifice of the Spanish Monarchy plunged into a revolutionary crisis which pushed Spain and her overseas territories to the brink of implosion. In a matter of weeks, the queen was toppled, a war of independence broke out in Cuba, and Puerto Rico experienced its first revolutionary attempt. Spain was shaken to the grounds. In the Peninsula, on September 17, 1868, a coalition of the parties that had been traditionally marginalized from the government—the Progressive Party, the Democratic Party, plus some elements of the Liberal Union—led by General Juan Prim, a war hero, former captain general of Puerto Rico (1847–8) and hero of the war against Morocco and a rising star in Spanish politics under the Progressive banner, started a revolution against Queen Isabella II for having explicitly supported the conservative Moderate Party as the party of power.

Beyond the queen's explicit support for the moderates, the Liberal Union cabinets of the 1860s had failed to gain any substantial benefit for Spain out of the many colonial adventures and proved unable to redress the economic crisis which unfolded from the international effects of the American Civil War and hit most European economies in the known as Panic of 1866. The Union Navy blockade of Confederate ports had caused a shortage of cotton for which the Spanish textile industry, essentially based in Catalonia, could hardly find any alternative supplier. As cotton prices soared in the international market, the textile industry entered a profound crisis, and the influx of foreign investment which nurtured the railways expansion—another vital sector of Spanish economy—ran short. Soon, unemployment grew, Madrid's stock exchange lost most of its value, and social unrest escalated into violent demonstrations and fueled radical liberal plotting for a general uprising.

In less than two weeks after the September 17 uprising, a revolution which became to be known as *La Gloriosa* (The Glorious) by its adherents ousted both the queen and the moderates, who had dominated Spanish politics intermittently since 1843, except for the Progressive Biennium (1854–6) and the Liberal Union long government (1858–63).[1] A new constitution was proclaimed in 1869, which declared Spain a kingdom—still without a king, passed male universal suffrage, and promised a series of reforms which included, among others, wider political rights for the Antilles and

---

[1] Durán. *La Unión Liberal y la modernización de la España isabelina*; V. G. Kiernan. *The Revolution of 1854 in Spanish History*. Oxford: The Clarendon Press, 1966.

solving the pending issue of slavery. Two soldiers and former captain generals of the Antilles became the strong men of the new regime. General Prim was elected head of Government, and General Francisco Serrano, former captain general of Cuba, was appointed regent until a king was found for Spain. Toppling the queen had been rapidly accomplished, but it unfolded civil wars in the Peninsula and the colonies, republican uprisings, several regime changes, and a permanent chaos sugarcoated by some social rights conquests over a six-year period known as *Sexenio Democrático*, or rather more accurately *Sexenio Revolucionario*.

The revolutionary forces, however, were riddled by division, for whereas progressives and liberal unionists thought toppling the Bourbons an accomplished goal, democrats considered it a starting point.[2] The revolution was further weakened by four main issues: a profound internal division surrounding the type of regime desired (monarchy or republic), a chronic political instability in the Peninsula, the unsolved issue of slavery, and a separatist war in Cuba. Consequently, the revolution of September 1868 gave birth to an extremely unstable regime. In only six years, Spain had a Regency (1868–71), a Monarchy (1871–3), a Republic (1873–4), and twenty different cabinets. Besides the war in Cuba, the country also underwent the Third Carlist War (1872–6), and the *Rebelión Cantonal* (1873–4), a federalist republican uprising aimed at breaking Spain into a hundred pieces only to reunite them again from below.[3]

Across the Atlantic, the Antilles were shaken by two revolutions aimed at severing ties with Spain. On September 23, 1868, Puerto Rico underwent its first uprising for independence, known as *Grito de Lares* (Proclamation of Lares). It did not escalate into a full-fledged war as it lacked substantial popular support and was quickly quelled by forces loyal to the Spanish Government. In Cuba, on the contrary, an uprising known as *Grito de Yara* (Proclamation of Yara) launched on October 10, 1868, turned into a long war that devastated the island: the Ten Years' War (1868–78). The aim of ending Spanish sovereignty in the island failed, but the traumatic experience of this war paved the ground for the abolition of slavery and was a foundational moment for Cuban nationalism.[4] Moreover, it also shaped the way in which the Volunteers would operate during the last decades of the Spanish presence in America.

The aim of the Antillean revolutions was clear: to sever ties with Spain. The revolutionary goals of *La Gloriosa* were more imprecise. There was only a vague consensus within the new ruling elite that more political and individual rights ought to be granted. This, of course, included the free inhabitants of Cuba and Puerto Rico. Nonetheless, the debates on people's rights also alluded to the enslaved inhabitants of the Antilles: *c.* 400,000 in Cuba, and *c.* 40,000 in Puerto Rico. These were the main issues that the new regime aimed at implementing in the Antilles through the Minister

---

[2] Miguel Tuñón de Lara. *Estudios sobre el siglo XIX español*. Madrid: Siglo XXI de España Editores, 1971, pp. 141–5.
[3] Raymond Carr. *Spain, 1808–1975*. Oxford: Oxford University Press, 1982, pp. 305–46; Josep Fontana. *La época del liberalismo*, in Josep Fontana, Josep & Ramón Viralles (dir.). *Historia de España*, vol. VI. Barcelona and Madrid: Crítica-Marcial Pons, 2007, pp. 351–408.
[4] Jorge Ibarra. *Ideología mambisa*. Havana: Instituto del Libro, 1967; pp. 9–76.

of the Colonies, Adelardo López de Ayala.[5] Nevertheless, the vagueness of goals and complex issues regarding the Spanish rule in the Caribbean rendered more difficult the elaboration of a coherent policy.

In the Antilles, there was only a vague consensus between *integristas* and reformists on the need to grant more political rights to free inhabitants of Cuba and Puerto Rico though they disagreed whether through assimilation or colonial autonomy. They also agreed the issue of slavery ought to be solved. It was still essential for the economy of both Cuba and Puerto Rico, especially the former, but both wings deemed slavery as untenable after the outcome of the US Civil War. The disagreement centered on how and when to implement the reforms. The *integristas*, with their armed wing the Volunteers, were most reluctant regarding the rapid implementation, or even any implementation at all. For them, the political and social changes pledged by the new government in the Peninsula were an open door to independence and for the outright abolition of slavery, if not a slave revolt. Their political stance was driven by a profound distrust toward the government and the reformists' goodwill.[6]

Counterrevolution in the Antilles

From the autumn of 1868 onward, the *integristas* in Cuba and Puerto Rico were engaged in an active counterrevolutionary effort. Cuba's *integristas* opposed two revolutions simultaneously, staged by the new authorities in the Peninsula and by creole separatists in the island. As to the former, their strategy was clear: to fight any movement aimed at severing ties with Spain. As to the new regime established in Madrid, the position was more complex. The uneven result of the anti-Spanish uprisings in Cuba and Puerto Rico determined not only Madrid's set of reforms for these islands but also the strategies with which the Antillean *integristas* tried to prevent them from being implemented.[7] The escalation of the Cuban uprising into a full-fledged war tempered the implementation of any major reforms. How to end the insurgency became a political battleground for confrontation between the Spanish Government and the *integristas*. The government considered that a generous set of reforms would end the war, whereas the *integristas*, on the contrary, considered that no reforms should be implemented until the rebels gave up their weapons.[8] It essentially became a debate on

---

[5] Mercedes García Rodríguez. *Con un ojo en Yara y otro en Madrid. Cuba entre dos revoluciones.* Havana: Editorial de Ciencias Sociales, 2012, pp. 62–4; Zaragoza. *Las insurrecciones de Cuba*, vol. II, pp. 734–6; Agustín Sánchez Andrés. *El Ministerio de Ultramar. Una institución liberal para el gobierno de las colonias, 1863–1899.* La Laguna: Centro de la Cultura Popular Canaria, 2007, pp. 43–64; Casildo Rodríguez Serrano. "Adelardo López de Ayala y el Ministerio de Ultramar," in Felipe Lorenzana de la Puente (coord.). *España, el Atlántico y el Pacífico y otros estudios sobre Extremadura.* Llerena: Sociedad Extremeña de Historia, 2013, pp. 237–50.

[6] Piqueras Arenas. *La revolución democrática (1868–1874). Cuestión social, colonialismo y grupos de presión.* Madrid: Ministerio de Trabajo y Seguridad Social, 1992, pp. 259–69.

[7] Ibid., pp. 295–9; Inés Roldán de Montaud. *La Restauración en Cuba. El fracaso de un proceso reformista.* Madrid: CSIC, 2000, pp. 1–10.

[8] Segundo Rigal. *A nuestros hermanos de la península.* Havana: 1871; Roldán de Montaud. *La Restauración en Cuba*, pp. 10–25.

trust and strategy. The new Constitution, passed on June 6, 1869, granted a temporary solution: no reforms would be implemented in Cuba and Puerto Rico until they sent representatives to the Spanish Parliament.[9] This reversed the exclusion of Antillean representatives at the Spanish Parliament in force since 1837. The new constitution sanctioned that Cuba would not elect its deputies and senators until the war was over, but Puerto Rico could rightly do so since the island was in peace.

In Puerto Rico, the swift quelling of the *Grito de Lares* introduced a different scenario. Local *integristas* could not openly oppose the implementation of reforms as there was no war on the island, or else this would have meant an open confrontation with the new government. Nonetheless, the *integristas* considered that these reforms should be as limited as possible, for they believed that prospects for another uprising were real. In fact, they accused the local reformists of harboring anti-Spanish sentiments and of plotting against the Mother Country. Thus, the *integrista* strategy became a sort of "conservative reformism," based on conditioning the government's policy toward the island, rather than posing a radical opposition to any reform.[10]

Though the scenarios in Cuba and Puerto Rico were quite different, the *integristas* of both islands rallied the Volunteers around the idea of the *Integridad Nacional*, or national integrity. This was a principle that considered Cuba and Puerto Rico members of the Spanish nation, rather than colonies. Its advocates wanted to keep Spain and her Antilles united, regardless of the political regime in Spain.[11] In real terms, the agenda of the *integrista* elites in Cuba and Puerto Rico was clearly directed against the reformist tendencies of the Spanish revolutionary government. In this context, the Volunteers were instrumental in the *integrista* strategy against the reforms.

However, beyond the basic agreement around the very idea of keeping the Antilles and metropolitan Spain under the same national unit, the Volunteers lacked a more solid cohesion in terms of social or political aspirations due to their very social-cross composition. The outbreak of war in Cuba challenged the strength of the Volunteers as a united force. War granted them a major role in Cuba and favored an incredible expansion beyond the realms of working-class *peninsulares* living in the island's big cities but made their internal contradictions the most evident. The Volunteers were a heterogeneous force only united by their commitment to the very idea of National Integrity.

Before 1868 the Volunteers had been chiefly dominated by *peninsulares*, but with the outbreak of the war, thousands of creoles joined it. United by patriotism, class was the main factor that divided the Volunteers at the start of the war.[12] Class differences

---

[9] *Constitución democrática de la Nación española*. Madrid: Imprenta de "El Imparcial," 1869, título X, art. 108; Alonso Romero. *Cuba en la España liberal*, pp. 36–8.
[10] Cubano Iguina. *El hilo en el laberinto*, pp. 59–70.
[11] Consuelo Naranjo Orovio. "Hispanización y defensa de la integridad nacional en Cuba, 1868–1898." *Tiempos de América: Revista de historia, cultura y territorio*, 1998, No. 2, pp. 71–92.
[12] For class E. P. Thompson's definition is followed, of class as a "social and cultural formation, arising from processes which can only be studied as they work themselves out over a considerable historical period." *The Making of the English Working Class*. London: Penguin, 1980 (first published in 1963), p. 11.

also translated into different political cultures, views, and practices. The Volunteers were made up of men that belonged to upper, middle, and lower classes. Each of them engaged in an intense struggle for political, social, and economic power, all within the umbrella of *integrismo* during the revolutionary period of 1868–78, especially in Cuba. This division proved a key element in the understanding of how the Volunteers resisted the challenges posed by the revolutionaries in Madrid and the Antilles.[13]

In 1868 the Volunteers were still an essentially urban phenomenon, both in Cuba and Puerto Rico. Chief officers and officers were for the most part members of the commercial, financial, landowning elite, as well as former army officers and civil servants of the colonial administration's highest ranks.[14] They were predominantly *peninsulares* who had settled in the Antilles after the 1820s and 1830s, thriving economically due to their involvement in the slave, sugar, and commercial trades. In Cuba, their leading figure was the Basque sugar baron, financier, and slaveowner Julián de Zulueta, and in Puerto Rico the creole José Ramón Fernández, the island's major sugar baron and slaveowner. Despite the opposition of these upper-class Volunteers to the reforms promised by the revolutionary government of *La Gloriosa*, some of them were well connected with the new regime in Spain. They were often granted major public contracts by the government, some of whose members had relatives among the Volunteers. For instance, Ramón López de Ayala, brother of the minister of the Colonies, was captain of Havana's 4th Volunteers Battalion.[15] This group was also well connected to the local Cuban elite through marriage, as most of them had wedded creole women that belonged to the island's old elite. This was a group deeply committed to the continuity of slavery, and a protectionist economic policy that kept the Antilles as captive markets for Spanish goods they traded with. Their opposition to the reforms promised by Madrid aimed to limit and restrict them as much as possible, trying to find a compromise with the Spanish authorities. Their views were often conveyed through the *Diario de la Marina*, Cuba's most important newspaper of the day. This *integrista* elite tried to dominate the Volunteers and use them to push forward their agenda, but the lower echelons often escaped their control, creating a political culture of their own. In Puerto Rico, class differences among the Volunteers were not as acute. The absence of war and the virtual nonexistence of an industry did not allow social and political tensions to grow as exacerbated as in Cuba. Thus, in the smaller of the Spanish Antilles the Volunteer elite generally managed to effectively control the whole of the militia.

Beneath this group, there were the middle-class Volunteers. They were also predominantly *peninsulares* who had arrived in the Antilles in the 1840s and 1850s and often had also married Cuban and Puerto Rican women. Most of them were shopkeepers and small business owners (such as bakeries, taverns, or transport companies), as well as cigar-making company owners. A good example of these men

---

[13] Roldán de Montaud. *La Restauración en Cuba*, pp. 30–5.
[14] María Dolores Domingo Acebrón. *Los Voluntarios y su papel contrarrevolucionario en la Guerra de los Diez Años en Cuba, 1868–1878*. Paris: L'Harmattan, 1996, pp. 53–6.
[15] José Joaquín Ribó. *Historia de los Voluntarios cubanos*. Madrid: Imprenta y Litografía de Nicolás González, 1872, vol. I, p. 334.

was the Catalan José Gener Batet, who had migrated to Cuba in the 1840s, and, after working for a few years as tobacco grower, established in Havana his own cigar-making company, *La Escepción*, which produced the famous *Hoyo de Monterrey* cigars, still much appreciated by cigar aficionados to this day.[16] In the 1870s he was captain of Havana's 6th Volunteer Battalion and was known for his fierce opposition to any form of concession to Cuban nationalism or even reformism. In fact, the political views of middle-class Volunteers tended to be far more intransigent and much more nationalistic than the upper-class. *La Voz de Cuba*, owned by the Asturian journalist and Volunteer Gonzalo Castañón, tended to represent the political views of this group.[17] These men coveted the superior social, cultural, and economic position of the elite, either *integrista* or reformist. During the war, they saw the opportunity to claim a greater share of power through violence. Politically, this group was highly heterogeneous. There were monarchists, as well as republicans, conservatives, and liberals, but all were radically committed to the continuity of Spanish rule. It was often the case that they supported the revolution of 1868 in Spain but not the colonial reforms it promised, as these were often perceived as a threat to Spain's presence in the Antilles. Rather than by politics, they were defined by their social position. Beyond opposing the political changes promised by Madrid and the *insurgents*, these middle-class Volunteers were also driven by an intense desire to ascend socially and economically. They considered the declining old Cuban elite as the most vulnerable enemy, for they had been displaced by the *integrista* elite from political power and were not supported by Spanish authorities. During much of the war, these Volunteers attacked the lives and properties of the declining creole upper-middle class. Repressing the political and social enemy, which often included seizing their property, required the indispensable collaboration of the working-class Volunteers, who would provide the brute force and the numbers. The influence of middle-class over working-class Volunteers was remarkable, both as officers and as employers.

Working-class Volunteers represented the lowest social echelons of this militia. They were mostly young *peninsulares* from Spain's northern regions, mostly Galicia, Asturias, and Catalonia, but also from the Canary Islands. For instance, in 1870 over 70 percent of Volunteers in Matanzas came from these four regions.[18] Usually, they had recently migrated to the Antilles and were often employed by middle-class Volunteers as shop assistants, store clerks, coachmen carters, cigar-makers, stevedores, or carters. They were relatively isolated from creoles, spending long hours "behind the counter" with their *peninsular* employees and tending to socialize with fellow countrymen in social clubs and regional associations. Also, due to their young age, they were generally not married, which was the usual way to integrate into the local society. This isolation often generated fierce anti-Cuban sentiments, which

---

[16] *El Moro Muza*, 31-03-1870, pp. 1–2.
[17] J. R. Betancourt. *Las dos banderas. Apuntes históricos sobre la insurrección de Cuba. Cartas al Excmo. Sr. Ministro de Ultramar. Soluciones para Cuba*. Seville: Establecimiento Tipográfico del Círculo Liberal, 1870, p. 63; García Rodríguez. *Con un ojo en Yara y otro en Madrid*, pp. 109–17.
[18] Manuel Moreno Fraginals & José J. Moreno Masó. *Guerra, migración y muerte (El ejército español en Cuba como vía migratoria)*. Colombres: Ediciones Júcar, 1993, p. 97.

were used by middle-class Volunteers to direct their violence against the old creole reformist elite.[19] They were generally poorly educated, and their political views often shaped by their employers and *La Voz de Cuba*. Since the 1860s these working-class Volunteers began to develop a greater class consciousness through their involvement in Cuba's organized labor movement. This was de facto constrained to Havana, where *La Aurora*, the island's first labor newspaper, had been created in 1865 by Saturnino Martínez, a migrant from Asturias who was employed at a tobacco factory and was himself a Volunteer.[20]

The reason for the intransigence of the rank-and-file Volunteer in the big cities is difficult to determine. It might have been caused by their generally poor education, and relative isolation from Cuban society, at least during their first years on the island. Most of the Volunteers in the big cities were young peninsular migrants, mostly employed in the commercial sector by other *peninsulares*, who often happened to be their relatives. Their working conditions tended to be quite harsh, spending long hours behind the counter, and often living in the shop backroom, with little contact with Cubans outside of their working hours. They often came to see in every Cuban a suspected rebel, who would potentially thwart their goal of making a living on the island. Thus, these young men were easy prey for the sort of radical rhetoric conveyed by *La Voz de Cuba* and other similar newspapers, which called for the "extermination" of the rebels.[21] Theirs was a noncompromising political attitude.

Volunteers' Days of Fury

In the autumn of 1868, Cuba's *integrista*s were caught between two revolutions, in Madrid and Cuba. Nonetheless, the instability of the central government and the scarce regular troops that Spain had in Cuba allowed the Volunteers to achieve a dominant position they had never enjoyed before. On October 10, 1868, a landowner and lawyer educated in Barcelona, Carlos Manuel de Céspedes, who eight years before had supported the Spanish intervention in Morocco, declared the independence of Cuba from his nearly broken sugar mill *La Demajagua*, nearby Manzanillo, in Oriente.[22] He was supported by a group of creole landowners highly indebted and who had lost faith in reforms under the governance of Spain.[23] In fact, some of them had been Volunteers during the early 1860s, when hope in reforms dominated Cuban politics. Francisco Vicente Aguilera, one of the wealthiest men of Bayamo and an important funder of the revolution, had been captain of the

---

[19] Áurea Matilde Fernández Muñiz. *España y Cuba, 1868–1898. Revolución burguesa y relaciones coloniales*. Havana: Editorial de Ciencias Sociales, 1988, pp. 135–56.
[20] Casanovas. *Bread, or Bullets!*, pp. 80–1.
[21] *La Voz de Cuba*, 30-01-1869, p. 1.
[22] María Victoria López-Cordón. *La revolución de 1868 y la I República*. Madrid: Siglo XXI de España Editores, 1876, pp. 114–15.
[23] AHN, Ultramar, 4417, exp. 90; 4349, exp. 48; 4347, exp. 63.

local Volunteer battalion by 1860, whereas Calixto García, leading commander of Oriente's rebel army, had been second lieutenant of Ojo de Agua's tiny Volunteer section before the war.[24]

In front of them, the man charged with organizing the repression was Captain General Francisco Lersundi (1867–9), a man at odds with the new revolutionary power in Spain. Lersundi was a First Carlist War veteran, former prime minister in 1853 in a conservative cabinet, and a staunch supporter of the ousted Queen. He did not recognize the new regime and continued signing decrees on behalf of Isabella II. Lersundi could not rely on many troops to quash the insurgency. On paper, he had 14,720 regular soldiers, 640 civil guards, 3,400 men from the Disciplined Militias, and 1,000 firemen with some military training.[25] In reality, almost two thirds of the soldiers were in hospitals as they had fallen ill to tropical diseases and most of the other units, except for the Civil Guard, had a poor military training after years of actual dereliction. On top of this, the loyalty of the mostly creole Disciplined Militias was at the very least dubious. Thus, the captain general turned at the Volunteers as a quick and cheap alternative to build a strong force with which to defend towns, allowing him to send regular soldiers to do the actual fighting against the rebels.[26] Keeping the cities under control was vital, for though the rebels occupied the countryside and had no material force to take a major town, they might get help in the form of men, weapons, and funds from the cities, where many *laborantes* worked for the success of the rebellion. These were the civilian agents of the insurgency who were called after an article wrote in support of Cuban independence by the journalist Rafael María Merchán in *El País* on November 15, 1868, entitled "Laboremus."[27] Discretely, they labored for Cuban independence throughout the war.

Calling the Volunteers was a great success, for their numbers rocketed. If there were 12,000 of them before October 10, they soon numbered 35,000 throughout the island only a month later, and rose to 70,000 by April 1869. They gathered an impressive force organized in 41 battalions, 162 companies, and 81 sections of infantry, 13 regiments, 38 squadrons and 16 sections of cavalry, and 1 artillery-mounted brigade.[28] At least during the first months of the war, only whites were allowed into the Volunteers, which means that being around 70,000, around a third of the 195,000 white males over 16—105,000 *peninsulares* and 90,000 Cubans—donned the uniform.[29] Fear that the *mambises*, as independence fighters were called, really wanted to wage a racial war and to establish a new Haiti, as *La Voz de Cuba* and other loyalist media soon claimed,

---

[24] *Cuerpos de Voluntarios de la isla de Cuba*, p. 34; José Abreu Cardet. *Apuntes sobre el integrismo en Cuba, 1868–1878*. Santiago de Cuba: Editorial Oriente, 2012, p. 48, note 137.

[25] Eugenio Vandama y Calderón. *Colección de artículos sobre el Instituto de Voluntarios de la Isla de Cuba*. Havana: Imp. Militar, 1897, p. 48.

[26] Otero Pimentel. *Memoria sobre los Voluntarios*, pp. 48–9.

[27] Eleuterio Llofriu y Sagrera. *Historia de la insurrección y guerra de la isla de Cuba*, vol. I. Madrid: Imprenta de la Galería Literaria, 1871, p. 51.

[28] *Cuerpos de Voluntarios de la Isla de Cuba*, p. 14. Navarro. *Las guerras de España en Cuba*. Madrid: Ediciones Encuentro, 1998, p. 28; Vandama y Calderón. *Colección de artículos*, p. 14.

[29] José María García de Arboleya. *Tres cuestiones sobre la isla de Cuba. ¿De dónde venimos? ¿Dónde estamos? ¿Adónde vamos?* Havana: Imprenta del Tiempo, 1869, pp. 14–15.

boosted the expansion of the Volunteers beyond the community of *peninsulares*, who only amounted to a tenth of Cuba's population. Thus, by recruiting thousands of white creoles, the war made the Volunteers a Cuban force truly, though only white, rather than a simple militia of *peninsulares* with a just a few locals.

The spectacular growth of the Volunteers, who outnumbered the regular army by far, had many *integristas* seeing them as the true armed representatives of their interests, rather than the government's regular troops. After all, most regular soldiers were poorly paid conscripts, if paid at all, commanded by a captain general appointed by officials in Madrid forced to fight a war they generally abhorred. On the contrary, the Volunteers were men who had stepped up in order to defend their very interests in a land where they had found their means of living, a home, and often a family. Because of this, they were more prone to be controlled by the local *integrista* elite, which not always coincided with Madrid's policy. Captain General Lersundi fully identified with the *integristas*, but due to his support for the ousted queen, his position was no longer tenable. Consequently, local institutions soon rushed to financially support the Volunteers so as not to make them fail due to political instability. The Spanish Bank of Havana gave 45,000 pesos on November 17, 1868, to pay for the expenses of 500 Volunteers for three months, probably thinking that the war would soon be over and that a strong local militia will be necessary to counter the foreseeable reforms. Their hopes of a short war soon proved wrong, and by 1872 the bank had already given 150,000.[30] The Catholic Church also contributed to the cause. The bishop of Havana, Jacinto María Martínez, had donated 32,000 pesos by early 1869.[31]

Soon, the new government in Madrid led by General Prim replaced Lersundi with General Domingo Dulce as their man in Havana in January 1869. Dulce was a well-known liberal soldier who had supported *La Gloriosa*, and who enjoyed a good relationship with creole reformists, with whom he had collaborated during his previous term as captain general between 1862 and 1866. He firmly believed that political representation and individual rights would convince Cuban rebels to give up the fight.[32] One of Dulce's first measures was to organize a meeting between representatives of the *integristas* and the reformists, headed respectively by Julián de Zulueta, by now colonel of Havana's 2nd Volunteer Battalion, and Miguel de Aldama, a wealthy reformist landowner who had conspired to annex Cuba to the United States in 1848.[33] Because of this, *integristas* hated Aldama, who needed the protection of fifty armed men granted by Dulce to defend his conspicuous palace in Havana.[34] The aim of the meeting was to build a common front between *integristas* and reformists over a

---

[30] Gil Gelpí y Ferro. *Álbum histórico fotográfico de la guerra de Cuba desde su principio hasta el reinado de Amadeo I*. Havana: Imprenta "La Antilla" de Cacho-Negrete, 1872, pp. 85–6; Inés Roldán de Montaud. *La banca de emisión en Cuba (1856–1898)*. Estudios de Historia Económica, No. 44. Madrid: Banco de España, 2004, p. 68.

[31] AHN, Ultramar, 4390, exp. 68; Rigoberto Segreo Ricardo. *Iglesia y nación en Cuba (1868–1898)*. Santiago de Cuba: Editorial Oriente, 2010, pp. 182–241.

[32] Joaquín Buxó de Abaigar. *Domingo Dulce. General isabelino*. Barcelona: Editorial Planeta, 1962, pp. 163–89.

[33] Chaffin. *Fatal Glory*, pp. 11–23.

[34] BNC, CM Ponce, No. 445.

set of reforms under Spanish sovereignty to counter the insurgents. This attempt was thwarted by incompatible strategies. The *integristas* would not have reforms without peace, whereas the reformists thought there would be no peace without reforms.

Beyond negotiations among elite members, the Volunteers' real power stemmed from their numbers. By the early months of 1869, once the regular army units had been dispatched to fight the rebels in eastern Cuba, Havana was a city of 210,000 inhabitants, of whom over 9,000 were armed Volunteers, the only force available to the captain general beyond the scant public order unit.[35] Despite knowing his weak position, Dulce pushed forward his reformist plans and issued a proclamation on January 12, 1869, declaring that the island would elect representatives to the Spanish Parliament, granting freedom of speech and reunion, and calling for an amnesty for the Cuban rebels.[36] This offerings were unacceptable to the radicalized middle-class and working-class Volunteers. Aware of Dulce's dependence on them, by the end of January 1869 they waged a wave of violence in Havana with a strong symbolic message directed against Dulce as much as against their actual victims.

Clashes between *integristas* and pro-independence Cubans had been relatively common in Havana since the start of the war, but the situation rapidly escalated sparkled by fear to Dulce's reformist plans. Freedom of speech allowed public displays of Cuban nationalism, which often conveyed its message through some of the more popular entertainments, such as theater plays. The Villanueva Theatre, very popular among creole nationalists for the political tone of many of the plays represented there, was ransacked by a group of Volunteers on January 22, ensuing a clash between them and theatergoers, during which one person was killed and eighteen were injured. The reason was that a line of *El Perro Huevero*, the play represented that very day, read "long live the freedom of the land which produces the cane," considered seditious at the time. Two days later, groups of Volunteers attacked the *Café del Louvre*, a popular meeting point among affluent Havana university students, many of whom harbored independence ideals. Right after attacking the *Louvre*, the assailing Volunteers looted the nearby impressive residence of the reformist leader Miguel de Aldama, beating his Black servants and raping one of them.[37] The day after, Aldama asked Dulce for personal protection before going into exile in the United States, a move followed by around 20,000 Cubans during the war. Havana was no longer a safe place for them. The rank-and-file Volunteers, often young men who worked long hours behind the counter, were driven not only by political opposition to Dulce's reforms and their supporters, but also by social hatred for people who, like Aldama and *El Louvre*'s university students, enjoyed a social position they could only dream of.

---

[35] Carlos de Sedano y Cruzat. *Cuba desde 1850 á 1873. Colección de informes, memorias, proyectos y antecedentes sobre el Gobierno de la Isla de Cuba, relativos al citado periodo y un apéndice con las Conferencias de la Junta Informativa de Ultramar, celebradas en esta capital en los años de 1866 y 1867*. Madrid: Imprenta Nacional, 1873, pp. 152–3; Olivar Bertrand. *Prim*. Madrid: Tebas, 1975, pp. 490–7.

[36] García Rodríguez. *Con un ojo en Yara y otro en Madrid*, pp. 124–36.

[37] AHN, 4933, exp. 1, No. 93 & 94.

The Volunteers' violence evidenced that the understanding between *integristas* reformists envisioned by Dulce was almost impossible. Indeed, tension between both factions ran high in Havana.[38] Assaults and murders became common in the city streets. Finding oneself in the wrong spot at the wrong time could be taken for a death sentence. Traditionally, Havana was not a city neatly segregated by race or birthplace, with just a few exceptions, but there were invisible borders better not to be crossed. A member of Havana's public order force reported to Dulce that, in some areas of the city where *integristas* were a minority, and especially in neighborhoods with a strong Black and mulatto community, the life of "honest men, especially the *peninsulares*, hung by a thread."[39]

With an ongoing war in Oriente, unstopped violence in Havana he was not able to control, and a lack of support from a government unable to send more men and weapons, Dulce's position soon became extremely weak. He needed the Volunteers, the very force which collaborated in undermining his authority. His complaints to Madrid against the Volunteers' violence went unheeded by the government. In his replies, Adelardo López de Ayala, minister of the Colonies, stated time and again that the Volunteers were the only force available in Havana, and that their officers had generously contributed to the Cuban treasury.[40] Dulce's complaints might be well-grounded, but his demands were not to be heard. He was alone against the Volunteers.

With the Volunteers out of control in Havana, and with no troops in the city to restore his authority, Dulce devised alternative ways to regain the upper hand, such as issuing a new regulation, or *reglamento*, for these men. So many new Volunteer units had been created since the war broke out that a reorganization was necessary. The new *reglamento*, published on April 21, 1869, confirmed the Volunteers' role in the Spanish military system in Cuba, but some of its articles were aimed at keeping them under a tighter scrutiny. While it kept much of the content of the 1856 *reglamento*, it created the *Subinspección General de Voluntarios*, an office overseeing the Volunteers located at La Fuerza Fortress, right next to the Captain's General Palace in old Havana. It was headed by the captain general's second-in-command, known as *segundo cabo*. While the *Subinspección* dealt with all the issues concerning the Volunteers, the captain general had the final decision over the Volunteers' promotion, the appointment of officers, or the creation and dissolution of units.[41]

Considering his weak position, the captain general sought to appease the Volunteers by adopting a harder line against the reformists and rebels.[42] In April he revoked the

---

[38] Gabriela dalla Corte Caballero & José Luis Luzón. "Espacio criollo y espacio colonial: los voluntarios y la batalla de La Habana en la Guerra de los Diez Años," in Centro de Investigaciones de América Latina (comp.). *De súbditos del rey a ciudadanos de la nación (Actas del I Congreso Internacional Nueva España y las Antillas)*. Castellón de La Plana: Univeristat Jaume I, Servicio de Publicaciones, 2000, pp. 339–68.

[39] ANRC, Asuntos Políticos, leg. 58, exp. 11.

[40] RAH, CCR, 9/7536, doc. 88 & 100.

[41] *Reglamento para los cuerpos de Voluntarios de la isla de Cuba* (1869), cap. II, art. 8-20.

[42] Alfonso W. Quiroz. "*Integrista* Overkill: The Socioeconomic Costs of 'Repressing' the Separatist Insurrection in Cuba, 1868–1878." *Hispanic American Historical Review*, 1998, vol. 78, No. 2, pp. 261–305.

freedoms granted by the decree of January 12 and deported 250 suspected *laborantes* to Fernando Poo, a tiny Spanish island in the Gulf of Guinea. Two dozen Volunteers were to escort them. The deported were mostly Havana liberal professionals and university students who supported wider reforms for Cuba, but not necessarily independence. These political nuances made no difference for the most radical *integristas*. In the tense atmosphere of early 1869, having shown discontent toward Spanish policy in Cuba was a reason for the *integristas* to consider anyone an enemy of Spain.[43]

Repressing them at home and expelling some of them to a far-flung African island was not enough to the most radical *integristas*, who considered that the physical appropriation of their wealth was the next step to take. Supporters of independence, or even reforms, were to be stripped of their properties. Yielding to pressures, Dulce created the Council of Sequestered Goods (*Consejo de Bienes Embargados*), on April 17, 1869, an office which would oversee the wealth transfer from free Cuba supporters to the hands of the advocates of Spanish Cuba.[44] The corrupt Spanish administration in Cuba soon made the council a hotspot for abuses and generalized corruption. Quite often the embargoed property ended up in the hands of prominent *integristas* with enough money to bribe the council's officials.[45] The symbolism of the *Consejo* was strikingly powerful: it represented the transfer of property from Cuban reformists and pro-independence supporters to *integrista* hands. On July 13, 1869, *La Voz de Cuba*, very popular among the Volunteers' most radical milieu, expressed it blatantly: "The traitors have enough goods to pay for the hardships undergone by the loyal."[46] The confiscation on goods, a common practice in wartime, became one of the cornerstones of Cuban nationalist fight against Spain. For *integristas* taking part in the *Consejo*, it was a basic form of affirming their predominant position.

From its very inception, Volunteer officers took part in the *Consejo*. It was headed by Dionisio López Roberts, political governor of Havana. Its speakers were Juan Atilano Colomé, Mamerto Pulido, and the Count of Pozos Dulces; Havana councilors José Cabarga, Juan Poey, and J. Pedroso; landowners and businessmen Fernando Illas, Bonifacio Blesa Jiménez, and Segundo Rigal; representative of the Cuban treasury, Agustín Genon. Its secretary was Justo Zaragoza. Segundo Rigal and Mamerto Pulido, two peninsular businessmen and Volunteer officers, were much respected by *integristas*.[47] However, rather than appeasing the Volunteers, the *Consejo* gave them a tool for rapid enrichment they were not willing to dispense with. In fact, the measures taken by Dulce against the corruption existing around the *Consejo* ended up precipitating his forcible resignation as captain general.

In Cienfuegos, an *integrista* stronghold in Las Villas and the most important port city in the Cuban southern coast, abuse on embargoed property, and summary

---

[43] AHM-M, Ministerio de la Guerra, sig. 5602.14.
[44] *Disposiciones relativas a bienes embargados e incautados a los infidentes*. Havana: Almacén de papel y efectos de escritorio de Castro Hermanos y Compañía, 1874, pp. 1–15.
[45] Alfonso W. Quiroz. "Corrupción, burocracia colonial y veteranos separatistas en Cuba, 1868–1910." *Revista de Indias*, 2001, vol. LXI, No. 221, pp. 91–111; RAH, CCR, 9/7536, doc. 156.
[46] *La Voz de Cuba*, 13-07-1869, p. 2.
[47] *El Pensamiento Español*, 13-05-1869.

executions, had become a common practice. To redress the situation, the captain general appointed Field Marshall Antonio Peláez as general commander of Las Villas Military District, where he clashed with local authorities. Colonel González Estéfani, the Havana-born head of the *Consejo*'s local branch, had been openly tolerating the illicit expropriation of embargoed properties by local sugar and trade barons, many of whom were Volunteer officers. When Captain General Dulce removed him in May 1869, these men spurred a coordinated action alongside fellow Volunteers from other towns such as Santa Clara, Matanzas, and Havana. Taking advantage of the secure railway communications of western Cuba, thousands of them gathered in Havana, donning their uniforms in a demonstration before the Captain General's Palace on May 30 asking for Dulce's resignation and harassing Peláez, who had been summoned to Havana, the following day.[48] Other *integristas*, mostly groups of civilians and army officers, joined them. The isolation of Dulce became evident when the scant army force guarding the palace refused to disperse the Volunteers, fearing that doing it would cause a bloodbath. Consequently, Dulce stepped down and left for Spain on June 3, 1869, after having appointed his second-in-command, Felipe Ginovés y Espinar, a man relatively popular among the Volunteers for his uncompromised loyalty to Spain, as the new acting captain general.[49]

Dulce's resignation meant a great victory for the Volunteers and the *integristas* in general. Without firing a shot, though with much coercion, they had forced the representative of the Spanish revolutionary government out of Cuba. Symbolically, they had expelled the reforms. After the expulsion, the real power in Cuba was held de facto by the Volunteers. For as long as Ginoés del Espinar remained acting captain general, waiting for a new governor to be appointed, the Volunteers' elite saw a window of opportunity to seize power at the local level. Only days after Dulce's departure, groups of Volunteers staged a campaign to forcibly remove reformists from many city and town councils across Cuba. For instance, the Basque Agustín Goytisolo, a Volunteer officer and a sugar baron with investments in the shipping industry, was appointed mayor of Cienfuegos in September 1869 after his comrades-in-arms stormed the town hall and forced the mayor and councilors, mostly Cuban reformists, out.[50] This was just an expression of the power they gained during Dulce's term and after his expulsion. The Volunteers wanted not only influence over the Captaincy General but also political power at the local level through councils. Thus, the forcible replacement of the captain general was followed by the violent removal of many mayors, who for the most part were Cuban reformists. The Volunteers' aim was to control all centers of power in Cuba.

Having expelled the captain general, and effectively controlling most of the city councils, the most radical *integristas* proceeded to create social institutions on their

---

[48] Antonio Peláez. *Contestación del general D. Antonio Peláez á las groseras calumnias que contiene el manifiesto á la nación por los Voluntarios de la isla de Cuba*. Madrid: Imprenta de D. Cárlos Frontaura, 1869, p. 44.

[49] García Rodríguez. *Con un ojo en Yara y otro en Madrid*, pp. 138–54; Pirala. *Anales de la Guerra de Cuba*, vol. I, pp. 548–9.

[50] Martín Rodrigo y Alharilla. *Los Goytisolo. Una próspera familia de indianos*. Madrid: Marcial Pons, 2016, pp. 96–7.

own. After politics, social influence would follow, and on June 11, 1869, the *Casino Español* was created in Havana.[51] The *casinos* were social clubs, spaces of sociability and relatively discreet political debate. The first one appeared in Madrid in 1836, but soon many were established all over Spain and the American countries with sizeable Spanish communities aimed at organizing and defending the social, economic, or political interests of their members.[52] For instance, a *Casino Español* had been created in Mexico City in 1863, during the reign of Emperor Maximilian I, in order to promote the many vested interests of the influential Spanish community in the former viceroyalty. In Cuba, the *integristas* wanted to establish a *Casino* on their own in order to have a social institution with which to promote their interests and most importantly to defend Spanish sovereignty in the island. Officially, Havana's *Casino Español* was a mere social club open to anyone supporting Spanish Cuba and able to pay the membership, but in fact it became the unofficial headquarters of the *integrista* elite and the Volunteers, and a sort of parallel authority alongside the Captain General's Palace. In fact, the *Casino Español* permanently reserved a hall for activities related to the Volunteers, from meetings to balls and banquets.[53] Most of well-to-do and respected Havana Volunteer officers flocked to join the *Casino Español*. They also represented a good deal of its board members. Thus, soon most of Havana's Volunteer chief officers and officers joined the *Casino Español*, setting an example to follow in other parts of Cuba. Volunteer officers in cities like Santiago de Cuba, Cienfuegos, Matanzas, and Santa Clara were instrumental in establishing a network of *Casinos Españoles*.[54]

After Dulce's resignation, it became an unwritten norm that major political decisions taken by the captain general had to be approved beforehand by the *Casino Español*. Beleaguered by instability at home and an ongoing war in eastern Cuba, the Spanish Government opted to accept the *integrista* ascendancy, rather than to open a second front against the unruly loyalists. Thus, Dulce's successors ought to be approved by the elite running the *Casino Español*. Ginovés del Espinar (1869), Antonio Caballero de Rodas (1869–70), the Count of Valmaseda (1870–2), and Francisco Ceballos (1872–3) were all made honorary Volunteers and often appeared in public donning the Volunteer uniform. Caballero de Rodas soon became one of the most popular among the Volunteers, if not the most. He selected a personal guard made up of chosen Volunteers, the so-called *Compañía de Guías*, commanded by José Olano y Caballero, a Cuban sincerely devoted to the cause of Spain.[55] Furthermore, in February 1870 Caballero de Rodas decreed that all the local branches of the Council

---

[51] Domingo Acebrón. *Los Voluntarios*, pp. 42–51.
[52] María Zozaya Montes. "El origen dieciochesco de los casinos españoles y su raíz italiana," in Francisco Núñez Roldán (ed.). *Ocio y vida cotidiana en el mundo hispánico moderno*. Seville: Universidad de Sevilla, 2007, pp. 617–30.
[53] Art. 9 of the *Fórmula o minuta de la escritura que habrá de otorgarse y bases bajo las cuales ha de constituirse la sociedad El Casino tan pronto como se halle suscrita la mitad de las acciones fijadas en el artículo tercero*. Havana: Imprenta del Avisador Comercial, 1872; Manuel Espadas Burgos. *Alfonso XII y los orígenes de la Restauración*. Madrid: CSIC, 1990, pp. 285.
[54] María José Portela Miguélez. *Redes de poder en Cuba en torno al partido Unión Constitucional, 1878–1998*. Cádiz: Servicio de Publicaciones Universidad de Cádiz, 2004, pp. 176–91.
[55] Otero Pimentel. *Memoria sobre los Voluntarios*, pp. 70–1.

of Sequestered Goods must have Volunteer officers among its members.[56] Not only he had accepted the Volunteers' fait accompli policy of seizing the institution, but he made their participation compulsory.

With the set of events following the expulsion of Dulce, the Volunteers had become the kings of Havana, while the war continued in Oriente. They had imposed their will over the first military and political Spanish authority in an island they could claim theirs. Enjoying such a privileged position, the Havana Volunteers may have felt entitled to determine who the enemies of Spain were, and proceed accordingly, sparing no condition or status, even of senior members of the Catholic Church. For instance, on April 12, 1871, they prevented Jacinto María Martínez, bishop of Havana, from entering the city on his way back from Rome, falsely accusing him of connivance with the Cuban rebels, stemming from the bishop's critical position toward their rebellious attitude.[57] Despite many rank-and-file Volunteers held radical ideals not particularly friendly with the Catholic Church, not allowing the bishop in was crossing a red line which shocked a mostly Catholic society. All the more so, when the bishop himself had contributed with thousands of pesos to fund the Volunteers at the beginning of the war. Despite the outrage perpetrated against the first religious authority of the capital of Cuba, acting captain general Buenaventura Carbó abstained from defending the bishop, for he had no regular troops available in the city and he feared the reaction of the 9,000 Volunteers garrisoning Havana.[58] A month after he arrived in the United States, where he found temporary shelter, Bishop Martínez declared to *The New York Herald* that "the Volunteers have all the power in the island and force the governor to do whatever they want."[59]

This included thwarting any prospects of negotiation that the Spanish and the rebel governments might hold. For instance, on January 26, 1869, Augusto Arango, a *mambí* officer commissioned by Céspedes to meet the Spanish authorities in Puerto Príncipe, was murdered by the Volunteers upon being arrested.[60] The Volunteers wanted a complete defeat of their enemies, not a reconciliation with them. Against the reality of a de facto Volunteer rule in Havana, after 1868 the Spanish Government had expressed a vague desire to broker a deal with the Cuban rebels through the promise of political and social reforms, including political representation and a controlled abolition of slavery. For the Volunteers, this was anathema, for they considered negotiations with the enemy a first step toward a total defeat. Reaching the enemy lines was vital for any hopes of negotiation to succeed, but anyone trying to negotiate a deal between sides was deemed a traitor and could even be executed by the Volunteers. This was the fate, for instance, of an acquaintance of General Prim, the Cuban poet Juan Clemente Zenea, who was captured by the Volunteers of Puerto Príncipe on New Years' Eve

---

[56] Zaragoza. *Las insurrecciones de Cuba*, vol. II, p. 813, note 7.
[57] Jacinto María Martínez. *Los Voluntarios de Cuba y el Obispo de La Habana, ó historia de ciertos sucesos que deben referirse ahora, y no después, y los refiere el mismo Obispo, Senador del Reino*. Madrid: Imprenta á cargo de D. A. Pérez Dubrull, 1871, pp. 167–73.
[58] Zaragoza. *Las insurrecciones de Cuba*, vol. II, pp. 587–8.
[59] AHN, Ultramar, 4934, exp. 2.
[60] Eladio Baldovín Ruiz. *Cuba. El desastre español del siglo XIX*. Astorga: Akrón, 2010, pp. 151–2.

of 1870, on his way back from a meeting he held with the president of the Republic in Arms, Carlos Manuel de Céspedes. Zenea, a man who had been in exile in New York since 1865 for his outspoken support for independence, was contacted by Nicolás de Azcárate, a Cuban collaborator of General Prim who advocated for the island's autonomy. He turned Zenea into a double agent, who began trying to negotiate a deal between Madrid, the rebel government in Cuba, and its delegates in New York on grounds of political autonomy for the island and the disarmament of the Volunteers. The two proposals were simply unacceptable for the Volunteers, for they regarded autonomy as the first step toward independence, and their disarmament the excuse that would allow the rebels to annihilate them. Without weapons and in a hostile political situation, the Volunteers would find themselves at the insurgents' mercy. Hence, they could not pardon Zenea's life, let alone let him act as middlemen between Madrid and the rebel representatives. Despite the safe conduct granted by the Spanish Government, the poet was handed by the Puerto Príncipe Volunteers over to their colleagues in Havana, where he was jailed and later executed on August 25, 1871.[61]

With an ongoing war and rumors that the authorities might use the Volunteers in a negotiation with the rebels, tensions continued to run high in Havana. Clashes with anyone who openly challenged the status quo became commonplace in the violent streets of the capital. One of the groups which most vocally protested the state of Cuba and supported its independence were university students. These young men were for the most part members of affluent families, often sons of peninsular fathers and creole mothers, many of whom surely embraced liberal ideals, sometimes including the independence of Cuba. Among them was José Martí, the galvanizing figure of Cuban independence in the 1890s. Son of a former sergeant in the Spanish Army from Valencia and a mother from the Canary Islands, Martí was able to become a university student thanks to the financial support of a family's friend. Paradoxically, the University of Havana, established by the Dominic Order in 1728 and protected by the Spanish Crown, had become the cradle of many generations of Cuban nationalists, especially after its secularization in 1842. It became an institution dominated by Cuban scholars, who by the 1860s represented twenty-four out of the University's twenty-seven lecturers.[62] An incident involving students and the tomb of an *integrista* idol escalated into the worst violent episode in the history of the Volunteers.

The events go back to November 23, 1871, when eight students of medicine at the University of Havana who were playing at the Espada Cemetery were falsely accused by the warden of desecrating the tomb of Gonzalo Castañón, director of *La Voz de Cuba*. An outspoken *integrista* and a Volunteer himself, Castañón had become a true idol for his comrades-in-arms due to his belligerent opposition to Cuban separatism. He had been murdered in January 1870 in Key West by a Matías Orozco, a Cuban nationalist who edited *El Republicano*, a newspaper which advocated for the island's independence. They were meant to have a duel because Castañón had allegedly insulted the honor of Cuban women exiled in the United States in an article. Having

---

[61] García Rodríguez. *Con un ojo en Yara y otro en Madrid*, pp. 282–324.
[62] Ribó. *Historia de los Voluntarios cubanos*, vol. II, p. 217.

traveled from Havana to Key West, Castañón was gunned down at his hotel in cold blood before the duel could take place. The murder of their idol in such a dishonorable way shocked the Volunteers. His funeral in Havana was a public display of *integrismo* that would not soon fade away. By the autumn of 1871 the memory of Castañón and the events surrounding his death were still fresh.[63]

The Espada Cemetery's warden's false testimony soon spread out in the streets of Havana, and the *integristas* demanded from the authorities a quick and firm action against the students. Only two days after the denouncement, Dionisio López Roberts, political governor of Havana, entered the university and ordered the arrest of forty-five students, among them the eight who had been playing at the cemetery. The students were jailed at the old prison nearby La Punta Fortress and put to trial before a military court made up of six army officers the day after. An army captain, Federico Capdevila, was charged with the defense of the students. Despite the lack of evidence, the court sentenced them to minor penalties, hoping to calm down the thousands of Volunteers that surrounded the court waiting for the verdict. Most of the Volunteers who had gathered to hear the sentence were members of Havana's 5th Battalion and were agitated by Captain Felipe Alonso, an old friend of Castañón who accompanied him to Key West as his second for the duel. Far from accepting the sentence, they threatened to storm the court unless at least some of the defendants were put to death.[64]

With Captain General Count of Valmaseda out of Havana, as he was commanding an important operation in Oriente, the Volunteers' pressure on the authorities soon become unsurmountable. The *segundo cabo*, Romualdo Crespo, a Cuban officer with a softer temperament and with barely regular troops at his disposal, gave in to the Volunteers' request. On 26 November, the forty-five students wet put before a military court anew, now made up of six army officers plus nine Volunteer officers. Fearing riots, members of the *integrista* elite tried to assuage the Volunteers' anger. Lorenzo Pedro, president of the *Casino Español* and a Volunteer officer himself, published an article in the *Diario de la Marina*, calling on the men to calm down, and let the judges do their job.[65] Being a farce trial, the students' lives hung on the Volunteer's mercy, despite the valiant defense put by Captain Capdevila. The Catalan José Gener, captain of the 6th Battalion and owner of the tobacco factory *La Escepción*, read the sentence: Two of them were acquitted, thirty-five sent to prison, and eight, cherry-picked, sentenced to death.[66] The eight, whose ages ranged from 16 to 21, were Anacleto Bermúdez, Carlos Augusto de Latorre, Pascual Rodríguez y Pérez, Carlos Verdugo, Ángel Laborde, Eladio González y Toledo, José de Marcos y Medina, and Alonso Álvarez de la

---

[63] Juan Ignacio de Armas y Céspedes. *Combate de Russell House o muerte de Castañón en Key West el 31 de enero de 1870*. New Providence: Im. del Nassau Times, 1870.

[64] Fermín Valdés Domínguez. *El 27 de noviembre de 1871*. Havana: Imprenta "La Correspondencia de Cuba," 1887, p. 181; Vital Fité. *Las desdichas de la Patria. Políticos y frailes*. Madrid: Imprenta de Enrique Rojas, 1899 p. 59.

[65] *Diario de la Marina*, 27-22-1871; *El Voluntario de Cuba*, 14-12-1870.

[66] A brief biography of José Gener can be consulted in Rafael Villa. *Álbum biográfico de jefes de Voluntarios*. Havana: Tipografía "La Universal" de Ruiz y Hermanos, 1888, pp. 52–4.

Campa. The two latter were the sons of peninsular Volunteer officers who tried to save the students' lives to no avail.[67] When the sentence was read, the Volunteers surrounding the court hall cheered.

On the morning of November 27, 1871, the eight students were taken to La Punta Fortress to face the firing squad, commanded by Volunteer Captain Ramón López de Ayala, senior official of the Spanish Post in Cuba, brother to the minister of the Colonies, and also an old friend of Castañón.[68] One by one, the students were executed, and their corpses taken to an undisclosed site—until it was discovered in 1887, in order to prevent it from becoming a sanctuary for Cuban nationalists. The Volunteer's thirst for revenge had been quenched, but their history had been stained forever, and their murderous action was widely criticized in Cuba as in the Peninsula, even by many of their comrades-in-arms.

The eight medicine students were the innocent victims of the revenge thirst that followed the murder of Castañón.[69] The likes of José Gener, Ramón López de Ayala, and Felipe Alonso might have been mistakenly driven by a desire to revenge the death of an old friend by choosing wrong victims.[70] But many of the Volunteers who surrounded the court and cheered the death of the students might have been guided by a mix of political and social resentment. The profile of the university students, young wealthy Cuban nationalists, had been targeted before during the fury days of 1869, with the storming of the Villanueva Theatre and the *Café del Louvre*. The students' privileged social position, alongside their political views, might have seemed unbearable to men who were often forced to take poorly paid jobs with scant social prestige, who spent long working hours behind the counter or the working table, who used to socialize with fellow *peninsulares*, and who firmly believed in the right of Spain to keep ruling Cuba.

The anger that these men might have felt toward the well-to-do students meant they did not even spare the life of a Volunteer's son. One of the students, Alonso Álvarez de la Campa, was the son of a well-known peninsular merchant and Volunteer officer. Right before the execution, Felipe Alonso, Castañón's friend, told the young student: "Ah, *Alonsito*, not even your father's millions will be able to spare you a bullet in the head!"[71] Quite a statement of crude violence, political hatred, and social resentment all in one.

Far from condemning it, the most radical *integrista* press claimed that the execution of the students was a rightful act of vengeance for the desecration of Castañón's tomb. On the very day of the assassination, November 27, 1871, *Diario de la Marina*, *La Voz de Cuba*, and *La Constancia* published a joint article in which they called the Volunteers to respect law and justice, but in which they wrote that all "Spanish hearts are full of anger against these dirty hyenas [the students]."[72] Radical Volunteers would not be

---

[67] Valdés Domínguez. *El 27 de noviembre de 1871*, pp. 45, 54 & 91.
[68] Ibid., pp. 38, 39, 45 & 50.
[69] Gelpí y Ferro. *Álbum histórico fotográfico*, pp. 327–34.
[70] Valdés Domínguez. *El 27 de noviembre de 1871*, p. 181; Vital Fité. *Las desdichas de la Patria. Políticos y frailes*. Madrid: Imprenta de Enrique Rojas, 1899 p. 59.
[71] Valdés Domínguez. *El 27 de noviembre de 1871*, p. 20.
[72] *La Voz de Cuba*, 27-11-1871, p. 1; Valdés Domínguez. *El 27 de noviembre de 1871*, pp. 60-2.

deterred by the authorities or the opinions of their comrades-in-arms, which did not approve of such savage actions. The assassination was not gratuitous, but symbolic. The students were but the scapegoat with which the lower echelons of the Volunteers, the most radical, showed their determination to claim their stake of power in Cuba.

Beyond these extremely radical circles, the assassination was widely condemned all over Cuba, Spain, and abroad, even by fellow Volunteers. Cuban-born Colonel Francisco de Acosta y Albear, a retired army officer who had raised a Volunteer battalion in 1869, strongly labeled the perpetrators as "social scum ... which have caused more damage to the national cause than all the *laborantes* together."[73] In the Peninsula, even Barcelona's *Círculo Hispano-Ultramarino*, the foremost representative of the colonial lobby in Spain, asked for the acquittal of the students still in prison, which was granted by the Crown on May 9, 1872.[74] Thus, this crime committed by a group of the Havana Volunteers was far from representative of the spirit of the whole militia or the *integristas*.

A Propaganda War

Below the institutions established by the *integrista* elite, more modest Volunteers also devised their own strategies to spread their views and forge alliances beyond the Antilles. Their lower economic and social position did not allow them to create well-funded stable institutions to exert a determinant influence over the Spanish Government and gather support from influential colonial lobbies in the Peninsula. To begin with, they lacked a coherent ideology of political interests, let alone the will to bring about a regime change in Spain, except for a firm defense of National Integrity. In fact, in the articles and books they produced among the Volunteers' most popular milieu, there was barely any explicit support for the monarchy as a system or for the Bourbon restoration. There was instead a constant defense of the union between Spain and her overseas territories, often vaguely wrapped with liberal and republican principles. Thus, the less educated and less established of the Volunteers, who often happened to be the most radical, bore a basic contradiction. Whereas they often supported the liberal revolution in Spain, they rejected the colonial reforms envisioned by the governments in Madrid. While they defended the existence of a Spanish Nation across the Atlantic, they did not believe in equal political rights for its citizenry. Fear that granting rights to subjects who had fought against Spain might undermine Spanish sovereignty was the basis underpinning this sheer contradiction.

Dozens of newspaper articles, pamphlets, leaflets, and even poems circulated across the Antilles and Spain supporting this contradictory notion of national unity. One of its finest examples was written by a freemason and a republican, José E. Triay. A native

---

[73] Francisco Acosta y Albear. *Compendio histórico del pasado y presente de Cuba y de su guerra insurreccional hasta el 11 de marzo de 1875, con algunas apreciaciones relativas á su* porvenir. Madrid: Imprenta á cargo de Juan José de Las Heras, 1875, p. 104.

[74] AHN, Ultramar, 4731, exp. 4.

of Cádiz, Triay had settled in 1860 Cuba, where he ended up becoming Gonzalo Castañón's successor as director of *La Voz de Cuba*. In *Las Glorias del Voluntario*, a poetry book published in Havana in 1869 and prologued by Castañón, aimed at audiences in Cuba and in Spain, Triay displayed a fervent Spanish nationalism matched by radical liberalism. He praised the liberty given to the Spanish people by *La Gloriosa* the year before, and considered the Volunteers heirs of Rafael de Riego, the Freemason colonel who imposed the Cádiz Constitution on Ferdinand VII through a coup in 1820 and became an icon of Spanish liberalism and republicanism. Quite conveniently, Triay avoided mentioning the effects this coup had in the independence of Spanish America, for Riego used against the king an army which was bound to embark for Venezuela to fight Simón Bolívar's insurgency. As much as he embraced the 1868 revolution in *Las Glorias del Voluntario*, Triay defended the existing status quo and tried to convince his readers that the abolition of slavery, a major promise of *La Gloriosa*, would ruin the island. He considered that freeing the enslaved would ruin the economy and create the conditions for a race war. Not that Triay opposed abolition for ideological reasons, but he found it inconvenient considering the local context. Despite this contradiction, the book essentially aimed at linking the fight of the Volunteers in Cuba with the struggle for liberal freedom in 1868 in the Peninsula and thus gain support for their fight among liberals and republicans across the Atlantic.[75] It was a discourse difficult to sell to some audiences, but it certainly had some supporters in Spain.

Despite their rebellious and violent spirit, the Volunteers could claim to be defenders of the Spanish national unity in far-flung Antilles. Undoubtedly, they garnered some degree of sympathy among parts of the Spanish society. Perhaps willing to instill patriotism in children, Barcelona toy makers began to sell cheap Volunteer-shaped paper dolls since at least early 1869.[76] They also made it into literature, becoming main characters in several theater plays and novels, such as J. Álvarez Pérez's *Aventuras de tres Voluntarios*, which narrated the adventures of three *peninsulares* who settled in Cuba and became Volunteers during the war. Álvarez Pérez was a relatively well-known author who published several novels set in the colonial context of the Antilles and Africa. His work on the Volunteers was meant to circulate among low-income readers as it only cost 4 *reales* in Madrid and 5 in other provinces.[77]

Composers of *habaneras*, a popular genre with lyrics usually expressing longing for the Antilles, took the Volunteers as a source of inspiration for writing several songs, for instance, *Los Voluntarios de Cuba* by Isidoro Hernández.[78] The Volunteers were also regularly mentioned in the popular press. All these were examples of popular culture that could potentially reach important audiences in the Peninsula. As much as they were controversial, the Volunteers also enjoyed some acceptance among the popular classes in Spain.

---

[75] José E. Triay. *Las Glorias del Voluntario. Ecos nacionales*. Havana: Imprenta La Intrépida, 1869; *La Correspondencia de España*, 01-11-1885, p. 2; *Boletín de Procedimientos*, 14-04-1896, p. 8; *El Imparcial*, 30-08-1900, p. 2; *El Liberal*, 06-03-1907, p. 3.
[76] ANC, Fons ANC1-160 / Pere Grañén i Raso, sig. 0978.
[77] J. Álvarez Pérez. *Aventuras de tres Voluntarios (guerra de Cuba)*. Madrid: Medina y Navarro Editores.
[78] BNE, MC/298/41.

But they also received harsh criticisms from Spain for their violent methods in Cuba, especially among republicans, who considered that more civil and political rights would end the war in Cuba, rather than repression. Despite many of the Volunteers sharing their broad political values, liberals in the Peninsula would not tolerate their behavior, for they generally accepted the existing political and social discriminations on the inhabitants of the Antilles, including slavery. On June 13, 1870, the republican representative Francisco Díaz Quintero declared at the Spanish Congress that he considered the Volunteers a stain on Spain's history in America. He blamed them for having executed two months earlier Francisco Esquembre, the presbyter of Yaguaramas, a small town nearby the loyalist stronghold of Cienfuegos, who had blessed a rebel flag presented by the *mambí* officer Germán Barrios in April 1869.[79] Díaz Quintero's speech provoked an immediate reaction by hundreds of Volunteers and their supporters in Cuba, Spain, and in the Spanish migrant communities in the Americas.[80]

The first reaction was publishing letters in the main newspapers vindicating the Volunteers' honor and disapproving Díaz Quintero's speech. The first letter was published in early July 1870 at *Diario de la Marina* by Captain José Gener, the man who would later read the death sentence against the eight medicine students executed in November 1871. In the letter to the *Diario*, Gener claimed that "without the Volunteers, the Spanish flag would not wave in the Morro Castle," and that the Volunteers were "Spaniards willing to lose everything before letting the enemies of their motherland triumph."[81] Captain Gener became a popular character among Cuba's *integristas*, even making it to the front page of *El Moro Muza*, a satirical weekly magazine very popular among Volunteers. The hundreds of letters that followed were collected and published by the journalist and Volunteer Joaquín de Palomino, the former owner of *El Eco del Comercio*, at the end of 1870, aimed at showing the support received by the Volunteers in the Antilles and Spain.[82] Concerned by public opinion in Spain regarding the Volunteers, in October 1870 Palomino created a newspaper in Madrid entitled *El Voluntario de Cuba*, aimed at propagating the idea that the Volunteers were true patriots and not criminals through articles and news on the Volunteers' main military actions in Cuba. This newspaper was financially supported from Havana by Miguel Suárez Vigil and other middle-class Volunteers, but it was short-lived due to the small number of subscribers and ceased to publish in January 1871.[83]

Opinions disapproving the Volunteers' methods strongly intensified after the assassination of the medicine students in November 1871. Member of Parliament

---

[79] AHN, Ultramar, 4402, exp. 55.
[80] AHN, Ultramar, 4726, exp. 33. The speech of Francisco Díaz Quintero in *Diario de Sesiones de las Cortes Constituyentes*, No. 305, 13-06-1870, p. 8806.
[81] *Diario de la Marina*, 02-07-1870, p. 2.
[82] Joaquín de Palomino. *Merecido ramillete que dedican los Voluntarios de la isla de Cuba al mal aconsejado diputado a Cortes Díaz Quintero, formado con las protestas, manifestaciones y composiciones poéticas publicadas en los periódicos de esta capital y precedido de varias dedicatorias en prosa y verso*. Havana: Imprenta y Encuadernación "Sociedad de Operarios," 1870; AHN, Ultramar, 4657, exp. 49.
[83] *El Voluntario de Cuba*, 18-01-1871, p. 1.

Francisco Salmerón y Alonso labeled the Volunteers brutal and cowardly for their involvement in this affair at the Congress during a debate on their role in the war held on October 14, 1872.[84] Ventura Olavarrieta, a former Volunteer and conservative deputy, replied Salmerón. Olavarrieta was a native of Asturias who had been lieutenant of the Volunteers' Light Battalion of Havana, where he befriended Gonzalo Castañón. Olavarrieta proclaimed his former comrades' role as the guarantors of Spain's presence in Cuba and accusing Salmerón of receiving "filibuster's gold," implying that he collaborated with the insurgents, or had been at least paid out by them.[85] This was the Volunteers' usual response to criticisms. Anyone disapproving of their behavior was considered a traitor to Spain. In November 1872, Francisco Matías Ruiz y López, a former Volunteer gunner, published *Cuba y sus enemigos* in which he accused Díaz Quintero, the republicans, and the abolitionists of defending the insurgents' cause in Madrid, and hence of being traitors to Spain.[86]

Despite the Volunteers' efforts to counter critical voices, the echoes of the assassination of the medical students reached South America. On December 28, 1872, the Buenos Aires newspaper *La República* published an article by Florentino González entitled "Cuba y las repúblicas americanas," which intensely disapproved of Spanish policy in Cuba. As well as supporting Cuba's independence and calling all Spanish American republics to fight for it, he called the Volunteers "mere assassins." González, who joined the University of Buenos Aires as law professor that very year after following a career as journalist and politician in his native Colombia, had a long record of supporting radical liberalism in the Americas. Among other activities, he had taken part in an assassination attempt against Simón Bolívar in 1828.[87]

This caused outrage among the Spanish community in Buenos Aires. Enrique Romero Jiménez, the editor of *El Correo Español*, a popular newspaper among Spanish immigrants, encouraged his fellow countrymen to give Florentino González a due response. Between January and February 1873 his newspaper published dozens of letters by Spanish migrants defending the honorable Spanish struggle in the Antilles.[88] The articles and letters exchanged between *El Correo Español* and *La República* reached a crescendo. Romero even urged the Argentinian president Domingo Sarmiento (1868–74) to force *La República* to apologize, or else he would "break up the social peace in Buenos Aires between the Spaniards and the Cuban insurgency-supporters," which included a good deal of Argentinians.

Among the letters published by *El Correo Español*, some disturbingly showed a blatant acceptance of violence and despise for the enemy even in a context of war.

---

[84] *Diario de Sesiones de las Cortes Constituyentes*, Nº 26, 14-10-1872, p. 537.

[85] Llofriu y Sagrera. *Historia de la insurrección y Guerra de la isla de Cuba*, vol. II, p. 574; *Diario de Sesiones de las Cortes Constituyentes*, Nº 27, 15-10-1872, p. 569.

[86] Francisco Matías Ruiz y López. *Cuba y sus enemigos. Defensa de los Voluntarios de la isla de Cuba contra los ultrajes proferidos en las Cortes españolas en detrimento de su honra publicada en la prensa de la Corte y de provincias*. Madrid: Imprenta de Lázaro Maroto, 1872, pp. 5–30.

[87] Matthew Brown. *The Struggle for Power in Post-Independence Colombia and Venezuela*. London: Palgrave Macmillan, 2012, p. 76.

[88] *Álbum dedicado a los heroicos Voluntarios de Cuba por los españoles residentes en la República argentina*. Buenos Aires: Establecimiento tipográfico de El Correo Español, 1874.

Perhaps the most striking was signed by Manuel Barros, who claimed to be former Volunteer who had settled in Buenos Aires after leaving Havana. His letter is one of the most extreme examples of radical *integrismo* found here. He rejected all the criticisms received by his former comrades-in-arms. Also, he considered that most Cubans supported the continuity of Spanish rule, and in relation to the murder of the medicine students, Barros boasted that "I would have executed not only eight students of medicine but forty."[89]

Romero Jiménez continued with his campaign and accused Norberto Ballesteros, the head of the Spanish diplomatic legation in Buenos Aires, of being a coward, for he was as "useless and ignorant as most of the diplomatic service appointed by the revolution of 1868."[90] The campaign asking for the removal of Norberto Ballesteros carried out by *El Correo Español* collected 6,700 signatures, which were sent to Cuba's captain general Blas Villate, who was very popular among the Volunteers, so that he could present the removal proposal in the Spanish Parliament.[91] This shows that similar views and attitudes of middle and working-class *peninsulares* were shared by part of the Spanish émigré community in Argentina, and probably in other countries with a sizeable Spanish population. They supported Spanish rule in Cuba, disapproved of *La Gloriosa*, and threatened to use violence, if necessary, to achieve their goals. Social class solidarity might also have played its part, for both the radical Volunteers in Havana and the men that supported them in Buenos Aires were young working-class men.

The radical pro-Volunteer propaganda seems to have faded away after 1873-4 when the *integrista* elite came to control the *casinos españoles* and impose its power in Havana. Of course, the class and political divisions among the Volunteers continued, but the voices of the middle and lower strata were not allowed to propagate their views, apparently. The works of the Volunteers that were published afterward reflected the views of the *integrista* elite, but also tended to praise the patriotism and bravery of the rank-and-file Volunteers. This was praised, but not given voice. This is the case, for instance, of the Volunteer José Joaquín Ribó Palandaries' *Historia de los Voluntarios Cubanos*. Published in two volumes between 1872 and 1877 and dedicated to Havana's *Casino Español*.[92] Ribó was a Catalan journalist who studied law in Madrid, where he became director of the conservative newspaper *El Eco de la Patria* (1863-71) and authored a few books on the Spanish policy in the Americas before settling in Havana between 1871 and 1873, where he joined the 5th Volunteers Battalion.[93] He was the nephew of Víctor Balaguer, the liberal minister of the Colonies who facilitated his entry in Cuba and recommended that Volunteer units provided him with documentation to write a sort of official history of the Volunteers. Ribó's approach to the Volunteers'

[89] Ibid., pp. 37-41.
[90] *Álbum dedicado a los heroicos Voluntarios*, pp. 15-18.
[91] Ibid., pp. 45-68; Domingo Acebrón. *Los Voluntarios*, pp. 67-9.
[92] AHN, Universidades, 4649, exp. 13; BVB, epistolario, sig. 7103958.
[93] *Cuatro palabras sobre la cuestión de Méjico y el General Prim* (1862) and *Postrimerías de la insurrección cubana* (1871).

history attempted to keep the balance between the rank-and-file and the elite Volunteers, stressing the issue that united the Volunteers: *integridad nacional*.[94]

A similar approach can be found in *Álbum de los Voluntarios*, a poetry book published in 1874 by the Volunteer Fernando C. Moreno Solano. He was a native of Matanzas who embarked on an ideological and legal journey by the early 1870s. In 1857 he had been convicted by the Spanish justice for forgery, leaving the island for Madrid in 1860, where he founded a reformist newspaper entitled *La Isla de Cuba*. In the Peninsula, during the revolution of 1868, he joined the banner of radical republicanism by becoming a member of the Federal Democratic Republican Party, which advocated for Cuba to become a state within the Spanish federal republic. As many other *integristas*, his radical liberalism in the Peninsula might have been tamed by events in the island, where he had settled back by the early 1870s in Cárdenas, nearby Matanzas. In Cárdenas he joined the local Volunteer Chasseurs Regiment and tried to develop a career as poet. His *Álbum de los Voluntarios* is a collection of poems on the most popular issues among the Volunteers, with verses devoted to the rank-and-file Volunteer, the members of the *Casino Español*, Spain, Cuba, and the *Integridad Nacional*. Above all, it was a chant to the "Spanishness" of Cuba. The very metrics and thematic treatment were inspired by the *romancero viejo*, a collection of orally transmitted popular stories which are the basis of Spanish popular poetry. Moreno stresses in almost every poem his condition as Volunteer and "good and proud Cuban loyal to his mother Spain."[95]

The campaign by the radical Volunteers to propagate their ideas went a long way. During their fury days in Havana over the first years of the war, their propaganda was markedly popular and rather exalted, stressing the Volunteers' patriotism and zeal in repressing whom they perceived as enemies of Spain. Since 1872, when the *integrista* elite began to take control of the *Casino Español* and emerged as the commanding group in Havana, Volunteers' propaganda assumed a more conciliatory tone. It began to stress the idea of patriotism and national integrity avoiding extremisms. An example of this moderated tone was provided by Luis Otero Pimentel, a native of Galicia and army officer with a long experience in Cuba, who wrote *Memoria sobre los Voluntarios* in 1876. Throughout this book, Otero Pimentel stressed the patriotic services rendered by the Volunteers in collaboration with the authorities, trying to avoid as much as possible the episodes of confrontation and extreme violence. In a similar tone, Ribó's second volume of *Historia de los Voluntarios cubanos*, published in 1877, highlighted the importance that both the militia and the government remained united in order to make Spanish rule in Cuba ever stronger. The most radical voices among the Volunteers and *integrismo* in general were overlapped and concealed over time by the more moderate tone of the loyalist elite, but their radicalism did not fade away. Instead, their views and demands were expressed by different means.

---

[94] Ribó. *Historia de los Voluntarios cubanos*, pp. 595–7.
[95] Fernando C. Moreno Solano. *Álbum de los Voluntarios*. Cárdenas: Imprenta "El Comercio" de E. Trujillo, 1874; AHN, Ultramar, 1715, exp. 2; *Revista hispano-americana*, 12-02-1865, p. 2; *La Discusión*, 19-11-1868, p. 3.

The Volunteers and Labor Movement

The rampant violence taking place in Havana and other Cuban cities during the first years of the war, away from the battlefields, showed the power of a working-class Volunteer magma which operated beneath the *integrista* elite of businessmen, Volunteer chief officers, and smoky social meetings at the *Casino Español*. These Volunteer laborers had shown a particularly radical form of *integrismo* and not much reluctance to resort to violence should it help their interests, as we have seen. They socialized in their own circles, read their newspapers, and grown their own political culture and social concerns. Also, they represented most of the militia. To put it in numbers, by 1872 there were 65,000 working-class Volunteers per 15,000 officers, either laborers or peasants.[96] Nearly 19,000 of them lived in Havana.[97]

In Havana, they were usually a peninsular migrant, usually employed by fellow *peninsulares* as a shop assistant, stevedore, coachman, or cigar-maker. The commerce was also a *peninsular* stronghold in Havana. No less than nine out of ten members of Havana's Shopkeepers Union (*Centro de Dependientes*) had come from the Peninsula.[98] Above this echelon, sergeants, and low-ranking officers (lieutenants and captains) were often lower-middle-class and middle-class *peninsulares*, who usually owned their own shop or small business, such as bakeries, or hardware stores. No consensus on the reasons why they would join the Volunteers exists. Some of them may have joined out of sincere patriotism.[99] Money was not even a concern for it was stipulated that they were not to receive any stipend, only in case of being mobilized to war. Truth is there were a variety of reasons for joining the Volunteers. Although an identification with the idea of the national integrity might have convinced some young men to step forward, better employability options and social prestige were the most important factors for a *peninsular* migrant to join the Volunteers.[100] In any case, patriotic sentiment might have been boosted by belonging to the Volunteers, in combination with gaining social status and relating to the dominant group.

According to the testimony of some of these men, to join this militia was almost a natural step upon settling in Cuba. The Catalan Narciso Maciá recalled joining the 1st Artillery Volunteer Battalion in Havana in 1873 at the age of 18 alongside his brother, persuaded by the owner of the shop where he was employed, a fellow Catalan, who was a lieutenant colonel in that unit. He recognized that donning the uniform, taking part in military parades, and carrying a weapon increased his patriotism.[101] The very hierarchy of trading companies was often reproduced in Volunteer units. For instance, Captain Antonio Ferrer y Robert of Santiago de Cuba's 2nd Volunteer Battalion recalled that the overseers in his shop, *La California*, the most important clothing outlet of the

---

[96] José Ferrer de Couto. *Cuba puede ser independiente: folleto político de actualidad*. New York: Imprenta de "El Cronista," 1872, pp. 85–6.
[97] Otero Pimentel. *Memoria sobre los Voluntarios*, p. 177; Casanovas. *Bread, or Bullets!*, pp. 119–24.
[98] Moreno Fraginals. *Cuba/España*, p. 267.
[99] Espadas Burgos. *Alfonso XII y los orígenes de la Restauración*, pp. 283–5.
[100] Uralde Cancio. *Voluntarios de Cuba española*, p. 60.
[101] Narciso Maciá y Doménech. *Vida y obra (1855–1933)*. Havana, 1954, p. 11.

city, were sergeants in his company, while his shopkeepers were troopers.[102] Birthplace also played an indirect part in the composition of some units. For instance, Captain Ferrer mostly employed young workers from his hometown Sitges, in Catalonia. Consequently, many of the men under his command at the battalion were from that town too. This correlation was to be repeated in many units throughout the island, especially in towns with a strong presence of *peninsulares*.

The reproduction of these hierarchies might have given more cohesion to the Volunteer companies but did not avert social tensions. On the contrary, many Volunteers were active members of the labor movement in Cuba. Cigar-makers were particularly active in this regard.[103] Indeed, being a Volunteer gave these men a sense of unity, cohesion, solidarity, and organization inherent to serving in the militia. The leader of the labor movement in Havana during the 1860s and 1870s, Saturnino Martínez, was himself a Volunteer who hailed from Asturias and had settled in Havana at a young age, where he had been employed by the Partagás tobacco factory as a cigar-maker. He had been promoting the creation of workers' associations at least since 1865 from the pages of *La Aurora*, Cuba's first workers' newspaper.[104]

The social and labor situation of workers in Havana worsened with the breakout of the war. The living conditions created by the Ten Years' War spurred the creation of labor associations. A higher tax pressure on the local industry to finance the war resulted in lower wages for the employees and shrinking income for the companies. This caused class tensions that partially explain the episodes of violence of 1869–71 by the Volunteers. Amidst this tension, both employers and employees began to organize for the defense of their own interests. The tobacco manufacturing industry, which employed *c*. 30,000 people throughout Cuba, particularly felt the tax pressure caused by the war. It became a sector where internal tensions between employers and employees were strongly felt. In 1870, the cigar factory owners created the Havana Tobacco Central Guild (*Gremio Central de Tabaco de La Habana*), which lobbied in Spain for the defense of its members' interests.[105] Only two years later, in 1872, their employees founded Cuba's first trade union, the Cigar Selector's Protection Society (*Sociedad Protectora del Gremio de Escogedores*), devoted to the defense of their members' interests.[106] Many union members had brought a strong culture of labor associationism along with their hopes for better life prospects from the Peninsula, where a great deal of Havana tobacco workers came from.[107] By the 1870s, regions like Catalonia and Asturias, which provided Cuba with thousands of migrants every year, had a long tradition of labor associations due to the early start of the industrial revolution in the Peninsula.

[102] AHMS, Fons Josep Carbonell i Gener, "Companyia de Voluntaris de Santiago de Cuba."
[103] Casanovas. *Bread, or Bullets!*, pp. 97–126.
[104] Ibid., pp. 80–1.
[105] Gremio Central del Tabaco en La Habana. *Informe del Comité permanente del Gremio Central del Tabaco en La Habana al Congreso solicitando la exención del pago de contribución municipal a las fábricas de tabacos puros y de cigarros*. Havana, 1871, pp. 1–10.
[106] Casanovas. *Bread, or Bullets!*, p. 109.
[107] Casanovas. *Bread, or Bullets!*, pp. 71–96; Josep Termes. *Anarquismo y sindicalismo en España (1864–1881)*. Barcelona: Editorial Crítica, 2000 (first published in 1965), pp. 285–95.

Almost inevitably, in a context of daily violence and imitating the actions of their colleagues in the Peninsula, other parts of Europe or the United States, the unions took their labor demands from the shops and warehouses to the streets. One of the earliest such actions paralyzed Havana on September 11, 1872, for the city's coachmen went on a strike, seriously disturbing the traffic of people and goods in a city which already had 210,000 inhabitants. Most of the strikers were *peninsulares* and members of the 5th Volunteer Battalion, and thus, a fair amount of them had a rifle at home and knew how to use it. All Volunteers had the right to keep at home the weapons they owned and carry them at any time with their militia uniform.[108] In a way, the working-class Volunteers could rightly have been considered to be "workers at arms."[109]

However, not all rank-and-file Volunteers shared ideals of class solidarity. Nor were these men sharply divided between powerful businessmen and their workers. In between, there was a middle class of shop owners and self-employed men, who usually filled the officers' low ranks, from second lieutenant to captain. The affirmative actions of the labor movement, such as strikes, affected their businesses as much as the company owners. In fact, these actions were regarded by them as unpatriotic actions which jeopardized the Volunteers' internal cohesion. The coachmen's struggle was just an example. For instance, José Gibert, a volunteer lieutenant who owned a bakery in the outskirts of Havana, wrote to his relatives in Catalonia that the strike had been caused by Captain General Francisco Ceballos' order to regulate transport coach fares, and by the propaganda spread by infiltrated agents of the International Workingmen's Association (IWA) who, according to him, had come to Cuba to disseminate their "terrible ideas."[110]

We do not know for sure whether there were IWA infiltrates among the Volunteers at all, but the early 1870s were certainly a period of rapid growth for the workers' movement in the Hispanic world, especially for anarchism. The anarchist idea was first introduced in Spain in 1868 by Giuseppe Fanelli, a Neapolitan commissioned by Mikhail Bakunin. Only two years later, in June 1870, the First Spanish Workers' Congress was celebrated in Barcelona, which became the main stronghold of Spanish anarchism due to its intense industrialization alongside rural Andalusia. It is thus likely that there were *peninsulares* disseminating the anarchist ideal in Cuba, especially considering the ongoing influx of migrants from Catalonia. Propertied members of the militia, even petty ones, considered the growing labor movement a threat. In fact, several *integrista* newspapers took part in creating an anti-AIT front alongside colleagues from the Peninsula in Madrid in October 1871, aiming at countering the powerful labor propaganda.[111] After all, disturbing memories of the many atrocities committed during the Paris Commune in the spring of 1871 were still fresh.

The threat from the labor movement might seem formidable, but workers were indeed pretty divided. Laborers defended their class interests separately by trade, rather than converging into a single trade union. This was the logical consequence of

---

[108] Moreno Fraginals. *Cuba/España*, p. 249.
[109] Ibid., p. 242.
[110] Letter to his relative Joan Font, 15 September 1872. Xavier Mas Gibert. *Cartes de L'Havana, 1872.* Canet de Mar: Els 2 Pins, 2013, p. 137.
[111] Josep Termes. *Anarquismo y sindicalismo en España (1864–1881)*. Barcelona: Crítica, 2000, p. 147.

the distinct working conditions of cigar-makers, coachmen, bakers, and other trades. Volunteer laborers did create mutual insurance companies as a common response to economic hardships and to provide some security to their members. The socially progressive ideals of the First Spanish Republic, proclaimed on February 11, 1873, after King Amadeus I stepped down, overwhelmed by Spain's chronic instability, facilitated the creation of these associations. For instance, in September 1873, Captain General Cándido Pieltain (1873), appointed by the republican government, approved the creation of *La Integridad Nacional*, a Volunteers mutuality which offered financial aid to its members and their relatives undergoing economic strain.[112] The idea was later implemented in other parts of Cuba. For instance, in 1882, Volunteer veterans in Oriente established the *Compañía Voluntarios Veteranos Reserva de Holguín* with a similar purpose.[113]

The creation of this insurance company gives the impression that Volunteer workers had a distinct identity of their own, based on their twofold condition of laborers and militiamen. Beyond the struggles of coachmen, cigar-makers, or shop dependents, still far from summoning efforts under a same banner by the early 1870s, working-class Volunteers were at least able to create a mutuality based on their very condition of militiamen. Their founders certainly had a strong esprit de corps, but also a clear idea that laborers needed not be controlled by the *Casino Español* or indirectly through other institutions dominated by the *integrista* elite, which also had social aid schemes for their members.[114] Rather than protection from their political akin, working-class Volunteers opted for independence from elite control.

From Cities to the Countryside: The Mobilized Battalions

In the cities, the Volunteers might have enjoyed a great power due to the scant presence of regular troops and the fact that they were often the only troops the authorities could count with. Also, they may indulge in acts of insubordination and unleash a wave of repression against independence supporters as the actual fighting was taking place in the distant fields and hills of eastern Cuba. But leaving the countryside to the mercy of the revolutionaries was no option. The wealth of Cuba, sugar, but also tobacco, was produced in mills and farms located in rural areas where they might easily fell prey to the torch of the *mambises*. Thus, while rank-and-file Volunteers may not be appealed to be deployed outside the cities' safety, their chief officers had much at stake in the mostly unprotected rural land. During the autumn of 1868, little reinforcements of regular troops could be expected from the Peninsula, for the new regime born of *La Gloriosa* still had to deal with resistance from opponents and the revolutionary

---

[112] BNC, Folleto C-1, No. 1, *La Integridad Nacional. Asociación Patriótica de Socorros a la Benemérita Clase de Voluntarios. Reglamento*, Havana, Imprenta del "Avisador Comercial," 1873; RAH, CCR, 1238, 2-12-1873, 1f; T. V, f. 269.

[113] AHPSC, leg. 2875, exp. 14.

[114] Tesifonte Gallego y García. *Cuba por fuera (apuntes al natural)*. Havana: La Propaganda Literaria, 1890, pp. 197–212.

impetus of some of its advocates. In fact, the first army expedition disembarked in Havana in January 1869. Thus, the *integristas* of Cuba needed to deploy their own resources and act quickly. Given the state and the small numbers of the island's army garrison, mobilizing the Volunteers to fight the rebels became a necessity. While during peacetime they could not be deployed outside their towns, during wartime the captain general could order their mobilization by assimilating them to regular troops in terms of rights and duties. Thus, the first mobilized battalions of Volunteers were created.[115]

On November 17, 1868, the battalions Volunteer Chasseurs "España" No. 1 and Volunteer Chasseurs "Orden" No 2 were created in the Cuban capital thanks to the financial help of the Bank of Havana. Since both battalions were meant to be deployed in the fields, their members were recruited among Volunteers with some military experience who would receive a stipend and were to be commanded by army officers.[116] The "España" was commanded by Francisco Méndez Benegasi, whereas the "Orden" was headed by Francisco de Acosta y Albear, a Cuban who had joined the army in 1827 and was resuming military life after having developed a career as landowner in Sancti Spíritus. The "España" was sent to operations to the main theater of war, in Oriente, to the area around Bayamo and Holguín, whereas the "Orden" was deployed in several locations of Las Villas, also known as Villa Clara, an area in the middle of Cuba which was crucial to tackle the rebel advance westward. On November 4, 1868, at Las Clavellinas, a small village only 15 km from Puerto Príncipe, the local rebels joined the insurrection, later followed by the uprising at Jagüey Grande on February 10, 1869, 80 km south of Matanzas. Despite the uprising at Jagüey Grande, west to Las Villas, the latter remained the frontier between rebel Cuba, where the insurgents controlled vast areas of the countryside, and loyal Cuba, which stood under Spanish control throughout the war. The biggest sugar mills, known as *ingenios*, and the main sugar-producing areas were located west to this area.[117] In this sense, the participation of mobilized Volunteers units responded to the basic need of defending big property which was essential for Cuban economy.

Soon, other Volunteer units followed the example, as the rebellion forces kept growing strong in Oriente and the Spanish garrisons in the war border located along Las Villas needed to be reinforced, especially in times of political uncertainty. On December 15, 1868, the very same day that it was known that Captain General Lersundi was going to be replaced by Domingo Dulce, the officers of Havana's 5th Volunteers Battalion offered Lersundi to send their men to the warfront in exchange for no stipend, only the daily ranch. In a matter of days, the Havana Mobilised 5th Volunteers Battalion was organized and sent to operations under the command of Major Luis Rubiales in Remedios, in Villa Clara, where numerous sugar mills needed protection.[118]

---

[115] "Expediente de los voluntarios movilizados en la Isla de Cuba." AGMM, CGC, SGV, sig. 5711.3
[116] The battalions were called *Orden* and *España*. RAH, CCR, 9/7536, doc. 104.
[117] AGMS, leg. A-210; Gelpí y Ferro. *Álbum histórico fotográfico*, p. 65; Llofriu y Sagrera. *Historia de la insurrección y guerra de la isla de Cuba*, p. 63.
[118] Llofriu y Sagrera. *Historia de la insurrección y guerra de la isla de Cuba*, vol. I, p. 106.

Indeed, protecting property was a major force behind the mobilization of Volunteers outside of the cities. Property in the form of sugar mills, sometimes tobacco farms, but also enslaved workforce, which could be counted in the hundreds of thousands in western Cuba, needed protection from the insurgents. Matanzas and its hinterland were the heart of Cuban sugar industry and slavery. By 1862, six years before the war started, there were 172,000 enslaved people working in 1,531 sugar mills across the island, of which 72,000 worked in the 456 *ingenios* of Matanzas, far exceeding any other region.[119] The owners of Matanzas' wealth had much to lose and thus much to protect. Though the main theater of war remained a few hundred miles eastward in Oriente, small insurgent parties were active around Jagüey Grande since February 10, 1869. Thus, the prospect of a generalized slave rebellion had the propertied class mobilizing its resources to protect their wealth without waiting for help from central authorities.

By early February 1869, 3,000 proprietors from Matanzas and its hinterland gathered at the city's main theater to appoint a 32-member Conservative National Committee which asked Captain General Dulce permit to raise their own Volunteer forces for the defense of their sugar mills and rural property.[120] Since the uprising at Jagüey Grande had forced the Civil Guard garrison to gather at the jurisdiction's seat, a committee member, Ricardo García Oña, quickly raised a 100-strong mobilized Volunteer squadron, mostly made up of army veterans, which sent platoons to each point of the area, bestowed with defending its many rural properties.[121] Some companies of the Matanzas Volunteer Battalion were also mobilized alongside regular army units, and the Committee showed its commitment to the Spanish cause by raising a Mobilised Volunteer Battalion that was sent to operations between Bayamo and Santiago de Cuba, in the very heartland of the insurrection.[122]

The use of mobilized Volunteers proved a success, as their wide presence across the region kept the insurgents at bay. A full-fledged revolutionary invasion seemed very unlikely, but small bands could still do harm. So much so that some proprietors raised their own personal Volunteer units, such as Francisco Ibáñez, a prominent *hacendado* who created the Socorro Mobilised Volunteers Party to protect his sugar mills of Socorro and Destino, nearby Matanzas, in November 1869.[123] The model was followed in other parts of the island, like in Oriente, where the Volunteer Battalion of Holguín, an *integrista* stronghold, detached one of its companies to be mobilized to the countryside alongside the regular army.[124] In fact, whereas most of the Volunteers garrisoned military hospitals, prisons, and forts in the cities, a very different type of war was being fought in rural Cuba.

---

[119] Rebecca J. Scott. *Slave Emancipation in Cuba. The Transition to Free Labor, 1860–1899*. Pittsburgh: University of Pittsburgh Press, 2000 (first published in 1985), p. 22, table 4.
[120] Llofriu y Sagrera. *Historia de la insurrección y guerra de la isla de Cuba*, vol. I, pp. 246–7.
[121] Ribó, vol. II, pp. 255–6.
[122] Ribó, vol. II, p. 251.
[123] AGMM, CGC, SGV, sig. 5712.8.
[124] AGMM, CGC, SGV, sig. 5806.71.

The Fight outside Havana: A Cuban Civil War

Rampant violence in Havana stemmed in part from the fact that the city had been spared from the worse hardships of war. Men and energy could be spent in street clashes as the front seemed far away. But outside the capital and other major cities, the conflict was quite different. It was a clash on property and the political and social future of Cuba. For the insurgents, it was a fight for ending Spanish rule as much as for getting rid of slavery.[125] Though most of the rebel army leading officers were propertied whites, who often owned enslaved people themselves, most of the troops were runaway former slaves and freemen from Oriente who identified free Cuba with their own personal freedom, either to gain it or to keep it. They understood that it was necessary to destroy Cuba's wealth to defeat Spain: from big sugar mills to the properties of peasants loyal to Spain.

On the loyalist side, it became a fight for the preservation of Spanish rule, their identity and property, which for a few included slavery, but for the most was the land they worked and depended for a living. Not only big property fought in Spain's side. The very need to protect their small tracts of land from the rebels' torch drew thousands of *guajiros* to join the Volunteer units created across the island.[126] Yet some of them might not have joined to defend their property but to escape from a revolution which had disappointed them. Some others might have joined out of fear of Spanish reprisals before the lack of actual victories from the rebel army.[127] The truth is that outside the big communities of *peninsulares* which existed in Havana and other major towns and nurtured the Volunteers, in the countryside, most of the defenders of the Spanish banner were sons of the country.

The enlistment of thousands of Cubans into the Volunteers was a big change brought about by war. In May 1870, Captain General Caballero de Rodas reported to the Ministry of War that Cuban peasants were joining the Volunteers in their thousands.[128] This means that the Cuban population did not rally unanimously behind the idea of expelling Spain from the island. On the contrary, it was split between those who fought for and against a Spanish Cuba. In fact, the Ten Years' War was a civil war as much as a war for independence. A civil war between "Spaniards from both hemispheres," and a civil war between Cubans.

Thousands of creoles queuing before the Volunteers' recruiting stations showed how divided the Cuban population was.[129] José Ferrer de Couto, a New York–based journalist from Galicia and a former Volunteer, claimed that out of the 80,000

---

[125] Ada Ferrer. *Insurgent Cuba. Race, Nation, and Revolution, 1868–1898*. Chapel Hill and London: University of North Carolina Press, 1999, pp. 15–42; Ibarra. *Ideología mambisa*, p. 51.
[126] Abreu Cardet. *Apuntes sobre el integrismo*, pp. 70–6.
[127] RAH, CCR, 462, letter to the minister of the Colonies, 24-06-1870, 11 f; T. III, ff. 168-178v.
[128] RAH, CCR, 402, letter to the minister of the Colonies, 15-05-1870, 5 f; T. III, ff. 105-109.
[129] Ramiro Guerra. *La guerra de los 10 años*, vol. I. Havana: Editorial Cultural, 1950, pp. 150–81; Ibarra. *Ideología mambisa*, pp. 42–58; Pérez, Jr. *Cuba. Between Reform & Revolution*, pp. 135–6; Fernando Redondo Díaz. "La Guerra de los Diez Años (1868–1878)," in *La presencia militar española en Cuba (1868–1895)*. Madrid: Centro de Estudios Superiores de la Defensa, 1996, pp. 33–65.

militiamen reported in 1872, at least 52,000 were Cuban.[130] Although it is extremely difficult to establish the exact numbers of the Cuban Volunteers, for not all units kept detailed records of their members, the surviving evidence suggests that creoles were important and even dominant in many Volunteer units across the countryside.[131]

In big towns, on the contrary, *peninsulares* made most of the Volunteers. In the area around the city of Matanzas there were *c.* 3,000 Volunteers by 1869. In the city, three quarters of them were *peninsulares*, and in nearby small towns, such as Sabanilla del Encomendador and Corral Nuevo, creoles represented more than half the numbers.[132] In the same area, the 550 men of Colón's Cavalry Volunteer Regiment were mostly Cubans.[133] Even in Oriente, the rebel stronghold, Volunteer units followed a similar pattern. In villages, such as Cuartón del Indio and Tiguabos, located around the city of Guantánamo, a loyalist stronghold, Cubans represented virtually every member of the local Volunteer sections. In the city of Guantánamo itself, well-to-do men created a cavalry unit known as Pando Hussars, where creoles filled half its ranks, while most of the infantry Volunteers Battalion were made up of *peninsulares*, chiefly Catalans.[134]

So many Cubans among the Volunteers in the countryside might have raised concerns among military commanders around the likelihood of desertions. There were cases in areas dominated by the revolution, in fact. In Jiguaní, a small town near Bayamo, the iconic symbol of the insurrection after it was burned in January 1869 by rebels before surrendering it to Spanish forces, dozens of its local cavalry Volunteer Regiment defected to the enemy.[135] But this was the exception rather than the norm, despite the war having from its very inception the cruel characteristics of a civil war, with families torn down the middle, but also with some loyalties swinging along the lines of family or town's position.

The siege of Holguín provides a good example. Between October 17 and November 6, 1868, the rebel forces, commanded by Julio Grave de Peralta, put this city in Oriente under siege.[136] The rebel commander had relatives among the besieged forces, for Grave de Peralta had been born in the town. A few days after the attack had begun, the only Spanish stronghold left was *La Periquera*, the house of Francisco Rondán, a Cuban merchant loyal to Spain. Several hundred other loyalists, among them army personnel, Volunteers, and their families, had taken shelter in Rondán's house and took up arms for its defense, commanded by the army Colonel Francisco Camps y Feliu. A few years later, Camps recalled that most of the people inside *La Periquera*

---

[130] Ferrer de Couto. *Cuba puede ser independiente*, pp. 85–6.
[131] Abreu Cardet. *Apuntes sobre el integrismo*, pp. 70–6.
[132] The data are taken from Benito González del Tánago. *Estadística de los Voluntarios existentes en 31 de julio de 1869 en Matanzas, Cabezas, Ceiba-Mocha, Corral-Nuevo, Canasí, Guanábana, Sabanilla del Encomendador, Bolondrón, Unión de Reyes, Madruga, Güira de Macuriges y Alacranes, con expresión de las clases, nombres y apellidos, edad, pueblos y provincias de donde son naturales*. Havana: Imprenta La Intrépida, 1869.
[133] Ribó. *Historia de los Voluntarios cubanos*, vol. I, p. 449.
[134] AGMM, Ultramar, Capitanía General de Cuba, Subinspección General de Voluntarios, caja 3007, Voluntarios de Guantánamo.
[135] ANRC, Donativos y Remisiones, leg. 474, exp. 10., and leg. 477, exp. 40.
[136] José Abreu Cardet. "La defensa del Imperio: Cuba 1868–1870." *Tebeto: Anuario del Archivo Histórico Insular de Fuerteventura*, 1994, No. 7, pp. 159–74.

were Cubans. Among them was Julio Grave de Peralta's grandmother, Josefa Cardet de Martínez, who died during the siege.[137] Only a few months later, one of these Cubans, the journalist Antonio José Nápoles Fajardo, wrote *El sitio de Holguín*, his own account of the siege.[138] Antonio José was the brother of Juan Cristóbal, a popular poet known as *El Cucalambé*, who joined the independence cause after having served as civil servant in Santiago de Cuba during the 1860s and who had his properties seized by the Council of Sequestered Goods in 1873.[139] Far from being a nationwide movement for independence embraced by all Cubans, the siege of Holguín is just one of the events that show how the war split local families down the middle.

The very existence of Cuban loyalists discredited the rebels' claim that the revolution was a fight between Cubans and Spaniards.[140] When captured after combat, insurgent commanders usually offered fellow Cubans either defecting from Spanish forces or death. Whereas a peninsular prisoner might be pardoned, Cubans loyal to Spain knew that death was the most likely outcome unless they joined the rebel army. During the 1871 *mambí* campaign on Guantánamo, self-proclaimed general Máximo Gómez, the former Dominican sergeant who had fought for Spain in his country but was now the military leader of the rebellion in Cuba, issued a call to his "fellow countrymen of Guantánamo" compelling them to join the insurgency, or else face death.[141] The message was clear: the Cubans defending Spain to the very last would not be forgiven. This attitude toward Spanish loyalists powerfully recalls the "War to Death" against all Spaniards proclaimed by Simón Bolívar in 1813. The difference was that whereas Bolívar promised clemency to all Americans and death to all *peninsulares*, regardless of their loyalty, the *mambís* would kill any Cuban supporting the cause of Spain.

In the countryside, Volunteers engaged in combat with the rebel army throughout the war. They were crucial in averting the insurrection from spreading to western Cuba, and in defending the Spanish positions in eastern Cuba, where the rebels had their main operational base.[142] For instance, the first attempt to bring the war westward, at Jagüey Grande on February 10, 1869, was quelled by the *Voluntarios Chapelgorris* of Guamutas.[143] In the east, the Volunteers helped the regular army to keep the cities and major towns under Spanish control. Throughout the war, the insurgents attacked all the towns in the region, except for Santiago de Cuba and Gibara, which became two loyalist strongholds surrounded by the revolution and with important bags of rebel supporters in the inside.[144]

---

[137] Francisco de Camps y Feliú. *Españoles é insurrectos. Recuerdos de la guerra de Cuba*. Havana: Imprenta de A. Álvarez y Comp., 1890, p. 396.
[138] *El sitio de Holguín* has been recently edited by Ángela Peña Obregón and José Abreu Cardet. *El sitio de Holguín: la pasión de un integrista*. Holguín: Ediciones Holguín, 2014.
[139] AHN, Ultramar, 4436, exp. 109; AHN Ultramar, 66, exp. 3.
[140] Francisco Pi y Margall. *Historia de España en el siglo XIX: sucesos políticos, económicos, sociales y artísticos, acaecidos durante el mismo, detallada narración de sus acontecimientos y extenso juicio crítico de sus hombres*, vol. IV. Madrid: Miguel Seguí Editor, 1902, p. 879.
[141] Pedro Pablo Rodríguez. *La primera invasión*. Havana: Editorial de Ciencias Sociales, 2012, pp. 113–14.
[142] Navarro. *Las guerras de España en Cuba*, pp. 22–37.
[143] Ribó. *Historia de los Voluntarios cubanos*, vol. 1, pp. 450–1.
[144] Abreu Cardet. *Apuntes sobre el integrismo*, pp. 37 & 82–5.

Local Volunteers were of great use to the Spanish military commanders, due to their thorough knowledge of the terrain. For instance, a group of Cuban fishermen from La Isabela, a small town in the central area of Las Villas, formed a company of Volunteers deployed to patrol the coast against the many attempts to disembark men and arms for the revolution.[145] Theirs was a vital task, for the insurgents used the many cays of the area to smuggle weapons and mercenaries into rebel territory, mostly coming from the United States, Jamaica, and Haiti.[146] For instance, on June 14, 1870, the Volunteers from the coastal town of Maniabón, commanded by Captain Aurelio López del Campo, captured the *George S. Upton* on the beach. This was a ship sent from the United States by Cuban exiles, loaded with men and weapons for Belisario Grave de Peralta, the rebel leader in the Holguín region.[147] The capture of the *Upton* became highly popular story among *integristas*, even making it to one of the pages of *El Moro Muza*, a Havana satirical magazine greatly popular among them. The Volunteers were also used to protect some of the key infrastructure in the countryside. For instance, a company from the local battalion of Puerto Príncipe, in the Camagüey region, protected the railway line that linked this city in central Cuba to the port of Nuevitas. Keeping the railway open was vital for the region's livestock industry, which exported its cattle though Nuevitas' port to other parts of Cuba, the Caribbean, and the United States.[148]

Forcible Mobilization

Far from the countryside, lack of discipline among the Volunteers in the cities had become a lingering problem for the authorities. The many riots and abuses committed by the Havana Volunteers between 1869 and 1871 had diminished, but not entirely faded away, as the war in the east went on, and fears that the rebels might make it to the rest of the islands seemed less unlikely. The situation remained extremely tense. The rebellion was not abating, and the capture by the Spanish Navy in October 1872 of the American ship *Virginius*, which transported 175 men, weapons, and ammunition for the rebels, brought Spain and the United States to the brink of war. The cause was that alongside four Cuban rebel leaders, 27 members of the ship's crew, including US and British citizens, had been executed in Santiago de Cuba in early November 1873.[149] To avoid war, the Spanish Government agreed to return the ship to the US authorities and

---

[145] Ribó. *Historia de los Voluntarios cubanos*, vol. 1, p. 459.
[146] María Dolores Domingo Acebrón. "El tráfico de armas durante la guerra de los Diez Años (1868–1878)," *Tebeto: Anuario del Archivo Histórico Insular de Fuerteventura*, No. 3, 1990, pp. 91–132.
[147] BNC, CM Pérez No. 2017, vol. A.
[148] For instance, the military records of the Volunteer Melitón Castelló Anglada report that the railway was severely attacked on July 20, 1869, when the *mambises* tried to cut Puerto Príncipe off from Nuevitas to seize the town. I am indebted for this information to his great-grandson Osvaldo Betancourt, who gave me Castelló's personal military records.
[149] Martí Gilabert. *La Primera República Española, 1873–1874*. Madrid: Ediciones Rialp, 2007, pp. 77–84.

to pay a compensation of $80,000 for the executions.[150] This was regarded as a betrayal by many Volunteers, who organized demonstrations against the Spanish Government for this agreement, between November and December 1873. They demanded that no compensation should be given to the US or British governments, for the nationals of these countries who participated in the *Virginius* expedition were helping to subvert Spanish sovereignty in Cuba. To back their demands, the Volunteers demonstrated donning their uniforms, and producing their weapons, claiming that they were ready to defend the island in case the United States declared war on Spain.[151] A message was also sent to the palace of the captain general: the events of 1869 could be repeated.

These demonstrations did not escalate, as Cándido Pieltain was replaced on November 5, 1873, by Joaquín Jovellar, a man respected by the *integristas* for his military record, honesty, and his known opposition to reform plans in the Antilles. He reassured the Volunteers of his firm commitment to defend Spanish rule in Cuba at any cost and asked them for a demonstration of patriotism in times of need. As the war continued, the situation had relatively calmed down regarding the Volunteers' rebellious spirit, but Jovellar took an unprecedented step toward a greater control and militarization of the militia. On February 10, 1874, he issued a decree on the *Gazeta de La Habana* official bulletin calling for the mobilization and deployment to the warzone of one in ten Volunteers for a period of six months, among other measures.[152] The decree also ordered the organization of two Volunteer cavalry regiments to protect sugar mills, tobacco and coffee farms in Santiago de Cuba, Guantánamo, and Las Villas, and to garrison Puerto Príncipe, Holguín, and Manzanillo. The aim was to use the Volunteers to cover at least two thirds of the garrisons throughout the island, and to deploy Volunteer gunners and engineers to man the artillery positions and to manage the forts. It also ordered that all Spanish men in Cuba, meaning both *peninsulares* and creoles, between the ages of 25 and 45 that were not serving in the army or the Volunteers should register as reservists in the Disciplined Militias. Additionally, he ordered the reorganization of the Colored Disciplined Militias, which would recruit its members among free Black men.

The reason was the shortage of men on the Spanish side during a period where almost no reinforcements could be expected to be sent from the Peninsula. The years of 1873–4 were critical for Spain. The proclamation of the Republic on February 11, 1873, following the stepping down of King Amadeus I, had only worsened the political instability the country had been living in since the Revolution of 1868. A new ruling elite divided between Unitarian and Federalist republicans, unable to stabilize the country and reluctant to impose discipline on the most basic institutions of the state, found itself in charge of a country facing a war in Cuba, a war against the Carlist army started in 1872, and a federalist uprising, the so-called *Rebellion Cantonal*, which aimed at breaking down Spain in many pieces only to reunite them afterward in a

---

[150] See Richard H. Bradford. *The Virginius Affair*, Boulder: Colorado Associate University Press, 1980; José Manuel Sevilla López. "Cuba 1873. La captura del 'Virginius'. El incidente Burriel-Lorraine." *Revista de Historia Militar*, 2017, Año LXI, No. 122, pp. 185–247.
[151] Maciá y Doménech. *Vida y obra*, pp. 11–15.
[152] *Gaceta de La Habana*, 11-02-1874.

federal republic. This meant that the already limited Spanish military resources could pay little attention to the war in Cuba, though it was still able to send 23,000 soldiers to the island.[153]

Before such difficult times for Spain, the mobilization order was implemented with no incidents. Nearly 8,000 Volunteers were readied and dispatched to the warzone.[154] Since most of them could only count on a superficial military training, Jovellar decided to organize auxiliary companies of mobilized Volunteers with these men and embed them into regular army battalions.[155] Thus, the Volunteers would not fight in independent units, but integrated into the regular army, whose members were fully militarized in terms of rights and discipline barely known by the Volunteers.

Mobilizing 8,000 Volunteers outside the cities could have caused a serious disruption in their regular lives. Most of them were laborers and peasants who could not afford to leave their jobs for half a year. Their absence from the workplace for a prolonged period would have also caused a serious problem to their employers, who often happened to be their officers in the militia. However, the pragmatism and flexibility of Volunteer companies provided the solution. Each battalion usually had from 100 to 200 men who had served in the army. Quite often, the Volunteers who did not want to fulfil their military duties paid these men a few pesos so that they would substitute them, even though this contravened the regulations.[156] Garrisoning military hospitals or prisons was an unpopular duty bestowed upon the Volunteers, let alone going to fight in an actual war. Thus, most of the Volunteers who ended up being mobilized by the February 7 decree were army veterans maintained by their colleagues.

This was a guarantee of discipline and better military performance, much more desirable than having 8,000 men who had never seen actual fighting and who were not especially prone to respect the authorities. As a result, the mobilized Volunteers contributed to the success of the Spanish forces. In Las Villas, 1,800 of them were deployed to cover the *trocha* linking the towns of Júcaro and Morón, which draw a line across the island north to south. The *trocha* was a fortified line that separated western from eastern Cuba, guarded by thousands of soldiers, with small forts every 50 meters, and its own train service. The aim of the *trocha* was to isolate western Cuba from rebellious Oriente.[157] Despite the many efforts poured into building the barrier, it soon proved crossable. Máximo Gómez and his forces crossed it on January 6, 1875, but failed to bring war to western Cuba, for the *trocha* did manage to impede any major invasion coming from the east.[158]

For a long period, the war became a sort of a stalemate, between a rebel army firmly established in the east, but unable to take any major city or thrust any decisive blow,

---

[153] Moreno Fraginals & Moreno Masó. *Guerra, migración y muerte*, p. 99.
[154] Gelpí y Ferro. *Historia de la revolución*, p. 281.
[155] Otero Pimentel. *Memoria sobre los Voluntarios*, pp. 152–6.
[156] Acosta y Albear. *Compendio histórico*, pp. 24–6.
[157] Luis de Sequera Martínez. "Las trochas militares en las campañas de Cuba (1868–1898)." *Revista de Historia Militar*, Año XL, No. 81, 1996, pp. 107–46.
[158] Navarro. *Las guerras de España en Cuba*, pp. 85–7; Evaristo Martín Contreras. *Los Voluntarios de la Isla de Cuba. Reconocimiento de su heroísmo y vindicación a su honor*. Valladolid: Imprenta, Librería Estéreo-galvanoplastia y Taller de Grabado de Gaviria y Zapatero, 1876, p. 25.

and a Spanish side in control of western Cuba and the major urban areas of Oriente, but not able to crush the insurgency. While Volunteers in Cuba remained as public order forces in the cities and auxiliary forces in the countryside, their colleagues in Puerto Rico took part in major political changes in the smaller of the Spanish Antilles.

Volunteers in Puerto Rico

Unlike Cuba, Puerto Rico remained mostly peaceful during the turmoil of the 1860s and 1870s, but similar political issues dominated the political and social scenario. Political rights for the island and the future of slavery were to monopolize the debate. Alike their colleagues in Cuba, Puerto Rican Volunteers were the armed wing of local *integrismo*, firmly committed to the defense of Spanish sovereignty and the status quo. Nonetheless, the relatively peaceful situation of Puerto Rico after the revolutionary autumn of 1868 conditioned the ways in which the Volunteers defended the interests of the *integristas*. Just as in Cuba, they adapted to local conditions.

The only revolutionary attempt in the island was the *Grito de Lares* on September 23, 1868, during which an ephemeral Puerto Rican Republic was proclaimed. Lacking any substantial popular support, it was rapidly quashed thanks to the participation of the Civil Guard. Once the possibility of a war had been halted by its rapid quelling, the political debate in Puerto Rico focused on two main issues: how to assimilate the island into the Spanish political system, and how to abolish slavery. The *integristas* were against these changes, whereas their political opponents, the reformists, favored them. The many captains general appointed by the Spanish Government for short terms of office alternated between supporting the former or the latter. This was a cause of deep instability, reflected in the fact that between 1868 and 1874 Puerto Rico had seven captains general: José Laureano Sanz (1868–70), Gabriel Baldrich (1870–1), Ramón Gómez Pulido (1871–2), Simón de la Torre y Ormaza (1872), Joaquín Enrile y Hernán (1872–3), Juan Martínez Plowes (1873), and Rafael Primo de Rivera y Sobremonte (1873–4). Political instability in the Peninsula was reflected in such a constant change of governors, which tensed the political atmosphere created in Puerto Rico after the Lares' failure. This context favored the reactivation of the Volunteers.

Although the first Volunteer battalion in Puerto Rico had been created in December 1864, it had been almost inactive since its inception. The creation of the Puerto Rican Volunteers was de facto triggered by the *Grito de Lares*. This was an uprising of nearly 600 peasants commanded by landowners in the town of Lares. After declaring the Republic of Puerto Rico on September 23, 1868, they arrested all the peninsular merchants in town, looted their shops, and proceeded to the nearby town of San Sebastián del Pepino, where they were subdued by a mixed force of the army and the mostly creole Disciplined Militias.[159] Knowing of the fate of their fellow countrymen in

---

[159] José Pérez Morís & Luis Cueto y González Quijano. *Historia de la insurrección de Lares, precedida de una reseña de los trabajos separatistas que se vienen haciendo en la Isla de Puerto-Rico desde la emancipación de las demás posesiones hispano-ultramarinas, y seguida de todos los documentos á ella referentes*. Barcelona: Establecimiento Tipográfico de Narciso Ramírez y Cº, 1872, pp. 127–35.

Lares, the *peninsulares* of the nearby towns of Arecibo, Aguadilla, and Camuy took up arms and organized companies of Volunteers. Men like Pedro Puig y Pí in Arecibo, José Ignacio Corujo in Camuy, and Francisco Juliá Palmeta in Aguadilla were appointed captains of local companies.[160] They were petty businessmen usually commanding their employees, who nevertheless rendered a good service. After a week, the uprising was over, and by December 1868 all its members were either imprisoned or in exile.[161]

The rebellion failed because it lacked popular support, and the Spanish forces acted swiftly.[162] Nonetheless, it was a sign of a certain level of discontent against Spanish rule. Rather than independence, the driving force pushing peasants toward the rebellion was their opposition to a system of forced employment known as the *libreta*.[163] This was a system by which the authorities forcibly turned the unemployed peasant workforce into cheap labor. As to the few landowners who supported the uprising, they were drawn in by fear of losing their properties to the peninsular merchants. In fact, due to the absence of banks in Puerto Rico, these *peninsulares* acted as moneylenders when the landowners needed capital to cover the costs of harvesting or buying new land. Quite often, when the debts could not be paid back, sugar and coffee crops, but also their plantations, ended up in their hands.[164]

The outcry of Lares also widened distrust toward creoles, despite the lack of popular support for the insurrection. But as a result, the Volunteers began to replace the Disciplined Militias in the military system of Puerto Rico, despite the latter's established record of defending Spanish rule on the island since the eighteenth century.[165] They had famously rejected the British attack on San Juan in 1797.[166] The reason was that several of the Lares' rebels had served in the Disciplined Militias, and that most of its members were creoles.[167] The Volunteers, on the contrary, were perceived by the Spanish authorities as a new loyal militia dominated by *peninsulares*.[168] Consequently,

---

[160] AHN, Ultramar, 5457, exp. 23; Rosado y Brincau. *Bosquejo Histórico*, pp. 11–18; González Cuevas. *¿Defendiendo el honor?*, pp. 64–9; David Jou i Andreu. *Els sitgetans a Amèrica i diccionari d'"Americanos".* Sitges: Grup d'Estudis Sitgetans, 2008, pp. 313–4.

[161] Jiménez de Wagenheim. *Puerto Rico*, pp. 163–76; Pérez Morís & Cueto y González Quijano. *Historia de la insurrección de Lares*, pp. 95–135.

[162] Brau. *Historia de Puerto Rico*, pp. 264–5; González Vales. "The Challenge to Colonialism," pp. 110–12.

[163] Juan Gualberto Gómez & Antonio Sendras y Burín. *La isla de Puerto-Rico. Bosquejo Histórico (desde la conquista hasta principios de 1891)*. Madrid: Imprenta de José Gil y Navarro, 1891, pp. 76–8; Brau. *Historia de Puerto Rico*, pp. 264–5; Gervasio Luis García. *Historia bajo sospecha*. San Juan: Publicaciones Gaviota, 2015, pp. 127–37; AGPR, Fondo Municipal de Arecibo, caja 49.

[164] Cubano Iguina. *El hilo en el laberinto*, pp. 35–9.

[165] Luis E. González Vales. "Las milicias disciplinadas. Guardianes de la soberanía española en Puerto Rico," in Rafael del Pino y Moreno, Gonzalo Anes y Álvarez de Castrillón (coord.). *La América hispana en los albores de la emancipación: actas del IX Congreso de Academias Iberoamericanas de la Historia*. Madrid: Marcial Pons, 2005, pp. 433–52; Nelson R. González Mercado. *Auge y decadencia de las Milicias Disciplinadas*. PhD. Thesis #37. San Juan: Centro de Estudios Avanzados de Puerto Rico y el Caribe, 2005.

[166] Héctor Andrés Negroni. *Historia militar de Puerto Rico*. Madrid: Siruela, 1992, pp. 108–17.

[167] González Mercado. *Auge y decadencia de las Milicias Disciplinadas*, p. 112.

[168] Labor Gómez Acevedo. *Sanz, promotor de la conciencia separatista en Puerto Rico*. Río Piedras: Editorial Universitaria, 1974, pp. 214–20.

while the Disciplined Militias were not allowed to recruit new members, new units of Volunteers were created throughout the island, in places like Caguas, Río Piedras, Carolina, Hato Grande, Ciales, and in the military departments of Aguadilla, and Humacao.[169] In spite of this, the expulsion of Domingo Dulce by the Havana Volunteers in June 1869 was an example too dangerous to be repeated. Such a fast growth needed to be controlled, and the first *reglamento* of the Puerto Rican Volunteers was published on August 5, 1869. It was harsher in terms of discipline than Cuba's, assimilating them to the army and ensuring dependence on the military authorities.[170]

After the events of Lares, Captain General José Laureano Sanz was the man in charge in Puerto Rico. He had been appointed by the Spanish Government to implement in the reformist policy promised by *La Gloriosa*. He would soon forget said promises and side with the *integristas* instead. They did not constitute a political party, but a group of powerful merchants, landowners, and officials, mostly *peninsulares* with some important Puerto Rican members. The island's biggest sugar producer, José Ramón Fernández, appointed Marquis of La Esperanza on February 5, 1869, for his proven loyalty to Spain, became their leader.[171] These *integristas* opposed the assimilation of Puerto Rico into the metropolitan political system sanctioned by the 1869 Constitution and rejected the abolition of slavery. Assimilation meant giving a voice to the reformists through press and assembly rights, and through the election of representatives to the Spanish Parliament, for the Constitution granted the right to vote to all adult males. As for the abolition of slavery, they argued that it would spur a race war, and that it would hamper the export economy. The fact is, however, that slavery had a very limited impact on Puerto Rican economy in comparison to Cuba.[172] Whereas 400,000 people, or one in four of the population, were enslaved there by 1868, only around 40,000 (6.5 percent of the population) were in the same position in Puerto Rico.[173] Most of them lived in the sugar-producing areas around the island's coast.

Opposing the *integristas*, the reformists were essentially a group of intellectuals and liberal professionals who, unlike many of their Cuban colleagues, were decidedly abolitionists, and had never conspired against Spanish rule. Some of their leaders, such as José Julián Acosta or Julio Vizcarrondo, were well connected with liberal politicians in metropolitan Spain and had been instrumental in the establishment in Madrid of the Spanish Abolitionist Society in 1864, the first association to advocate the end of enslaved workforce in nineteenth-century Spain.[174]

The first challenge posed by political assimilation was the election of representatives to the Spanish Parliament, sanctioned by the new constitution, for the first time since the expulsion of the Antillean deputies in 1837.[175] Since the *peninsulares* were

---

[169] Rosado y Brincau. *Bosquejo Histórico*, pp. 19–29.
[170] Isla de Puerto-Rico. *Reglamento para los cuerpos de Voluntarios de la misma*, cap. VII, art. 43–75; González Cuevas. *¿Defendiendo el honor?*, p. 68.
[171] Alejandro Ynfiesta. *El marqués de la Esperanza, jefe del partido español de Puerto Rico*. San Juan: Tipografía de González, 1875, p. 17.
[172] AHN, Ultramar, leg. 5164; Cruz Monclova. *Historia de Puerto Rico*, t. II, vol. II, pp. 285–7.
[173] Schmidt-Nowara. *Empire, and Antislavery*, pp. 16 & 38.
[174] Ibid., pp. 100–25.
[175] Piqueras Arenas. *Sociedad civil y poder en Cuba*, pp. 80–2.

the backbone of *integrismo*, and they represented only 2 percent of Puerto Rico's population, their political success necessarily depended on electoral manipulation, in connivance with captains general.[176] Thus, in the elections of January 15, 1869, the *integristas* won eight of the eleven seats that Puerto Rico sent to the Congress of Deputies. Among them were the Marquis of La Esperanza and Colonel Juan Bautista Machicote of the San Juan Volunteer Battalion.[177] Although 11 deputies in a Spanish Parliament of 352 seats could do little, the *integristas* would send a firm voice against the reforms to Madrid.

This victory gave the *integristas* little influence in altering Madrid's policy in Puerto Rico. Amid accusations of electoral manipulation, Captain General Sanz was replaced by the liberal Gabriel Baldrich (1870–1). In just a few months, Baldrich established the local Provincial Council (*Diputación Provincial*), in equal terms with the other Spanish provinces, appointed reformists in the administration, embarked on a campaign against corrupt officials, and allowed the creation of political parties.[178] Under Baldrich's supervision, the elections of June 20, 1870, were clean. The *integristas*, now organized under the banner of the Conservative Liberal Party, suffered a severe defeat, clinging onto only two out of the fifteen deputies sent to Madrid, including José Laureano Sanz.[179]

The lessons that the *integristas* could have taken from the election were evident. On the one hand, the electoral victory of 1869 had not translated into real power on the island. On the other, non-manipulated elections on the island meant a landslide victory for the Liberal Reformist Party. Hence, to protect their agenda, the *integristas* would need to practice politics outside of parliament. If they wanted to control Puerto Rican politics, the captain general needed to be an ally, and Baldrich was not. Aiming at ousting him, they launched a campaign to undermine his authority. The *Boletín Mercantil*, Puerto Rico's main *integrista* newspaper, bitterly criticized Baldrich for protecting the reformists.[180] It was edited by José Pérez Morís, an Asturian journalist and telegraphist who had been a reformist in Cuba but who adopted a staunchly *integrista* stance after the *Grito de Yara*. At the same time, Volunteers throughout the island began to parade more often, aiming to intimidate their opponents. These actions added to rising tensions, causing some degree of opposition among reformists too. For instance, in the town of Ciales, the local company of Volunteers was stoned by a group of drunken men on February 17, 1871, after a ceremony they held to swear allegiance to the new Amadeus I, who had been proclaimed king of Spain the month before.[181]

---

[176] AHN, Ultramar, 1134, exp. 52; Brau. *Historia de Puerto Rico*, pp. 267–9; González Vales. "The Challenge to Colonialism," pp. 112–13; Jiménez de Wagenheim. *Puerto Rico*, pp. 176–8;

[177] ACD, Serie documentación electoral: 61, No. 18.

[178] Jesús Lalinde Abadía. *La administración española en el siglo XIX puertorriqueño*. Seville: Escuela de Estudios Hispano-Americanos de Sevilla, 1980, pp. 147–50; AHN, Ultramar, 5094, exp. 19; 5113, exp. 4, 19, 46, 50, 51, 55, & 56.

[179] Reece B. Bothwell. *Orígenes y desarrollo de los partidos políticos en Puerto Rico*. San Juan: Editorial Edil, 1987, pp. 3–4; ACD, Serie documentación electoral, 65, No. 4.

[180] Brau. *Historia de Puerto Rico*, pp. 269–70.

[181] Rosado y Brincau. *Bosquejo Histórico*, pp. 36–7.

The *integristas* accused the captain general of being permissive with such behavior. Despite Baldrich's complaints to Madrid against the provocative attitude of the Volunteers, they continued their campaign of intimidation. On June 22, 1871, the captain general wrote to the minister of the Colonies that most likely he would be impelled to take "forceful dispositions after the elections."[182] The most serious incident occurred on July 23, 1871, when an accidental shot by a Volunteer in San Juan sparked a massive street fight between his comrades-in-arms and a group of Blacks and mulattoes of the area who had shouted at them. The brawl ended up with the Volunteers randomly beating reformist suspects and shouting out against the captain general. As this dangerously resembled the events of 1869 in Havana, Baldrich declared a state of siege in San Juan for three days, taking the army to the streets, and rapidly controlling the situation. However, the Spanish Government wanted to avert a repetition of Dulce's expulsion by appeasing the anger of the Volunteers and the *integristas* in general. Thus, by September 1871, Baldrich was replaced by Gómez Pulido.[183]

Unlike what happened in Cuba after the expulsion of Dulce, Baldrich's substitution did not translate into *integrista* control of Puerto Rico. They might have been a coercive power in support of Spanish rule but were by no means an essential force to keep cities under control. As war reinforced the Volunteers in Cuba, peace in Puerto Rico weakened them. In fact, more governors committed to the reformist agenda were sent from the Peninsula. In that scenario, the options for the *integristas* to dominate Puerto Rican politics were to promote a change of government in Madrid or to forge alliances against the captain general. They chose to join forces with the Cuban *integristas*, with conservatives in metropolitan Spain, and to use the press against the authorities, often employing a menacing tone. For instance, on January 21, 1873, the *Boletín Mercantil* reminded Captain General Joaquín Enrile that "true Spaniards," as they considered themselves, would always be willing to use the Volunteers to make sure that Puerto Rico remained part of the Spanish nation, should the authorities fail to do so.[184]

This thorny relationship would be particularly tense during 1873. The reason was the proclamation of the First Spanish Republic, and the abolition of slavery in Puerto Rico, passed by the Spanish Parliament on March 22, 1873. The abolition was not a surprise, as it was the logical consequence of the gradual transition to free labor promoted by the ruling elite now in power. Besides, the abolition was enacted on moderate terms: the 2,000 slaveholders would be compensated, the c. 30,000 freed enslaved people would have to work for their former masters for a period of three years, and they would not enjoy political rights for five years.[185] The *integristas* would try to thwart its full implementation. They usually argued that freed slaves would take revenge against their former legal owners. Additionally, they thought that alike in the US South during the Reconstruction era which followed the Civil War, Blacks might be granted political rights in the future, which could benefit the reformists for

---

[182] BVB, Epistolario, sig. 7102075.
[183] AHN, Ultramar, 5113, exp. 5.
[184] *Boletín Mercantil*, 21-01-1873.
[185] Díaz Soler. *Historia de la esclavitud negra en Puerto Rico*. San Juan: Editorial de la Universidad de Puerto Rico, pp. 349-71.

their well-known abolitionist record.[186] Stemming from this, the *integristas* were also afraid that should their opponents become dominant in Puerto Rican politics, they would have the Volunteers dissolved. They had already expressed their desire to do so. In January 1872, Puerto Rican reformist representatives in the Spanish Congress had formally asked the government for the dissolution of the Volunteers on grounds that they were not necessary and hampered social cohesion between *peninsulares* and creoles in a peaceful island.[187]

The strategy followed by the *integristas* to thwart complete abolition was to pretend that there was a serious threat to Spanish sovereignty on the island and to label all reformists as conspirators. For instance, on February 13, 1873, a group of Volunteers and Civil Guards seized the country house of Cayetano Estrella, near the town of Camuy, alleging that the reformists that regularly met there were conspiring against Spain.[188] The reformists were armed, and the assault ended with twelve of them being killed, several arrested, plus a Volunteer and a Civil Guard injured.[189] The actual purposes of the Camuy reformists are unknown, and there were even rumors that the story had been manufactured by the *integristas*.[190] Whatever the case, it was conveniently exploited by the *Boletín Mercantil*. It published several articles for a few days after the Camuy events, claiming that this proved "a new Lares" was on its way.[191] The Volunteers were presented as the eternal saviors of the Spanish *integridad nacional*.[192]

The Camuy affair did not represent a victory for the *integristas*, though. Despite public speeches praising their collaboration with the Civil Guard, Captain General Martínez Plowes did not trust them entirely. He feared that the Volunteers might have been exaggerating information and rumors on supposed anti-Spanish conspiracies to claim a greater influence and undermine his authority. After all, Martínez Plowes was the representative of a government which had recently abolished slavery and given more political rights to all the free inhabitants of Puerto Rico. The memories of Havana's Volunteers' behavior in 1869 were still too fresh. In April 1873, Martínez Plowes wrote to the minister of the Colonies, José Cristóbal Sorní y Grau, that he was trying to keep the Volunteers under control.[193] The captain general had to keep a delicate balance between the reforms promised by the Spanish Republic to Puerto Rico in the form of abolition of slavery and more civil rights, and the local *integristas*' mounting pressures.

Quite cleverly, the Martínez Plowes took a sugar-coated measure to achieve this. On March 4, 1873, he issued a decree making the Volunteers "reserves of the Army." In that very decree, he praised the Volunteers for their loyal services to Spain but reminded them that they must abide by military discipline, and only the supreme authority on the

---

[186] Cruz Monclova. *Historia de Puerto Rico*, t. II, vol. I, pp. 257–78; John Hope Franklin. *Reconstruction after the Civil War*. Chicago and London: Chicago University Press, 1961, pp. 104–26.
[187] *Altar y Trono*, 28-01-1872.
[188] Negroni. *Historia militar de Puerto Rico*, pp. 125–6.
[189] AHN, Ultramar, 5103, exp. 62 & 63; Rosado y Brincau. *Bosquejo Histórico*, pp. 57–60.
[190] Brau. *Historia de Puerto Rico*, p. 272.
[191] *Boletín Mercantil*, 11-02-1873.
[192] *Boletín Mercantil*, 19-02-1873, 21-02-1873, 23-02-1873.
[193] AHN, Ultramar, 5113, exp. 16; Gelpí y Ferro. *Historia de la revolución y guerra de Cuba*, pp. 257–8.

island, the captain general, was to decide on the gravity of the rumors and threats that circulated around the island. He warned that he would not tolerate disturbances caused by these very ungrounded news.[194] The *reglamento* of 1869 established that causing public disorder for no apparent reason could be punished with arrest for a few days, or expulsion from the Volunteers. However, Martínez Plowes reminded them that he could decide whether a Volunteer must be judged by a military court, and according to the army ordinances, the punishment for public disorder would be imprisonment. According to their ordinances, the Volunteers must stand trial before a military court in case of war, sedition, or under any circumstance deemed grave by the captain general.[195]

So far, all the strategies adopted by the *integristas* had failed. Neither electoral participation nor the tension strategy had worked out for them. With the proclamation of the First Republic, their situation only worsened. In fact, the first captain general appointed by the new regime, Rafael Primo de Rivera, was a well-known liberal who worked intensely to implement a reformist policy on the island.[196] He had some qualities especially fit for the task. He was a creole born in Montevideo in 1813 who had held posts in the Spanish Antilles and was committed to the Revolution of 1868. In addition to this, in 1869 he had quelled a federalist uprising as captain general of Valencia. Thus, he was a liberal soldier of order. In just a few months, he decreed freedom of the press (April 30, 1873), of public gatherings (May 5, 1873), and the Municipal Law (July 25, 1873), which sanctioned the appointment of mayors by popular election. All of this benefited the reformists, for it allowed them to express in the press and at the polling stations the popular support they actually enjoyed.[197] Aware that they could never beat them cleanly, the *integristas* decided to abstain from participating in elections.[198] This meant that the reformists would have the monopoly of the representatives in Madrid, the Provincial Court, and town councils. In fact, the decision to abstain was taken in August 1872, but was confirmed after the arrival of Rafael Primo de Rivera. During his term, the elections for the Spanish Parliament were held between May 10 and 13, 1873, and for the Provincial Court between October 6 and 9, 1873, without the participation of *integristas*.[199] Thus, by refraining from participating in political institutions, they yielded to reformists all political power in Puerto Rico save for the captaincy general.

Despite abstaining electorally, the *integristas* were determined to take back control by other means. Having failed in all their strategies, they concluded that the problem rested in Madrid. To prompt a change of policy in Puerto Rico, it was necessary to change the regime in Madrid. This was a conclusion shared by the *integristas* in Cuba, and the conservatives in Spain who opposed to the political situation unfolded by *La Gloriosa*. Consequently, they decided to coordinate their efforts to change Spain's political regime.

---

[194] *Provincia de Puerto Rico. Instituto de Voluntarios*, p. 19; González Cuevas. *¿Defendiendo el honor?*, pp. 70–1.
[195] *Reglamento para los cuerpos de Voluntarios de la isla de Puerto Rico*, cap. VII, art. 72.
[196] AHN, Ultramar, 5113, exp. 21.
[197] Cruz Monclova. *Historia de Puerto Rico*, t. II, vol. II, pp. 278–373.
[198] *Boletín Mercantil*, 25-04-1873.
[199] Bothwell. *Orígenes y desarrollo*, pp. 8–9.

5

Fighting the Revolution across the Atlantic

To organize the opposition to the much-feared reforms envisioned by the Spanish Government, *integristas* conducted their counterrevolution in the Antilles but also forged alliances with groups with similar interests across the Atlantic in Spain, but also in American countries with sizeable Spanish communities. The governments of the *Sexenio Revolucionario* had been less revolutionary than expected, but the promises of equal political rights and slavery abolition outlined by the minister of the Colonies Adelardo López de Ayala in October 1868 were still regarded by the *integristas* and their counterparts in the Peninsula as open doors to the end of Spanish sovereignty in the Antilles and an economic collapse of a whole system.[1]

In the Peninsula, a strong opposition to the successive cabinets was gradually taking shape around the remnants of the Moderate Party that had been kicked out of power in September 1868. Many early supporters of the revolution disappointed with the incapacity of the new regime to stabilize Spain joined the opposition. Local industrial and agricultural bourgeoisie was also opposed to the new regime due to the free trade policy advocated by the minister of the Treasury Laureano Figuerola (1868-9) and continued with some nuances by his successors. Flour producers of Santander, wheat producers of Castile and Andalusia, and most notably the Catalan textile industry depended on a protectionist policy to keep Spain and the Antilles as captive markets for their products.[2] Among them, there were numerous *peninsulares* who had settled back in Spain, known as *indianos* or *americanos*, after having accumulated fortunes in the Antilles, where they generally kept significant vested interests.[3] Opposition groups in Spain began to gather around the idea of restoring the monarchy to Prince

---

[1] García Rodríguez. *Con un ojo en Yara y otro en Madrid*, pp. 62-4; Zaragoza. *Las insurrecciones de Cuba*, vol. II, pp. 734-6.

[2] Jordi Nadal. *El fracaso de la revolución industrial en España, 1814-1913*. Barcelona: Ariel, 1975, pp. 189-225; Jordi Maluquer de Motes. "La burgesia catalana i l'esclavitud colonial: modes de producción i pràctica política." *Recerques: Història, economia, cultura*, 1974, No. 3, pp. 83-126; Martín Rodrigo y Alharilla. "Cataluña y el colonialismo español (1868-1899)," in Salvador Calatayud Giner (coord.). *Estado y periferias en la España del siglo XIX. Nuevos enfoques*. Valencia: Universitat de València, 2009, pp. 315-56; Antón Costas Comesaña. "El viraje del pensamiento político-económico español a mediados del siglo XIX: la 'conversión' de Laureano Figuerola y la formulación del librecambismo industrialista." *Moneda y Crédito*, 1983, No. 167, pp. 47-70.

[3] Áurea Matilde Fernández Muñiz. "Los indianos: su incidencia en la economía peninsular y en la política colonial." *Trocadero: Revista de historia moderna y contemporánea*, 1992, No. 4, pp. 21-36.

Alphonse, son of Isabella II, the queen dethroned in 1868, a project they shared with the *integrista* elite in Cuba and Puerto Rico. Both groups coordinated efforts to end the political instability started in 1868 and restore the Bourbon dynasty.[4] After a few years of impossible coexistence, they reached the conclusion that the revolutionary regime was Spain's first obstacle for stability and a threat to their interests.

To push forward this agenda, the efforts to dismantle the regime established after September 1868 were being articulated through networks and institutions across the Atlantic. Personal networks, shared ideas and strategies were put to work to attain goals in common. *Integristas* in Cuba took had taken the lead with the creation of the *Casino Español* in Havana June 1869, followed by many more across the island, and even with a colleague institution in San Juan de Puerto Rico. In the Peninsula, *alfonsinos*, supporters of restoring the Bourbons on Prince Alphonse, created a network of the *círculos hispano-ultramarinos* across Spain, in every major city with substantial interests in the Antilles. The Volunteers, the *casinos*, and the *círculos* revolted around the basic set of ideals enshrined by *integrismo*. While the institutions pushed forward the agenda by political and economic lobbying, the militia represented its armed wing, thus establishing many links between them.

Casinos Españoles

Havana's *Casino Español* was created on June 11, 1869, by three peninsular merchants, Juan Toraya, Antonio C. Tellería, and Rufino Sainz, and the treasurer Juan de Ariza. They were middle-class Volunteers who envisioned the *Casino* as a power center with which to pressure the Spanish authorities and challenge the *integrista* elite's upper hand. The *Casino* imitated a formula already existing in other American countries with influential Spanish communities, such as Mexico and Argentina.[5] Purportedly, the aim of the *Casino Español* created in Havana was to "provide a meeting venue for all these persons [Spanish loyalists], to address privately the issues that concern the moral and material interests of the country, promote and collaborate with projects that favour and provide its members means of instruction and leisure; everything within the law and always helping the action of the authorities."[6] Actually, the *Casino Español* soon became the political center for radical *integristas*.[7] Before long, a network of thirty-one *Casinos* was created throughout Cuba, somehow coordinated by the *Casino* of Havana, in cities like Matanzas, Cárdenas, Santiago de Cuba, Cienfuegos, Trinidad, or Guantánamo, but also in towns such as Guanajay, Remedios, Colón, Manzanillo,

---

[4] Espadas Burgos. *Alfonso XII y los orígenes de la Restauración*, pp. 271–99.
[5] For an overview of Spanish associationism in America, see Juan Andrés Blanco Rodríguez. "Aspectos del asociacionismo en la emigración española a América," in Juan Andrés Blanco Rodríguez (ed.). *El asociacionismo en la emigración española a América*. Salamanca: UNED Zamora/Junta de Castilla y León, 2008, pp. 9–30.
[6] BNE, HA/71063. *Reglamento del Casino Español de La Habana*, 1893, Art. 1.
[7] Fernández Muñiz. *España y Cuba*, pp. 156–63.

Caibarién, Baracoa, Santiago de Las Vegas, Gibara, Bemba (Jovellanos), Isla de Pinos, Limonar, Santa Clara, El Recreo, Alacranes, Bejucal, San Antonio, Sagua la Grande, Sancti Spíritus, Holguín, Placetas, Hato Nuevo, and Morón.[8] Despite the *Subinspección General de Voluntarios* remained at Havana's La Fuerza Fortress, the *Casino Español* of the city became a sort of an officious headquarters for the Volunteers, and the *Casinos* across Cuba basic spaces of socialization. Since some Volunteer units did not have barracks of their own, the *Casinos* soon became the place to meet, discuss, and organize events, beyond the traditional taverns.

The success of the *Casinos*, with their rapid spread throughout Cuba and their growing influence, was soon coveted by the *integrista* elite. During the years of the Volunteers' uncontrolled violence in Havana (around 1869 and 1872) the *Casino* in Havana was kept under the umbrella of the most radical sectors of *integrismo*. After a period where this elite disputed its control with the middle-class Volunteers that created it, the *Casinos* finally came under the control of the wealthy *integristas* in 1872, when Julián de Zulueta was appointed its president. Seizing the *Casino* had become only possible thanks to the removal of Captain General Blas Villate in 1872. The middleman of the *integrista* elite in Madrid, Manuel Calvo, had been lobbying before the Crown and the government at least since 1870. They perceived Villate as a threat. Not only he was tremendously popular among the rank-and-file Volunteers, but he had also openly and repeatedly denounced the corruption of the wealthiest *integrista* groups before the Spanish Government.[9]

Once in power, the elite opted not to clash with the elements that had controlled the *Casino* before them, perhaps fearing that the anger thrusted against Captain General Dulce in 1869 could easily be turned against them. Middle-class *integristas* were integrated into the lower positions of the board.[10] The latter had lost control over the institution, but somehow their voices would still be heard. The social profile of the *Casino*'s directors had changed, but not their purpose. It became a center of greater influence thanks to the prominent social position of its leaders. The *Casino Español* exerted a great influence on both captains general and the Spanish Government, as well as advising them on the Cuban situation, to the extent that the appointment and removal of captains generals could hardly be peacefully done without its approval. For instance, even Prime Minister Juan Prim (1869–70), politically considered a liberal, often consulted with the presidents of the *Casino* about the convenience of certain policies for Cuba.[11] But the *Casino* put the interests of *integrismo* before any other consideration. There have even been insinuations that the men of the *Casino Español*

---

[8] Ribó. *Historia de los Voluntarios cubanos*, vol. I, pp. 571–86; Mayela Velázquez Díaz. "El legado social hispano en Guantánamo: el Casino Español," in José Manuel Azcona Pastor & Israel Escalona Chadez (dir.). *Cuba y España. Procesos migratorios e impronta perdurable (siglos XIX y XX)*. Madrid: Dykinson, 2014, pp. 144–61.
[9] Fernández Muñiz. *España y Cuba*, p. 158.
[10] Portela Miguélez. *Redes de poder en Cuba*, p. 176.
[11] BNE, sig. HA/10478(24), *Carta del Presidente del Casino Español de La Habana, de 15 de noviembre de 1869, al Excmo. Sr. D. Juan Prim, Presidente del Consejo de Ministros*, 1869.

might have organized the assassination of Juan Prim in December 1870, for there were insistent rumors that he was trying to sell the island to the United States.[12]

The firm position of the *Casino Español* as the center of Cuban *integrismo* was maintained throughout the *Sexenio Democrático* and beyond. Coinciding with the visit to Cuba of the First Republic's Minister of the Colonies Santiago Soler y Pla (1873-4) in November 1873, the *Casino* reaffirmed its compromise to trying to keep Cuba out of the upheaval that irresponsible reforms might bring. This attitude was praised by the *integrista* press. The *Diario de la Marina* considered the *Casino* the firmest stronghold of Spain in Cuba, and the staunchly *integrista* newspaper *La Voz de Cuba* considered that Cuba would be Spanish for as long as the Volunteers and the *Casino Español* existed.[13] Both the Volunteers and the *Casinos Españoles*, the armed wing and political headquarters of *integrismo* respectively, came to be regarded as the bulwarks of Spanish Cuba against the reformist policies envisioned by the First Republic.[14]

Many initiatives by Cuban *integristas* were followed in Puerto Rico. In 1871 a *Casino Español* was established in San Juan by the same elite that had created the Volunteers in 1864. Its aims and purposes were the same as in Cuba: staunch defense of national integrity and opposition against reformists in the Peninsula and Puerto Rico. In fact, the influence of the Cuban *Casinos* was not merely theoretical. Juan de Ariza, one of the founders of the *Casino Español* in Havana, went to Puerto Rico to help establish the local branch in San Juan. He also partook in the organization of some of its activities, such as the celebration of the appointment of Alphonse XII as King of Spain in 1875.[15] Also, the relationship between the *Casino* and the Volunteers in Puerto Rico was as close as in Cuba. Many of the men who created the Volunteer Battalion in San Juan back in 1864 were found among the founders of the *Casino Español*, headed by the Marquis of La Esperanza.[16] Nonetheless, due to the weaker position of the Puerto Rican *integristas* in comparison to their Cuban colleagues, the *Casino* did not have as much influence over the authorities. However, it did act as a lobby in defense of its members' interests. For instance, in October 1877 it formally asked the government to reduce the tariff applied to Puerto Rican sugar entering the Peninsula, for many sugar barons were members of the *Casino*.[17]

---

[12] Espadas Burgos. *Alfonso XII y los orígenes de la Restauración*, pp. 285–91; Juan Pando Despierto. "Las conversaciones Prim-Sickles: España-Cuba-Estados Unidos en 1868–1870." Juan Pablo Fusi & Antonio Niño Rodríguez (coord.). *Antes del desastre: orígenes y antecedentes de la crisis del 98.* Madrid: Universidad Complutense de Madrid, 1996, pp. 359–78. Recently, Juan Pérez Abellán has argued that the Regent Francisco Serrano plotted to kill President Prim, to become King of Spain. *Matar a Prim.* Barcelona: Editorial Planeta, 2015, pp. 131–45.

[13] Alfonso Rodríguez Aldave. *La política ultramarina de la República del 73.* Havana: Nuestra España, 1940, p. 37; Roldán de Montaud. *La Restauración en Cuba*, pp. 91–3.

[14] Martí Gilabert. *La Primera República Española*, pp. 77–84.

[15] *La Época*, 04-01-1875.

[16] Jaime M. Pérez Rivera. *Asociacionismo, prensa y cultura entre los inmigrantes españoles de San Juan, 1871–1913*, Ph.D. Thesis. Río Piedras: Universidad de Puerto Rico, Recinto de Río Piedras, 2002, pp. 82–144.

[17] AHN, Ultramar, 6302, exp. 2-5.

Círculos Hispano-Ultramarinos

Just as the *integristas* had created their own organizations in the Antilles, the groups with interests in the Antilles created their own version in metropolitan Spain. Apart from having been a Spanish territory for centuries, Cuba was a land of provision for many *peninsulares*. During the second half of the nineteenth century, hundreds of thousands of *peninsulares* had settled in Cuba looking for better life prospects, which in turn ended up generating remittances back to their families which revitalized the impoverished economies of many towns in Galicia, Asturias, or Catalonia. As well as to maintaining families, remittances were also employed to pay for basic infrastructures such as sewerage, lighting, schools, or hospitals.[18] But above this basic economic binding between Cuba and the Peninsula, important sectors of the local economy had much at stake in the Antilles. Whereas Cuba essentially depended on the US market, some producing sectors in the Peninsula depended on the Cuban market. By the early 1870s, while the Peninsula imported 8 percent of its trade from Cuba, the island absorbed 14 percent of its exports.[19] The economic dependence was not evenly distributed throughout the Spanish geography, for it was heavily concentrated in industrial areas. Certainly, wheat producers in Castile, flour exporters from Santander, and wine exporters from Andalusia had their shares in the trade with Cuba, but Catalonia outstood with its textile industry and shipping lines. Some of their most relevant members had amassed a fortune in Cuba due to slave trade, among other activities, whose continuity was also one of the bedrocks of colonial lobbyists in the Peninsula.

In order to defend their vested interest in Cuba, these groups created the *Círculos Hispano-Ultramarinos*. These were institutions aimed at defending the Antillean market, financially supporting the Spanish soldiers and Volunteers in Cuba, and opposing the outright abolition of slavery.[20] The creation of the *Círculos* was a reaction to the Moret Law on July 4, 1870. This law, named after Segismundo Moret, minister of the Colonies, paved the way for the gradual abolition of slavery.[21] It sanctioned that enslaved people over 60 and those born after September 1868 should be immediately freed.[22] In a way, the *Círculos* of the Peninsula were similar to the *Casinos* of the Antilles. Both were social clubs, but the *Círculos* explicitly served as a platform with which to defend the colonial interests, lacking the educational or socialization purposes of the *Casinos*.

---

[18] Martín Rodrigo y Alharilla. *Indians a Catalunya: capitals cubans a l'economia catalana*. Barcelona: Fundació Noguera, 2007, pp. 17–40.
[19] José A. Piqueras. *Cuba, emporio y colonia. La disputa de un mercado interferido*. Madrid: Fondo de Cultura Económica, 2003, p. 222.
[20] Maluquer de Motes. "La burgesia catalana i l'esclavitud colonial," pp. 116–19; Christopher Schmidt-Nowara. "National Economy and Atlantic Slavery: Protectionism and Resistance to Abolitionism in Spain and the Antilles, 1854–1874." *The Hispanic American Historical Review*, vol. 78, No. 4, November 1998, pp. 603–29.
[21] Concepción Navarro Azcúe. *La abolición de la esclavitud negra en la legislación española, 1870–1887*. Madrid: Ediciones Cultura Hispánica/Instituto de Cooperación Iberoamericana, 1987, pp. 37–123; José Antonio Piqueras Arenas. *La esclavitud en las Españas. Un lazo transatlántico*. Madrid: Los Libros de la Catarata, 2012, pp. 234–51.
[22] Espadas Burgos. *Alfonso XII y los orígenes de la Restauración*, pp. 286–9.

The first *Círculo* was created in Madrid in November 1870 by the Marquis of Manzanedo, an *indiano* that had made a fortune in Cuba as a slave trader. The rules of the *Círculo* established that its members must have lived in the Antilles and needed to maintain active interests there.[23] Its first president was José Laureano Sanz, the former governor of Puerto Rico who had quelled the Lares uprising attempt and so harshly repressed creole reformists. Due to personal issues, Sanz was soon replaced by Manzanedo in 1871. The model of the Madrid *Círculo* was rapidly copied, and by the end of 1872, ten more branches had been created in Barcelona, Cádiz, Seville, Málaga, Santander, Valencia, Avilés, Bilbao, Zaragoza, and Cáceres.[24]

The most important of the *Círculos* was Barcelona's, established in December 1870. Catalonia was, by far, the region with the strongest economic ties with the Antilles.[25] For the Catalan textile industry, keeping the Antilles a captive market was essential for its survival. Unable to compete with British clothing's price and quality, high tariffs and protective commercial laws were the pillars of Spain's most important industrial cluster. The creation of the Barcelona *Círculo* had been promoted by National Production Promotion (*Fomento de la Producción Nacional*), the main employers' association created in 1868 to fight against the free trade policy defended by the minister of the Treasury Laureano Figuerola, himself a Catalan.[26] *Fomento* continued the work of the Industrial Institute of Catalonia, which had been created in 1848 by Juan Güell. *Fomento*'s first president and vice-president were Juan Güell y Ferrer and Antonio López, respectively. Güell had been Spain's most remarkable advocate for protectionism, and López the country's most important shipbuilding tycoon of the nineteenth century.[27] He established the Compañía Trasatlántica Española in Barcelona, which transported migrants, soldiers, and goods between the Peninsula and Cuba.[28]

---

[23] Rafael Portell de Pasamonte. "Don Juan Manuel Manzanedo y González, I Duque de Santoña, I Marqués de Manzanedo." *Monte Buciero*, 2004, No. 10, pp. 87–102; José Gregorio Cayuela Fernández & Ángel Bahamonde Magro. "Trasvase de capitales antillanos y estrategias inversoras. La fortuna del Marqués de Manzanedo (1823–1882)." *Revista Internacional de Sociología*, No. 1, 1987, pp. 125–48.

[24] Cáceres. Fernández Muñiz. *España y Cuba*, p. 159.

[25] Maluquer de Motes. "La burgesia catalana i l'esclavitud colonial"; Carlos Martínez Shaw. "Los orígenes de la industria algodonera catalana y el comercio colonial," in Gabriel Tortellà & Jordi Nadal Lorenzo (coord.). *Agricultura, comercio colonial y crecimiento económico en la España contemporánea: actas del Primer Coloquio de Historia Económica de España, Barcelona, 11–12 Mayo 1972*. Barcelona: Ariel, 1974, pp. 243–67; *La Convicción*, 28-12-1871; José Miguel Sanjuan. "El tráfico de esclavos y la élite barcelonesa. Los negocios de la Casa Vidal Ribas," in Lizbeth J. Chaviano Pérez & Martín Rodrigo y Alharilla (eds.). *Negreros y esclavos. Barcelona y la esclavitud atlántica (siglos XVI-XIX)*. Barcelona: Icaria, 2017, pp. 131–58.

[26] Espadas Burgos. *Alfonso XII y los orígenes de la Restauración*, p. 288.

[27] Martín Rodrigo y Alharilla. "Los marqueses de Comillas, 1817–1925," in Carmen Almodóvar Muñoz (ed.). *Presencia de Cuba en la historiografía española actual*. Madrid: Ediciones Doce Calles, pp. 141–54; Jaume Vicens Vives. *Industrials i Polítics (segle XIX)*. Barcelona: Ediciones Vicens Vives, 1991 (first published in 1958), pp. 337–44.

[28] César Yáñez. "Los negocios ultramarinos de una burguesía cosmopolita: los catalanes en las primeras fases de la globalización 1750–1914," *Revista de Indias*, 2006, vol. 66, No. 238, pp. 679–710.

Apart from the shared interests of the *Casinos* and the *Círculos*, there were personal connections too, which helped to establish the latter, and to keep the links with the former. Juan Bautista Machicote, former colonel of Puerto Rico's first Volunteer Battalion and co-founder of the *Casino Español* in San Juan, became a member of the *Círculo Hispano-Ultramarino* in Madrid.[29] In Seville, Rafael Torres-Pardo, former Volunteer and member of the *Casino Español* of Havana, gave a passionate speech in the local branch of the *Círculo* in April 1872 defending their former comrades-at-arms from the attacks that kept coming from the reformist Spanish press.[30]

Though the *Círculos* pretended not to be political beyond the defense of Spanish national unity, they became overwhelmingly dominated by the *alfonsinos* who wanted to restore Monarchy toppled in 1868.[31] This gave the *Círculos* an ideological cohesion around issues such as the defense of slavery or the return of the Bourbons. De facto, this meant the exclusion of republicans, who had historically advocated for the abolition of slavery. For instance, the republican member of the Congress Baldomero Lostau was kicked out of the first meeting of the Barcelona *Círculo Hispano-Ultramarino* for having outspokenly defended the end of slavery.[32]

The cohesion of the *Círculos*, therefore, was the result of the collusion between *integristas* and *alfonsinos*. This became even more evident with the creation of the National League (*Liga Nacional*), a sort of coordinating platform for all the *Círculos Hispano-Ultramarinos*. This platform was created by the *Círculo* of Madrid on February 7, 1873.[33] It was the last attempt to tackle the abolition of slavery in Puerto Rico, which was much more feasible for the peaceful situation of the island. In Cuba, serious discussion about slavery's future would still have to wait until the end of the war. Though the economic impact of slavery in Puerto Rico was limited, due to the relatively slight importance of enslaved labor for the island's economy, members of the *Círculos* feared that the measure would soon be extended to Cuba, where slavery was still profitable.[34] The National League organized demonstrations and presented thousands of signatures against the abolition of slavery. Setting the enslaved people free in Puerto Rico was a strategic compromise of the government, for it wanted to

---

[29] *Memoria que presenta á los señores socios del Centro Hispano-Ultramarino de Madrid el Presidente Excmo. Sr. Marqués de Manzanedo. 20 de enero de 1873*. Madrid: Imprenta de Andrés Orejas, 1873, p. 31; AHN, Ultramar, 5457, exp. 23.

[30] Rafael Torres-Pardo. *Discurso en defensa de los Voluntarios de Cuba, leído en la Junta General del Círculo Hispano-Ultramarino de Sevilla y su provincia, celebrada el 14 de abril de 1872, por D. Rafael Torres-Pardo, socio del mismo*. Seville: Imprenta de Salvador Acuña y compañía, 1872, pp. 3–8; AHN, Hacienda, 3147, exp. 96.

[31] Eloy Arias Castañón. "El Centro Hispano-Ultramarino de Sevilla y la Guerra de Cuba (1872–1881)," in *Actas del II Congreso Internacional de Historia Militar*, vol. III. Zaragoza: Servicio de Publicaciones del EME, 1988, pp. 213–29.

[32] *La Igualdad*, 02-02-1872, pp. 2–3. Baldomero Lostau Prats (1846–1896) was elected to the Congress for the districts of Gracia (1871–2) and Vilafranca del Penedés (1893–4), ACD, Serie documentación Electoral, 62, No. 10 & 107, No. 8.

[33] Espadas Burgos. *Alfonso XII y los orígenes de la Restauración*, pp. 285–8; Maluquer de Motes. "La burgesia catalana i l'esclavitud colonial," pp.119–22.

[34] Rebecca J. Scott. *Slave emancipation in Cuba*, pp. 77–110.

earn the support of local reformists. After three years of discussions, the Spanish Parliament finally passed the law abolishing forced labor in Puerto Rico on March 22, 1873. The cabinet headed by Manuel Ruiz Zorrilla (1872–3) not only honored a political compromise but also considered that it would convince Cuban insurgents to give up their fight in exchange for political rights and promise of abolition. Having been defeated in its attempt to thwart the end of enslaved labor in Puerto Rico, the National League was dissolved shortly afterward.[35]

The National League did not succeed, but it established a pattern of collaboration between *integristas* and *alfonsinos*, two forces which aimed at changing the regime in force in Spain since 1868. Along with defending their vested interests in the Antilles, members of the National League had been actively working for the return of the Bourbon dynasty to Spain. Both forces believed that a conservative government under the restored monarchy of Prince Alphonse would bring peace and stability to Spain and the Antilles. Consequently, the profile of many members of the National League was the same that supported the Bourbon's restoration to the throne: a mixture of politicians, army officers, civil servants, and middle-class businessmen disappointed with the evolution of the 1868 regime, and conservatives who had never hosted any hopes on it.[36] The president of the National League, General Francisco Serrano, former regent (1868–71) and its vice-president Adelardo López de Ayala, former minister of the Colonies, were among the men disappointed by the successive revolutionary governments' inability to stabilize Spain. Among the conservative politicians who had opposed *La Gloriosa* from the very beginning, Antonio Cánovas del Castillo, former minister of the Interior (1864) and of the Colonies (1865–6), became the mastermind behind the proclamation of Prince Alphonse as King Alphonse XII. Disregarding concerns from leading members of the opposition, who advocated for a peaceful return of the Monarchy led by civilians, General Arsenio Martínez de Campos staged a coup on New Year's Eve 1874 in Sagunto, a town north to Valencia, proclaiming Alphonse of Bourbon king of Spain. Martínez de Campos brought the king back, but Cánovas was the true architect of the operation, and the mastermind behind the regime which followed, the Restoration (1874–1923), the most stable regime in modern Spanish history.[37]

Aiming at establishing a strong Crown and a strong government which could guarantee national unity and—ironically—end with military coup culture, the new regime set upon the task of pacifying Spain. Rather than Cuba, the priority for Cánovas was the Peninsula. First, it devoted thousands of soldiers and *pesetas* to end the war

---

[35] Eduardo Galván Rodríguez. *La abolición de la esclavitud en España. debates parlamentarios, 1810–1886*. Madrid: Dykinson, 2014, pp. 166–87.

[36] Melchor Fernández Almagro. *Historia política de la España contemporánea*, vol. I. Madrid: Alianza Editorial, 1968, pp. 242–7; Carr. *Spain, 1808–1875*, pp. 348–55; Espadas Burgos. *Alfonso XII y los orígenes de la Restauración*, pp. 357–98; Ramón Villares & Javier Moreno Luzón. *Restauración y Dictadura*. Josep Fontana & Ramón Villares (dir.), *Historia de España*, vol. VII. Barcelona and Madrid: Crítica/Marcial Pons, 2009, pp. 5–24.

[37] Carr. *Spain, 1808–1875*, pp. 348–55; José Luis Comellas. *Cánovas*. Madrid: Ediciones Cid, 1965, pp. 147–212; Jesús Neira. "El régimen político de la Restauración," in *Cánovas y la vertebración de España*. Madrid: Fundación Cánovas del Castillo, 1998, pp. 35–78.

against the Carlist army started in 1872.[38] Only when the Peninsula was pacified after the Carlist defeat in 1876 would Cánovas devote any major military effort to end the war in Cuba.[39] Between 1876 and 1878, the Ministry of War was able to send to Cuba around 80,000 troopers, many of whom had been recently fighting the Carlists and were thus seasoned soldiers. The military direction of the war was bestowed to Arsenio Martínez de Campos, who beyond the regular army could count on around 80,000 Volunteers to end the Cuban rebel resistance. Much divided and torn after ten years of unstopped fighting, the *mambises* accepted to capitulate on the promises of political reforms and the end of slavery for Cuba. On February 10, 1878, Martínez de Campos and representatives of the Cuban rebel government signed the *Pacto del Zanjón*, ending a ten-year war which had cost over 150,000 lives and was an immense blow to the economy of Cuba and Spain.[40]

Once Cuba was pacified, the Spanish Government set to implement a series of deep reforms in the island between 1878 and 1881. These reforms were not perceived as a threat by the *integristas*, for they knew that the reforms envisioned by the Conservative Party headed by Cánovas were to be much less ambitious than the reformist policies of the revolutionary governments of 1868–74. Cuba was assimilated into the Spanish political system, following the example set for was Puerto Rico in 1869. Thus, Cuba would elect its own representatives to the Spanish Parliament for the first time since 1837. But assimilation did not mean equal rights, let alone political fairness. Political assimilation of Cuba into the Spanish political system did not mean ending colonial practices of abuse. The narrow electoral census in the Peninsula was even more restricted in Cuba and Puerto Rico to assure the predominance of the *integrista* elite through a complicated mechanism of taxes and requisites made to favor a certain population segment. Also, Cuba was not to elect their representatives as such. Instead, the island was divided into six provinces, each with its own Provincial Council, also dominated by *integristas*, who often happen to be *peninsulares*. Granting political rights to all free inhabitants of Cuba, a long aspiration of reformists, had ended up providing *integristas* with more elements of political power and control.

Beyond political rights, the major pending issue in Cuba was the fate of slavery. It had been the most-welcomed victim of the Ten Years' War, for keeping it the way it was before 1868 was unattainable. Abolition of slavery had been a rebel promise which drew support of thousands of Cubans of African descent, who had shed way too much blood to be forgotten. The passing of the Moret Law in 1870 and the abolition of slavery in Puerto Rico in 1873 could not be isolated from the future of the "peculiar institution" in Cuba. Hence, the fate of slavery in Cuba by the late 1870s was clear.

---

[38] For the presence of *Carlismo* in the Spanish Empire see Fernando J. Padilla Angulo. "El carlismo en Ultramar," in Daniel Montañà & Josep Rafart (eds.). *Fronteres del carlisme: del Berguedà a Ultramar. IV Simposi d'Història del Carlisme. Avià, 7 de maig de 2016*. Avià: Centre d'Estudis d'Avià, 2016, pp. 209–29.

[39] Josep C. Clemente. *Las guerras carlistas*. Madrid: Sarpe, 1986, pp. 184–97; Julio Aróstegui, Jordi Canal & Eduardo González Calleja. *El carlismo y las guerras carlistas*. Madrid: La Esfera de los Libros, 2003, pp. 76–85.

[40] Casanovas. *Bread, or Bullets!*, pp. 119–24; Navarro. *Las guerras de España en Cuba*, pp. 87–112; Otero Pimentel. *Memoria sobre los Voluntarios*, p. 177.

After much technical negotiations, the law abolishing slavery in the island was passed by the Congress on February 13, 1880. Thus, after centuries, all Spanish territories became slave-free. De facto, slavery in Cuba had been destroyed by war. Thousands of enslaved men and women became actually free by joining the insurrection; a good deal of the agricultural system in eastern Cuba had been shattered. Also, the high costs of maintaining enslaved workers—feeding, surveillance, and fear of a rebellion—convinced slaveowners to accept abolition without much protest.[41] It was a relatively smooth transition to free labor, for abolition did not mean immediate freedom for the enslaved people. A so-called Trusteeship Law (*Ley del Patronato*), passed almost immediately after the abolition bill, established a period of eight years during which enslaved people, around 230,000 souls in 1880, were forced to work for their former owners as *patrocinados*, under conditions that powerfully resembled unfree labor. Two years before the deadline, in 1886, the 25,000 *patrocinados* left were finally freed.[42]

Consequently, *integristas* in the Antilles and the colonial lobbies in the Peninsula felt secured and protected by the new regime in power. Wider political rights to the people of the Antilles were granted, and abolition had been sanctioned, but in a way that it did not severely affect neither Spanish sovereignty nor their interests. Between 1876 and 1881 all the *Círculos Hispano-Ultramarinos* were dissolved. The first was the branch of Madrid, for its members, mostly former officials of the Spanish administration in Cuba and army chief officers, were chiefly concerned with bringing a conservative regime to power, and that had already been achieved in 1875.[43] The last *Círculo* to dissolve was Barcelona's, for its members, basically, Catalan *indianos* with a strong interest in the Antillean economies, were clearly interested in securing from the government an economic policy friendly to their interests. Only in January 1881, a few months after the issue of slavery had been settled, the *Círculo Hispano-Ultramarino* of the Catalan capital was dissolved. In a letter to Prime Minister Cánovas del Castillo, the president of the Barcelona *Círculo*, José Munné, considered that the institution was no longer necessary, since the government was making the reforms required to boost Cuban economy while they felt their property was well protected.[44]

---

[41] Scott. *Slave Emancipation in Cuba*, pp. 111–24.
[42] Scott. *Slave Emancipation in Cuba*, 127–41; Knight. *Slave Society in Cuba*, pp. 154–79; Galván Rodríguez. *La abolición de la esclavitud en España*, pp. 195–221.
[43] *El Imparcial*, 21-01-1876, p. 2.
[44] *Diario oficial de avisos de Madrid*, 26-01-1881.

6

The Volunteers and the Reconstruction of Cuba

As Máximo Gómez, commanding general of the rebel army during the war, observed the harbor of Santiago de Cuba from a boat on February 14, 1878, the 3,000 Cubans donning the Volunteer uniform who had gathered at the port to receive injured Spanish regular soldiers from the San Quintín Battalion had him famously exclaim that "Cuba cannot be free."[1] Gómez, who had been commissioned to have an interview with Antonio Maceo in order to convince him to lay down weapons, would soon go into exile alongside many of his men. The regular soldiers were to be shipped back to the Peninsula within a few weeks. As most Cubans, the Volunteers had to stay in the island, keeping on with their ordinary lives, coping with the bitter legacy of a ten-year civil war and the many challenges posed by peace. A new period full of uncertainties was unfolding in Cuban history.

To begin with, it was unclear whether peace was to prevail at all. The Pact of Zanjón reached on February 10, 1878, between General Martínez de Campos, commander-in-chief of the Spanish Army in Cuba, and the representatives of the Government of the Republic in Arms was rejected by part of the rebel forces in Oriente, the revolution's stronghold. Men like Antonio Maceo and Calixto García rejected the pact and continued the fight. The vague promises of granting Cuba the same political rights enjoyed by Puerto Rico since 1869—political representation in the Parliament and the implementation of the 1876 Constitution—and freedom for the enslaved population and Asian indentured servants who fought for the revolution were not enough for men who had shed blood for ten years in the name of independence and outright abolition.

After Calixto García had been captured and Máximo Gómez had accepted the terms of the Zanjón following rebel government orders, Antonio Maceo remained as the sole insurgent commander with the reputation to stand against the peace with Spain. After holding an interview with Martínez de Campos, Antonio Maceo, who still commanded a few thousand beleaguered fighters, issued the Protest of Baraguá on March 23, 1878, thereby rejecting the Zanjón's terms and unrecognizing the government of the Republic in Arms. He ordered the drafting of a new constitution which would only allow the new

---

[1] Máximo Gómez. *El Convenio del Zanjón. Recopilación de los artículos publicados en "El Imparcial de Trinidad."* Trinidad: Imp. de "El Imparcial," 1884, p. 19.

government to accept peace based on independence and abolition. Virtually exhausted by ten years of bloody war, after a few weeks Antonio Maceo agreed to give up the fight and took the exile offer posed by the Spanish authorities. He left the island vanquished, but not surrendered. Too much blood had been spilled for the independence ideals to easily fade away.

On June 14, 1878, Martínez de Campos entered Havana alongside his men victoriously, passing under a triumphal arch built by the *Casino Español* and where one could read in big letters "to the pacifiers of Cuba."[2] The man who had brought back Prince Alphonse to Spain in 1874 and vanquished the last Carlist strongholds in 1876 had also defeated Cuban insurgents and offered them an acceptable peace. Men from Havana's Volunteer battalions escorted him along the road from the harbor to the Captains General's Palace, surrounded by thousands of *habaneros* who cheered the men who had put a long war to an end.

Despite the pomp and circumstance, the peace was frail. The Spanish Government was not too committed to the promises given by Martínez de Campos to the rebels. Some considered it was too soon to grand full political rights in an island where a good deal of its inhabitants supported independence, and a few thousand of them had fought for it. In a canny move, Cánovas del Castillo stepped down as prime minister in February 1879 and recommended to King Alphonse XII that Martínez de Campos should be appointed in his place. It was a way to have the general away from Cuba and entertained in the troubled waters of Spanish politics. The king heard Cánova's suggestion, but as expected, Martínez de Campos proved a better soldier than a politician. Only ten months after having resigned, the king called for a new government and Cánovas del Castillo was back in power, while Martínez de Campo's prospects of a political career in Madrid had been shattered.

With the Pacifier, as Martínez de Campos was popularly known, out of Cuba, Spain still had a large array of experienced generals to rule the island. The man appointed was Lieutenant General Ramón Blanco y Erenas, who had earned the title of Marquis of Peña Plata during the Third Carlist War. Blanco was a man of wide colonial experience, having served in Cuba, Santo Domingo, and the Philippines, where he showed tactful political skills as governor of Mindanao, an island mostly populated by Muslims where only the Christians of the coast recognized Spanish sovereignty. A Freemason, Blanco was regarded as a liberal who agreed with his predecessor that reforms was the best way to win the hearts and minds of Cubans for Spain.[3] As a gesture toward creoles who had fought for Spain, he issued two orders on June 7 and 10, 1879, sanctioning that the 125-strong Volunteer Cavalry Squadron of Camajuaní, in Las Villas, should be permanently mobilized alongside the army and the Civil Guard in keeping order in that important area of central Cuba.[4] Most of the men in the

---

[2] *La Ilustración española y americana*, 22-08-1878, p. 40.
[3] Francisco López Casimiro. "Ramón Blanco Erenas, capitán general de Cuba y la masonería." *Boletín de la Real Academia de Extremadura de las Letras y las Artes*," 2009, t. 17, pp. 109–22.
[4] *Colección legislativa del Ejército. Año 1879*, Madrid: Imprenta y Litografía del Depósito de la Guerra, 1895, núm. 425, p. 617.

squadron were Cubans who earned the trust of Spain's top authority in the island after their gallant performance during the war.

Yet not all Spanish commanding officers thought alike. In fact, some of them considered that even those who had joined the Volunteers during the war were not entirely reliable. Field Marshall Camilo García de Polavieja, governor of the recently created province of Puerto Príncipe (1878–9), which had become the main rebel stronghold after Oriente, warned Captain General Blanco in June 1879 that wide areas of rural Cuba remained in a "latent state of insurgency."[5]

Polavieja was a soldier in his early forties who had built an impressive military career from scratch. He joined the army as a private in 1858, fought in the war against Morocco and had scaled the ranks up by taking part in the War of Santo Domingo, the Ten Years' War and the Thirst Carlist War. Polavieja had a deep firsthand knowledge of Cuba, men, and war. He had taken part in the preliminary negotiations that led to the Pact of Zanjón and generally distrusted Spain's capacity to affirm its sovereignty in Cuba, which he considered bound for independence. Because of his experience, he was appointed governor of Oriente, where pro-independence feelings were widespread. From Santiago de Cuba, seat of the province, he insisted to Blanco of the perils of a new insurrection. Polavieja considered that insecurity in rural Cuba stemmed from the fact that "weapons of the Volunteers in the countryside have not been collected properly, and God knows where they might end up."[6] Volunteers had the right to keep weapons of their property at home, but the authorities often had to provide them with firearms whenever they were too poor to purchase a rifle. In this case, state-owned rifles had to be stored at barracks, at least in theory. This was rather difficult to comply with in rural and isolated areas. Thus, having thousands of weapons astray in a region which had generally supported the rebellion was an evident danger. Disaffected Volunteers were also a possible source of trouble. They had received no compensation for their war effort, except for some personal decorations, whereas rebel veterans were granted jobs and there were rumors that they would get tracts of land for having laid down weapons. The extent of discontent among the Volunteers in Oriente wasn't known, but there were some signs of it.

All of this might have nurtured Polavieja's distrust for Cubans. He reckoned that only a minority sincerely supported Spain, whereas most of those who claimed to be loyal to the Mother Country simply wanted to avoid having problems with the authorities. Despite the decisive contribution of Cuban loyalists to the Spanish victory in 1878, he argued that all Blacks and mulattoes, plus half the whites, supported independence from Spain.[7] These were not optimistic prospects for the person who represented Spanish authority in Oriente. But facts did not entirely contradict him.

---

[5] Letter to Captain General Ramón Blanco Erenas (1879–1881), June 4, 1879, AGI, Diversos, Leg. 9B, No. 155.
[6] *Relación documentada de mi política en Cuba. Lo que vi, lo que hice, lo que anuncié*. Madrid: Imprenta de Emilio Minuesa, 1898, pp. 43–8.
[7] ANRC, Donativos y Remisiones, leg. 474, exp. 10; id., leg. 477, exp. 40.

The Little War

Polavieja's distrust was not entirely unfounded, as rebel veterans who rejected the terms of the Zanjón peace kept planning the organization of a new uprising. Guillermón Moncada, born into a freemen's family, headed the conspiracy in Oriente, recruiting men, gathering weapons, and securing funds in collaboration with the exile community in New York. After a bag full of weapons had been discovered in Santiago de Cuba by a mulatto policeman in late August 1879, the plotters escaped to the mountains and declared war on Spain less than one year and a half of a relative peace. The swift and firm reaction of the troops under Polavieja managed to control the situation and reduce the war to a series of unimportant skirmished in the mountains of Oriente. After slightly over a year of fighting, the Spanish Army forced the capitulation of the rebel leader, Calixto García, in September 1880.[8] Perhaps in comparison to the previous ten-year-long war, this was soon called *Guerra Chiquita*, or Little War. Though brief, this war made clear that the danger of a new insurrection in Cuba and a certain level of disaffection among Cuban loyalists for Spain were not mere suppositions of Polavieja.

There was indeed some discontent among Volunteers in the countryside, as they might have felt neglected by Spanish authorities. In many areas, they had been the only forces fighting the rebels without help from regular troops. In small towns throughout hilly Oriente, clashes often engaged a section of Volunteers between 30 and 50 men, poorly armed and barely military trained, against a mounted force of 200–500 insurgents. Since Volunteers generally defended their towns but were not mobilized away from them, they were neither paid nor provided with food. Only mobilized Volunteers were. Consequently, these Volunteers might have felt undervalued by the Spanish authorities. In addition to this, there might have been a racial issue playing with disaffection. Although the Volunteers did not usually keep records on its member's race, there are a few exceptions. The documentation produced by the Volunteer infantry section of Cuartón del Indio, a small village nearby Guantánamo, shows that in 1876 around a third of its members were of African descent. Out of eighty-seven men, eighty-five were Cubans, including six mulattoes and twenty-two Blacks. In the nearby village of Palma de San Juan, in the only recorded case, one of his men was reported as a native of Africa, probably a former slave who had managed to attain the status of Spanish subject, as it was a requirement to join the Volunteers.[9] In this sense, the Volunteers in Oriente's countryside were the product of a society that had the highest percentage of people of African descent of Cuba.

In the cities, life for the Volunteers was much safer. Urban battalions, mostly made up of *peninsulares*, were still protecting key infrastructures such as military forts,

---

[8] Baldovín Ruiz. *Cuba. El desastre español del siglo XIX*, pp. 251–9; Enrique Collazo. *Desde Yara hasta el Zanjón. Apuntaciones históricas*. Havana: Tipografía de "La Lucha," 1893, pp. 139–56; José Luis Prieto Benavent. "La Guerra Larga y las consecuencias de la Paz del Zanjón," in Manuel Moreno Fraginals (coord.). *Cien años de historia de Cuba (1898–1998)*. Madrid: Editorial Verbum, 2000, pp. 11–34; Pérez Guzmán & Sarracino. *La Guerra Chiquita*, pp. 178–254.

[9] AGMM, Ultramar, Capitanía General de Cuba, Subinspección General de Voluntarios, caja 301.

hospitals, and prisons, but saw little action. For instance, Captain Antonio Ferrer Robert of the 2nd Volunteer Battalion of Santiago de Cuba reported no military action in the diary he kept during the Little War. The only event he reported apparently related to the conflict was the kidnapping of one of his corporals after a lunch he offered to his men in a hacienda in the coastal town of Daiquirí.[10] Yet Volunteers officers in the cities were still relevant characters, very valuable for their social influence and their ability to gather information, as many of them owned shops and companies which earned them many acquaintances within local society, into which they were often married. Cástulo Ferrer Torralba, another one of the many sons of Sitges who had settled in Santiago de Cuba, was the colonel of the 2nd Volunteer Battalion. He had arrived in Cuba in 1846 at the age of 13 and became a prominent social figure in Santiago thanks. He had largely invested in coffee production and railway development in Oriente. A well-known loyalist, Ferrer had been involved in local politics in Santiago for some years, and was a man trusted by the authorities. During the Little War he provided Polavieja with accurate information on the whereabouts of the rebel forces and convinced several young members of affluent Cuban families from Santiago not to join the rebellion. This earned him several decorations awarded by the Ministry of War at the request of Polavieja, who highly valued the power of influence and information in a land of swinging loyalties.[11]

Yet in the countryside, the situation was starkly different. Polavieja relied on regular army soldiers rather than on Volunteers to crush the rebels. Around 28,000 soldiers were shipped from Spain during the Little War in an effort not to protract the conflict and quell the rebellion swiftly. He approached the war as a conflict of maneuver and not position. This means that army columns chased the rebels while the Volunteers were left alone to defend the small towns.[12] The Volunteers were in a general state of dismay, distrusted by the authorities they owed obedience to, and harassed by the rebels who threatened their lives unless they joined the insurgency. They felt rather abandoned by the authorities. All these factors might have pushed a few hundred Volunteers to perform the largest defection of their history. Only two weeks after the war started, over 1,200 of them deserted. On September 9, 1879, 800 of them turned coats in El Arpón, a small village nearby Santiago de Cuba; four days later, 400 Volunteers from Mayarí, nearby Holguín, followed their steps.[13] This level of desertions had never been seen in the history of the Volunteers.

Such large numbers defecting to the enemy might have been caused by discontent toward the Spanish authorities rather than by sincere support for independence.[14] At least, this was Polavieja's view. During November and December 1879, he reported to the minister of the Colonies, Salvador Albacete, that he had found that Volunteers

---

[10] AHMS, Fons Josep Carbonell i Gener, "Companyia de Voluntaris de Santiago."
[11] AGI, Archivo de Camilo García de Polavieja y del Castillo, Diversos, 9B, R. 1, D.57; AHN, Ultramar, 4786, exp. 9; Jou i Andreu. *Els sitgetans a Amèrica*, pp. 290–1.
[12] Navarro. *Las guerras de España en Cuba*, pp. 115–28.
[13] Pérez Guzmán & Sarracino. *La Guerra Chiquita*, pp. 201–2; Navarro. *Las guerras de España en Cuba*, pp. 123–5.
[14] Pérez Guzmán & Sarracino. *La Guerra Chiquita*, pp. 203–4.

outside the urban areas were resentful because of some privileges granted to the capitulated rebels after Zanjón, such as tax exemptions and land allotments.[15] After all, they had shed blood for Spain in exchange for despise and neglect. The clumsy policy of appeasing the rebellion by rewarding the former enemy and neglecting the loyalists was bound to backfire. The message sent by Volunteer deserters was clear. Not even the most loyalist elements would keep their word should Spain keep neglecting them while treating its former enemies so generously. Clearly, Spanish authorities needed a different strategy to secure the loyalty of their own in a region riddled by a latent discontent with Spain.

Reconstructing Cuba

Years of war had not only torn families apart and destroyed thousands of human lives; they had also devastated large tracts of land in central and eastern Cuba, where most of the fighting had taken place. Most of the industry was concentrated in the west, but the destruction inflicted upon the rest of the island acted as a burden for the whole Cuban economy. Out of a hundred sugar mills which existed in Oriente in 1868, only thirty-nine were left in 1880. In Puerto Príncipe the destruction had been more dramatic: from 100 *ingenios* in 1868 to only 1 in 1880.[16]

Cuban agriculture needed to be reconstructed. Political and military authorities and landowners embarked in a series of projects aimed at reviving a beleaguered economy in a depressed atmosphere.[17] But their aspirations did not always coincide. Whereas the latter aimed to attract cheap labor force and expand sugar production, the former prioritized the creation of Spanish loyalist rural communities in the countryside.[18]

Among the Volunteer chief officers there were prominent landowners who showed little interest in using their men to reconstruct the island's agricultural industry. Instead, they thought of alternative sources for cheap labor. One of the Volunteer founders in 1855, José Eugenio Moré, Count of Casa Moré, submitted in 1879 a project proposing that the Cuban Treasury pay for the import of 30,000 Chinese indentured servants and 10,000 *peninsulares* to work the land.[19] In 1880, Francisco F. Ibáñez, Count of Casa Ibáñez and the colonel of a Havana Volunteer battalion, suggested that the public budget be used for establishing fifty sugar mills throughout

---

[15] BNC, CM Guerra, No. 10.
[16] Le Riverend. *Historia económica de Cuba*, p. 453–8; Pérez, Jr. *Cuba. Between Reform & Revolution*, pp. 129–36.
[17] Naranjo Orovio. "Trabajo libre e inmigración española en Cuba, 1880–1930." *Revista de Indias*, 1992, vol. 52, No. 195–196, pp. 749–94.
[18] Imilcy Balboa Navarro. "Colonización e inmigración. Dos realidades enfrentadas en la Cuba de fin de siglo," in Francisco Morales Padrón (ed.). *III Coloquio de Historia Canario-Americana, VIII Congreso Internacional de Historia de América (AEA) (1998)*. Las Palmas de Gran Canaria: Cabildo de Gran Canaria, 2000, pp. 452–70, pp. 452–70.
[19] AHN, Ultramar, 278, exps. 2 & 3; *Cuerpos de Voluntarios de la isla de Cuba*, p. 35; Naranjo Orovio. "Hispanización y defensa de la integridad nacional," p. 77.

the island and importing 1,000 families from the Peninsula to work them.[20] A few years earlier, in 1871, Ibáñez had thought of bringing rural workers from Annam to compensate the workforce shortage caused by the war.[21] Similar views for the future of Cuban agriculture, shared by many landowners who were also Volunteer commanding officers, were well represented by the *Círculo de Hacendados*, an association aimed at promoting, defending, and protecting the interests of the island's landowning elite.[22]

The Volunteers and the Military-Agricultural Colonies

The authorities, on their side, had other plans to reconstruct the countryside. Their aim was to fill rural Cuba with Spanish loyalists who would work the land and pose a first defensive line against the war's revolutionary stronghold. A few months before the end of the war, a Royal Decree of October 28, 1877, promoted the creation of colonies, settled in order of preference by army veterans and Volunteers who had been demobilized from military operations, civilian loyalists who had lost their property due to the war, and former rebels who had asked for pardon.[23] With the explicit purpose of "averting another rebellion in Cuba," these colonies were meant to mix all these elements rather than establishing separate settlements. Mixing was merging, or so they thought.

On paper, Volunteers in the countryside were ideal material for settling the agricultural colonies in a context where peace had to be rebuilt. They were mostly Cuban *guajiros* who were theoretically loyal to Spain, knew how to work the land, and most likely had family ties with the rebels. In places like Cuartón del Indio and Tiguabos, nearby Guantánamo, the agricultural heartland of Oriente, virtually all the local Volunteers were Cuban peasants.[24]

The military colonies, aimed at "turn rebel Cuba Spanish," apparently commenced with weak foundations.[25] Beyond the lack of material means, the authorities in Havana and Santiago disagreed over the real prospects of success. Despite the reluctance of Polavieja, he had to obey the captain general's faith in the project. For one such colony created in Puerto Príncipe during his term as governor, five more were established in Oriente between 1879 and 1881, nearby the villages of Jibacoa, Zarzal, El Congo,

---

[20] AHN, Ultramar, 340, exp. 15.; Francisco Feliciano Ibáñez, *Observaciones sobre la utilidad y conveniencia del establecimiento en esta isla de Grandes Ingenios Centrales para salvar nuestra agricultura é industria azucarera por el aumento de producción y disminución de gastos y bases para la formación de una Compañía para la fácil realización de este objeto*. Havana: Imprenta y Lit. Obispo, 1880, p. 27; Consuelo Naranjo Orovio & Armando García González. *Racismo e inmigración en Cuba en el siglo XIX*. Aranjuez: Ediciones Doce Calles/FIM, 1996, pp. 175-8; César Aenlle. *De todo un poco*. Havana: Imprenta Mercantil de los Herederos de Spencer, 1889, pp. 31-5.
[21] AHN, Ultramar, 94, exp. 23.
[22] Fernández Prieto. *Espacio de poder*, pp. 55-78.
[23] *Gaceta de Madrid*, 28-10-1877, No. 501, p. 303.
[24] AGMM, Ultramar, Cuerpo de Voluntarios, caja 3557, "Cuartón del Indio" and "Tiguabos."
[25] Naranjo Orovio. "Hispanización y defensa de la integridad nacional," pp. 71-91.

Calicito, Vega Botada, and Guantánamo.[26] They were essentially established for Cuban peasants of African descent. Out of the 364 men with their families, 356 were Cuban, out of which 239 were Black. Both the total numbers and the participation of the Volunteers were rather modest though. Six years after being created, the colonies only hosted sixty-one Volunteers plus their families.[27] In Jibacoa, nearby Manzanillo, there were 37 Volunteers among the 144 settlers, which were all Black and Cuban except for 2 *peninsulares* and 5 whites.[28] Thus, the massive presence of *guajiros* of African descent in the settlements reflects that the Volunteers in this area of Cuba stemmed from local society, which was of Black descent at a percentage of around 85 since the 1860s.[29]

The creation of six colonies in two years in such a wide area didn't take a quick path. Certainly, they were not a priority for Spanish authorities, but lack of interest was not just the only cause. In his reports to Havana and Madrid, Polavieja constantly attributed such slow progress to inefficient bureaucracy and informal land ownership.[30] The *reglamento* that established the organization of the colonies (1877) had two institutions involved in the process: the *Inspección de Montes* and the *Juntas de Socorro*. The former was part of the national administration and had to demarcate the land allotments to be granted. The latter depended on city councils, which were mostly trusted to Cubans after 1878, thus returning to the situation prior to 1868, when numerous towns all over the island were seized by *integristas*, often *peninsulares*, to secure local power for Spain. It was a reason for Polavieja not to entirely trust them. The *inspecciones* organized land distribution, and, in some cases, were controlled by Volunteers officers.[31] For instance, in Manzanillo, it was presided by Lieutenant Juan de Meza.[32] But it wasn't an efficiency guarantee either. In 1881, the delimitation of land plots around Manzanillo had still not been completed.

By the mid-1880s, the colonies might have been regarded as a failure. Despite the efforts of a special commission created in Madrid between the ministries of War and the Colonies in 1881 to reactivate the colonization, its projects were never implemented due to the weak confidence posed in the military settlements by the authorities on the ground, beginning with Polavieja.[33] Gradually, the colonies' future began to fade away, and the landowners' enterprise of importing a cheap workforce from metropolitan Spain began to take the lead.[34]

---

[26] Balboa Navarro. "La inmigración como forma de presión política: Polavieja, los hacendados y la colonización por la vía militar. Cuba, 1878–1892," *Illes i Imperis*, 2004, No. 7, pp. 133–55.

[27] Balboa Navarro. "Tierras y brazos. Inmigración, colonización y fuerza de trabajo. Cuba, 1878–1898." *Illes i Imperis*, 2002, No. 6, pp. 67–76, pp. 69–70.

[28] Ibid., p. 69.

[29] Javier Laviña. "Santiago de Cuba, 1860: esclavitud, color y población," *Boletín de la Asociación de Geógrafos Españoles*, 1992–1993, No. 15–16, pp. 17–32.

[30] García de Polavieja. *Relación documentada*, p. 17; ANRC, Gobierno General, leg. 46, exp. 1959, and leg. 48, exps. 2137 & 2138.

[31] *Gaceta de Madrid*, No. 536, p. 622, December 2, 1877; García de Polavieja. *Relación documentada*, p. 50.

[32] ANRC, Gobierno General, leg. 39, exps. 1634, 1636 & leg. 46, exp. 1956.

[33] AGMM, Ultramar, caja 3078, "*Establecimiento de Colonias Militares en Ultramar*, 1883."

[34] Naranjo Orovio. "Hispanización y defensa de la integridad nacional," pp. 749–94; Balboa Navarro. "Colonización e inmigración," pp. 452–70.

Despite the relative failure of the agricultural colonies thus far, the Volunteers would play a central role in the attempt to revive them under Captain General Manuel Salamanca y Negrete (1889-1890). Salamanca, a man of no colonial experience who was sent to Cuba at the end of his military career, believed that better organization might make a success of these settlements. He thought that Volunteers, and not licensed conscripts from the regular army, should be the human material with whom to staff the colonies. In general, he considered that theirs should be most of the responsibility for defending Spanish sovereignty in Cuba.[35] On a report sent to the Ministry of the Colonies in August 1889, Salamanca proposed a plan of colonization aimed at combining the immigration of *peninsulares* with the creation of loyalist communities.[36] He aimed at staffing the colonies with migrants and making them Volunteers. He trusted on the unstopped influx of *peninsulares*. Despite a slowing down in their arrivals due to a worsening economic situation and an unclear political future, between 1886 and 1890, 97,000 of them settled in Cuba, apart from the 27,000 conscripts who served their military service in the island. First, Salamanca resorted to metropolitan migrants to settle the new colonies.[37] And he wanted all the males between 18 and 50 to join the Volunteers.[38]

Despite his efforts and good spirit, the lingering problem of an inefficient and slow bureaucracy hampered the future of the colonies. In just over a year, 887 settlers had been allotted land in the colonies, but the authorities had them in a complete state of neglect.[39] So much so that most of Salamanca's settlers ended up abandoning the colonies and finding petty jobs in Havana or in the sugar mills as cheap laborers.[40] After almost twenty years of attempts, the military colonies had clearly failed. Although other governors like Polavieja (1890-2) and Alejandro Rodríguez Arias (1892-3) tried to retrieve the project, the military settlements had been a failure due to the authorities' mismanagement. The Volunteers and their families, alongside the other settlers, were not provided with the seeds, farm implements, and proper housing promised by the authorities, causing many of them to abandon the colonies and settle in the cities, where there were more work opportunities.[41]

---

[35] AHN, Ultramar, 247, exp. 7.
[36] Balboa Navarro. "Asentar para dominar. Salamanca y la colonización militar. Cuba, 1889-1890." *Tiempos de América*, 2001, No. 8, pp. 29-46, pp. 29-46; AHN, Ultramar, Sección Fomento, leg. 247, No. 7.
[37] Albert García Balañá, "'The Empire is no longer a social unit': Declining imperial expectations and transatlantic crisis in metropolitan Spain, 1859-1909," in Alfred W. McCoy, Josep M. Fradera & Stephen Jacobson (eds.). *Endless Empire. Spain's Retreat, Europe's Eclipse, America's Decline*. Madison: The University of Wisconsin Press, 2012, pp. 92-103; Moreno Fraginals & Moreno Masó. *Guerra, migración y muerte*, p. 121.
[38] Balboa Navarro. "Asentar para dominar," p. 33.
[39] Ibid., p. 44.
[40] AHN, Ultramar, leg 174, 13.
[41] García de Polavieja. *Relación documentada*, p. 324; AFAM, leg. 489, carpeta 8, Alejandro Rodríguez Arias a Antonio Maura, 20-06-1893.

7

The Volunteers and the Emergence of Party Politics

With the end of the Cuban war in the late 1870s, the Spanish Antilles were entering a new era. The countryside needed to be reconstructed after ten years of destruction, but the political system binding Cuba and Puerto Rico to Spain ought to be restructured. Since 1837, the two Spanish overseas territories had been excluded from the Spanish Parliament in exchange for protection of slavery. The war had exacerbated the paramount position of the mostly peninsular *integrista* elite at the expense of the mostly Cuban reformist bourgeoisie which had challenged the status quo in different ways. Thousands of men had fought, spilled blood, and lost friends and relatives for and against the Spanish sovereignty in Cuba. But after the war, all this needed to be overcome. Slavery was dying a slow but certain death, and reconciliation between *integristas*, reformists, and nationalists was an absolute necessity. The Volunteers may have been as happy as anyone in Cuba to get back to their ordinary lives, but the future of the militia in the Antilles was far from clear. The very idea of a Spanish transatlantic nation had to be reinvented.

One of the biggest changes was the reintegration of Cuba into the Spanish constitutional system, following the status granted to Puerto Rico in 1869. Ending with over forty years of exclusion, both islands were to be fully reintegrated into the Constitution. While Puerto Rico was already an overseas province with its own Provincial Council, Cuba was divided into six provinces in 1878: Pinar del Río, Havana, Matanzas, Santa Clara, Puerto Príncipe, and Santiago de Cuba, each with its own Provincial Council. The organic laws in force in metropolitan Spain were sanctioned in the Antilles after undergoing due adaptations to local conditions. Cuba, following the steps of Puerto Rico, was also given back the right to send representatives to the Spanish Parliament, which implied the emergence of a political party system. And this was a threat to the Volunteers' paramount role in the Antilles.

The assimilation of Cuba and Puerto Rico into the Spanish constitutional system was in fact a move toward a stronger bond between the European and Caribbean territories of the Spanish Monarchy. In theory, this favored the very concept of national integrity the Volunteers had fought for. In practice, the establishment of a political party-based system ousted the Volunteers from the very center of Spanish colonial policy. During wartime they had been the armed wing of *integrismo*, a force the Spanish authorities could not dispense with, even though they had forced captain generals to step down, had imposed their violent ways in Havana, and had shown a rebellious spirit more than once. But now, during peacetime, political parties were to take the central stage of Caribbean politics, sending the Volunteers to the margins of power. Of course, they were still a militia which could summon thousands of men in Cuba and Puerto Rico, but the new political situation had made them just another element, though important, of Spanish rule in the Antilles.

Cuba and Puerto Rico were to have a two-party system following the same model existing in the Peninsula, which in its turn was inspired in Britain's model, the very blueprint of most parliamentary systems in Europe. Whereas in metropolitan Spain the two dominant parties were the conservative and the liberal, in the Antilles the political arena was disputed between the forces that demanded wider reforms and autonomy and those who opted for limited political and social reforms.[1] Both forces shared a consensus on the need for basic economic reforms and the continuity of Spanish rule. Their main difference laid in which element they accentuated. The true limit of the regime was Spanish sovereignty. The pro-independence movement, which was virtually nonexistent in Puerto Rico but considerable in Cuba, had to operate outside the system as they were not legally allowed in Spain and the Antilles. Spain was not to have the Antillean version of the Irish political parties which had seats at Westminster. The Cuban separatists had to have their operational basis in the exile, especially in the United States.[2]

The forces advocating for deeper reforms were the Reformist Liberal Party in Puerto Rico (created in 1870) and the Liberal Party in Cuba (1878), soon to be both known as autonomists, whose social basis was mostly made up of Antillean liberal professionals and some landowners with wider economic ties with the United States than with Spain.[3] In the other political aisle, Antillean conservatism was represented by the Conservative Party in Puerto Rico (established in 1870) and the Constitutional

---

[1] Alonso Romero. *Cuba en la España liberal*, pp. 46–51; Fernando Bayón Toro. *Elecciones y partidos políticos de Puerto Rico (1809–1976)*, Madrid, Instituto de Cultura Hispánica de Madrid, 1977; Bothwell. *Orígenes y desarrollo*, pp. 1–49; José A. Piqueras Arenas. *Sociedad civil y poder en Cuba. Colonia y poscolonia*. Madrid: Siglo XXI, pp. 157–64; Roldán de Montaud. *La Restauración en Cuba*, pp. 121–55.

[2] Gerald E. Poyo. *"With All, and for the Good of All." The Emergence of Popular Nationalism in the Cuban Communities of the United States, 1848–1898*. Durham and London: Duke University Press, 1989, pp. 52–69; Paul Estrade. "El papel de la emigración patriótica en las Guerras de Independencia de Cuba (1868–1898)." *Tebeto: Anuario del Archivo Histórico Insular de Fuerteventura*, No. 11, 1998, pp. 83–102.

[3] Marta Bizcarrondo & Antonio Elorza. *Cuba/España. El dilema autonomista, 1878–1898*. Madrid: Editorial Colibrí, 2001, pp. 121–98; Marta Bizcarrondo. "El autonomismo cubano. Las ideas y los hechos (1878–1898)." *Historia Contemporánea*, 1999, No. 19, pp. 69–94; Luis Miguel García Mora. "La fuerza de la palabra. El autonomismo en Cuba en el último tercio del siglo XIX." *Revista de Indias*, 2001, vol. LXI, No. 223, pp. 715–48. For the Puerto Rican Reformist Liberal Party (later 'Puerto Rican Autonomist Party) see Astrid Cubano Iguina. "El autonomismo en Puerto Rico, 1887–1898: notas para la definición de un modelo de política radical," in Consuelo Naranjo Orovio, Miguel A. Puig-Samper & Luis Miguel García Mora (eds.). *La nación soñada, Cuba, Puerto Rico y Filipinas ante el 98: actas del Congreso Internacional celebrado en Aranjuez del 2 al 28 de abril de 1995*. Madrid: Ediciones Doce Calles, 1996, pp. 405–16; "Política radical y autonomismo en Puerto Rico: conflictos de intereses en la formación del Partido Autonomista Portorriqueño (1887)." *Anuario de estudios americanos*, 1994, vol. 51, No. 2, pp. 155–73.

Union Party in Cuba (1878). They essentially drew support from the propertied classes with closer ties to Spain, often but not exclusively *peninsulares*, administration officials, army officers, and *integristas* in general.[4]

Since the latter stood for ever stronger ties with Spain, the Volunteers became closely associated to the conservative forces, though their members were far from embracing the same ideology. The political leanings of the owner of a tobacco company or sugar mill could hardly be the same as the political opinions of a cigar-maker or a coachman. Conservatives, liberals, monarchists, republicans, and even *carlistas* donned the Volunteers' uniform, but in the Antilles, the need to defend the Spanish sovereignty operated as the essential unifying factor. There were, of course, Volunteers who considered that reformism was the best way to ensure Spain's continuity in the Antilles. For instance, José Suárez García, a *peninsular* who was appointed captain of Volunteers during the Ten Years' War and established the Liberal Party committee in Güines, nearby Havana. Carlos Saladrigas, a leading member of the Cuban Autonomist Party, as the Liberal Party was renamed in 1881, was a colonel of Volunteers.[5] But they were the exception.

Generally, the Volunteers sided with the conservatives unequivocally. Each one of the leaders of the conservative parties in the Antilles were Volunteer officers. In Cuba, the leaders of the Constitutional Union—the creole José Eugenio Moré (1878-90), the Basque Vicente Galarza (1890-2), and the Cuban Julio de Apezteguía (1892-8)—were all colonels of Volunteers. The creole José Ramón Fernández (1871-80) and the Basque Pablo Ubarri (1880-94), leaders of the Puerto Rican conservatives, were also Volunteer colonels.[6] But as anywhere else in the liberal systems of the late nineteenth century, politics remained the realm of the propertied classes with only a tiny room for popular participation. Consequently, the Volunteers did not participate en masse during elections. Just as anywhere else in the liberal regimes of the late nineteenth century, the right to vote was very restricted in the Antilles, even more than in the Peninsula. By 1889, for instance, slightly over a fifth of Spanish males over 25 had the right to vote in metropolitan Spain. In Cuba, the percentage was 3.82 and in Puerto Rico 0.52.[7] This was the result of the June 9, 1878, Royal Decree sanctioning that the Spanish Antilles were to adopt the Electoral Law of July 20, 1877, but adapted to local conditions.

---

[4] On the Cuban Constitutional Union, see Inés Roldán de Montaud. *La Unión Constitucional y la política colonial de España en Cuba (1868-1898).* Madrid: Universidad Complutense de Madrid, 1991, PhD Thesis 91/296; Portela Miguélez. *Redes de poder en Cuba.* On the Puerto Rican Conservative Liberal Party (*Partido Liberal Conservador*) created in 1870 and renamed "Unconditional Spanish Party" (*Partido Incondicional Español*) in 1880 there is no recent bibliography. However, some information can be consulted in Cubano Iguina, *Puerto Rico,* pp. 541-58; Bothwell. *Orígenes y desarrollo,* pp. 1-49; Bayón Toro. *Elecciones y partidos políticos de Puerto Rico,* pp. 190-212; José Julián Acosta. *Los partidos políticos. Artículos publicados en "El Progreso."* San Juan: Imprenta y Librería de Sancérrit, 1875;Francisco Mariano Quiñones. *Historia de los partidos reformista y conservador de Puerto-Rico.* Mayagüez: Tipografía Comercial, 1889, pp. 22-3.

[5] Raimundo Cabrera. *Cuba and the Cubans.* Philadelphia: The Levytype Company, 1896, p. 366; *Don Circunstancias,* 04-12-1881, p. 390.

[6] Bothwell. *Orígenes y desarrollo,* pp. 4-40; Portela Miguélez. *Redes de poder en Cuba.*

[7] S. Andrés. *La reforma electoral en nuestras Antillas.* Madrid: Imprenta de la "Revista de España," 1889, p. 23.

Rather than counting votes, the key issue was making voters. The very purpose of the electoral system in force in the Antilles after 1878 was to provide friendly electorates for the parties which unconditionally supported the continuity of an unchallenged Spain rule. This meant securing the voting upper hand to *peninsulares*, since creoles were thought to be generally supportive of reformist options which demanded more decision-making power over their own affairs. Before 1890, when universal male suffrage was established in metropolitan Spain, any male over 25 who paid a yearly tax contribution of 25 pesetas was granted the right to vote, but in the Antilles the contribution threshold was five times as much. As well, taxes stemming from commerce overweighted those who came from agriculture, thus making more voters in the cities, where *peninsulares* tended to settle in comparison to a countryside overwhelmingly populated by creoles.[8] As a result, the imbalance between creoles and *peninsulares* as to the effective right to vote was too scandalous in some places. For instance, in Güines, a 13,000-inhabitant town in the Havana Province, 500 *peninsulares* represented 90 percent of the electoral census.[9]

Since a real electoral competition did not exist in the Antilles, even less than in Spain, political power for the *integristas* political parties had to be attained, built, and secured through other means and in collaboration with certain institutions. The network of *Casinos Españoles* provided conservatives with a gathering space and many of its leading ranks, while droves of *integrista* newspapers spread their principles. But brute force, if deemed necessary, was also an option. And in this, the Volunteers had a role to play. For instance, in October 1886, the local committee of the Constitutional Union in Cienfuegos sent a few dozen Volunteers to storm the theater where autonomists were holding a meeting to discuss the strategy to regain control of local town councils at the expense of *integristas*.[10] This was a notorious act of political violence, but not the only one. Not even the most important, for the place where political tensions became really heated in the mid-1880s was Puerto Rico.

Repressing the Autonomists: The Puerto Rican "*compontes*"

Political tensions ran high in Puerto Rico at the end of the 1880s between *integristas* and autonomists. Lieutenant General Romualdo Palacios y González, who had been appointed captain general on January 17, 1887, by the liberal cabinet headed by Práxedes Mateo Sagasta, was an essential part of the problem. A man in his sixties, Palacios had wide experience in the colonies, having fought in Morocco and in Cuba, where he had been appointed *segundo cabo* by the First Spanish Republic in September 1873. He also fought the *carlistas* as captain general of Valencia during the 1870s, which earned him the *Gran Cruz de San Fernando*, the highest military decoration of

---

[8] Inés Roldán de Montaud. "Política y elecciones en Cuba durante la Restauración." *Revista de Estudios Políticos*, 1999, No. 104, pp. 245–87.
[9] Cabrera. *Cuba and the Cubans*, p. 192.
[10] David Sartorius. *Ever Faithful*, pp. 157–86.

the Spanish Army. Proven loyalty to the army went hand in hand with a long-standing career as conspirator. Palacios was known for being a radical democrat who took part in the Progressive Party's role in ousting Queen Isabella II in 1868 and had supported the ill-fated Republic in 1873.[11] But in Puerto Rico, Palacios showed no sympathy to forces which conspired to challenge the status quo.

As with many other liberal radicals, crossing the Atlantic turned Palacios into a staunch advocate of Jacobin ideals of Spanish national unity against any force that might aspire to change the relationship between Spain and her Antilles. This position necessarily had to clash with the rising autonomist movement which was redefining the Puerto Rican Liberal Party. After almost twenty years of party politics in which *integristas* had the upper hand due to the unfair electoral law and the protection of the authorities, Puerto Rican liberals were exploring ways to make their case for greater political rights and more economic freedom to trade with the United States more visible and robust. Convinced that allying with their ideological peers in the Peninsula was not the best way to push forward their agenda, Puerto Rican liberals openly embraced the ideal of autonomy at the convention held at Ponce between May 7 and 9, 1887. It was the birth of the Puerto Rican Autonomist Party.[12]

Tensions in the island ran high, and apparently minor incidents were almost automatically attributed to political tensions between autonomists and *integristas*. For instance, the *integrista* press denounced that, in November 1886, during the funeral of a Volunteer in Ponce, groups allegedly associated with the autonomists stoned the attendants while insulting Spain and those who defended it. Refusing to take the blame, Francisco Cepeda, editor of *La Revista de Puerto Rico*, which followed the lines of the Autonomist Party, didn't hesitate to label the Volunteers as "social scum." The insult was more the grave coming from a peninsular and a former Volunteer. Cepeda was a native of Asturias who had served in the 1st Battalion of Sagua la Grande, Cuba, in the 1870s, where he owned the newspaper *El Sagua*. A sincere republican, he had defended Cuban autonomy as editor of *La Revista Económica de las Antillas* (1877–82), which had him being deported to Madrid, where he defended the same ideas as editor of *La Revista de las Antillas* (1882–6) before settling in Puerto Rico in 1886.[13] The fact

---

[11] Bizcarrondo & Elorza. *Cuba/España*, pp. 154–97; Portela Miguélez. *Redes de poder en Cuba*, pp. 169–97; Sartorius. *Ever Faithful*, pp. 177–86; *Gaceta de Madrid*, No. 247, 04-09-1873, p. 1597; No. 327, 23-11-1883, p. 571; No. 17, 17-01-1887, p. 157; No. 40, 09-02-1899, p. 506; Juan Mañé Flaquer. *La revolución de 1868 juzgada por sus autores*. Barcelona: Imprenta de Jaime Jepús, Editor, 1876, p. 143; Antonio Pirala. *Historia contemporánea. Anales desde 1843 hasta la conclusión de la última guerra civil*, vol. III. Madrid: Imprenta y Fundición de Manuel Tello, 1876, p. 90.

[12] Lidio Cruz Monclova. *Historia del año de 1887*. Río Piedras: Ed. Universitaria, 1958, pp. 157–97; Astrid Cubano Iguina. "Política radical y autonomismo en Puerto Rico: conflictos de interés en la formación del Partido Autonomista Portorriqueño (1887)." *Anuario de estudios americanos*, 1994, vol. 51, No. 2, pp. 155–73; Antonio S. Pedreira. *El año terrible del 87. Sus antecedentes y sus consecuencias*. San Juan: Biblioteca de Escritores Puertorriqueños, 1937, pp. 26–40.

[13] Gómez & Sendras y Burín. *La isla de Puerto-Rico*, pp. 142–3; Ribó. *Historia de los Voluntarios cubanos*, vol. I, p. 286; Quiñones. *Apuntes para la historia de Puerto Rico*. Mayagüez: Tipografía Comercial Aduana, 1888, pp. 52–3; *Revista de Puerto Rico*, 6-11-1886; Rosado y Brincau. *Bosquejo Histórico*, pp. 122–9.

that the armed wing of *integrismo* was so openly insulted by one of its former members indicated that the staunch defenders of Spanish rule might have to face difficult times.

The *integristas* of Puerto Rico regarded the autonomists as an existential threat to Spanish rule in the island, despite the latter rejected independence and placed their hopes in structural changes within the Spanish Monarchy. The *integristas* considered that autonomy was but an excuse to take a first step toward independence. Also, the community of business owners which was the backbone of Puerto Rican conservatives considered closer economic ties with the United States as a threat to their vested interests. Feeling under threat, they turned to the captain general for protection and readied the Volunteers and the press to launch a campaign against the autonomists' puissance. It was the onset of the *Compontes*, a brutal campaign of repression against the autonomists which took part in the late summer of 1887.[14] But first, they needed to create an enemy.

On August 21, 1887, the *Boletín Mercantil*, the San Juan's newspaper which was considered to speak for the *integrista* elite, published an article signed by Policarpo Echevarría in which he claimed that an autonomist-supported secret society dubbed *Los Mojados* was planning to kill all the *peninsulares* in Juana Díaz, a small town near Ponce.[15] Similar accusations were published in other *integrista* newspapers, such as *La Bandera Española* and *La Integridad Nacional*.[16] Echevarría stressed the necessity for all *peninsulares* and "good Puerto Ricans" to rally under the banner of the Spanish Unconditional Party, as conservatives were now known, and to regard the autonomists as mere separatists in disguise.

The profile of the article's author gave the warning the highest credit. Policarpo Echevarría had been the mayor of Juana Díaz since 1868. He was regarded as a diehard of the Unconditional Party and a close friend of its leader, the Basque businessman Pablo Ubarri. Echevarría had joined the administration in 1850 and was the captain of the 2nd Company of the 10th Volunteers Battalion, stationed in Juana Díaz. In fact, he had created the company back in 1872. More importantly, Echevarría was a native of Puerto Rico and the mayor of a town located in the heartland of autonomism. His loyalty to Spain was beyond any doubt, and being a Puerto Rican, he could not be accused of peninsular sectarianism.[17] He was very well positioned to warn about the very intention of autonomists. However, the very existence of a conspiracy to kill all *peninsulares* is more than doubtful, but the article served to the purpose of anathemizing the autonomists, precisely in a context in which the political tide seemed to be turning against the *integristas*.

Soon, the authorities put its mechanisms to work in with all the swiftness and diligence of an operation that seems to have been planned beforehand. Only nine days after the article, on August 30, 1887, the Civil Guard of Juana Díaz sent a report to the

---

[14] AHN, Ultramar, 5143, exps. 15-19.
[15] *Boletín Mercantil*, 21-08-1887; Pedreira. *El año terrible del 87*, p. 43.
[16] Gómez & Sendras y Burín. *La isla de Puerto Rico*, p. 168.
[17] AHN, Ultramar, 5117, exp. 30; Rosado y Brincau. *Bosquejo Histórico*, p. 42; *Ejército de Puerto-Rico. Estado militar de todas las armas e institutos y Escalafón General de todos los Jefes y Oficiales de Infantería*. Puerto-Rico: Imprenta de la Capitanía General, 1888, p. 71.

captain general informing him about the arrest of Cristiano Aponte, Cleto Mangual, and fifty other members of *Los Secos*, another supposedly secret society which was planning to kill all *peninsulares* and proclaim the Republic of Puerto Rico. Due to the lack of evidence, the judge who first heard the case at the Court of Puerto Rico dismissed all charges against the detainees, but the captain general forced his replacement for José García de Paredes, a well-known *integrista* who formally charged them with plotting against Spain. As a result of these events, Captain General Palacios issued a note on September 5, 1887, published in the *Gaceta de Puerto Rico* three days later, stressing that he would not tolerate the "political ideas that promote these criminal acts," a not very subtle reference to autonomism.[18] Indeed, Palacios sent the Civil Guard and the Volunteers to arrest, lock down, and torture hundreds of autonomists. The *compontes* were a brutal violation of the constitutional rights of individuals for being members of a political party which was legal under Spanish law. It was authored by the captain general and supported by local *integrismo* but was neither authorized nor tolerated by the Spanish Government. Quite conveniently, the governor of Puerto Rico blocked all communications with the Peninsula.[19]

As much as it was an outright violation of Spanish law, the *compontes* seem to have been popular among members of the Spanish Unconditional Party, the *incondicionales*. It is difficult to know whether they truly believed there was an ongoing conspiracy, but the fact is that all the Volunteer units and most local committees of the Unconditional Party from across Puerto Rico sent telegrams to Palacios supporting his decided campaign to repress autonomists, publicly launched in the note published on 8 September at the *Gaceta de Puerto Rico*.[20] Only a day later, droves of telegrams and letters began to pour into the General Government of Puerto Rico and the main *integrista* newspapers praising the captain general's determination to defend national integrity at any cost. The Basque businessman Pablo Ubarri, leader of the Unconditional Party, sent a telegram of support "As Chief Officer of the 1st Volunteer Battalion, and on behalf of its members, I warmly congratulate you for the important note published in the *Gaceta* of the 8."[21] The captain general also earned support from humbler Volunteers, men who might have developed a certain siege mentality in areas dominated by autonomism and were thus prone to believe conspiracy theories about an imminent risk for the lives of all *peninsulares*. For instance, the *Boletín Mercantil* published a letter signed on October 26 by fourteen Asturians, members of the 9th Volunteers Battalion, who dwelled and worked in the Hacienda San José, near Ponce, the heartland of autonomism. "We are devoted to our humble occupations in order to make an honest living, living completely apart from politics, but we do not forget that we are sons of Spain," hailing the captain general for "his worth praise and patriotic

---

[18] *Gaceta de Puerto-Rico*, 08-09-1887, p. 1.
[19] Cruz Monclova. *Historia del año de 1887*, pp. 199–345; Pedreira. *El año terrible del 87*, pp. 44–5; Francisco Mariano Quiñones. *Apuntes para la historia de Puerto Rico*, pp. 65–80; *Revista de Puerto Rico*, June 21 and 22, 1887.
[20] AGPR, Asuntos Políticos y Civiles, "Felicitaciones de varios pueblos de los comités del Partido Incondicionalmente Español por los sucesos de Juana Díaz y Ponce, 1887."
[21] *Manifestaciones del elemento español de Puerto-Rico con motivo de los sucesos de Juana Díaz*. Puerto Rico: 1887, pp. 4–5.

behaviour has to earn as it does the applause from anyone who loves order and institutions, nowadays represented by the zealous and energic governor who happily rules the destinies of this island."[22] Of course, the autonomist press denounced the *compontes*, causing the fury of *integristas*. A group of Puerto Ricans and *peninsulares* affiliated to the Unconditional Party in San Sebastián, in the hilly interior of the island, labeled the campaign by the autonomist *Revista de Puerto Rico* against the captain general as "unjustified and calumnious."[23]

Indeed, the *Revista de Puerto Rico* took the lead in denouncing the abuses inflicted upon autonomists as an outrageous violation of their rights as Spanish citizens. This outright opposition to Palacios led to the arrest of its editor, Francisco Cepeda. With all the communications with the Peninsula blocked, it was of vital importance for the autonomists to spread the word about the situation outside the island. Thanks to a young autonomist who managed to escape to Spain and spread the word, Juan Bautista Arrillaga Roqué, the *compontes* were first denounced in the Spanish Congress on October 12, 1887, by the Puerto Rican representative Julio Vizcarrondo. He was a highly respected politician who had been instrumental in the creation of the Spanish Abolitionist Society in 1864, a founder of the Autonomist Party, and representative of Ponce, where the repression had hit the hardest. His witness before the parliament caused a political turmoil over the autumn which eventually brought about the release of the arrestees in December 1887 and the removal of Romualdo Palacios in early January 1888.[24]

What started as a wave of repression against autonomists, ended up as a major political defeat for *integristas*. Their methods had been exposed before the Spanish public opinion. The electoral system in the Antilles might have been designed to prevent the autonomists to win elections, but violating their constitutional rights so blatantly was a red line the Spanish Government was not willing to cross. It may alienate a good deal of Cubans and Puerto Ricans from the idea that reforms under Spanish sovereignty were possible. In a context as sensible as the Antilles, breaking the feeble political equilibrium could have disastrous consequences for Spain. Madrid feared that autonomists might want to retaliate, reinforcing the discontent toward Spain that might end up in their resorting to violence to achieve their objectives.

These fears were well grounded, as political tension in Puerto Rico escalated. Though the autonomists had been duly released, some people paid a toll for having supported the *compontes*. Policarpo Díaz, the mayor of Juana Díaz, had his house burnt down by groups allegedly linked to the Autonomist Party, whereas attacks on property owned by *incondicionales* who partook in the repression became commonplace in Puerto Rico over the spring of 1888.[25] Furthermore, aimed at undermining their prominent

---

[22] Ibid., pp. 74–5.
[23] *Boletín Mercantil*, 26-10-1887, p. 2.
[24] Schmidt-Nowara. *Empire, and Antislavery*, pp.100–25; ACD, *Diario de las Sesiones de Cortes*, Serie Documentación Electoral, 103, No. 6; Juan Bautista Arrillaga Roqué. *Memorias de antaño*. Ponce: Tip. Baldorioty, 1910, pp. 16–17 & 154–5.
[25] *Puerto-Rico por dentro. Cartas abiertas, por XXX. Julio y agosto de 1888, con la sentencia dictada por la Audiencia de Puerto-Rico en 2 de junio de 1888*. Madrid: Imprenta de José Gil y Navarro, 1888, p. 24; Cruz Monclova. Historia de Puerto Rico, t. III, vol. I, pp. 204–5 & 273.

economic position in the island, groups within the Autonomist Party launched a boycott campaign against shops and companies owned by *incondicionales* which lasted intermittently until the US invasion of July 1898.[26]

Far from crushing the autonomist movement, the *compontes* widened the existing gap between *incondicionales* and autonomists, thus making any potential political transaction very unlikely. The Volunteers had played a central role in this affair. They collaborated with the authorities in the repression and showed their explicit support for such a measure. During peacetime, violence backfired. Rather than reinforcing Spanish rule and the *integristas'* privileged position, the *compontes* strengthened the autonomist movement and undermined the economic position of the staunchest supporters of Spain's presence in Puerto Rico.

The Volunteers and the Right to Vote

As much as the emergence of party politics had sent the Volunteers to the margins of power, the force of events of a manipulated electoral system in such a complicated scenario as the Antilles brought them back into the center of political debate. From their very creation, the Volunteers had become a powerful symbol with contradictory political readings. For the forces supporting the status quo, they were the bedrock of Spanish nationality in the Antilles, despite the excesses that they committed. On the other aisle of the political spectrum, while there were some autonomists who held prominent positions in the militia, the Volunteers were generally regarded as the epitome of everything which was wrong with how Spain ruled the Antilles. Throughout the Ten Years' War, emissaries of the insurgents, but also Cuban reformists, had demanded the dismantlement of the Volunteers as a condition to start negotiations.[27] In January 1872, shortly after the murder of the eight medicine students in Havana which shook Spanish public opinion, the representatives of the Puerto Rican Liberal Party at the Spanish Congress formally requested the disarmament of the Volunteers. Julián Blanco, who presented the proposal, labeled the Volunteers as an "unnecessary force" made up of "social scum" who could only serve to alter social cohesion and peace in the Antilles.[28] As the war ended and projects of independence seemed to be fading away over the 1880s, the heated political debate on the Volunteers' role in the Antilles tended to get colder, until by the end of the decade discussions about the extension of the political census brought the Volunteers back into the center of politics.

As we have seen, the electoral census was way more restricted in the Antilles than in the Peninsula, thus establishing a grievance which had become extremely difficult to justify. Representatives of Puerto Rico could justly allege that the island had never underwent a revolutionary process since the pro-independence forces were virtually

---

[26] Fernando Picó. *1898. La guerra después de la guerra*. San Juan: Ediciones Huracán, 2013 (first published in 1987), pp. 36–9.
[27] García Rodríguez. *Con un ojo en Yara y otro en Madrid*, pp. 336–42.
[28] ACD, *Diario de las Sesiones de Cortes*, 22-01-1872, p. 34.

non-existent, whereas Cuban autonomists could argue that ten years had passed since the end of the last war in 1880 and that no major attempts at starting a new insurgency had taken place. Both islands were in peace and there was no reason to believe that extending the electoral census would favor forces which advocated for weakening ties with Spain. Yet this was precisely the fear of the Spanish ruling class when the country prepared to widen the right to vote to all males over 25, which became law in June 1890, though only in the Peninsula.[29] Since the Antilles were also integral members of the Spanish nation, they could not be left outside the debate, but neither given the same status as the Peninsula in terms of voting rights. Fear was that it would sentence *integristas* not to win an election again, thus paving way for the autonomists to become dominant and favor policies which would loosen the ties between Spain and the Antilles in the long run.

To avert this, while at the same time enlarging the electoral census, Manuel Becerra, minister of the Colonies (1888–90), thought the Volunteers could provide a solution by granting all of them the right to vote. Becerra was an old politician about to turn 70 who had been involved in all liberal conspiracies since the 1850s and was aware of the intricacies of Antillean politics after he had already been minister of the Colonies in 1869–70. Though liberals were in theory more prone to extend political rights than conservatives, in relation to Cuba and Puerto Rico both parties generally shared a distrust toward creole political participation. But they could neither block reforms. By the late 1880s, the regime in force in the Antilles had become somehow obsolete politically and economically. Even *integrista* political parties understood that the moment had come for changes. On March 31, 1888, the Constitutional Union of Cuba called through an open letter for embarking in a series of wide political, economic, and administrative reforms, in a political switch which could have seemed unthinkable a few years earlier.[30] The time was ripe for change.

Becerra presented the project for widening the census before the Spanish Congress on February 15, 1889, only introducing the clause about the Volunteers' right to vote on June 15, 1889. As the electoral census in the Antilles was not a priority for the Spanish Parliament, it was not discussed until April 2, 1890.[31] Becerra's project aimed at granting the right to vote to civil servants with a salary over 100 pesos, all active and retired army and navy officers, taxpayers who contributed with at least 8 pesos stemming from rural property or 12 for urban property, commerce owners and employees, and, most controversially, to the Volunteers, though with nuances. According to the project, Volunteers in Puerto Rico with over six years of service were to be granted voting rights regardless of

---

[29] Domingo Vivanco y Argüelles. *La reforma electoral. Ley electoral para diputados á Cortes en la península de 26 de junio de 1890 aplicable á las elecciones de concejales y de diputados provinciales, precedida de un Índice de sus títulos y capítulos y seguida de un Repertorio alfabético con notas y observaciones*. Madrid: Imprenta de los Hijos de J. A. García, 1890.

[30] Fernández Almagro. *Historia política de la España contemporánea*, vol. II, p. 95.

[31] Luis Estévez y Romero. *Desde el Zanjón hasta Baire. Datos para la historia política de Cuba*. Havana: "La Propaganda Literaria," 1899, pp. 651–5; Roldán de Montaud. "Política y elecciones en Cuba," pp. 245–87.

the rank. In the case of Cuba, only Volunteer officers who had also been serving for at least six years, or Volunteers of all ranks who had been decorated, were to become voters.[32]

Such a project was taken as an offense by Cuban and Puerto Rican autonomists, precisely at a time when the parliament was debating over universal male suffrage, one of their historical aspirations. Reflecting a few years later, Luis de Estévez y Romero, a Cuban autonomist lawyer and sugar baron, considered that Manuel Becerra had well deserved to be considered a "recalcitrant enemy of the Cubans for his Volunteers' vote project."[33] The unfairness of the electoral law in force meant that 1 in 21 males voted in the Peninsula, for 1 in 51 in Cuba and 1 in 250 in Puerto Rico. There had been previous attempts to enlarge the census, but to no avail. In June 1887, the former minister of the Colonies, the Catalan historian Víctor Balaguer, registered a bill project at the Congress to widen the electoral basis to large layers of Antillean society, mostly deemed autonomist. It was not even discussed due to the opposition of the Conservative Party and large sectors of his own Liberal Party, which shared a basic consensus as to the necessity to prevent the autonomists from winning elections.[34]

In such a context, the autonomists launched a campaign to present the Volunteer's vote clause in the bill as a brute attempt to keep securing victories for the *integristas* and preventing the ideas purportedly shared by most Cubans and Puerto Ricans to be heard in Madrid. Even the discrimination of Cuban Volunteers in comparison to their Puerto Rican colleagues was designed to tackle autonomist voices. Whereas the formers were conservative almost with no exception, in Cuba the Volunteers presented a much more heterogeneous group in political terms with the presence of many radical liberals and even republicans. In addition, to this, controlling the around 5,000 Volunteers of Puerto Rico was much more feasible than guiding the vote of around 66,000 Volunteers in Cuba.[35] This was pointed out by autonomist representatives for Puerto Rican constituencies such as Rafael María de Labra and José Celis Aguilera, who denounced that whereas "all of the Puerto Rican Volunteers are conservatives, in Cuba, there are strong pockets of liberal Volunteers in Las Villas and Oriente."[36] In fact, since the creation of the Unconditional Party in 1870, it was an unwritten rule that only their members and supporters could join the Volunteers in Puerto Rico.[37]

---

[32] ACD, *Diario de las Sesiones de Cortes*, Appendix No. 6, 15-06-1889; Roldán de Montaud. *La Restauración en Cuba*, pp. 414–19; Estévez y Romero. *Desde el Zanjón hasta Baire*, pp. 362–8.

[33] Estévez y Romero. *Desde el Zanjón hasta Baire*, p. 535.

[34] Roldán de Montaud. *La Restauración en Cuba*, pp. 370–3; Víctor Balaguer. *Memoria que precede á los dos volúmenes de documentos que publica el Excmo. Sr. D. Víctor Balaguer acerca de su gestión en el Ministerio de Ultramar durante el desempeño de su cargo como ministro del ramo desde 11 de octubre de 1886 hasta 14 de junio de 1888*. Madrid: Imprenta y Fundición de Manuel Tello, 1888, pp. 33–4; S. Andrés. *La reforma electoral*, p. 11; ACD, Serie Documental Electoral, 60, No. 8.

[35] AGMM, Documentación de Puerto Rico, sig. 5195.1; Gallego y García. *Cuba por fuera*, p. 229.

[36] ACD, *Diario de las Sesiones de Cortes*, No. 140, April 17, 1890, p. 4312. See Catherine Davies & Sarah Sánchez. "Rafael María de Labra and *La Revista Hispano-Americana* 1864–1867: Revolutionary Liberalism and Colonial Reform." *Bulletin of Spanish Studies: Hispanic Studies and Researches on Spain, Portugal and Latin America*, 2010, vol. 87, No. 7, pp. 915–38; ACD, *Diario de las Sesiones de Cortes*, 21-04-1890, pp. 4434–9; ACD, Serie Documentación Electoral: 103, No. 6.

[37] Ángel Rivero Méndez. *Crónica de la Guerra Hispano-Americana en Puerto Rico*. Madrid: Sucesores de Rivadeneyra, 1922, p. 450.

Labra reckoned that the bill, as it had been presented, would have given the right to vote to 5,000 Volunteers over a census of 24,000. In Cuba, the impact would have been ever greater, for the Volunteers with the right to vote might have gone up to 40,000 for a census of 98,500 voters in the whole island.[38] Consequently, the autonomist representatives rejected the project for the huge impact it would have had on the Puerto Rican electoral census.

Paradoxically, the same argument was used by supporters of the bill.[39] For instance, *Cuba Española*, an *integrista* newspaper of Holguín, in Cuba, rejected the argument that granting the right to vote to the Volunteers would favor the conservatives for there were, indeed, many of them who supported the Autonomist Party in Oriente and Las Villas, and elsewhere in the island.[40] In the Peninsula, the military press also supported the bill, often publishing articles penned by Volunteer officers. For instance, *El Correo Militar* published in late May a letter by the Canary islander Eugenio Vandama y Calderón, colonel in a Havana Volunteer battalion, who defended the right to vote as a well-deserved reward for the many "generous and continuous services rendered by the Volunteers to the Motherland."[41] At the Congress, General Luis Manuel Pando, a veteran of the Ten Years' War who had been elected for Santiago de Cuba, defended the Volunteers' right to vote as a reward for the many services they had rendered to the cause of Spain in the Antilles. He argued that the very existence of autonomists among the Volunteers was a proof that the militia was not partisan, which demonstrated that Becerra's bill was not aimed at securing victories for the *integristas*.[42] In the same line, General Manuel Cassola, a liberal-minded former minister of war, briefly defended the bill on April 25, 1890, stressing that the right to vote would be given to all the Volunteers meeting the requirements, born either in the Peninsula or in the Antilles, whether they be white, mulatto, or Black, for he reminded the autonomists that there were many races donning the uniform in defense of Spain. That very day, the clause on the Volunteers' vote was passed by the Congress.[43]

After two months of debates, the bill was passed by the Congress on May 5, 1890, stating that Volunteers of all ranks with over six years of service, and all Volunteers who had been awarded a war medal regardless of service time, were granted the right to vote.[44] Despite having gone through the first step in a bicameral system, the bill underwent substantial changes in the Senate. On July 2, when the high chamber debated the bill, the proposal of granting the right to vote to the Volunteers had been removed by the senatorial electoral commission, alleging that the captain general of Cuba and the leader of the Constitutional Union, the Count of Casa Moré, had renounced to demand it in order to avoid escalating tensions with the autonomists.[45] Despite the

---

[38] ACD, *Diario de las Sesiones de Cortes*, 22-04-1890, p. 4493.
[39] Andrés. *La reforma electoral*, p. 23.
[40] The article was reproduced in *El Correo Militar*, June 7, 1890, p. 1.
[41] *El Correo Militar*, 29-05-1890, p. 1.
[42] ACD, *Diario de las Sesiones de Cortes*, 18-04-1890, p. 4362.
[43] ACD, *Diario de las Sesiones de Cortes*, 25-04-1890, p. 4611.
[44] ACD, *Diario de las Sesiones de Cortes*, 05-05-1890, Apéndice 3º al núm. 154, art. 17, punto 5º.
[45] AS, *Diario de Sesiones a Cortes*, 02-07-1890, pp. 4156-70.

many protests by the advocates of the bill, and the fact that Puerto Rico's Volunteers had not refused to be granted the right, the Senate did not reconsider its position, and kept the Volunteers' issue outside the bill. The military press, which generally supported granting the right to vote to the Volunteers, accused the autonomists of having maneuvered to convince senators with little to no knowledge on Antillean affairs to vote against the bill on grounds that it would hamper social peace in Cuba and Puerto Rico.[46]

In any case, the legislature was close to be called off, as Premier Sagasta was forced to step down on July 5 due to the controversial involvement of his wife in the construction of a railway in Cuba.[47] Conservative leader Antonio Cánovas del Castillo was appointed premier anew that very day. His new cabinet had little interest in pushing forward a project launched by the Liberal Party, letting it die a natural death after the legislature was called off two days after assuming power. The military press blamed the autonomists and the peninsular political parties for not pushing forward a just reward to the Volunteers, thus depriving the most loyal of the Spanish loyalists in the Antilles in what they labeled a "suicidal policy."[48] The project was never resumed by the conservative-dominated parliament between 1890 and 1892, when the liberals got back in power.

In the Antilles, the Volunteers made no effort to stand for their right to vote. In any case, it remained as a lingering issue in Spanish politics, ready to be used by conservatives and liberals rather than by the Volunteers themselves. It would be Antonio Maura, the minister of the Colonies (1892-4) in the new liberal cabinet headed by Sagasta, who would bury the Volunteers' vote project. He simply ignored the issue and let it die a natural death. Maura, a young lawyer from Majorca, was committed to implementing a wide set of reforms in the colonies, aimed at giving more political rights to their inhabitants but keeping them under Spanish sovereignty.[49] In a way, he wanted to loosen the ties between the Peninsula and the Antilles through decentralization in order to gain the hearts and minds of reformist creoles. Consequently, Maura wanted to impede the *integristas* from using the Volunteers as an electoral weapon against their rivals. For instance, the new electoral reform bill presented before the Congress on December 28, 1892, increased the Cuban electoral census from 21,000 to over 50,000 voters, but it did not include any special voting right for the Volunteers, although they

---

[46] *El Correo Militar*, articles from July 2 to 4, 1890.
[47] Fernández Almagro. *Historia de la España contemporánea*, vol. II, pp. 123–7; Javier Rubio. "Cánovas ante el gran reto antillano," in Emilio de Diego García et al. *Cánovas y la vertebración de España*. Madrid: Fundación Cánovas del Castillo, 1999, pp. 199–232.
[48] *El Correo Militar*, 04-07-1890, p. 1.
[49] James Durnerin. *Maura et Cuba. Politique coloniale d'un ministre liberal*. Besançon: Annales Littéraires de l'Université de Besançon/Les Belles Lettres, 1978; Emilio de Diego García, "¿La última oportunidad política en las Antillas?," in Emilio de Diego García (dir.). *1895, la guerra en Cuba y la España de la Restauración*. Madrid: Editorial Complutense, 1996, pp. 99–118; Pérez Cisneros. *El reformismo español en Cuba*, pp. 116–28; Fernando Maura. "Autonomía para Cuba: el proyecto Maura (1893)." *Razón española: Revista bimestral de pensamiento*, 2014, No. 184, pp. 169–84; Javier Tusell Gómez. "Maura: una propuesta para la solución del problema de Cuba," in José Ramón Cervera Pery et al. *La presencia militar española en Cuba (1865-1905)*. Madrid: Ministerio de Defensa / Instituto Español de Estudios Estratégicos, 1995, pp. 111–24.

could still vote should they meet the general requisites applied to anyone else eligible.[50] This meant that most of the rank and file, just as any other Spanish citizen with a low income living in the Antilles, would not have the right to vote. Furthermore, Maura wanted to end with political leverage of the Volunteers at the local level by banning them from holding public office in city and town councils. At least since the Ten Years' War, many Volunteer officers had been appointed councilors and mayors in Cuba. This naturally caused certain discontent among *integristas*. Ramón Barrios, the governor of the Havana Province and the whole Western Region of Cuba, complained to Maura in February 1893 that this decision had forced him to replace several mayors, including some who had shown great managing skills, such as the mayor of Santiago de los Baños and colonel of the local Volunteer battalion, who had been appointed in 1869.[51]

Maura wanted the institution of the Volunteers out of politics. He did not want the militia to become a force which could be used for electoral purposes, especially when he needed a more controllable electoral basis to push forward his reform plans. Perhaps as a gesture to assuage the upset that this might cause among the Volunteers, he included their most veteran colonels into the Administration Council alongside the captain general, the archbishop of Santiago de Cuba, the navy commander in Cuba and Puerto Rico, the *segundo cabo*, and the re-elected provincial deputies. This council was an advisory body that saw to any major political issue regarding the Antilles.[52]

After over a decade of party politics, the actual capability of the Volunteers to mobilize thousands of men for political purposes had been nearly shattered. The close ties between the Volunteers and politics that had predominated since the Ten Years' War, and was reinforced by the Restoration regime in the Antilles, had been seriously eroded by Maura's reforms. They were deprived of local political power, and it had become clear that the government was unwilling to make them a privileged electoral group. The Constitutional Union fiercely opposed Maura, even warning him that the effect of these measures on the Volunteers might endanger Spanish rule in areas where Cuban nationalists were in a majority. Román Martínez, head of the party's local branch in Santiago de Cuba, complained to Maura by warning him that the effects of his reforms had "deeply affected the Volunteers," and that the consequences could be "deplorable."[53] As the minister refused to reconsider his position, the entire local party committee in Santiago de Cuba resigned in August 1893.[54]

Despite rumors insisting that the Volunteers were preparing violent demonstrations against the authorities, they generally accepted Maura's reforms, though begrudgingly.[55] The dissociation between the Constitutional Union's claims and the Volunteers'

---

[50] Roldán de Montaud. "Política y elecciones en Cuba," p. 275; Pérez Cisneros. *El reformismo español en Cuba*, p. 120; AHN, Ultramar, 4944, leg. 19; *Gaceta de Madrid*, 28-12-1892.
[51] AFAM, leg. 358-1, carpeta 5, Ramón Barrios a Antonio Maura, 28-02-1893.
[52] Pérez Cisneros. *El reformismo español en Cuba*, pp. 123–4.
[53] AFAM, leg. 166, No. 10, letter from Román Martínez to Antonio Maura, 12-11-1893.
[54] *El Noticiero Balear*, 17-08-1893, p. 3.
[55] AFAM, leg. 335-1, carpeta 5, telegram from Captain General Alejandro Rodríguez Arias to Antonio Maura, 12-06-1893.

attitudes seemed to indicate that there was widening gap between the Volunteers and the *integrista* political elite. It does not mean that the Volunteers had necessarily accepted Maura's thesis, but rather that they shied away from open confrontation with reformists and autonomists. Besides, the debates on the Volunteers' right to vote had left out all the non-decorated rank-and-file members with less than six years of service, which might cause frictions between them and their commanding officers. Beyond the politicized atmosphere of the cities, the right to vote might have been less a concern for the thousands of peasant Volunteers, who were more affected by the neglected state of the countryside than by political maneuvering in Havana and Madrid.

8

The Volunteers and the Military Challenges of Peace

After having played a central role in the Antilles during the Ten Years' War, during peacetime the Volunteers had to redefine their military role. The new context following the Zanjón Pact placed them in a situation somehow similar to the period between the annexationist threats of the mid-1850s and the revolutionary outburst of 1868. Back then, their financial and logistic support of the military campaigns in Morocco and Santo Domingo justified their very existence, but no colonial war was in sight by the early 1880s. Consequently, after 1878, since this militia lacked a clear military role, service in the Volunteers became less appealing, their raison d'être at least dubious, and their morale low.

Right after the war, the excess of regular military personnel in Cuba was easily solved. Units were merged, conscripts were licensed, and entire battalions were shipped back to the Peninsula. In just two years, the 85,000-men garrison of 1878 was reduced to 30,000 in 1880.[1] What to do with the remaining 85,000 Volunteers was another question.[2] They were just too many for peacetime. Whereas the units created during the war could be dissolved, their members could be neither stripped of their uniform nor shipped somewhere else, for these men were civilians not subjected to military laws during peacetime, and more importantly, they continued to live in Cuba, where they had found employment and often a family.[3] Certainly, they cost virtually nothing to the treasury, but the use of such a large militia during peacetime remained an unsolved issue. The victorious colonial state attempted to square this circle. Throughout 1878 several Volunteer units were dissolved, and the officers that had been mobilized were offered the possibility of joining the regular army or being recommended for appointments in the island's administration by the Royal Decree November 7.[4] Joining the army could mean being sent to the Peninsula or to a far-flung colony in Asia or the Gulf of Guinea, so this option scarcely appealed to men who depended on their regular

---

[1] Andrés Mas Chao. *Evolución de la infantería en el reinado de Alfonso XII*. Madrid: Servicio de Publicaciones del EME, 1989, pp. 158–81.
[2] Otero Pimentel. *Memoria sobre los Voluntarios*, p. 177.
[3] *Reglamento para los cuerpos de Voluntarios de la isla de Cuba* (1869), art. 64, p. 22.
[4] Mas Chao. *Evolución de la infantería*, pp. 165–6; *Gaceta de Madrid*, 8-11-1878, No. 512, t. IV, p. 373.

jobs and were well settled in Cuba.⁵ At a certain age, having a family to sustain, most Volunteers would be hardly attracted to the idea of starting a military career anew.

In Puerto Rico, even more than in Cuba, the military purpose of keeping the Volunteer militia alive was unclear. The island had not undergone a war, and the pro-independence movement hardly existed. The threat of an uprising was minimum, and new recruits were hardly to be found. In this context, a symbolic gesture seemed a proper way to revive the Volunteers esprit de corps and make them an attractive unit to be part of. Pablo Ubarri, the Basque businessman, leader of the Spanish Unconditional Party and colonel of the San Juan's 1st Volunteer Battalion, suggested to Captain General Eulogio Despujols (1878–81) to reward all the local Volunteers with a medal to foster their social status.⁶ At the captain general's request, the Ministry of the Colonies created a medal that acknowledged the patriotism of local Volunteers on August 27, 1880.⁷ It was to be a silver medal engraved with the *Voluntarios de Puerto Rico* phrase, to be awarded to any Volunteer who had served for at least ten years with a flawless record.⁸ On March 11, 1881, the medal, which came to be known as Constancy Medal (*Medalla a la Constancia*), was delivered to several thousand men from all the fourteen Volunteer battalions of Puerto Rico during a public ceremony held in the wide fields standing in front of San Felipe del Morro, the iconic fortress that had protected San Juan's bay since the late sixteenth century.⁹ According to the *Boletín Mercantil*, the ceremony was an enthusiastic demonstration of loyalism and a proof of the Volunteers' good shape.¹⁰

The medal seemed indeed a good way to cheer the morale up. Probably inspired in Puerto Rico, the Ministry of the Colonies created another Constancy Medal through a Royal Decree published on July 22, 1882, to reward Volunteers of all ranks in Cuba.¹¹ But the truth is that medals were not getting much new recruits. In Puerto Rico, by 1884, there were only around 4,700 Volunteers for a population of 810,000. This meant that there was 1 Volunteer for every 172 inhabitants, whereas in Cuba in 1877, shortly before the end of the war, the ratio was one Volunteer for every 16 people.¹² Certainly, the situation of both islands was not comparable, for the lingering legacy of war was

---

⁵ For instance, in 1877 58 percent of the men of the Tiguabo's Infantry Volunteers Section were married, AGMM, Ultramar, Capitanía General de Cuba Subinspección General de Voluntarios, caja 3057, "Sección de Voluntarios de Tiguabos."
⁶ Jesús Martín Ramos. "Bosquejo histórico-biográfico de Pablo Ubarri y Capetillo, Conde de San José de Santurce," in Octavio Ruiz-Manjón Cabeza & María Alicia Langa Laorga (eds.). *Los significados del 98: la sociedad española en la génesis del siglo XX*. Madrid: Biblioteca Nueva, 1999, pp. 201–12.
⁷ *Colección legislativa del Ejército. Año de 1880*. Madrid: Imprenta y Litografía del Depósito de la Guerra, 1896, núm. 363, pp. 727–8.
⁸ *Colección legislativa del Ejército. Año de 1880*, núm. 365, pp. 729–30.
⁹ AHN, Ultramar, 5114, exp. 12; Rosado y Brincau. *Bosquejo Histórico*, pp. 71–83; González Cuevas. *¿Defendiendo el honor?*, pp. 72–7.
¹⁰ *Boletín Mercantil*, 24-03-1881.
¹¹ Ministerio de la Guerra. *Colección legislativa del Ejército*. Madrid: Imprenta y Litografía del Depósito de la Guerra, 1898, pp. 341–6.
¹² Luis A. Figueroa. *Sugar, Slavery, and Freedom in Nineteenth-Century Puerto Rico*. Chapel Hill: The University of North Carolina Press, 2005, p. 48, table 2.1; Fe Iglesias. "El censo cubano de 1877 y sus diferentes versiones." *Santiago*, 1979, No. 34, pp. 167–214; *Ejército de Puerto-Rico* (1884), p. 7.

still a heavy burden in Cuba, but Volunteers in Puerto Rico stood way behind in terms of social presence. To revert this, in December 1884, Captain General Luis Dabán (1884–7) urged the officers to recruit more men and to improve military training, which had been generally neglected. The bad shape of the Volunteers might give a bad impression which had negative political implications, especially in those areas where *integrismo* was most weak, especially around the area of Ponce, the autonomist heartland. The state of the 6th Volunteer Battalion, based precisely in that city, was so precarious that statistics on the actual shape of its weapons or even on membership were not to be trusted. Many of its members simply didn't show up for drilling, and officers seemed not to care much. The battalion was not dismantled simply for political reasons, for it would have dismayed *integristas* and encouraged autonomists.[13]

The symbolic implications of letting the Volunteers go derelict in Puerto Rico for Spanish rule were too evident. Captain General Dabán decided to work closely with Pablo Ubarri to put back the militia in good shape.[14] One of the first measures was to write the story of the Volunteers to give them a place in the history of Puerto Rico. Army officer Rafael Rosado y Brincau was commissioned by the Captaincy General to write *Bosquejo histórico de la Institución de Voluntarios en Puerto Rico*, published in 1888. It offered a laudatory version of the Volunteers and insisted on its key role in keeping Puerto Rico Spanish at least since they were reorganized in September 1868 to quell the uprising attempt which ensued the *Grito de Lares*.[15] Though naturally biased, it gave a thorough account of the many events which had taken place during two decades, giving a special place to the "good Spaniards" who created companies whenever and wherever it was most needed.

The publication of the Volunteers' history book was important, but to keep the organization of the militia in good order was essential. Since the reorganization of October 20, 1874, eight Volunteer battalions were established, one per each military district. These were numbered: 1st in San Juan, 2nd in Bayamón, 3rd in Arecibo, 4th in Aguadilla, 5th in Mayagüez, 6th in Ponce, 7th in Guayama, and 8th in Humacao. After a decade, their numbers were not even, ranging from 355 men in Humacao to 856 in Mayagüez.[16] The somehow vague Volunteer *reglamento* of 1869 and their lack of a concrete purpose had shaped a militia with serious deficiencies in terms of uniformity, weaponry, military training, and membership. For instance, in 1886 the 1st Battalion still had 497 beleaguered 12mm Chassepot rifles with their bayonets, which had been bought to Italy in 1870. There was no ammunition to feed them, for its production had ceased in 1875.[17] The Chassepot had been the staple rifle of the French infantryman during the Franco-Prussian War, but by 1886 it was an outdated weapon, even for an auxiliary militia in the Antilles.[18] Considering that the San Juan battalion

---

[13] AGMM, Documentación de Puerto Rico, sig. 5179.24, 5199.2, 5202.2; Rosado y Brincau. *Bosquejo Histórico*, pp. 95–105.
[14] Rosado y Brincau. *Bosquejo Histórico*, pp. 125–51.
[15] Ibid., pp. 153–61.
[16] González Cuevas. *¿Defendiendo el honor?*, p. 71; *Ejército de Puerto-Rico. Estado militar …* (1884), p. 7.
[17] AGMM, Documentación de Puerto Rico, sig. 5193.3.
[18] Roger Ford. *The World's Great Rifles*. London: Brown Books, 1998, p. 23.

was considered the Volunteers' finest in Puerto Rico, one can imagine the state of the others in the rest of the island.

Willing to redress the situation, Captain General Dabán created a committee in November 1886 including army officers and Volunteer chief officers to study feasible solutions.[19] The main task was to reorganize the units, and after a year the committee produced a new *reglamento* that was submitted to the Ministry of War for approval and was sanctioned by a Royal Decree on July 10, 1888. The eight battalions were turned into fourteen, with almost even numbers, clear norms as to the possession of weapons, which usually was afforded by the Volunteers themselves, and military training. The new scheme consisted of the 1st Battalion in San Juan, the 2nd in Bayamón, the 3rd in Río Piedras, the 4th in Arecibo, the 5th in Aguadilla, the 6th in Mayagüez, the 7th in Maricao, the 8th in Sábana Grande, the 9th in Ponce, the 10th in Coamo, the 11th in Guayama, the 12th in Hato Grande, the 13th in Humacao, and the 14th, labeled "Tiradores de la Altura," in Utuado. Additionally, an independent company was established in the island of Vieques.[20] Each battalion had its headquarters in the seat of the military department and was made up of four companies scattered in smaller towns, covering virtually all of Puerto Rico.

The *reglamento* of 1888 ensured a much more organized, coordinated, and fit force. It also succeeded in attracting more recruits. In four years, nearly 1,000 new men joined the Volunteers, from 4,412 members in 1884 to 5,328 in 1888. This was more than enough for an island that had no serious external threat and already had a regular army garrison aided by the Civil Guard. In this shape, the Volunteers remained practically untouched until the dissolution of the militia in 1898 at the end of Spanish rule in Puerto Rico. Undoubtedly, other factors helped the new reorganization to become a success. First, managing around 5,000 men in a 3,515 sq. miles island, almost a tenth of Cuba's geography, made the fulfilment of orders of joint maneuvers easier in logistical terms. Second, a strong cohesion facilitated by a neat, yet unofficial, identification with the Spanish Unconditional Party and an undisputed leadership, shared by both the party and the militia. Pablo Ubarri, colonel of the 1st Battalion and leader of that political party, was the mastermind behind the whole process of reorganizing the Volunteers, which he saw as inextricably associated with the *incondicionales*.[21] Third, due to the smaller importance of sugar and tobacco production, and the small workforce needed by coffee farms, Puerto Rico had no proletariat as such by the end of the nineteenth century.[22] The

---

[19] The committee was presided over by Juan Contreras y Martínez (*Segundo Cabo*), Colonel Juan Álvarez Arenas (Staff Chief), Colonel Fernando Alameda Liancourt (Engineers deputy inspector), Colonel Luis López Ballesteros (infantry), Major Eduardo Valera y Vicente (artillery), Lieutenant Colonel Pablo Ubarri (1st Volunteer Battalion), Lieutenant Colonel Bernardo Pérez Méndez (2nd Battalion), Lieutenant Colonel Manuel González Fernández (3rd Battalion), Lieutenant Colonel Ulpiano Valdés (8th Battalion), and the Secretary Lieutenant Colonel Juan de Zibikowski y Tello (infantry). Rosado y Brincau. *Bosquejo Histórico*, pp. 130–1.

[20] *Isla de Puerto-Rico. Reglamento para los cuerpos de Voluntarios* (1888); Rosado y Brincau. *Bosquejo Histórico*, pp. 143–51.

[21] Rosado y Brincau. *Bosquejo Histórico*, pp. 235–9; AHN, Ultramar, 5100, exp. 12, 13, 19, 34; 322, exp. 4, 5; 428, exp. 48-52, 54.

[22] Gervasio L. García & A. G. Quintero Rivera. *Desafío y solidaridad. Breve historia del movimiento obrero puertorriqueño*. San Juan: Ediciones Huracán, 1982, pp. 13–34.

absence of a strong labor movement, the logical consequence of the absence of a strong industry, also spared the Puerto Rican Volunteers from much social conflict between employers and employees, who often coincided in the companies and battalions. In Cuba, however, the situation was rather different.

Serving in the Volunteers under the Military Service Law of 1885

A military service bill passed by the Spanish Parliament in 1885 explored new ways of collaboration between the army conscription system and the Volunteers, aiming at making service in the militia more attractive. The units needed men, at least in Cuba, as their numbers seemed to have been declining since the end of the war in 1880. In a way, it renewed a relationship which had been explored before. For instance, on April 2, 1878, shortly after the Pact of Zanjón, the Ministry of War sanctioned that, for as long as the state of war remained in force, the time served in the Volunteers should be discounted from the military service in the army.[23] Later on, on December 11, 1880, shortly after the end of the Little War, a Royal Order stated that as long as exceptional circumstances lasted in Cuba, the Volunteers who had joined the militia after June 12, 1878, could also Benefit from the April 2, 1878, Royal Decree in order to shorten the military service.[24] This only affected *peninsulares*, for Spanish citizens from outside the Peninsula, that is, Cubans and Puerto Ricans, were not subject to comply with military service. Volunteer officers were also offered ways to join the army or at least have some advantages as a reward for their contribution during the war. On November 7, 1878, the government decreed that the officers of militias who had fought in the war should be classified into three categories: fit to join the regular army, able to remain in their units, and fit for being appointed as civil servants.[25]

These benefits were only linked to the Volunteers' service during the wars in Cuba, but anyone who had joined the militia after the end of the war could not enjoy any of the benefits linked to war service. In this regard, military service law passed on July 11, 1885, introduced a change that could theoretically benefit these men. It allowed the *peninsulares* that had been serving in the Volunteers for at least one year to fulfil their military service in their units instead of joining the army or the navy, where the service lasted for four years.[26] In case they opted for it, they would have to serve in the Volunteers for six years, in comparison to four years in the army or the navy. Still, it was more attractive for a young man who had emigrated from the Peninsula to serve in the Volunteers, as it was possible to combine the service with a paid regular job and to stay at his new home. Service in the regular army, instead, meant living in barracks doing an unpaid job for four years, and likely be sent to a far-flung colony to fight local insurgency, or a new Carlist uprising in the Peninsula. As well, the military service law

---

[23] *Colección legislativa del Ejército. Año 1878.* Madrid: Imprenta y Litografía del Depósito de la Guerra, 1894 1878, núm. 91, p. 216.
[24] *Colección legislative del Ejército. Año 1880*, núm. 524, pp. 890.
[25] *Colección legislativa del Ejército. Año 1878*, núm. 338, p. 610.
[26] *Gaceta de Madrid*, 13-07-1885, No. 194, additional article No. 3, p. 123.

was aimed at reverting the outflux of thousands of young *peninsulares* who migrated to South America, mostly Argentina and Brazil, or Africa, away from Spanish national territory, to avoid being drafted for the army or the navy. Between 1882 and 1885, over 100,000 Spaniards had migrated to South America, whereas less than 50,000 had settled in Cuba.[27] In French Algeria, the Spanish colony rose from 114,000 in 1881 to 157,000 in 1889.[28]

Contrary to other powers, such as Britain, France, or the Netherlands, which mostly relied on volunteer armies for colonial campaigns, the many wars fought in and by Spain required the participation of thousands of conscripts who had paid unbearable death tolls. Of the 180,000 men who were sent to Cuba during the Ten Years' War, only around a half managed to get back home, not to mention the many hardships underwent in campaigns like Morocco, Santo Domingo, or the Third Carlist War. Tropical diseases, unpaid service, and poor food were staple features of conscript military service in the nineteenth-century Spanish armed forces. Consequently, military service had become hugely unpopular in Spain.[29] A life of adventures in far-flung colonies, which might be appealing for professional soldiers, was, on the contrary, a deterrent to potential Spanish conscripts.[30]

The 1885 military law had little impact on Puerto Rico, where the *peninsulares* had never been more than a tiny community. By 1860, they were only 13,000 for a population of 600,000, and the numbers decreased to nearly 8,000 for a population of 950,000 in 1899.[31] Consequently, by 1886 only nine *peninsulares* were serving in the 806-strong Volunteer 1st Battalion under the terms of the 1885 military service law.[32] As to Cuba, on the contrary, the law had an immediate impact. The migration trend of previous years was reversed, and nearly 90,000 *peninsulares* settled in Cuba in 1886–90, for 60,000 in 1881–5.[33] But the 1885 law and the incoming influx of new *peninsulares* had side effects for the Volunteers' social fabric and esprit de corps. The average Volunteer had never been a war-loving individual, but he stepped up to fulfil military duties and had been mobilized to warzone during the 1870s. Yet the kind of new Volunteer who had joined the ranks under the terms of the 1885 law did it so precisely to avoid a heavy military burden. In October 1885, Jaime Cañameras y Ferrer, a young member of Santiago de Cuba's 1st Volunteer Battalion, wrote to his uncle Antonio Ferrer, a Volunteer captain veteran who had settled back in Sitges, that many

---

[27] AHN, Ultramar, 120, exp. 5; Nicolás Sánchez-Albornoz. "La emigración española a América en medio milenio: pautas sociales." *Historia Social*, 2002, No. 42, pp. 40–57; Moreno Fraginals & Moreno Masó. *Guerra, migración y muerte*, p. 121.

[28] Eloy Martín Corrales. "La emigración española en Argelia." *Awraq: Estudios sobre el mundo árabe e islámico contemporáneo*, 2012, No. 5–6, pp. 47–63.

[29] Fernando Puell de la Villa. *El soldado desconocido. De la leva a la "mili" (1700–2012)*. Madrid: Biblioteca Nueva, 2012, pp. 251–8.

[30] García Balañá. "The Empire is no longer a social unit," pp. 92–103.

[31] Cubano Iguina. *El hilo en el laberinto*, table 1, p. 156, taken from US War Department, *Report on the Census of Puerto Rico, 1899*, Washington D.C., Government Printing Press, 1900, pp. 34, 43, 62, 94; Pérez Morís & Cueto y González Quijano. *Historia de la insurrección de Lares*, p. 223.

[32] AGMM, Documentación de Puerto Rico, sig. 5193.3.

[33] Moreno Fraginals & Moreno Masó. *Guerra, migración y muerte*, p. 121.

of his young peninsular colleagues were joining the Volunteers "for the sole purpose of avoiding military service in the regular army" and that "[they] lack the motivation required to fulfil their duties effectively."[34]

Hand in hand with low morale, politics were involved too. Indeed, alongside the determination to avoid military service, many young *peninsulares* coming from industrialized areas in Spain, such as Catalonia, Biscay, and Asturias, had crossed the Atlantic with socialist and even anarchist ideals which would feed an emerging labor movement in places like Havana. Social tensions within a militia where tobacco factory owners and cigar-makers, shop owners and shopkeepers met, were bound to happen.[35] Many young Volunteers held ideas of class solidarity, like the Basque Ramiro de Maeztu, son of a well-to-do liberal from Cienfuegos, who arrived to Cuba as a socialist, though later in life he became a leading thinker of Spanish conservatism.[36] Shortly after having settled in Havana, Maeztu found a job as shop assistant and in May 1893 he joined the Chapelgorris del Cerro, a Volunteer battalion mostly made up of fellow Basque migrants who lived in the outskirts of Havana. Socialization with fellow employees and Volunteers provided Maeztu with acquaintances who introduced him into the Havana's thriving labor movement.[37]

The Volunteers' Social Unrest

Indeed, labor demands were rising in a context of social tension and huge unemployment. By the end of the 1880s, Havana had become a harder place to make a living. The greater influx of jobseekers from the Peninsula only worsened the fact that in a city of 250,000 people, no less than 20,000 were unemployed. Social unrest was often mixed with discontent with an endemically corrupt colonial administration which did little to assuage the situation and meeting the needs of the island's people.[38] In fact, the working-class *integristas* who fed the Volunteer ranks often blamed the inefficient administration for undermining the very basis of Spanish rule in Cuba. Identifying with a sort of "plebeian nationalism," these men combined a staunch defense of Spain and a raw criticism of its colonial administrators hand in hand. It was a Cuban replica of the combination of populism and nationalism which had nurtured the discourse of

---

[34] Copiador de cartas de Antonio Ferrer Robert. Jaime Cañameras Ferrer a Antonio Ferrer Robert, 11-10-1885. I thank Lluís Riudor Gorgas for letting me consult the private correspondence of his great-grandfather Antonio Ferrer Robert.
[35] Casanovas. *Bread, or Bullets!*, pp. 203–21; Frank Fernández. *El anarquismo en Cuba*. Madrid: Fundación de Estudios Libertarios Anselmo Lorenzo, 2000, pp. 23–46; Pérez, Jr. *Cuba. Between Reform & Revolution*, p. 132.
[36] In 1934 he published *Defensa de la Hispanidad*, in which he defined the concept of Spanishness as a single cultural unity embracing both the Spanish and Portuguese-speaking worlds.
[37] AGMS, leg. M-147.
[38] Jean-Philippe Luis. "Les employés: une horde prédatrice ?," in Jean-Philippe Luis (ed.). *L'État dans ses colonies. Les administrateurs de l'empire espagnol au XIXe siècle*. Madrid: Casa de Velázquez, 2015, pp. 227–52; Xavier Huetz de Lemps. "Un cas colonial de corruption systémique: les Philippines à la fin du XIXe Siècle." *Illes i Imperis*, 2014, No. 16, pp.135–46.

democrats and republicans in the Peninsula against conservatives since the 1840s.[39] In Cuba, the *integristas*' commitment to the Spanish Nation was used to legitimize demonstrations against those who they perceived as elitist, corrupt, colonial civil servants, who undermined Spain's rule in Cuba and damaged the interest of working-class Volunteers. This combination of nationalism with social demands was not unique to Cuba, of course. For instance, a similar example can be found in the *Boulangist* movement in France (1885–9), whose supporters considered the Third Republic an elitist, corrupt, and anti-national regime.[40] Havana's working-class Volunteers had very similar thoughts on the colonial authorities in Cuba.

Ideas were followed by actions. For instance, between August 23 and 27, 1887, around 5,000 young workers, mostly *peninsulares* and Volunteers, took to the streets in Havana to demand the removal of acting captain general Sabas Marín (1887–9) for his cynical connivance with corrupt officials. The demonstrators demanded the arrival of Manuel Salamanca, who had already been appointed as the new captain general but was being stalled in the Peninsula by the government for having declared in early August to *El Resumen,* a Madrid newspaper, that he was going to eradicate corruption in Cuba.[41] The situation became incredibly difficult to handle, for calming down young men with some military training who had the right to keep a personal weapon at home was not easy. Nearly twenty years had passed, but everyone remembered the forcible removal of Captain General Dulce in 1869. Though regular cavalry units were deployed in central Havana to ward off demonstrators, the protests were called off only after intense negotiations between the captain general, Volunteer officers, and their subordinates, who were promised that the authorities had listened to their demands for proper administration of public affairs.[42]

Widespread corruption was almost a staple feature of any colonial administration, and Cuba was no exception. The main example had been slave trade, which kept importing enslaved Africans until the mid-1860s in connivance with the authorities, though it was illegal since 1820. Slavery itself was gone in 1886, but by the end of the century many still benefited from other sorts of corruption, from the public accountant who embezzled money from the island's treasury to the Customs official who accepted bribes; from the trader engaged in smuggling to the consumer who could purchase cheaper goods by avoiding paying due taxes. In 1887, the journalist Francisco Moreno published *El país del chocolate*, a highly controversial book which openly denounced

---

[39] Xavier Andreu Miralles. "El pueblo y sus opresores: populismo y nacionalismo en la cultura política del radicalismo democrático, 1844–1848." *Historia y política: ideas, procesos y movimientos sociales*, 2011, No. 25, pp. 65–91; Philip G. Nord. *The Politics of Resentment. Shopkeeper Protest in Nineteenth-Century Paris*. New Brunswick and London: Transaction Publishers, 2009, pp. 261–301; Albert García Balañá. "Clase, Pueblo y Patria en la España liberal: comunidades polisémicas y experiencias plebeyas en la Cataluña urbana, 1840–1870," in Fernando Molina Aparicio (coord.). *Extranjeros en el pasado. Nuevos historiadores de la España contemporánea*. Vitoria: Servicio de Publicaciones de la Universidad del País Vasco, 2009, pp. 97–128.

[40] Michel Winock. *Histoire de l'extrême droite en France*. Paris: Seuil, 1994, pp. 51–82.

[41] *El Resumen*, 6-8-1887; Casanovas. *Bread, or Bullets!*, p. 183.

[42] ANRC, Asuntos Políticos, leg. 105, exp. 4; Casanovas. *Bread, or Bullets!*, pp. 183–5.

the immorality of Cuba, not only of its administrators: "today one doesn't go to Cuba to seek some comfort or make a modest living, but to steal; to steal, yes, as this raw phrase condenses unequivocally [...] the aspiration of every emigrant." It was so utterly unfair to put all *peninsulares* in the same boat that Moreno nuanced the statement a few pages later by claiming that he meant those who crossed the Atlantic "with a credential."[43] He meant, of course, officials who came to Cuba with a recommendation letter. Such a generalization might have been unfair as well, but it certainly reflected the mood of the day and a certain state of affairs.

Rank-and-file Volunteers shared the mood, and their officers and chief officers, who often had close links with the administration, were not spared from criticisms. Of course, the influx of young *peninsulares* more interested in joining the labor movement than to fulfil military duties might have fueled discontent among Volunteers, but the truth is that some of their officers engaged in corruption scandals too big to be ignored.[44] Though it undermined the inner cohesion, division between rank-and-file and officers could play into the hands of reformist-minded colonial authorities who thought leading *integristas* not fit to meet Cuba's need of reforms. In 1890, Captain General Manuel Salamanca wrote to Prime Minister Sagasta stating that "all the Volunteers in here [Havana] and in the provinces, are entirely on my side." Instead, he considered men like the Count of Casa Moré and Leopoldo González Carvajal, Marquis of Pinar del Río, leading members of the Constitutional Union and Volunteer chief officers, to be his true enemies.[45] Salamanca considered that men of their profile represented the intimate relationship between economic power, political influence, and administrative corruption which was alienating many Cubans from supporting Spanish sovereignty.[46]

In relation to this, corruption was not pushing Volunteers away from the very concept of Spanish national unity, but it certainly was eroding their loyalty toward colonial authorities. Some governors wrongly confused identifying the national ideal with supporting its representatives. Camilo García de Polavieja, who was appointed captain general of Cuba in August 1890, recalled a few years later that upon arriving to the island he had found that the Volunteers lacked "the good spirit they used to have. Peace had undermined their enthusiasm and politics had them divided; within their ranks there were already socialists and anarchists, and because of these, separatists too."[47]

Actually, Polavieja had never trusted entirely the Volunteers, not even when he resorted to them to organized some military agricultural colonies in Puerto Príncipe and Oriente at the end of the war in 1878–80. But he was not all wrong, for there were indeed Volunteers holding more radical ideas of social emancipation, hardly

---

[43] Francisco Moreno. *El país del chocolate (la inmoralidad en Cuba)*. Madrid: Imp. de F. García Herrero, 1887, p. 11 & 13.
[44] See, for instance, AGMM, Subinspección General de Voluntarios, caja 2997, 2998.
[45] AFAM, leg. 488, carpeta 14, carta del general Salamanca al presidente del Consejo de Ministros (Práxedes Mateo Sagasta); Villa. *Álbum biográfico*, pp. 15–17 & 21–4.
[46] Quiroz. "Corrupción, burocracia colonial y veteranos separatistas en Cuba, 1868–1910," pp. 91–111.
[47] García de Polavieja. *Relación documentada*, pp. 76–7.

compatible with being member of a paramilitary militia created for defending the sovereignty of the State. There were, indeed, anarchists among the Volunteers, some of whom actively participated in promoting such political projects. For instance, Eduardo González Bobés, who gave a speech in the first Labour Congress in the history of Cuba held on January 15–19, 1892, in Havana, in which anarchist theories predominated among the speeches delivered, some of which did not explicitly reject the idea of separation from Spain.[48] Naturally, Volunteers present in the congress did not embrace secessionist ideals, but the fact that they were able to share the same platform with fellow workers who did was a worrying symptom of the militia's morale. In any case, cases like González Bobé's remained the exception, for most labor associations in which the Volunteers were involved were demanding the betterment of labor conditions rather than revolutionary breakups with Spain. Associations of cigar-makers, coachmen, or shopkeepers, not anarchist cells, kept attracting most of working-class Volunteers.[49] But the authorities still regarded these men with great suspicion.

Captain General Polavieja thought that pure repression was the proper way to deal with labor demands, which he mixed up with separatism and aspirations of social subversion. Luckily for him, shortly after he assumed power in Cuba, he had the chance to implement his policy. On October 11, 1890, barely a month after his appointment, the coachmen of Havana went on strike and were soon joined by tram and cab drivers, cigar-makers, bakers, and other trades which mostly employed *peninsulares*. They demanded better salaries, less regulations, and, hence, fewer taxes.[50] Without transportation, laborers living in working-class neighborhoods in the outskirts of Havana could hardly make it to their workplaces, and many goods could not be transported from and to the port. Officials could neither reach their offices, and well-to-do ladies would be forced to walk through the muddy streets of Havana. Without transportation, shops would soon run out of employees and stock to sell. In short, Havana was facing the likely prospect of a general strike.

Coachmen were a particularly mobilized group of workers. Many of them were *peninsulares*, often also Volunteers, and very active in defending their interests. Almost twenty years before, on September 11, 1872, the coachmen of Havana, many of whom were members of the 5th Volunteer Battalion, had gone on strike, paralyzing the city's transport and hence the economy for a few days. As well, in 1881 they had established their first mutual insurance company, the *Sociedad de Socorros Mutuos de Cocheros Blancos*, only for white coachmen. This society provided its members with financial assistance in case of accident, medical attention, a burial, and a ticket back to the Peninsula if necessary.[51]

---

[48] Casanovas. *Bread, or Bullets!*, pp. 217.

[49] Rubén Lahullier Chaviano. "La transformación de los espacios de sociabilidad en la Cuba finisecular: el caso de la Asociación de Dependientes del Comercio de La Habana (1880–1898)." *Minius: Revista do Departamento de Historia, Arte e Xeografía*, 2006, No. 14, pp. 171–90.

[50] José Luis Luzón. "Estado, etnias y espacio urbano: La Habana 1878." *Boletín americanista*, 1991, No. 41, pp. 137–50; Casanovas. *Bread, or Bullets!*, table 8, p. 39.

[51] ANRC, Gobierno General, leg. 97, exp. 4468; Moreno Fraginals. *Cuba/España*, p. 249.

Hence, by 1890, the Havana coachmen had a certain sense of an inherited decades-long history of fighting for their rights, reinforced by the arrival of young *peninsulares* imbued with social emancipation ideals. In his reports to the minister of the Colonies, Antonio María Fabié (1890–1), in relation to the Volunteers' involvement in the strike, Polavieja explicitly accused the conscripts who were serving in the Volunteers under the 1885 recruitment law terms of being the instigators and organizers. Polavieja's distrust of the Volunteers was widely known. He was against using them to repress their comrades, as he could not guarantee they were entirely loyal to the authorities. He warned the minister that clashing with them at this point could have terrible consequences for public order, since "every Volunteer has a rifle and 70 cartridges at home." He insisted on the necessity of placing the conscripts of the 1885 law out of the Volunteers and into regular army battalions, hence under stricter military discipline, as he considered them a pernicious social element. As the Ministry of War rejected transferring the Volunteer conscripts to army units, Polavieja opted to use regular soldiers to replace the strikers in the tramlines and as coachmen. He also threatened Volunteer officers with revoking their privileges should they fail to convince their subordinates to give up. Pressure on commanding officers seems to have worked out, and as transportation slowly returned to normality, the strike was eventually called off after four days. As usual, strikers attained none of their goals, other than being given vague promises.[52]

The end of the strike was a defeat for the Volunteers, but they had shown a remarkable capacity of mobilizing different working sectors and causing trouble to the authorities. As much as he distrusted Volunteers in the countryside when he tried to establish agricultural military colonies in 1879–80 in eastern Cuba, Polavieja did not rely on the Volunteers' loyalty to the authorities ten years later. He considered that they had been infiltrated by socialists and enemies of order, leading him to believe that "in Cuba, everything conspired against Spain."[53] Despite the distrust, in his reports to Madrid, Polavieja never suggested suppressing the Volunteers. They were too important a force to be dispensed with, considering the exiguous numbers of the regular garrison in the island. By 1889, there were 22,000 regular soldiers, many of whom were unfit for service due to an unbearable high ratio of tropical diseases, for 60,000 Volunteers.[54] Instead, he considered that the Volunteers ought to be thoroughly reorganized as a reserve militia to serve as the main auxiliary force of the Spanish Army in Cuba. He was not the only one holding such idea.

Reform Projects for the Volunteers

More than ten years without a clear military role had not left the Volunteers unscarred. Since the end of the war in 1880, they had been marginalized by political parties, had been involved in unsuccessful plans to reconstruct the Cuban countryside, had been

[52] AGMM, Ministerio de la Guerra, sig. 5851.19; Casanovas. *Bread, or Bullets!*, pp. 210–11.
[53] AGMM, Ministerio de la Guerra, sig. 5851.19.
[54] Casanovas. *Bread, or Bullets!*, table 9, p. 45.

stained politically by repressing the Puerto Rican autonomists, and had been involved in a political turmoil in relation of their right to vote. Nothing really related to defending military Spanish sovereignty in the Antilles, which was their true raison d'être. Their general state by the late 1880s and early 1890s was of derelict. Anyone interested in the Volunteers' good shape was aware that a thorough reform was desperately needed. The main problem was that the main institutions with real power to implement reforms did not seem really interested, even when the bad shape of such basic elements as weapons were involved. For instance, the *Subinspección General de Voluntarios*, the organism which oversaw the Volunteer units in Cuba, sent a report to the Ministry of War on October 10, 1889, informing about the poor state of most of their weapons. Since most of the Volunteer units consisted of sections and companies scattered throughout the island made up of men with little financial resources, keeping a strict control over them was virtually impossible. Hence, the *Subinspección* requested that the ministry took care of replacing and repairing the weapons. On December 28, 1889, two months after the request reached Madrid, the official answer was that the Volunteers should take care of the weapons themselves. Clearly, the state of a colonial militia was not a priority for the Ministry of War.[55]

But in the Antilles, there were people who were indeed concerned about the Volunteers' problems. Beyond the need to renew weaponry, many of them coincided that the lack of discipline and low morale were the main problems the Volunteers needed to overcome in order to have a proper place in the Spanish military system. This was the opinion of Alejandro Menéndez Acebal, captain of the 1st Volunteer Chasseurs Battalion of Cárdenas, in the Matanzas Province. A native of Asturias and a former army officer, Menéndez Acebal had lately developed a career as journalist and was the editor of *El Eco de Cárdenas*. Due to his background, he was aware of the importance of discipline and reputation for the success of an armed force. According to him, a low military spirit was undermining the Volunteers from bottom to top. Aiming at readdressing this, in 1890 he published the *Cartilla del Voluntario*, a sort of guidebook for Volunteers in which he stressed the importance of knowing the ordinances, respecting the officers, and fulfilling their military duties properly.[56] The former army officer wanted his subordinates to behave as soldierly as possible.

Other Volunteer officers held similar opinions. For instance, Eugenio Vandama y Calderón, who had not served in the army but was the quintessential Volunteer. Born in the Canary Islands in 1849, he had settled in Cuba in 1865 where he had found a job behind the counter and became an active member of the Canary community in Havana. He first joined the Volunteers in January 1869, having seen some action during the war which earned him some military decorations. Since 1886, Vandama was the commander of Havana's 2nd Artillery Volunteer Battalion.[57] He knew the

---

[55] R.O. 28-12-1889, nº 657. Ministerio de la Guerra. *Colección legislativa del Ejército*. Madrid: Imprenta y Litografía del Depósito de la Guerra, 1889, pp. 970–1.
[56] Alejandro Menéndez Acebal. *Cartilla del Voluntario*. Cárdenas: Establecimiento Tipográfico, 1895, 2nd ed. (first published in 1890), pp. 9–13.
[57] Villa. *Álbum biográfico*, pp. 33–5; *Diario de Tenerife*, 15-04-1887, p. 2.

militia from bottom to top and could understand very well the nature of the Volunteer. A regular contributor to military newspapers, after more than two decades of service Vandama considered that the Volunteers had fallen into a state of chaos. Veterans and men who sincerely felt patriotism formed in the same companies with unmotivated young conscripts, and while Volunteers in the cities still fulfilled their main duty of protecting key infrastructures, in the countryside they did not do much.[58]

Vandama also considered that the Volunteers were suffering from an excess of pomp and circumstance. According to him, there were way too supernumerary officers, who enjoyed the privileges of the uniform in exchange of a few pesos. Supernumerary officers were men who undertook no military service, but paid a membership fee which was used to pay for the companies' regular costs, such as uniforms and weapons. In many cases they were Volunteer veterans unfit for service due to their age. They were men like Segundo Álvarez, owner of *La Corona* cigar factory and president of Havana's Chamber of Commerce, who paid a monthly fee amounting to 20 pesos as supernumerary captain of a battalion.[59] Their main reason for becoming a Volunteer supernumerary officer was the social status and manly reputation it garnered. Keeping a bond with the militia could also be a good reason. Not coincidentally, Álvarez had moved his factory to the palace of Miguel de Aldama after it was ransacked by the Volunteers in January 1869.[60]

Vandama advocated for turning the Volunteers into the colonial reserve of the army in Cuba, which should be made up of Spanish conscripts, both *peninsulares* and creoles, Black and white, between the ages of 18 and 40.[61] This would have altered the very nature of the militia. Actually, Vandama wished to make the Volunteers a colonial army in all but in name. He was not alone in thinking that Spain needed a sort of a more professional colonial militia. Julio Álvarez Chacón, an army officer with experience in Cuba, had stressed in an 1882 essay the importance for Spain of having a professional or semi-professional militia in the Antilles, made up of volunteers and conscripts, if necessary, to keep public order and assume most military needs of the island.[62]

By the end of the nineteenth century, the Spanish military policy had its particularities in the colonial context of the day. As such, there was no colonial army in the Antilles, mostly because Cuba and Puerto Rico were not colonies, but overseas provinces, part of the national territory. Also, perhaps more importantly, because the permanently stressed Spanish treasury could not afford it. The Spanish Army in

---

[58] Vandama y Calderón. *Colección de artículos*, pp. 39–66.
[59] ANRC, Donativos y Remisiones, leg. 418, exp. 29.
[60] García de Polavieja. *Relación documentada*, p. 251; J. C. Prince. *Cuba illustrated with the biography and portrait of Christopher Columbus containing also general information relating to Havana, Matanzas, Cienfuegos, and the island of Cuba with illustrations and maps together with an Anglo-Spanish vocabulary*. New York: Napoléon Thompson & Co., 1893–4, p. 121; *Gaceta de La Habana*, 28-04-1871.
[61] Vandama y Calderón. *Colección de artículos*, pp. 45–66.
[62] Julio Álvarez Chacón. *España gran potencia por su organización militar*. Santiago de Cuba: Sección Tipográfica del E.M. de la Comandancia General, 1882, pp. 41–4.

Cuba and Puerto Rico and in the Peninsula had the same structure and relied on professional officers and conscript soldiers. The only differences laid on duration of the military service, the officers' pay, and quicker promotions for those serving in the Antilles. As to the Volunteers, they could be hardly compared to colonial forces of other powers, such as Britain and France, for they were not professional soldiers, were deployed locally, and were essentially used to keep public order. Britain had created a semi-professional Volunteer Force in Cape Town in 1853 which had taken part in the South African wars against the Boer and the Zulu ever since, but mostly trusted the defense of the empire to a mix of British and native soldiers commanded by British officers, such as the British Indian Army or the many local regiments of the British Caribbean.[63] France, on its turn, had essentially built her empire after 1870 thanks to its Army of Africa, which mixed European and Muslim professional soldiers in the Foreign Legion, the African Chasseurs or the *Tiralleurs*, among other units.

Despite lacking some of characteristics of these British and French imperial forces, some voices among the Volunteers considered that taking part in a colonial adventure might in fact reinforce the very existence of the militia and redefine its role in the defense of Spain, in the Antilles and elsewhere. The chance was provided by Morocco, the southern neighbor with which Spain has had frictions from time to time. Since the peace treaty of 1860, relationship between Spain and Morocco had been generally calm, despite minor attacks launched by Berber clans every now and then against the enclaves of Ceuta and Melilla. But by 1889, the relationship deteriorated bringing both countries to the brink of war due to a series of attacks on Spanish ships and their crews by coastal Berber and Arab clansmen, plus the assassination of the sister of a Spanish diplomat in Casablanca.[64] As both governments seemed unable to reach an agreement on these issues, rumors of war began to spread. Amid these tensions, Volunteer officers saw an opportunity to renew their commitment to defending Spain.

Over the autumn of 1889, newspapers in the Peninsula and the Antilles published dozens of letters penned by Volunteers offering their men to serve the country fighting the Moroccans if necessary. On September 21, 1889, *El Correo Militar* published a letter by Volunteer Major Ramón Elices Montes, from Puerto Rico, entitled "The African Problem and the Volunteers of Cuba and Puerto Rico." Elices, a former army officer, wrote that himself and his "80,000 warrying" comrades would gladly volunteer to fight alongside the army in Africa for the glory of Spain.[65] Only two days later, the same newspaper published a letter by Pablo Ubarri offering Puerto Rico's 1st Volunteer Battalion to be sent to fight in Morocco as an "act of patriotism."[66] More letters in the same tone reached the newspaper in the following weeks coming from Cuba and Puerto Rico claiming that all the Volunteers would gladly join a good fight in Africa.[67]

---

[63] Thomas Pakenham. "The Contribution of the Colonial Forces," in Crawford & McGibbon. *One Flag, One Queen, One Tongue*, pp. 58–73.
[64] Fernández Almagro. *Historia política de la España contemporánea*, vol. II, pp. 105–6.
[65] *El Correo Militar*, 21-09-1889.
[66] *El Correo Militar*, 23-09-1889.
[67] *El Correo Militar*, 06-11-1889.

Such a display of patriotism and will to fight for Spain in Africa was mocked by the autonomist press in Cuba and Puerto Rico as a pie in the sky. Despite the rebuke by Elices himself, published by *El Correo Militar*, the truth is that Volunteers could have been hardly mobilized across the ocean to fight in Morocco.[68] Essentially, the Volunteers were not professional soldiers, had only a superficial military training, and providing for the logistics of transporting them across the Atlantic would have been too costly. The Spanish Army had thousands of men just across the Moroccan northern coast ready to intervene if necessary. And more importantly, the Volunteers were not needed in Africa because escalating tensions between Spain and Morocco cooled down in 1890, at least for a while. In October 1893, the Berber clans around Melilla attacked the city in protest against the construction of a fort on the grounds of a marabout's tomb, which was being built in its turn to give protection to the enclave's outskirts. After weeks of intense fighting during which the governor of Melilla, General Margallo, died, the government sent Arsenio Martínez de Campos to defeat the clans and settle peace with the sultan, signed in March 1894, thus ending the so-called Margallo's War.

A New *reglamento* for the Cuban Volunteers

Colonial dreams of deploying thousands of Volunteers to Africa to fight the old Moroccan foe soon faded away, if they were ever genuine, but the need to reorganize the Volunteers in Cuba remained, especially after their Puerto Rican colleagues had taken the lead. The case of Puerto Rico might have served as an example. The new *reglamento* of 1888 had successfully reorganized the Volunteers in the smaller of the Antilles, providing uniformity as to weapons and structure, and had increased its members by a firth. Puerto Rico had some advantages when it came to dealing with the Volunteers in comparison to Cuba. First, it only counted with 5,000 members; second, there were only infantry forces; third, since their very inception there had been one battalion per military department; fourth, and in relation to the latter, there had always been a more centralized command. Thus, it was easier and cheaper to provide the Volunteers of Puerto Rico with uniforms, weapons, and a coherent structure. In Cuba, on the contrary, the Volunteers were a group made up of nearly 66,000 men organized in scattered regiments, battalions, companies, squadrons, batteries, and sections of infantry, cavalry, and artillery throughout the biggest island of the Caribbean. They had been growing organically since the very creation of the militia in 1855, and whereas they had a good structure in the big cities, in the countryside the panoply and state of uniforms, weapons, and varying degrees of military instruction was the norm.

Aware of the need to put the Volunteers in order, the determination of Captain General Polavieja followed the steps of the Puerto Rican militia and called for a commission bequeathed with the task of writing a new *reglamento*. The *reglamento* of 1869 still in force had been written a bit on the rush, during the first months of the Ten

---

[68] *El Correo Militar*, 06-12-1889.

Years' War, when the Volunteers grew in a matter of weeks from a few thousand men militia mostly centered in the cities to an 80,000-strong force with units of all arms scattered across the island. It was a text aimed at providing with some order a militia which was growing organically at great speed. Understandably, the over-twenty-year-old *reglamento* lacked some more detail on organization, weaponry, and other day-to-day aspects referring to the functioning of the Volunteers.

The mix of Volunteer and army officers appointed by Polavieja to elaborate the text put up a new *reglamento* which was finally sanctioned by the Ministry of War on July 7, 1892.[69] It did not follow the path suggested by people like Vandama, in the sense that the militia should become a colonial reserve army combining volunteers and conscripts. The 1892 *reglamento* neither turned the Volunteers into a reserve army nor counted with conscripts to fill its ranks. The minister of War (1890-2), Lieutenant General Marcelo Azcárraga Palmero, a Filipino mestizo with a wide colonial experience, considered that reshaping the Volunteers as a colonial reserve army which existed nowhere else in the Spanish Monarchy could bring round unwanted political consequences. Since Cuba was de jure a Spanish national territory, having a militia so different from others in Spain might be taken as a sign that the island was drifting away from the rest of the nation. Beyond this concern, Polavieja and Azcárraga feared that combining volunteers and conscripts might mean the entry of thousands of Cuban separatists who might take advantage of getting military training which could be later used against Spain.[70] However, the new *reglamento* gave the Volunteers a more defined organization, and clarified several aspects regarding promotions, punishments, and duties that facilitated the coordination within the units and among them. The *reglamento* of 1892 attempted to tackle the problems in the esprit de corps and military capacity originating in the influx of young *peninsular* conscripts according to the law of 1885, and the growing class tensions among the Volunteers caused by the labor movement. It a nutshell, the *reglamento* of 1892 aimed at reading the Volunteers for the upcoming security challenges in Cuba.

The Volunteers and the Fight against Banditry

Far from the social tensions-riddled world of Cuban cities, the thousands of Volunteers who still existed in the countryside by the early 1890s were suffering alongside the rest of the population an endemic phenomenon which had intensified after the destruction of the agricultural system during the wars for independence: banditry. Too much fighting had destroyed hundreds of sugar mills, cattle ranches, tobacco farms, and many other forms of agricultural production, thus forcing thousands of peasant families to flee their homes looking for better prospects in the cities or in the areas less affected by the war. Banditry mostly affected the western part of Cuba, for although it had not been

---

[69] *Manual de Instrucción Militar y Reglamento comentado para el Instituto de Voluntarios de la Isla de Cuba*. Havana: Imprenta del Diario del Ejército, 1892.
[70] AGI, Diversos, 13, R.2, D.7.

the main theater of war, most of the sugar mills on which thousands of peasants depended were located there. Once the industrial production was gone, so was the agricultural. In the eastern part, on the contrary, a subsistence economy proved much more resilient to the destruction caused by over ten years of fighting.

The destruction of production systems and entire communities, which depended on the production of sugar, tobacco, or other goods, left many families deprived, thus pushing many young men to resort to banditry to make a living, but also as a form of popular response to the new economic and social situation. But banditry was also interpreted by Cuban separatists as an expression of popular support for independence, as social subversion went hand in hand with political changes. Actually, many among the bandits claimed to be robbing, extorting, and kidnapping for the freedom of Cuba.[71] For Spanish authorities, however, bandits were but simple criminals who tried to fish in troubled waters, taking advantage of an existing social unrest to justify their criminal activities. In a letter to Azcárraga, Polavieja insisted that the bandits who claimed to support Cuba's independence were merely "legitimizing their crimes."[72]

This might well have been the case, but the truth is that there were many links between banditry in Cuba and the nationalist émigré community in the United States, with its two main colonies of New York and Florida, in Tampa and Key West. After years of unsuccessful attempts at summoning efforts to launch a new campaign to liberate Cuba, the early 1890s were years of intense separatist activity. Shortly before Polavieja was appointed captain general, in 1890 Captain General Salamanca, as an act of conciliation, allowed the former rebel leader Antonio Maceo to visit Cuba, where he met with old friends and potential supporters. Almost upon arriving to Havana, Polavieja expelled him after finding that the veteran *mambí* was contacting people in order to gather money and men for a new uprising.[73]

But the very mastermind of the renewed separatist activity was José Martí, son of a Spanish sergeant, who had supported Cuban independence since his early youth and had become the undisputable rising star of the separatist movement. A very talented writer and political commentator, Martí had lived in exile for most of his adult life, in the Peninsula and in Spanish America before settling in the United States, where he created the Cuban Revolutionary Party in 1892, in South Florida.[74] Considering that any form of social unrest might help the cause, the nationalist exiles financially supported the most important bandits in Cuba, such as Manuel García, nicknamed the "King of the Cuban Fields," who claimed to be waging an irregular war against Spanish

---

[71] Eric Hobsbawm. *Bandits*. New York: Pantheon Books, 1981 (first published in 1969), p. 17; Rosalie Schwartz. *Lawless Liberators: Political Banditry and Cuban Independence*. Durham and London: Duke University Press, 1989, pp. 19–50.
[72] AGI, Diversos, Archivo de Camilo García de Polavieja y del Castillo, Diversos 19, carta al ministro de la Guerra Marcelo Azcárraga Palmero, 19-06-1892.
[73] Mármol. *Antonio Maceo. El Titán de Bronce*. Miami: Ediciones Universal, 1998, pp. 91–9.
[74] Jorge Mañach. *Martí el apóstol*. Madrid: Espasa-Calpe, 1968 (first published in 1942), pp. 198–205; Pérez, Jr. *Cuba. Between Reform & Revolution*, pp. 143–55; Rubén Pérez Nápoles. *Martí. El poeta armado*. Madrid: Algaba Ediciones, 2004, pp. 249–79; Piqueras Arenas. *Sociedad civil y poder en Cuba*, pp. 219–27.

colonialism.⁷⁵ García, who claimed for himself the title of general of Cuba's western department, even issued a war declaration on Spain on April 27, 1891, in Melena del Sur, a town in the Province of Havana. It was written in Spanish and in broken English, allegedly to reach an audience in the United States. Interestingly, he grounded his declaration in the lack of fulfilment of the Pact of Zanjón, the importation of Chinese immigrants instead of white ones, the scarce presence of Cubans in the administration, the burden of high taxes, and some other minor demands. Instead of declaring outright independence, Manuel García proclaimed the Republic of Cuba annexed to the United States and asked the US Government for help and Remington rifles.⁷⁶

But south to Florida, right on the spot, in rural Cuba, banditry was not at all that popular. Sugar mill owners were the most attractive targets for bandits, for the bounty they might represent, but were by no means the only victims. Humble *guajiros*, who often depended on a subsistence economy, were the easiest prey. Being stolen a cow, a few pigs, of half a dozen of rice sacks might mean not having food for weeks. Historically, small landowners had collaborated with the authorities to suppress any form of unrest in the countryside. In 1852, in the annual report to the authorities in Madrid, Captain General Gutiérrez de la Concha noted that *"the* guajiros *of Cuba have always been the first and foremost repressive force against the Black people uprisings: among them we find the plantation overseers who control the govern of the slaves, and whom consequently are entitled to carry on the punishments."*⁷⁷ Gutiérrez de la Concha referred to the case of rebellious enslaved people, but the *guajiros* had been also traditionally used to chase bandit gangs. Small towns sections of infantry Volunteers had been sent to capture bandits at least since the 1850s.⁷⁸ They were an ideal human material to do so. In the countryside, where most Volunteers were Cuban peasants, they knew the terrain like the back of their hands and belonged to local communities. Hence, they enjoyed a perfect knowledge of local society, its fears and aspirations, and often had family of friendship ties which might provide them with valuable information used to chase the bandits.⁷⁹ Consequently, they might inspire more confidence to their akin than public order forces sent from big cities if not from the Peninsula.

Banditry had been endemic in Cuba since the mid-nineteenth century, but it had become a major problem because of the wars of independence. Yet, the authorities did not address it as something more than a problem of public order until the arrival of Polavieja to the Captaincy General in 1890. Captain General Sabas Marín had declared the state of war in the provinces of Pinar del Río, Havana, Matanzas, and Santa Clara between April and July 1888, but it did not translate into effective policy of patrolling the countryside. Polavieja extended the state of war to Oriente in September

---

[75] Pérez, Jr. *Lords of the Mountain*, pp. 3–57; Schwartz. *Lawless Liberators*, 98–120.
[76] AGI, Archivo de Camilo García de Polavieja y del Castillo, Diversos 19, D. 9.
[77] José Gutiérrez de la Concha. *Memorias sobre el estado político, Gobierno y administración de la isla de Cuba*. Madrid: Establecimiento Tipográfico de D. José Trujillo, 1853, p. 24.
[78] AGMM, Ultramar, caja 3194, Febrero 1880; Paz Sánchez, Fernández Fernández & López Novegil. *El bandolerismo en Cuba*, vol. I, pp. 89–101.
[79] Gallego y García. *Cuba por fuera*, p. 216.

1890. Only Puerto Príncipe, barely affected by banditry, was left out of the scheme.[80] More importantly, Polavieja established an agency solely aimed at fighting bandits: the Particular Cabinet (*Gabinete Particular*).[81] It was created on September 22, 1890, as an autonomous organism within the Captaincy General that coordinated forces of the army, the Civil Guard, and the Volunteers throughout Cuba. Alongside constant patrols, persecutions, and detentions, bribing also became a tool for the Particular Cabinet. Most famously, the former *mambí* general Julio Sanguily collaborated under the table with the authorities while publicly opposing Spanish rule, and most probably played the double game, as Polavieja and other top officials suspected.[82]

Whereas the Civil Guard carried out most of the operations, the Volunteers joined patrols alongside them and the army and protected infrastructures from bandits, such as sugar mills, tobacco farms, railways, and telegraphic cables.[83] As much as they rendered good services, their participation was often problematic. According to the *reglamento*, Volunteers had to be only deployed locally, thus allowing their members to combine their military duties with their regular jobs. Only in case of war they could be mobilized outside their towns and hence put under the same military rights and duties of the regular army, which meant that they were fed and paid a stipend. But the Particular Cabinet often had them chasing bandits outside their villages without providing them with food or stipend. Town councils were also a source of trouble for the Volunteers, for local authorities often asked them to conduct permanent patrols which did not allow them to keep on with their jobs. In big towns, Volunteer battalions had men enough to rotate patrols, but in small villages, the local force of Volunteers was often a section of around 20 men, clearly not enough to protect permanently wide areas. In Tapaste, in the Province of Havana, the mayor had demanded the local Volunteers to patrol the surroundings for ten hours a day. The answer of Lieutenant Volunteer Gerónimo Rodríguez, commander of the local section, was blatantly sincere: "donning the uniform and defending the Nation is an honour for the Volunteers […] but my men are poor peasants and shopkeepers, who have to work hard every day to sustain themselves and their families. Hence, it would be extremely difficult for them to keep this service for much longer."[84]

---

[80] Paz Sánchez, Fernández Fernández & López Novegil. *El bandolerismo en Cuba*, vol. I, pp. 161–225.

[81] Paz Sánchez, Fernández Fernández & López Novegil. *El bandolerismo en Cuba*, vol. I, pp. 226–36; José Joaquín Gallego Jiménez. "La protesta rural y los mecanismos para su represión por parte del Gobierno del Capitán General Camilo García de Polavieja en Cuba: (1890–1892)." *Americanía: revista de estudios latinoamericanos de la Universidad Pablo de Olavide de Sevilla*, 2011, No. 1, pp.219–34.

[82] AGI, Diversos 19, D.7, "Parte reservado de 10 de diciembre de 1890"; AFAM, leg. 334, carpeta 3, carta de Antonio del Moral a Antonio Maura, 28-02-1893; Manuel de Paz Sánchez, "Julio Sanguily y Garritte (1846–1906) y los alzamientos de febrero de 1895 en el Occidente de Cuba." *Revista de Indias*, 1996, vol. LVI, No. 207, pp. 387–428.

[83] AGM, Ultramar, Capitanía General de Cuba, caja 3195, Bandolerismo 1890–1895, Comandancia Militar de Guanabacoa, 11 de Septiembre de 1890; caja 3195, Bandolerismo 1890–1895, Compañía de Bomberos de San José de las Lajas, 10 de diciembre de 1890; caja 3195, Bandolerismo 1890–1895, Comandancia Militar de San Antonio de los Baños, 3 de marzo de 1891; caja 3195, Bandolerismo 1890–1895, Comandancia Militar de San Antonio de los Baños, 3 de marzo de 1891; caja 3007, Güines, 1887, Comandancia Militar de Güines, Nota 5.

[84] AGM, Ultramar, caja 3195, Bandolerismo 1890–1895, Comandancia Militar de Jaruco, 15-09-1890.

The unrest caused among Volunteers by these kinds of pressures from local authorities nurtured the long-standing distrust Polavieja had always held toward them. He was especially suspicious of commanders in the smallest villages, for he considered that at least some of them were conniving with the bandits and supported a free Cuba as well.[85] Facts seem to contradict Polavieja, for there is only one case reported of connivance with bandits but with no political connections. Eustasio Méndez Rey, commander of the Volunteers in Las Vueltas, a small town nearby Havana, took part in the kidnapping and assassination of a landowner with the sole purpose of extorting the family.[86] Any connection with separatism seems unlikely. As Méndez Rey was arrested and sentenced to death by the courts, Volunteers across the island set up a campaign demanding that the penalty be commuted. Thousands of them demonstrated in Havana before the palace of the captain general, but to no avail, as Méndez Rey was executed on September 2, 1891.[87]

Such harsh measures would not end with banditry, which continued throughout the decade, despite Polavieja's successor, Emilio Calleja (1893–5), dismantled the Particular Cabinet in October 1893 in order to give a false impression of security in the countryside before the Spanish Government. Banditry was part of a state of latent insurgency in the countryside, and even made it to the start of the war. Manuel García, the "King of the Cuban Fields," kept pillaging and looting small towns around Havana and Matanzas after 1893, and quite symbolically was lowered down by a Spanish column in Ceiba Mocha, nearby Matanzas, on February 24, 1895, the very day the last war for Cuban independence started.[88] With the death of the most famous of the Cuban bandits, the fight against banditry gave way to a full-scale war.

---

[85] Paz Sánchez, Fernández Fernández & López Novegil. *El bandolerismo en Cuba*, vol. I, p.230.
[86] AGI, Archivo de Camilo García de Polavieja y del Castillo, Diversos 19, D.10; Paz Sánchez, Fernández Fernández & López Novegil. *El bandolerismo en Cuba*, vol. I., pp. 265–75; Schwartz. *Lawless Liberators*, pp. 210–12.
[87] *El León Español*, 01-09-1891.
[88] Otero Pimentel. *Memoria sobre los Voluntarios*, pp. 147–8; Paz Sánchez, Fernández Fernández & López Novegil. *El bandolerismo en Cuba*, vol. I., pp. 206–24.

9

The Volunteers' Last Stand (1895–8)

The last years of the Volunteers were marked by success and disaster. Due to the outbreak of a new war in Cuba, they played a key role in the military events, creating new units, and reaching around 90,000 members, the highest in their history. In Puerto Rico, the local Volunteers were mobilized for the first time to take up arms against the invasion of the US Army. Even in the Philippines, as we will see, imitating the example of their colleagues in the Antilles, local volunteer units were created during the Filipino Revolution. Finally, the Volunteers had a presence in all Spanish overseas territories at stake, but their fate was intrinsically associated to the continuity of Spanish sovereignty, and it was unavoidably contested. The geopolitical context paved the way for its disastrous end. The colonial distribution system set up to control the scramble which followed the Berlin Conference, which had avoided war among European powers by scrambling Africa and Asia, was exhausted by the 1890s, in favor of the English-speaking empires. The distribution exhaustion and the Anglo-Saxon puissance explained the British Ultimatum to Portugal in 1890, the Fashoda Incident of 1898, and favored the long-coveted US intervention against the Caribbean and Asian dominions of Spain, a "dying nation," in the words of the British prime minister Lord Salisbury.[1]

In the *fin de siècle* context, with no support from a great power after years of following an isolationist foreign policy, Spain may well have been considered a dying nation, but it was rather a diehard. Between 1895 and 1898, Spain faced anticolonial wars in Cuba (1895–8) and the Philippines (1896–8), which resulted in the military intervention of the United States in April 1898, and the termination of the old Spanish Empire. After this war, Cuba, Puerto Rico, and the Philippines fell under the American aegis; the United States emerged as a new colonial power; and Spain lost its empire, entering a political, military, and national crisis that has come to be known as the Disaster of 1898 (*Desastre del 98*).[2]

---

[1] Andrew Roberts. *Salisbury. Victorian Titan*. London: Phoenix, 2000 (or ed. Weidenfeld & Nicolson, 1999), pp. 689–93.
[2] Carlos Serrano. "Conciencia de la crisis, conciencias en crisis," in Juan Pan-Montojo (coord.). *Más se perdió en Cuba. España, 1898 y la crisis de fin de siglo*. Madrid: Alianza Editorial, 1998, pp. 335–403.

With the end of Spanish rule in the colonies, the Volunteers were also gone, but not without a hard fight. Thousands of them fought in Cuba, the Philippines, and Puerto Rico, both against the insurgent armies and the US invading forces. In all, around 103,000 Volunteers took up arms in the Spanish overseas territories: 90,000 in Cuba, 8,000 in Puerto Rico, and 5,000 in the Philippines. In Cuba, they defended the cities, the key infrastructure (railroads, harbors, etc.), and agricultural property which was the main target of the rebels. They defended the sugar mills and tobacco farms, whereas the regular army carried out most of the military operations. In Puerto Rico, where war only arrived with the US troops, the Volunteers were a key element in assisting the regular army in preparing for war against the new imperial power. In the Philippines, they became essential to the defense of Manila, the goal around which the whole war gravitated.

These wars in Cuba, the Philippines, and Puerto Rico demanded from Spain the most intense military effort in men and resources of its whole troublesome nineteenth century. More than 230,000 soldiers, mostly conscripts, were dispatched from the ports in the Peninsula to fight in Cuba and the Philippines, where no more than 30,000 irregular fighters in each territory held them at bay for more than three years until the US intervention determined the result of the war.[3] Such a vast mobilization of men implied a great capacity of sending resources, but a weak position in the war scenarios, for too many men were needed to fight too few—though extremely able—forces. In this context, the Volunteers were the symbol of a relatively strong loyalism, which persisted even when State control was weak. Indeed, it is understood that the central military role played by the Volunteers during the wars was a sign of the State's weakness but the strength of Spanish patriotism.

War in Cuba

On February 24, 1895, while the island was celebrating a carnival Sunday, a group of *mambises* launched the *Grito de Baire* (Proclamation of Baire), a remote town of Oriente, announcing the rebirth of the Cuban Republic and the start of a new war for independence for the third time in three decades. About sixteen small gangs followed the signal all over the island, and took to the *manigua*, the mountain areas which were the mythical stronghold of Cuban independence fighters. This new rebellion had been organized under the leadership of two veterans of the Ten Years' War, Máximo Gómez and Antonio Maceo, and the political guidance of José Martí, the intellectual that created the Cuban Revolutionary Party in 1892 whilst in exile in the United States. The main guidelines of the new uprising were outlined by the Manifesto of Montecristi (March 25, 1895), written in the Dominican Republic, where Máximo Gómez was in exile and reunited with the other rebel leaders. It declared a renewed struggle

---

[3] Baldovín Ruiz. *Cuba*, pp. 423–71; Enrique de Miguel Fernández. "Discurso de apertura del XXXI curso de Historia y Cultura valenciana: las tropas españolas en la guerra de Cuba. De las estimaciones especulativas a la cuantificación." *Anals de la Real Acadèmia de Cultura Valenciana*, 2010, No. 85, pp. 243–71.

to free Cuba from Spanish rule, called to all Cubans to gather under the banner of independence, advocated for helping Puerto Rico to gain its freedom, and promised a quick and humanitarian war. It was signed by José Martí as the political leader of the revolution and Máximo Gómez as its military commander. Antonio Maceo, a mulatto, perhaps the most brilliant soldier of the revolution, was appointed *ad hoc* a military rank, *lugarteniente general*, as Gómez's second-in-command. Prominent white revolutionaries opposed appointing a man of African descent as general, for it might shy whites away from joining the uprising, and foster ideas of social emancipation among black Cubans.

This new attempt at the liberation of Cuba was built on a profound disaffection toward Spain. The failure of both the low-tariff agreement between the governments of Madrid and Washington DC (1891–4) and the ill-fated reformist plan advocated by the Minister of the Colonies Antonio Maura in 1892–4 had convinced wide sectors of the Cuban population that a better political and economic situation was unattainable under Spain's rule.[4] The renewed fight, thus, was as much a long-standing aspiration as the offspring of frustrated expectations.

The initial reaction by the Spanish authorities was not to give too much importance to the uprising, as the insurgent movement in western Cuba was rapidly quelled, or so it seemed. Captain General Emilio Calleja had been aware of war preparations at least since the autumn of 1894. On October 7, 1894, Calleja informed Maura that he had received information on plans for a new uprising that Máximo Gómez was organizing in Santo Domingo. Additionally, the governor of Santiago de Cuba, General José Lachambre, told Calleja that insurgent veterans of the Ten Years' War, such as the Sartorius brothers and Guillermón Moncada, were recruiting able men in Oriente. The captain general reported to Madrid that he did not issue any arrest warrant as the alleged plotters had not broken the law yet, to the dismay of the government.[5] Such was the spirit of the high Spanish authority in Cuba shortly before the war.

An expedition project known as *Plan de La Fernandina*, overseen by José Martí, had been thwarted on January 12, 1895, when the US authorities, uninterested in sparkling a diplomatic conflict with Spain, seized three boats loaded with men, weapons, and ammunition which had departed from three points of the US coast and were bound for La Fernandina, Florida, and from there to Cuba. But in February 1895, war had started for good, and by early March, dozens of parties were waving the banner of independence, recruiting men, and fighting small Spanish outposts across eastern Cuba.[6] *Integristas* often blamed Captain General Calleja for his slowness in crushing the rebellion, and the Liberal Party, in power in Spain since 1892, for having somehow

[4] Elorza & Hernández Sandoica. *La Guerra de Cuba*, pp. 161–79; Louis A. Pérez, Jr. *Cuba Between Empires, 1878–1902*. Pittsburgh: University of Pittsburgh Press, 1983, pp. 3–38; José Antonio Piqueras Arenas. *Cuba, emporio y colonia*, pp. 303–8.
[5] AGP, Sección Reinados, Fondo Alfonso XIII, caja 12.832, exp. 15-A: "Telegramas entre el Gobernador General de Cuba y el ministro de Ultramar," 07-10-1894, 23-02-1895, and 24-02-1895.
[6] José Abreu Cardet & Juan José Tartaglia Redondo. "La Guerra del 1895 en el Oriente de Cuba," in Rafael Sánchez Mantero (coord.). *En torno al "98": España en el tránsito del siglo XIX y XX: actas del IV Congreso de la Asociación de Historia Contemporánea*. Huelva: Universidad de Huelva, Servicio de Publicaciones, 2000, pp. 435–48.

tolerated the free movement of Cuban separatists for the sake of reconciliation. Francisco Álvarez, a shop owner in Havana and Volunteer sergeant, wrote to his family in Valladolid that "Calleja is dominated by his wife," and that the rebellion was the fault of "reforms devised by politicians who know nothing of Cuba."[7]

In the countryside, there was little time for political debate. In many remote areas of Oriente, a local section or company of Volunteers, often made up of Cuban *guajiros*, was the only Spanish garrison. From the very beginning of the war, they became the main target of the so-called Liberating Army (*Ejército Libertador*). By the onset of the war, all the Volunteer units in Cuba could gather around 60,000 men, but far from the city, a section of less than 30 men, if lucky a company of 100, usually was the only force they could assemble.[8] From the very first moments of the war, they engaged with the enemy. A day after the war began, the *mambises* attacked the town of El Caney, famous for its fruit production, only 10 km from Santiago de Cuba.[9] War was yet to arrive to the western part of the island, but in the east the rebellion was knocking at the very doors of the main Spanish stronghold.

The lack of regular military presence in the countryside, though, necessarily weakened the forces that stood loyal to Spain. After all, Volunteers in the area were mostly peasants-at-arms, poorly trained in military tactics, and surrounded by an ocean of popular support for the rebellion. They knew from the previous wars that they could expect no mercy from fellow Cubans in case of getting caught in combat. They had relatives and their only home in Cuba, and usually the nearest Spanish force of Civil Guard or the army was miles away. Fearing the reprisal of the *mambís* and not expecting any readily assistance from regular troops, these men often opted not to directly confront the insurgency. Insurgents were not particularly well armed or disciplined, but being mostly cavalry units, they moved quickly and could attack by surprise. Often, groups of 200–300 rebels attacked villages defended by 30 Volunteers. Fighting them back was unlikely to happen, but not providing them with weapons was an alternative way to hamper their advance. For instance, Volunteer Captain Cayetano de La Maza, in Veguitas, a village just 10 km from Las Tunas, found himself alone when a 500-strong rebel party which operated in the area north to Manzanillo, headed by Esteban Tamayo and Bartolomé Masó, entered the town in early March 1895. None of the local Volunteers answered the call to take up arms. After asking for instructions from the military commander of Manzanillo, the only answer he received was to "act following your instinct and patriotism." De La Maza decided to disable 150 Remington rifles and 10 ammunition boxes so that the insurgents could not use them.[10] Events like this one are quite telling of the state of bewilderment of the Spanish authorities in the areas directly threatened by the

---

[7] Letter to his cousin Hermenegildo Álvarez, March 3, 1895. María Luisa Martínez de Salinas Alonso. *Noticias de Cuba. Cartas de emigrantes vallisoletanos en la segunda mitad del siglo XIX*. Valladolid: Instituto Interuniversitario de Estudios de Iberoamérica y Portugal, 2007, pp. 126–7.

[8] Eugenio Antonio Flores. *La guerra de Cuba (apuntes para la Historia)*. Madrid: Tipografía de los Hijos de M. G. Hernández, 1895, p. 333.

[9] ANRC, Donativos y Remisiones, leg. 418, exp. 63.

[10] *El Eco de Sitges*, 24-03-1895.

insurgency. Before a clear act of insubordination by the Volunteers, the authorities did not know how to react and only relied on the common sense and the guts of their men-on-the-ground.

The Cuban situation was clearly and rapidly getting out of hand, rendering Captain General Calleja in no position to hold back. Neither did the liberal cabinet in Madrid. It had failed at implementing any viable reforms in Cuba, it had not avoided war, and was uncapable of handling it. The government of Sagasta had failed both in peace and war. Consequently, the prime minister resigned in March 1895, and Queen Regent Maria Christina of Austria, widow of Alphonse XII, appointed a conservative cabinet headed by Antonio Cánovas del Castillo.[11] He was a man not opposed to reforms in the Antilles, but was sincerely convinced that military victory must precede a political solution for Cuba. Looking for a rapid victory, Cánovas appointed a prestigious soldier as the new captain general. Arsenio Martínez de Campos, the man who defeated the Carlist insurrection in 1876, who ended the war in Cuba in 1878, and who solved the Melilla imbroglio in 1894, arrived to Havana in April 1895 to assume command in the island for the second time in his career. Over 6,000 soldiers accompanied the "Pacifier," as the rebellion kept advancing.

Mobilizing the Volunteers

By April, the war was afoot. The commander of the Spanish forces was in Cuba. So were the leaders of the insurrection. On April 1, 1895, Flor Crombet, the man appointed by José Martí to lead the uprising in Oriente, accompanied by Antonio Maceo, landed in Duaba, a remote beach north to Baracoa. Máximo Gómez, the insurgent military leader, and José Martí, the mastermind of the rebellion, landed ten days later, on April 11, in Cajobabo, south to Baracoa. They brought men, weapons, ammunition, and the hope to summon most of the Cubans to the fight for independence. Soon they knew that the quick, humanitarian, and civilized war which Martí had promised was wishful thinking. So was the idea that all Cubans would join their banner.

The expeditionary were met by local guerrilla forces made up of Taínos, the last pockets of native Cubans who lived in small settlements around the town of Baracoa, the first city founded by the Spaniards back in 1512, and stood loyal to the Crown. Flor Crombet was killed fighting them on April 10 in Alto del Palmarito. The very descendants of those who were conquered by the Spaniards four centuries before were now fighting the sons and grandsons of Spaniards, but also of enslaved Africans, who battled for the independence of Cuba. Much embittered by the dramatic symbolism of Taínos' loyalty, Martí wrote in his campaign diary that "Those pigs fight for the peso they're paid, a peso a day [...] They are the bad neighbors of the villages, or those who have pending counts with the courts, or vagrants who do not want to work, and a few Indians from Batiquirí and Cajuerí."[12]

Flor Crombet was immediately replaced by Antonio Maceo, the so-called Bronze Titan, a veteran of the Ten Years' War, a native of Santiago de Cuba who knew well

[11] Fernández Almagro. *Historia política de la España contemporánea*, vol. II, pp. 237–43.
[12] José Martí. *Obras completas*, vol. 19. La Habana: Editorial de Ciencias Sociales, 1991, p. 222.

its region and a fighter extremely popular among independence supporters. Martí, Gómez, and Maceo held a meeting to decide the war strategy at a sugar mill called "La Mejorana" on May 5, not to meet again. The war was going to be neither humanitarian nor quick. In an encounter with regular Spanish forces at Dos Ríos on May 19, 1895, José Martí, an intellectual who rejected being put in a safe place during battle, was killed in action. In just over a month, the revolution had lost its mastermind and the commander of Oriente. But the roots of the rebellion lied deep, and despite the setbacks the fight for a free Cuba went on, as the Spanish control of Oriente grew weaker.

By the summer of 1895, the revolutionary forces dominated most of Oriente, except for the main towns, and parties of insurgents popped up in all provinces of Cuba. Supporters of Spain could only feel safe in the cities, controlled by soldiers and Volunteers. On the countryside, their situation was desperate, while the *mambí* army held ground in eastern Cuba, where troops were much needed. Regular troops garrisoning western Cuba had to be dispatched eastward, leaving wide areas almost unprotected. In this situation, the Volunteers seemed a very likely candidate to replace the regular troops in some areas where sugar mills, railways, and other infrastructures needed protection. To this purpose, on August 8 the captain general ordered that the Volunteer battalions in Havana send 100 men each to Las Villas. Each battalion disposed that a captain, 2 first lieutenants, 2 second lieutenants, 4 sergeants, 8 caporals, 2 bugles and 85 volunteers, plus 130 mounted men from the two cavalry Volunteer regiments, be sent outside of the city for at least a month.[13]

Considering that most Volunteers in Havana were not trained soldiers who depended on their regular jobs, the battalions decided to collect money in order to pay a stipend to those who wanted to see some action, or were perhaps in desperate need of some income. Soldiers and caporals were to be paid 30 pesos, sergeants 35, and the officers' pay was the same as their army colleagues.[14] Paid for by their battalion comrades and put under military discipline, a force amounting to 1,300 Volunteers paraded in front of the captain general and thousands of *habaneros* along the Parque de la India, in downtown Havana, on August 11, 1895, before taking a train at the Villanueva Station for Las Villas, where hundreds of *ingenios* and *centrales* waited for their protection. Surrounded by an electric atmosphere of flags hanging from balconies and military bands playing patriotic songs, Martínez de Campos dispatched them declaring that "True Cubans must be the first to defend property rather than destroy it."[15] Both the colonial authorities and the insurgency knew that the rebels could not rout the Spanish Army out of Cuba, but it could inflict severe damage to the very economic foundations of the Spanish edifice in the island. The war was above all other considerations a war on property in which the Volunteers were to play a key role, leaving the bulk of fighting to regular soldiers.

Soon, to acknowledge the men who had switched the working tool for the rifle, the press in Cuba and in the Peninsula wrote stories about the Volunteers' gallant

---

[13] *El Imparcial*, 23-08-1895.
[14] *La Ilustración Ibérica*, 05-10-1895, p. 631.
[15] *El Imparcial*, 26-08-1895.

defense of small towns and sugar mills in Las Villas against parties of insurgents. For instance, *El Imparcial*, the most widely read newspaper in the Peninsula, published a piece on September 16, 1895, about how fifteen mobilized Volunteers commanded by Lieutenant Enrique Maseda, entrenched in the church rooftop of a village called Salamanca, defended the town from a big group of "mostly black" insurgents who were forced to lift the attack.[16]

Over the autumn of 1895 more Havana Volunteers were sent to reinforce the mobilized garrisons in Las Villas, while the rebels hold ground in Oriente and kept advancing westward. In a clash that has come to be known as Mal Tiempo Battle, on December 15, 1895, the *mambís* defeated a Spanish force in Cruces, in the heart of Las Villas, only 28 km from the important city port of Cienfuegos, where fear was more likely seizing many. According to the press, the Havana Volunteers offered the captain general to send more men to reinforce the sugar mill garrisons, so that the regular army could put more men on the field against the insurgents. Attempting to appease their anxiety, Martínez de Campos might have fueled it even more by recognizing that he did not control the situation. In a speech delivered on January 4, 1896, to the Volunteers, he declared that though he thanked their offerings he needed them to defend Havana and its surrounding towns from the enemy, but also to keep public order. In a clumsy way to encourage the fighting men, the captain general declared that he counted on the Volunteers to fight house to house in case the rebels forced their entry into Havana.[17] Admitting such a possibility, even in an allocution to the troops, was a clear hint that despite counting on thousands of soldiers across Cuba, the Spanish forces were far from keeping the insurrection under control in the countryside.

Volunteers on the Spot

Due to their presence across the island, the Volunteers were permanently targeted by the insurrection. From major urban centers to small remote towns, they were engaged in all fronts. Actual fighting took place in the countryside, but an intense campaign of clandestine propaganda was also waged in the cities by *laborantes*, the undercover agents of the independence movement living in the cities. In Havana, Santiago, Matanzas, or Cienfuegos, the agents of rebellion tried to foster friction between the Volunteers and the Spanish authorities. They knew that convincing the Volunteers to join the rebellion was almost a pointless effort, but exploiting any frictions they may have with the captain general might be worth the effort. Commitment to the idea of Spanish national unity did not necessarily mean loyalty to the authorities. Almost a quarter of a century had passed since the expulsion of Dulce in 1869 or the execution of the medicine students in 1871, but the new war context might renew the rebellious spirit of the Volunteers.

---

[16] *El Imparcial*, 15-09-1896, p. 1
[17] *El Imparcial*, 05-01-1896, p. 1.

In the countryside, Volunteers were kept in a permanent state of alarm due to the frenetic activity of the enemy. Despite the major loss of the revolutionary political leader José Martí in May 1895, Gómez and Maceo kept the war going. Fighting became almost a daily affair in many areas of eastern Cuba. During the first months of the war, regular army units were still concentrated in the main urban areas, thus leaving the wide rural Cuba for the Volunteers to defend. According to the *reglamento* of 1892, a Volunteer section had 26 men, and a company between 94 and 140, and these were the units most common in the countryside. Thus, Volunteer garrisons of between 26 and 140 men were often the only force in the way of the *mambís*' main strategy: to burn the island down. To destroy the economy was vital for the success of their fight. Antonio Maceo, the *lugarteniente general*, or second-in-command of the rebel army, famously declared that "to annihilate Cuba, is to defeat the enemy."[18] The strategy of the *mambís* was to conduct a guerrilla warfare aimed at making it clear that Spain was no longer capable of controlling the situation. Cuba's independence needed the island to become unprofitable for Spain. Aware of their inferiority in men and weapons, but having a strong popular support in the countryside, the insurgents avoided direct clashes with the regular army; destroyed sugar mills, tobacco farms, telegraphic lines, bridges, and railways; harassed the population still loyal to Spain; and lived on the peasants' logistic support, either voluntarily or by force.[19] On February 6, 1897, the leader of the rebel army, General Máximo Gómez, summed it up in a nutshell in a letter to one of his subordinates: "it is necessary to destroy Cuba to make it free."[20]

Volunteer units scattered around the countryside had little means. They were few men defending wide areas, were poorly armed, and had barely any proper military training. Still, they had to get ready to face the *mambises*. For instance, in Sagua de Tánamo, a town in Oriente, the 75-strong local company organized a permanent force of 50 men plus a reserve of 25. Most of these men were peasants who depended on their neighbors' charity to survive since their military duties barely allowed them to work.[21] Aware of this, the town council gave them 1 *peso* per day for six days, which was not enough to provide for food. To remedy this, sixteen neighbors collected 326 *pesos* to maintain the Volunteers for two weeks, the time they reckoned it would take an army force to arrive. Facing these men, the *mambís* were fully devoted to waging war, whereas Volunteer *guajiros* had to combine their regular jobs with the armed defense of their towns, lives, and properties. Stemming from their weaknesses, the insurgents deemed that their weapons and ammunitions could be taken easily. Besides, the rebels considered that since there were thousands of Cuban Volunteers, they could be induced or forced to join the insurgency. After all, Cuba was the only land they knew. Unlike *peninsulares*, they generally had no family in Spain they could go back to in case the situation got ugly. All their family and property, if at all, were in Cuba. But beyond this reckoning, Cubans loyal to Spain knew that should they be

---

[18] Luis de Armiñán. *Weyler*. Madrid: Editorial "El Gran Capitán," 1946, p. 89.
[19] Tone. *War and Genocide in Cuba, 1895–1898*. Chapel Hill: The University of North Carolina Press, 2006, pp. 57–68.
[20] BNC, CM Gómez, No. 6.
[21] AHPSC, leg. 737, exp. 7.

captured in combat, they were most certainly going to be murdered cold-bloodedly by the *mambís*, who regarded them as mere traitors. Only in joining the rebel ranks could they hope to keep the heads over the shoulders. Therefore, the presence of army troops in small towns was so vital for the military performance of local Volunteers. Fighting alongside a regular battalion meant that the chances of resisting the attack were much higher. For a section or a company of Volunteers, having to fight a rebel force of a few hundred men on their own was almost a guarantee of defeat. Thus, the stronger the presence of regular troops, the better the military performance of the Volunteers.

In the cities, the war looked much different. As the *Ejército Libertador* swept across the countryside in Oriente, in the urban centers and in the west of the island the war had yet to arrive, at least during the early months of the conflict. In cities like Havana, Matanzas, or Santiago, independence agents tried to exploit as much as possible the inner weaknesses and divisions of their enemy. *Laborantes* tried to promote any possible conflict between the Volunteers and the authorities, hoping that the fury days of 1869 could be repeated. Captain General Martínez de Campos was not a liberal revolutionary of the likes of 1868 by any means. He staged the coup in December 1874 to speed up the returning of the Bourbons to the throne. But he was a man of compromise, prone to negotiation. In February 1878, he had negotiated with representatives of the rebel government the end of the Ten Years' War, and in 1894 he headed the Spanish embassy and concluded a peace treaty with the Sultan of Morocco after Margallo's War. Martínez de Campos was appointed by Cánovas del Castillo for conducting a firm military action, but considering his background, the door for negotiation might remain open.

Negotiations between the captain general and the rebels did not take place, but *laborantes* tried to exploit a mobilization decree which might have upset the urban Volunteers, barely willing to take part in real fight. With only 15,000 regular troops at his disposal, and with the rebellion growing strong in Oriente, on May 19, 1895, Martínez de Campos decreed that the conscripts called in 1892–4 who were serving in Volunteers units in Havana had to quit their units and join the regular army.[22] These young men, around 670, were used to raise a third battalion each to the initially two-battalion infantry regiments of Alfonso XIII and María Cristina, deployed in Ciego de Ávila to reinforce the *trocha*'s defenses.[23] Cubans were not subject to military service. This decree affected exclusively young *peninsulares*, who were mostly employed by fellow countrymen in the island's main cities, and who depended on their job for a living. Being called to quit their companies and join the army during wartime might have a negative effect on men who had chosen the Volunteers precisely for being able to find a regular job and to avoid the hardships of military life. Seeking to exploit the discontent, the network of *laborantes* quickly began to circulate in Havana a pamphlet accusing Martínez de Campos of abusing the Volunteers and calling them to take up arms against Spain.

---

[22] *Gaceta de La Habana*, 19-05-1895, p. 2.
[23] *El Correo Militar*, 31-07-1895, p. 2; *Diario de la Marina*, 28-05-1895, p. 2.

The authors of the pamphlet must have been aware that its chances of convincing any volunteer to join the rebellion were virtually inexistent, but they could fuel discontent among young *peninsulares* toward the captain general. Conscripts had taken up most of the fight during the Ten Years' War or the recent Margallo's War in Melilla. Additionally, they were forced to conduct unpaid work for three years, and were much more restricted in terms of social life and freedom of movement. The authorities knew that calling the Volunteers to join the rebellion would have no success, but nevertheless, the *Gaceta de La Habana* published on May 24 a message addressed by the captain general to the Volunteers, reminding them of their services to Spain in the past, and stressing that their contribution was much needed to quash the rebellion.[24] There is no evidence of any Havana Volunteer defecting to the insurgency during the war, but the authorities were not willing to allow the circulation of enemy propaganda among them.

The fact is that combat morale among the Volunteers was not at its peak. Not many young men were willing to join the militia, especially in the cities, which were spared from war effects for a good deal of 1895. Although it was commonly assumed that the rebellion was stronger than admitted by the authorities and published by newspapers, war was still a distant issue as seen from Havana, Cienfuegos, or Matanzas. Encouraged by the Captaincy General, the *Diario de la Marina* published an article in late June 1895 calling for more men to join the Volunteers. Quite verbosely, the newspaper called on the young Spaniards to imitate the deeds of the French that rallied to defend the Revolution in 1789, the volunteers who flocked to join the Union Army at the start of the war against the Confederacy, and the fellow Spaniards who took up arms against the Napoleon's French Army in Madrid on May 2, 1808, in defense of Spain's independence.[25] However, it seems that the morale of the Volunteers could not be lifted by an article. Growing discontent among the Volunteers affected by the decree became a great concern for their officers, who feared violent demonstrations or desertions en masse. Hence, a delegation of the Havana Volunteer units' commanders met with Martínez de Campos at the Palace of Captains Generals seeking to modify the decree without undermining his authority. The captain general soon became aware that the moral among Volunteers was very far from the one he knew twenty years before and agreed to revoke the decree, but still feared that some spirit of insubordination might be left. Instead of being transferred to the army, 150 Volunteers would be drafted in the city and dispatched to reinforce the garrisons of several sugar mills in the Province of Havana.[26]

In areas of the countryside still controlled by Spanish authorities, rebel propaganda was not very useful, for its inhabitants were largely illiterate. Instead, propaganda of the deed was much more effective. Due to the limited presence of regular army troops, and the fact that most of Volunteers in the rural areas were Cuban born, the insurgents could threaten these men, allure them by claiming kinship or even family

---

[24] ANRC, Asuntos Políticos, leg. 84, exp. 24.
[25] *Diario de la Marina*, 22-06-1895.
[26] *El Eco de Sitges*, 26-05-1895.

ties, or just by infiltrating them. In some cases, infiltration had been part of the very war preparations. Ricardo Batrell Oviedo, a young Black man who joined the *Ejército Libertador* and authored the only war memoirs by a Cuban of African descent, recalled that a Volunteer from Sabanilla del Encomendador, a small town in the Province of Matanzas, smuggled weapons from his company to the rebels as early as March 1895.[27]

The fact is whether voluntarily or forcibly, some Volunteers in remote areas had collaborated with the rebellion. As well, the very presence of rebel troops in the vicinity might have restrained many peasants from joining the Volunteers out of fear of reprisals. This situation was only worsened by Arsenio Martínez de Campos's strategy of distributing small garrisons across Cuba to defend sugar mills and railroads, the heart and veins of Cuban economy, in order to keep the landowners' support.[28] This strategy of disseminating troops, which included the use of Volunteers, made the Spanish position weak everywhere but strong nowhere. It resulted in poorly defended sugar mills and railroads, and small towns left to the only defense of the Volunteers, often badly fed and ill-trained. In Matanzas, Cuba's sugar heartland, mills were usually garrisoned by 15–20 poorly trained Volunteers who usually had to defend their position against forces of 50–100 *mambises*. Beyond this essential difficulty, providing them with ammunition and feeding them also became a major problem, for sugar mills were often surrounded by *mambí*-controlled areas, which meant that peasants were not allowed to trade with anyone in a Spanish-held position. On their part, peasants who traded food with Spanish forces often ended up hanging from a palm tree.[29] The only option left for the Volunteers garrisoning sugar mills was to conduct razzias in nearby towns, or wait for a convoy to arrive, often at the cost of a fight and several deaths.

In this situation, the strategy of disseminating forces to protect sugar mills and railroads soon proved untenable. The insurgent army kept gaining control of the countryside, at the cost of undermining the Spanish position and morale. Very few men dared to join the Volunteers, trade with Spanish forces, or even to admit publicly of supporting the Spanish cause, at the cost of one's own life. A conscript passing by the small town of Tuinucú, in Las Villas, with his battalion, recalled finding the quartered corpse of an Asturian who had been hacked to death by the *mambís* for the mere fact of being a *peninsular*, according to townsfolk accounts.[30] And it was not a rare case. News soon reached the cities by mail or mouth-to-ear accounts, which contradicted the victorious tone of the press. Francisco Álvarez, a Volunteer sergeant and a shop owner, wrote from Havana to his cousin in Valladolid that "The war the *mambís* are waging on us is barbaric, for they show no respect. They catch the wounded, hack them to pieces, rape women, kill every shop employee for the crime of being a Spaniard, burn and

---

[27] René González Barrios. *Apuntes autobiográficos de la vida de Ricardo Batrell Oviedo*. Havana: Editorial de Ciencias Sociales, 2014, pp. 8–10.
[28] Tone. *War and Genocide*, pp. 113–22.
[29] AGMM, Capitanía General de Cuba, Asuntos Generales, Gobierno Militar de Matanzas, Destacamentos, cajas 3079, 3080, 3081.
[30] José Moure Saco. *1102 días en el Ejército español. Recuerdos de un soldado en la Guerra de Cuba*. Havana: Ediciones Boloña, 2001, p. 41.

destroy anything they find on their way."[31] As the countryside was rapidly becoming rebel land, the general impression was that the situation was getting out of hand, and that the captain general was unable to cope with the war waged by the *mambises*.

Attempting to redress the situation in Oriente, Martínez de Campos organized a tour across the region to visit and encourage the main garrisons. One of the first steps was to take him alongside Brigadier Santocildes from the port town of Manzanillo to Bayamo, an iconic city for Cuban nationalism for it was the cradle of the 1868 insurrection, and the city they made martyr by burning it to the ground before abandoning it to the enemy in January 1869. On their way, the around 1,500-strong convoy was attacked by over 1,000 *mambís* commanded by Antonio Maceo himself, in the town of Peralejo on July 13, 1895. Though the convoy made it to Bayamo, Brigadier Santocildes was killed alongside many of his men, and with them Martínez de Campos's confidence in his own ability to win the war. A few days later, on 25 July, St. James Day, Saint Patron of Spain, Martínez de Campos sent a letter to Prime Minister Cánovas del Castillo, telling him that "the few Spaniards that there are on the island, only dare to call themselves as such in the cities," and that "there are only a few men that still want to join the Volunteers in the countryside." In the same letter, he observed that most of Cuba's population supported the rebel army. To counter that, he pointed out the possibility of putting peasants, on whom the rebels relied for logistic support, into concentration camps. Additionally, he admitted that he was not a man up for this task, as he could not take such a measure as the representative of a "civilised nation." Instead, he suggested Valeriano Weyler as the man to carry out such a war.[32] Blatantly, Martínez de Campos was admitting that he was unable and unwilling to turn the war tide in favor of Spain, and hence was asking to be replaced.

These words seem to have accurately depicted the situation, which was precisely the result of Martínez de Campos's policy. The vulnerability of the Spanish presence in the countryside allowed the insurgency to consolidate the rebellion in Oriente, and to begin the most daring military action of the entire war: bringing the war from east to west in the campaign known as Invasion of the West (*Invasión a Occidente*). A main cause for rebel defeat in 1878 was that war remained mostly constrained in eastern Cuba, due to regional and racial divisions within the insurgent army and the ability of the Spanish authorities to exploit them. Most of whites from west Cuba, where they represented two thirds of the population, deeply distrusted, and despised the overwhelmingly Black and mulatto troops coming from Oriente. On top of this, the very notion of Cuban nationhood was still on the making, as attachment to one's region was much stronger than a vague idea of a Cuban nation. As a result, *mambí* soldiers often refused to fight outside of their native area and deserted when they were forced to trespass the borders of their region.

---

[31] Francisco Álvarez to Hermenegildo Alonso, 20-09-1895. Martínez de Salinas Alonso. *Cartas de Cuba*, pp. 141–5.

[32] AGP, Sección Reinados, Fondo Alfonso XIII, caja 12.832, exp. 9: "carta de Arsenio Martínez de Campos a Antonio Cánovas del Castillo, 25-07-1895"; Elorza & Hernández Sandoica. *La Guerra de Cuba*, pp. 194–5.

But in 1895, rebel leaders were determined to overcome these divisions by taking war from east to west. On October 22, 1895, Antonio Maceo gathered the so-called Invading Army (*Ejército Invasor*) in Mangos de Baraguá, the small town where he had rejected Martínez de Campos's peace offers back in 1878, and started the conquest of the west. Starting the campaign that very day, this army swept across Cuba from east to west, fighting its way nearly 1,100 km until they entered Mantua, in the easternmost province of Pinar del Río, on January 22, 1896.[33] Although the rebels took no major city during the campaign, their biggest success was to bring the war to western Cuba, the heart of Spanish power on the island, with its political center in Havana and sugar and tobacco heartlands in Matanzas and Vuelta Abajo, in Pinar del Río. The *Invasión* also revealed the Spanish incapacity to keep the countryside under control. The rebel army never exceeded 30,000 men in arms during the war, so it avoided a major battle with an army that could count on more than 150,000 in the island, although many of them were in the hospitals languishing from tropical diseases. Instead, they opted for selective attacks and staged the so-called *campana de la tea*, or torch campaign. They focused on burning cane fields and sugar mills, tobacco farms, blowing up railways, cutting telegraph lines, and looting towns, which were often defended by the Volunteers.[34]

Small towns were particularly easy prey for the insurgents, for the weak defense posed by Volunteers in some cases, the tiny army garrisons—if any at all, a good share of sympathizers, and the possibility to loot shops and houses which could provide weapons, ammunition, clothing, and food, but also, either voluntarily or by force, and recruits and women, often prey to raping and all kind of abuses. Before this, the response of the Volunteers and the local population often depended on the support provided by the regular army, and was determined by the fact that the Volunteers, which were predominantly Cuban in small towns, could expect no mercy from the rebels in the event of being caught in combat. The *mambís* felt a deep hatred for fellow Cubans who stood loyal to Spain, especially the Volunteers, regarding them as traitors to the cause of a free Cuba.[35] Simply possessing travel documents issued by the Spanish authorities could lead to loyalist Cubans being killed. The *mambí* officer Enrique Loynaz del Castillo hanged two Cubans in Colón (Matanzas) in July 1897, for the mere fact of bearing two Spanish safeguards.[36] When captured alive in combat, Cuban Volunteers were systematically hacked to death or hanged. Only on some occasions they were given the chance to join the rebel forces in order to save their lives.[37]

Consequently, when there was no army garrison at all in the town, local Volunteers often surrendered to the *mambís*, especially as news of the atrocities committed by the advancing rebel army reached the west. San Antonio de los Baños, a town famous among Havana's affluent families for its hot springs, was taken by Antonio Maceo and

---

[33] José Miró Argenter. *Cuba: crónicas de la guerra*. Havana: Editorial de Ciencias Sociales, 1970 (first published in 1909), pp. 116–281.
[34] Tone. *War and Genocide*, pp. 139–52.
[35] Ibid., pp. 139–41.
[36] Enrique Loynaz del Castillo. *Memorias de la guerra*. Havana: Editorial de Ciencias Sociales, 1989, p. 497.
[37] Ibid., pp. 145–52.

his men on January 6, 1896. The only defense was a local company of Volunteers, who gave up without firing a shot, and surrendered around 500 rifles plus ammunition. Not posing resistance was a clear violation of the ordinances which could be severely punished by a military court, but this was a threat more distant than the rebels who were to enter the town. The Volunteers had taken positions in the fortified church but decided not to resist the attack after the pleas of their fellow townsfolk, who yelled at them that to resist would mean having the town burnt down by the rebels.[38] By giving up their weapons, they might also probably avoid being hacked to death, and perhaps sparing their relatives and akin from being robbed, their homes looted, their shops assaulted, and their women abused. Finally, the *mambís* entered the town; seized weapons, ammunition, food, and clothing; and get some new recruits, but spared the town from looting and a bloodbath. Though the local Volunteers refused to put up a fight, none of them joined the rebel ranks.[39] There must have been a mix of feelings among the inhabitants of San Antonio de los Baños as the *mambís* left the town after a few hours. Certainly, many of the people welcomed them as fighters for Cuba's freedom, whereas many others felt they had been invaded by a force which stood for a cause they rejected, or at least did not support. When the people begged the Volunteers to not resist the rebels, sparing the town from disaster, rather than supporting the fight for independence, was their major concern. Such was the nature of the civil war that was being fought in Cuba.

When the Volunteers fought side by side with regular troops, the situation was drastically different. The combination of regular army fighting with the Volunteers as auxiliary troops made towns much more impenetrable for insurgent forces. A good example of this was provided by the combat for Candelaria. A town about 50 km east to San Antonio de los Baños, Candelaria stood in the Province of Pinar del Río, in the area known as Vuelta Abajo, heart of the Cuban raw tobacco production, which was mostly produced by Canary islanders and their descendants, plus a sizeable community of free Black people. In 1896, it was defended by a four-company Volunteer battalion commanded by Colonel Remigio Humara, a local merchant, two Volunteer squadrons, and fifty men from the San Quintín Battalion, one of the army's finest. On February 5, 1896, the town was put under a thirty-hour attack by a rebel force commanded by Antonio Maceo, which clashed against a fierce resistance put up by the local garrison. The local Volunteers were a mixture of Basques and Cubans, among whom many of African descent, who also donned the distinctive Basque beret, or *boina*, of their comrades. Their combativeness enraged Maceo, who yelled at their troops that all Black Volunteers were to have the throat cut should they take the town. Far from weakening it, this menace possibly intensified the defense, which was labeled as "heroic" by the *mambí* chronicler José Miró Argenter, a Catalan journalist who joined Maceo's forces since the early stages of the war.[40] Despite having taken several of the blockhouses which conformed the outer defenses of Candelaria, and burnt several houses, the

---

[38] AGMM, Ultramar, Capitanía General de Cuba, Subinspección General de Voluntarios, caja 3001, Encausados Sumariados, 1896.
[39] Miró Argenter. *Cuba: crónicas de la guerra*, pp. 222–9.
[40] Ibid., pp. 328–42.

rebels withdrew after realizing the impossibility of taking the town. Candelaria was an example of the good fighting skills of the Volunteers fighting alongside army soldiers, better military trained, and another example that, in the countryside, the war pitted Cubans versus Cubans.

The combat of Candelaria was a good example of the collaboration between Volunteers and soldiers, but it was also a reminder that the war was not going well for Spain. Since the *Ejército Invasor* had reached the easternmost tip of Cuba on January 22, 1896, when Maceo entered the town of Mantua, it had been fighting Spanish forces back and forth, much superior in numbers. Retrieving the concept of the Júcaro-Morón military line of the Ten Years' War, a new 50-km *trocha* built between Mariel and Majana and garrisoned by around 15,000 men, managed to enclose Maceo in Pinar del Río, but was proving not enough to capture him. In the rest of the island, the cities remained under Spanish control, but wide regions of the countryside became rebel land.

In Cuba, the situation remained stuck during the last half of 1895, the idea of replacing Martínez de Campos began to take shape. In the Peninsula, the press, the bourgeoisie with Antillean interests, and conservatives in power insistently demanded that he be replaced. In Cuba, the Volunteers, especially commanding officers, were at the forefront of opposition against Martínez de Campos. But lower ranks were also permeated by the idea that the "Pacifier" would not be able to end the ongoing war. His plan to combine fighting while leaving an open door for negotiations was proving a disaster. In September 1895 *El Correo Militar*, the most popular newspaper among the military, published an anonymous letter from "a merchant and Cuban Volunteer officer" who summed up the militia's feeling toward the captain general and his approach to war: "Thinking about politics in Cuba in the current circumstances, it feels to me like a house owner discussing minor reforms with the architect while the house is aflame. Let's extinguish the fire first, and then we'll have time to discuss the rest after we've learnt the due lesson, if is ever proves useful to us."[41]

The fact is that insisting rumors of a coup against Martínez de Campos began to circulate by late 1895. Saber-rattling in Havana's Volunteer battalions became dangerously persistent.[42] One of these men wrote to his relatives in Spain that "all good Spaniards [...] know that Martínez de Campos would like to make a shady deal with the rebels," but he does not because he "knows the Government would not allow to it, and we [Volunteers] would stop him."[43] The continuity of Martínez de Campos, who had admitted himself his failure in the mentioned letter to Cánovas del Castillo, was untenable. His replacement suggestion was heard, and Valeriano Weyler was appointed new captain general of Cuba. *El Correo de España*, a Buenos Aires newspaper very

---

[41] The letter was first published in *La Justicia*. *El Correo Militar*, 25-09-1895, p. 1.
[42] Andreas Stucki. *Las guerras de Cuba. Violencia y campos de concentración (1868–1898)*. Madrid: La Esfera de los Libros, 2017 (or. *Aufstand un Zwangsumsiedlung. Die Kubanischen Unabhängigkeitskriege (1868–1898)*. Hamburg: Hamburger Edition, 2012), p. 100.
[43] Francisco Álvarez to Hermenegildo Alonso, November 1895. Martínez de Salinas Alonso. *Noticias de Cuba*, pp. 146–9.

popular among the local Spanish community, hence not subject to the tight censorship imposed upon press published in Spanish territory, considered the stepping down of Martínez de Campos a victory of the Volunteers.[44]

Weyler's Total War

Valeriano Weyler y Nicolau, a veteran soldier who, at 58, had not missed a war fought by Spain since 1858, was politically considered a liberal. He was a soldier of a vast experience, both in the Peninsula and in the colonies. He had commanded troops during the war of Santo Domingo, the Ten Years' War, and the Third Carlist War. He had been captain general of the Philippines between 1888 and 1891, where he expanded Spanish control of the archipelago's southern islands by quashing Muslim resistance. Between 1893 and 1896, right before arriving to Cuba, Weyler had been appointed captain general of Catalonia, where he was charged with repressing the wave of terrorist attacks carried out by anarchists in Barcelona.[45] When he took command of Cuba, Weyler was a man in his late fifties hardened after decades of assuming control of extremely difficult areas. He had been forged in war and was instructed by the government to do whatever it took to keep Cuba Spanish. This included locking peasants into camps. Either voluntarily or forcibly, rural populations provided information and logistics to the rebels. In any guerrilla war, the collaboration of the rural inhabitants proves vital for the insurgency. Ready to tackle it, Weyler assumed Cuba's command on February 10, 1896.

Upon arriving aboard the *Alfonso XIII* to the harbor of Havana, Weyler declared to the press that "I am not here to deliver candies." Everyone understood. On his way to the harbor to the palace of the Captaincy General, escorted by hundreds of Volunteers who provided for security, *integristas* cheered Weyler on their thousands, whereas supporters of independence made up their minds that they needed to commit to a harsher war. The autonomists, who considered that political reforms and negotiations could end the war, were forced to take sides. In his inauguration speech, he exposed neatly that one could be either with him or against him: "To me, in Cuba, there are only Spaniards and separatists. My mission in relation to this will be telling friends from foes, making a clear distinction between those who love Spain and those who fought against it."[46] Hence, no room for reformists, autonomists, or negotiations were to be expected under Weyler's command.

His strategy rested on two pillars. On the one hand, he was to wage a maneuver war, placing his forces in an offensive position. The army was to be taken from the cities to the countryside, where columns of around 200 regular soldiers were to chase rebel parties with the help of guerrillas, locally recruited units made up of

---

[44] *El Correo de España*, 26-01-1896, p. 5.
[45] Gabriel Cardona & Juan Carlos Losada. *Weyler. Nuestro hombre en La Habana*. Barcelona: Editorial Planeta, 1997, pp. 15–153.
[46] *El Imparcial*, 11-02-1896, p. 1.

peasants who knew every inch of the territory and did not differ much from the rebel soldier. Weyler also allowed landowners to pay for the protection of small groups of soldiers and Volunteers. In the cities, the Volunteers were to be given more military training and bestowed with the defense of most towns with the assistance of minor army garrisons. As part of this strategy, Weyler convinced a group of Havana's elites of bankers, businessmen, and top officials to create a Volunteers unit to keep public order in the city, which would allow much of the local garrison to be sent to operations. In February 1896, the 1,200-strong Urban Volunteers Battalion was created, rapidly deploying its companies to protect key areas of the city. It was commanded by Ramón de Argüelles, a prominent Asturian businessman, banker, and member of the Constitutional Union. But Weyler also thought the Volunteers as a force able to increase army garrisons and join them in the fight. To this effect, he created two mobilized Volunteer battalions, dubbed Gallegos and Matanzas, who were recruited among the existing units in Havana, and sent to reinforce the operational forces stationed in Las Villas.[47] So persistent was the participation of Volunteers in mobilized garrisons outside their areas that by the end of 1897, there were no less than 22,000 of them defending key infrastructures across the island.[48]

On the other hand, he was to implement the *reconcentración*, the Spanish word for relocating the entire peasant population into fortified areas, aimed at depriving the enemy of the logistical support that *guajiros* provided either voluntarily or forcibly.[49] This was undoubtedly the most controversial measure conducted during the war. Concentrating prisoners of war was a common practice in nineteenth-century warfare. Captured soldiers were used as a pressure mechanism against the enemy. Concentration camps had been established in the United States during the Civil War, and in Spain during the Third Carlist War, for example. But relocating civilians into camps was uncommon. In Cuba, limited and localized concentration of rebel leaders' relatives had been conducted during the Ten Years' War. But the scale of the population relocation Weyler intended to carry out was unseen. Out of a population of about 1.5 million for the whole island, around 400,000 peasants were *reconcentrados*, out of whom *c*. 150,000 perished of starvation and maladies.[50] Thus, one in ten inhabitants of Cuba was killed due to the concentration of Weyler, who began to be dubbed "butcher" by Cuban nationalists and by the press in the United States and elsewhere.[51]

The basic idea of the *reconcentración* was not to annihilate Cuba's peasants, but to impede them from providing support to the rebel army by locking them into camps which were to have their own crops, allowing them to trade with the cities,

---

[47] Valeriano Weyler y Nicolau. *Mi mando en Cuba (10 Febrero 1896 a 31 Octubre 1897). Historia militar y política de la última guerra separatista durante dicho mando*. Madrid: Imprenta, Litografía y Casa Editorial de Felipe González Rojas, 1910, vol. I, p. 145.

[48] Valeriano Weyler y Nicolau. *Mi mando en Cuba (10 Febrero 1896 a 31 Octubre 1897). Historia militar y política de la última guerra separatista durante dicho mando*, vol. V. Madrid: Imprenta, Litografía y Casa Editorial de Felipe González Rojas, 1910, p. 42.

[49] Stucki. *Las guerras de Cuba*, pp. 106–29; Tone. *War and Genocide*, pp. 153–78.

[50] Jordi Maluquer de Motes. *España en la crisis de 1898: de la Gran Depresión a la modernización económica del siglo XX*. Barcelona: Península, 1999, p. 39.

[51] Tone. *War and Genocide*, 153–78.

and promoting the participation of peasants in the defense of the camps. A negligent implementation in providing proper housing, clothing, and feeding, and the precarious health conditions in Cuba, which were decimating the Spanish Army as well, were the main cause of the terrible tragedy experienced by *reconcentrados*.

In fact, Weyler's policy was meant to put some order into the chaotic waves of refugees who had been settling disorderly in towns since the start of the war. Thousands of *guajiros* had been trying to escape from war hardships by leaving the countryside for the cities, where no combats were fought. Many in rural Cuba might support the idea of independence, but not much were willing to undergo what it entailed. Some others, probably a minority, also escaped the countryside for being sincere supporters of Spain. Among the refugees there were Volunteers too. Crammed into shanty towns improvised around major cities, no formal steps were taken by the authorities to assuage the poor living conditions of the refugees. Stacked into huts and with no resources available, begging and prostitution usually became the only way out of starvation when charity was not enough.[52] Town councils set up improvised soup kitchens and basic housing with the Catholic Church's assistance, but city dwellers generally regarded the *reconcentrados* with suspicion as infection bearers, and even by some as independence supporters, and by others as collaborators of Spain.

The formal *reconcentración* envisioned by Weyler was meant to organize this chaos, though its actual implementation was more often characterized by corruption, negligence, and a lack of basic coordination. Hence the terrible death toll. The first concentration decree was issued on February 16, 1896, affecting the eastern provinces of Santiago de Cuba and Puerto Príncipe, plus the Sancti Spiritus jurisdiction in the Santa Clara province. These were the areas where the rebellion was strongest, but since the *mambises* kept fighting, the measure was extended to the rest of Cuba on October 21, 1896, covering the provinces of Havana, Matanzas, Pinar del Río, and all of Santa Clara.

The Spanish authorities bear most of the responsibility for the horrors experienced by the thousands of peasants who were forcibly relocated into camps far from their homes. But the tragedy stemmed to a certain degree from the type of war waged by the *Ejército Libertador*.[53] By "destroying Cuba in order to make it free," the whole economic system of the countryside was shattered. The burning of sugar mills, tobacco farms, and cattle ranches directly affected the landowning elite, who generally sided with the Spanish authorities, but also deprived humble peasants from some of their best clients by interrupting the production-consumption flow. In addition to this, the *mambís* strictly prohibited peasants from trading with the Spanish-controlled areas, impeding peasants from selling their products in urban markets, let alone feeding the thousands of Spanish regular soldiers. Máximo Gómez and other rebel leaders explicitly ordered that any peasant trading outside *mambí*-controlled areas be hanged, claiming the lives of unknown droves of *guajiros*. Some rebel leaders were lenient with regards to this,

---

[52] Josep Conangla. *Memorias de mi juventud en Cuba. un soldado del ejército español en la guerra separatista (1895-1898)*. Barcelona: Ediciones Península, 1998, p. 174; Miró Argenter. *Cuba: crónicas de la guerra*, pp. 629-37; Pérez Guzmán. *Herida profunda*, pp. 39-59;

[53] Ibid., pp. 90-8.

but some others went further. Even before Weyler's formal *reconcentración*, Carlos Roloff, a Polish veteran of the US Civil War and the Ten Years' War who was appointed chief of the rebel army in Las Villas, had ordered in August 1895 that all peasants living within a mile of any Spanish garrison be put to death.

This harassment of peasants from both Spanish and rebel armies forced them to either flee to the cities or to join the insurgent ranks. Ricardo Burguete, a Spanish Army officer who commanded a guerrilla made up of Cuban peasants, admitted that Weyler's forcible relocation and property destruction policy had driven entire families into the rebel ranks. On the other side, a young officer in the US Consulate in Havana admitted to a revolutionary agent that the *reconcentración* had been the most effective recruiter for the rebel army.[54] The other side of this were the thousands of *guajiros* who fled to the cities, and in crude war logic, they became a problem for Spanish authorities for they were droves of people who needed food, housing, clothing, and were often infected by maladies out of their poor living conditions.

In this catastrophe, the Volunteers played a twofold role. On the one hand, they assisted the regular army in enacting the forcible relocation of peasants from the countryside into Spanish-controlled towns. Hence, they partook in the destruction of peasants' houses, the burning of crops, the killing of cattle, and, on some occasions, the many types of abuses inflicted upon unarmed men, women, and children. This was the price paid by families who refused to leave their homes and had to be violently forced to do so. Many of these families probably supported the fight for a free Cuba, but many others simple rejected to quit the only home they knew.

On the other hand, among the thousands of country people who took refuge in the cities fleeing from the rebels, there were many Volunteers with their relatives. Beyond the war hardships underwent by all in the countryside, being a Spanish supporter in small towns controlled by the *Ejército Libertador* was a quick shortcut to the grave, let alone being a Volunteer. Entire families fled to army-controlled areas, and formed camps nearby and around the cities, and along the *trochas*, who were often attacked by *mambí* forces who regarded them as traitors. Some of them formed close-knit communities who openly admired Weyler's harsh policy against the rebels. For instance, the villagers of the tobacco-producing Luis Laso Valley in Pinar del Río, many of whom were descendants of Canary islanders and had formed local Volunteer units, renamed the area as "Weyler's Valley" in a clear political statement.[55]

All of Cuba was affected by the war, but some provinces endured more hardships than others. Pinar del Río was particularly affected. From January 1896 until the death of Antonio Maceo in December of that very year, Pinar del Río was the center of constant military action between Spanish troops and insurgent forces that burnt down or ransacked most of the towns.[56] Despite having far more men than the rebels, the

---

[54] See Fernando J. Padilla Angulo. "*Reconcentración* in Cuba (1895–1898)," in Fernando Puell de la Villa & David García Hernán (eds.). *War and Population Displacement. Lessons of History*. Brighton, Portalnd & Toronto: Essex University Press, 2018, pp. 117–35.

[55] *Diario de la Marina*, 29-04-1896, p. 29.

[56] Miró Argenter. *Cuba: crónicas de la guerra*, pp. 420–508 & 523–654; Tone. *War and Genocide*, pp. 179–92.

Spanish forces were unable to expel the rebels from Pinar del Río. More than 16,000 Spanish regular soldiers were incapable of defeating the 4,000 *mambís*, mostly cavalry forces. Their high mobility and skillful management of attacks by surprise allowed them to destroy farms and ransack towns throughout that year.[57] As in eastern Cuba, the Spanish forces were widely disseminated throughout the territory, and the rebels only attacked a town when they outnumbered the defenders. One estimate was that there were 12,000 Volunteers in the province, remaining trapped in an enclosed warzone and stuck in their hometowns.[58] Seeking to isolate the province and "cleansing" it of rebel forces, Weyler ordered the construction of the Mariel-Majana *trocha*. The works began on March 18, 1896, stretching along 50 km north to south with a series of forts and outposts garrisoned by 15,000 men.[59]

Loyalist *Reconcentrados*

Within enclosed Pinar del Río, thousands of peasants were suffering from *reconcentración* harsh effects and *mambí* harassment. Most of them had been displaced forcibly, including independence supporters and people who perhaps had no clear ideological leaning but refused to leave their home behind. For some others, however, the *reconcentración* was the only way to save their lives, for their known allegiance to Spain. This was the case for the *reconcentrados* in some of the fortified towns that were built along the valleys and coast of Pinar del Río.

One of them, Dimas, was a small settlement in the northern coast of the province, about 90 km east to the town of Pinar del Río. It had a garrison consisting of Marines, some men from the Wad Ras Battalion. A gunboat named *Flecha* patrolled its coast. Thanks to the reports sent by Lino Galán, the town military commander, to the brigadier in charge of the area, we know that *guajiros* loyal to Spain had been flocking to Dimas even before the formal concentration decree of October 1896. Most of them were Volunteers and *guerrilleros* who took their families to a safe place, escaping from the harassment of the rebel army which had entered Pinar del Río in January 1896. According to Lino Galán, they feared reprisals from their own neighbors as well. He considered that most of the countryside collaborated with the insurgents as they reckoned their victory over the Spanish troops was imminent, but not because they sincerely supported the independence movement.[60] Consequently, only those who had openly supported Spain and could expect nothing but death by the rebels sought shelter in Dimas. Since mid-1896, Dimas began to attract more loyalists from the nearby towns of Mantua, Remates, Bajas, and Guane. These men and their families contributed to their own alimentation and defense since their arrival. They

---

[57] Manuel Piedra Martel. *Mis primeros 30 años*. Havana: Editorial de Ciencias Sociales, 2001 (first published in Minerva, 1943), pp. 97–100.

[58] Arturo Amblard. *Notas coloniales*. Madrid: Ambrosio Pérez y Compañía, 1904, p. 163.

[59] Miró Argenter. *Cuba: crónicas de la guerra*, pp. 242; Weyler. *Mi mando en Cuba*, vol. I, pp. 131–9.

[60] AGMM, Ultramar, Capitanía General de Cuba, Subinspección General de Voluntarios, caja 4123, Dimas.

not only ploughed the crop zones established around the town but also surrounded it with a barbed-wire fence, built several forts, and took part in the defense alongside regular soldiers.

The very existence of a place like Dimas was a symbol against the rebel's claim that all Cubans backed them in their fight for the island's independence. And it was a symbol which could not be ignored. In his report, Galán informed of the many attacks suffered by the village's outer forts and crops. The attacks could have been aimed at securing food with which to feed the rebel ranks, but also were a vengeance against these *reconcentrados* loyal to Spain, who ought to be deprived of food and protection, according to the insurgents.[61] Cubans fighting for Spain had to pay for it. The fact is that Dimas could only rely on its own resources. Regular soldiers, Volunteers, *guerrilleros*, and their relatives worked the land and defended the town. Not much help could be expected to arrive from Pinar del Río or Havana, beleaguered as the war went on. Despite this, or perhaps because of this, Dimas was a success story. Its dwellers knew that failure was not an alternative, and more and more loyalists settled in the area, to the extent that Galán warned his superior that "due to the arrival of new people, we cannot fit them into the town." Thus, new crop areas and fortified settlements were built around the original area of Dimas, most notably in Tumbas de Estorino. Dimas and the settlements around it became self-sufficient, even establishing proper municipalities. One of these settlements, Bartolo, had a mayor and a town council appointed, which even considered constructing a telegraphic line to connect all the settlements around Dimas.[62] The settlement held its ground, and even after the formal end of the concentration decreed by Weyler's successor in March 1898, the town continues to exist to this day.

Stalemate

As the war went on to its second year, it got stuck in a sort of stalemate by 1897. The previous year had been extremely intense. While the rebel army extended the war across Cuba and kept Spanish positions on their toes, both sides engaged in a maneuver war of marches and countermarches, especially in central Cuba under the able command of Máximo Gómez and Valeriano Weyler. In the west, Antonio Maceo had been enclosed in Pinar del Río, but after crossing the Mariel-Majana *trocha* in order to meet with Gómez to discuss the war strategy, he was killed in combat by a column commanded by Major Cirujeda on December 7, 1896, in Punta Brava, only 25 km from Havana. This was a major loss for the *Ejército Libertador*, who lost its most formidable commander. While Cuban nationalists mourned the death of Maceo, among Spanish supporters many hoped that it would end the war. Church bells were rung from Havana to Madrid, from cathedrals to small towns' churches, and thousands of people gathered around the newspaper's offices to get the latest news on the event, while patriotic demonstrations were organized.

[61] Stucki. *Las guerras de Cuba*, pp. 185–93.
[62] AGM, Ultramar, Gobiernos Militares de La Habana y Pinar del Río, Memoria sobre la reforma de la Comandancia de Dimas, caja 3223.

But in fact, the war was far from over. The rebels might have lost a great commander, but they still had Máximo Gómez and around 20,000 men-in-arms willing to fight for Cuba's independence until the very end and were able enough to prevent any major battle. Instead, they kept with the hit-and-run guerrilla warfare that had proven successful until then. They were in no position of ousting the Spanish forces out of Cuba, but by avoiding a major defeat, they were in a way successful. With their little means, they were able to keep the fight on. The Spanish forces, despite its far superior numbers, proved unable to inflict them a decisive blow. During 1896, Spain had an army of around 85,000 men in Cuba, but almost half of them had fallen ill of tropical diseases, usually yellow fever, and dysentery, which counted for over 90 percent of its casualties during the war. Military hospitals across the island were crammed, while operational units had only half its strength.

With an army occupying the hospitals and chasing the rebels, the over 60,000 Volunteers were responsible for the defense of the cities. Though Havana, Santiago, Matanzas, or Cienfuegos were spared from direct fighting, smoke columns stemming from burning sugar mills could be seen from the cities. The insurgency got to the cities' gates. This led to the creation of new volunteer units solely devoted to reinforcing the city's defenses, but also the establishment of volunteer units to be sent to increase the army garrisons in the countryside. Due to the shortage of able men, Weyler promoted the creation of two Volunteer units for that purpose. On October 30, 1896, two *Tercios de Voluntarios y Bomberos Movilizados* were set up in Havana, of over 500 men in total. They were made up of a mix of Volunteers and firemen, recruited among the already existing companies, who would be deployed to the areas where more men were needed to fight the insurgents, such as Pinar del Río, where they reinforced the Mariel-Majana *trocha*. Among these men, Weyler chose thirty Blacks to form his personal guard, in order to show his support for "this race, who used to be so addicted to Spain."[63]

After nearly two years of continued fighting, both sides were exhausted, and in 1897, the war entered a stalemate period of positional fighting in an almost voided space. The *reconcentración* nearly emptied the countryside of peasants and Spanish forces, which were concentrated in both in towns and in military positions. Meanwhile, the insurgency controlled vast areas of rural Cuba, although the destruction of the agricultural system had seriously affected the combative capacity of the *mambís*.[64] Throughout most of 1897, the war entered a less intense period, in which the shortage of food and casualties caused by illnesses were the major problems for both sides. The insurgents kept control of the countryside, and the Spanish forces remained entrenched in the cities, which were barely attacked by the *mambises*. In a situation of stalemate, the military operations were halted. Volunteer units barely reported any action beyond the regular garrisoning of key infrastructures and the odd shooting with rebel parties approaching the town. Narciso Maciá, a Catalan officer of Havana's Artillery Regiment, summed up the year 1897 in his diary with a succinct "nothing

---

[63] Weyler. *Mi mando en Cuba*, vol. III, p. 6.
[64] Laird W. Bergad. *Cuban Rural Society in the Nineteenth Century: The Social and Economic History of Monoculture in Matanzas*. Princeton: Princeton University Press, 1990, pp. 151–95.

new happened this year [...]. The war kept on with its hardships, paralysing every activity, increasing poverty, made even worse by the *reconcentración*, and making life in Cuba extremely difficult."⁶⁵

The only military action of some relevance was the falling of Victoria de Las Tunas on August 14, 1897, to the hands of the eastern rebel army commanded by Calixto García. Las Tunas was the head of one of the island's thirty-two *jurisdicciones*, the administrative unit above the municipality and below the province, and thus a city of relative importance in northern Oriente. The rebel army greatly boasted its conquest, for it was the only city it took during entire war, but the fact is the importance of the rebel taking of Las Tunas was more symbolic than strategic. For the first time since 1868, soldiers of free Cuba had conquered a town. But stemming from their victory, they also sent another kind of symbolic messages. The garrison defending Las Tunas capitulated after the *mambís* promised to spare their lives, transport them to Puerto Padre to be dispatched to Havana by sea, and grant them the right to keep their weapons. Moments after both sides agreed on the capitulation, the forty Volunteers of the garrison were isolated form the rest of the men, surrounded by armed rebels and hacked to death, for they could expect no mercy from Free Cuba, even from Calixto García, a former Volunteer himself who had defected in 1868.⁶⁶

Void of any major military actions, 1897 was intense in the political ground, for Weyler's harsh conduction of the war undermined his position in Spain and abroad. Major press campaigns against the "butcher" were conducted by independence agents in the United States and Europe. The war was entering a new and more political stage which was to bring deep changes in the political and military conduct of the war.

US Intervention Looming in the Horizon

Although the removal of peasants had almost brought the war to a halt, its brutality fueled public opinion in the United States against Weyler and the continuance of Spain in Cuba. There was not much need to exaggerate the calamitous state of peasants in Cuba because of Weyler's methods, but yellow press north of the Florida Straits started a sensationalist campaign against him in particular and Spanish rule in general which boosted among American readers the idea that their troops had to intervene in the island to stop the brutal ruler, paving the road for war with Spain.⁶⁷ Two New York newspapers, William Randolph Hearst's *New York Journal* and Joseph Pulitzer's *World*, were the leaders of this disinformation campaign.⁶⁸ The extent of their propaganda

---

[65] Maciá. *Vida y obra*, p. 26.
[66] *La Correspondencia Militar*, 14-09-1897.
[67] Philip S. Foner. *The Spanish-Cuban-American War and the Birth of American Imperialism*. New York and London: Monthly Review Press, 1972, vol. I, pp. 281–310; Tone. *War and Genocide*, pp. 225–38; Trask. *The War with Spain in 1898*. New York: Macmillan Publishing Co., 1981, pp. 1–29.
[68] Sylvia L. Hilton. "The Spanish-American War of 1898: Queries into the Relationship between the Press, Public Opinion and Politics". *REDEN: Revista Española de Estudios Norteamericanos*, 1994, No. 7, pp. 71–87; John Patrick Leary. "America's Other Half: Slum Journalism and the War of 1898." *Journal of Transnational American Studies*, 2009, vol. 1, No. 1, pp. 1–33.

permeated among voters, helping the republican candidate William McKinley winning the presidential elections of November 3, 1896.[69]

McKinley's victory was not good news for Spain, for his open support for intervention in Cuba greatly differed from his predecessor, the Democrat Grover Cleveland (1893–7). Cleveland had indeed tried to secure an influential position for the United States in relation to the war in Cuba but was very adamant to support the rebel side or to alienate the goodwill of Spain. For instance, he decided not to bring into effect a series of declarations in favor of recognizing belligerent rights to the Cuban rebel army passed by both chambers of the US Congress between February and April 1896, though these were supported by an overwhelming bipartisan majority. Resisting mounting pressure, Cleveland insisted instead that the United States should try to break a deal between the Spanish Government and his rebellious Cuban subjects. For instance, on April 4, 1896, Secretary of State Richard Olney sent a note to Spain's plenipotentiary minister in Washington DC, Enrique Dupuy de Lôme, proposing to open negotiations with the insurgent government based on granting wide autonomy to Cuba within the Spanish Monarchy.[70]

Contrary to Cleveland's administration, President McKinley (1897–1901) was an open advocate of US intervention in favor of the insurgents for the sake of liberty, humanitarianism, and American power. He assumed the office on March 4, 1897, giving a good example from the very beginning of the Manifest Destiny ideology, and he was not alone. Assistant secretary of the navy Theodore Roosevelt, Senator Henry Cabot Lodge, and Admiral Alfred T. Mahan were just the most prominent representatives of a group of hawks who staunchly advocated for the creation of an American Empire at the expense of a weak rival like Spain.[71] Mahan, who authored the influential book *The Influence of Sea Power in History* in 1890, famously declared that the United States needed a powerful navy in order to control commercial lines and build its own empire. Accordingly, since the early 1890s the United States Navy Department had been planning an imperial expansion which included not only Cuba but also Puerto Rico and the Philippines as parts of a chain that would allow the United States to dominate the seas from the Caribbean to the South China Sea through an already projected Panama Canal, as theorized in Mahan's influential book.

Throughout 1897, McKinley showed his willingness to intervene in Cuba while cynically maintaining diplomatic manners. He alternated offerings of mediating into a negotiated peace to the Spanish and rebel governments, while threatening Spain with bringing into effect the April 1896 US Congress resolution recognizing belligerent rights to the rebel army should Spain rejected the US meddling in the war.[72] McKinley's unconcealed eagerness for intervening in Cuba severely deteriorated the relationship

---

[69] Amblard. *Notas coloniales*, pp. 208–17; Richard F. Hamilton. *President McKinley, War and Empire*, vol. I. New Brunswick and London: Transaction Publishers, 2006, pp. 105–47.

[70] Foner. *The Spanish-Cuban-American War*, vol. I, pp. 177–207.

[71] Evan Thomas. *The War Lovers. Roosevelt, Loge, Hearst, and the Rush to Empire, 1898*. New York, Boston and London: Little, Brown and Company, 2010, pp. 31–61; Tone. *War and Genocide*, pp. 239–49.

[72] Hamilton. *President McKinley*, vol. I, pp. 213–38.

between both governments in Madrid and Washington DC to a breaking point. On September 18, 1897, the US ambassador in Madrid, Stewart L. Woodford, posed the Spanish Government an ultimatum: unless Madrid ended the *reconcentración*, granted Cuba political autonomy, and ended the war, the United States would intervene.[73] Ending the forcible relocation of peasants and granting Cuba home rule were feasible measures for the Spanish Government, but ending the war was wishful thinking. The rebel army, despite only counting with a few thousand men and facing dire problems to provide its troops with due logistics, had been showing a strong determination to fight to the end for over two-and-a-half years. Everyone knew that Spain could not meet this demand, and that consequently the US Government was utterly decided to launch a military intervention in Cuba.

In Spain, although these demands were formally rejected, the government was aware that not meeting at least some of them would probably lead to a war against the United States. Forced by such a prospect to change his basic principle of no concessions without peace, Prime Minister Antonio Cánovas del Castillo presented a set of reforms before the Spanish Parliament in February 1897.[74] The project partially retrieved a reforms' plan that had been presented by the former minister of the Colonies, the Cuban Buenaventura Abárzuza (1894–5) on February 24, 1895, the same day the war broke out, before the Spanish Parliament and was consequently ignored. But before McKinley's aggressive policy, the Cánovas presented a project which had the parliament debating for most of 1897 issues like amnesty for the rebels, administrative autonomy, and wider political rights for the island's inhabitants, when a bullet thwarted the plans. Antonio Cánovas del Castillo, the strong man of Spanish politics since 1875, was assassinated by an anarchist at the Santa Águeda spa in Cestona, in the Basque province of Guipúzcoa. Michele Angiolillo, a London-based Italian anarchist, gunned down the prime minister in retaliation for the Montjuich Process, a trial which ruled the execution of five anarchists and the imprisonment of another 19 in April 1897. The sentences stemmed from the bomb launched against procession-goers on June 7, 1896, Feast of Corpus Christi, in front of a church in Barcelona, killing twelve and injuring thirty-five. The trial and the executions were highly publicized by anarchist networks across Europe, labeling the Spanish Government as the new Inquisition, and convincing a man of action like Angiolillo to engage in a terrorist act, which was not uncommon for anarchists by the end of the nineteenth century. Looking for contacts who might help him carry out the assassination, on his way from England to Spain he contacted in Paris with Ramón Emeterio Betances, the old Puerto Rican plotter who acted as representative of the Cuban insurgents in France and gave Angiolillo funds and contacts in Spain.[75]

---

[73] Foner. *The Spanish-Cuban-American War*, vol. I, pp. 217–18.
[74] Elorza & Hernández Sandoica (1998), pp. 285–306; John L. Offner. *An Unwanted War: the Diplomacy of the United States and Spain over Cuba, 1895-1898*. Chapel Hill: University of North Carolina Press, 1992, pp. 37–53.
[75] Francisco J. Romero Salvadó. *¿Quién mató a Eduardo Dato? Comedia política, tragedia social*. Granada: Comares, 2019, pp. 1–55; Demetrio Ramos. "El antillanismo extremista: Betances y los 'velos' que cubrieron la muerte de Cánovas," in Diego García, Emilio de &). *Cuba, Puerto Rico y Filipinas en la perspectiva del 98*. Madrid: Editorial Complutense, 1997, pp. 73–110.

The assassination of Cánovas del Castillo shocked Spain, for the country lost the mastermind of the Restoration regime at a very crucial point in the war in Cuba, when the Spanish and rebel forces seemed to have reached a stalemate and conflict with the United States was looming on the horizon. Only Cánovas had earned the respect of the Spanish ruling class necessary to advocate for a military solution for Cuba while at the same time presenting a set of reforms which might keep the United States away from intervening in the island, risking that these would fail. Acknowledging that no other conservative politician had neither the charisma nor the respectability to replace Cánovas, Regent Queen Maria Christina appointed Práxedes Mateo Sagasta, the liberal leader who had alternate power with Cánovas since 1881, as head of the government in October 1897.[76]

The coming to power of the liberals profoundly changed Spain's policy in the Antilles. Contrary to Cánovas del Castillo, who relied on a military solution for Cuba, Sagasta believed that the war should have a political solution, which necessarily meant meeting some of the US demands: ending the *reconcentración* and granting political autonomy, thus making Weyler's position untenable, as he represented Cánovas' harsh policies.

The man chosen to carry out the new policy in Cuba was Ramón Blanco y Erenas, marquis of Peña Plata, who arrived to Havana on October 31, 1897. He was a veteran soldier with wide experience in combat, four times captain general of the political tactful-needed Catalonia, and former governor of colonial territories. He had dealt with the Little War as captain general of Cuba (1879–81) and saw the beginning of an anticolonial revolution as captain general of the Philippines (1893–96). Though Blanco was known to be a liberal, and everyone knew that he had been sent to Cuba to end Weyler's tougher policy, the prestige of some of them men he took with him to the island seemed to assuage the anxiety of the Volunteers. Lieutenant General Luis Manuel Pando, head of the General Staff, and Division General Julián González Parrado, *segundo cabo*, earned the praise of the *integrista* press in Havana, at least during the first weeks, for they were regarded as guarantors that Blanco's reforms would not endanger Spanish sovereignty. *Los Voluntarios*, a newspaper created at the start of the war in Havana to represent the interests of the Volunteers, considered that during the military parade carried out to welcome the new authorities, General Parrado "applauded us and admired us [the Volunteers] with sincere warm."[77] On November 4, 1897, the chief officers of Havana's Volunteer battalions paid a visit to show their confidence to the *segundo cabo* who flattered them back in very warm terms.[78] But good relationship would soon deteriorate.

On November 13, 1897, only weeks after assuming command, following instructions from the government, Blanco issued a decree allowing the *reconcentrados* to return to their villages as long as these were in Spanish-controlled areas. This was a humanitarian gesture toward the *reconcentrados* but also toward the US Government.

---

[76] Fernández Almagro. *Historia de la España contemporánea*, vol. II, pp. 7–23.
[77] The article was reproduced by *El Correo Militar*, 20-12-1897, p. 1.
[78] *El Correo Militar*, 29-11-1897, p. 1.

The sufferance inflicted upon the *reconcentrados* was appalling, and Blanco wanted to inform the government with detailed information about it. In November 1897, he requested reports on the state of the relocated peasants to provincial authorities, who reported the dramatic situation they had to deal with. The governor of the Pinar del Río Province, where formal *reconcentración* had started in October 1896, and who only counted with reliable data from 10 of the 25 municipalities of his area, reported that at least 35,000 peasants had been displaced, out of a population of 225,000 souls, and that he reckoned the entire province had lost about half its pre-war population.[79] Before such a dramatic situation, and in order to reach peace and avert the prospects of US intervention, the Spanish Government considered that the *reconcentración* had to be over.

Another of the US Government's demands was met with a political major change. On November 25, 1897, the Spanish Government granted Cuba and Puerto Rico a generous political autonomy.[80] Self-rule had been a longtime demand from Cuban reformists in order to avoid revolution, at least since the 1830s, when the island's representatives were excluded from the Spanish Parliament, but it was now granted in order to end a war. Extending the measure to Puerto Rico was not politically necessary, for the island was in peace, but it was a personal compromise of Sagasta, who had promised it to Puerto Rican autonomists in exchange for support in the Spanish Parliament. As a part of the agreement, the Autonomist Party had to become the Puerto Rican branch of the Liberal Party, thus losing its distinct identity. This caused the secession of the so-called orthodox autonomists, led by José Celso Barbosa, who rejected an absorption by a monarchical metropolitan political party and created a political platform which advocated for the integration of Puerto Rico into the United States.[81]

Granting autonomy to Cuba was highly controversial among *integristas*, for many among them regarded it as an open door to independence. They thought the rebels would understand it as concessions stemming from weakness, not strength. In fact, following the assassination of Cánovas, measures to assuage the suffering of "reconcentrados" and to grant Cuba political autonomy were implemented amid mounting pressure from the United States. Rather than a generous gesture toward the vanquished enemy, Sagasta's Antillean policy was an attempt to avoid a war with the United States that Spain could not possibly win, despite the intense press campaigns that convinced Spanish people otherwise.

In Cuba, war had made these political compromises much harder to achieve. Over two years and a half of blood spilling made any concession to the enemies of Spain much difficult to accept. The Constitutional Union had always rejected autonomy demands, and it considered it would not bring peace, for the *mambís* were fighting

---

[79] AGMM, Ultramar, caja 5809, exp. 1, letter from the governor of Pinar del Río to Ramón Blanco, 28-11-1897.
[80] José Trías Monge, chief justice of the Supreme Court of Puerto Rico (1974–85), considered in 1997 that the autonomy granted by Spain in 1897 "was much greater in several aspects than what the United States has been willing to concede up to the present." *Puerto Rico. The Trials of the Oldest Colony in the World.* New Haven and London: Yale University Press, 1997, p. 13.
[81] Bothwell. *Orígenes y desarrollo*, pp. 30–2.

for independence, not home rule within the Spanish Monarchy. Despite not counting much real popular support, electoral manipulation had granted the Constitutional Union the role as Spain's party in Cuba since the incorporation of the island into the political system in 1878. The party controlled most of Cuba's town and city councils, the provincial councils, and sent most of Cuban representatives to the Spanish Parliament thanks to an electoral system which indirectly excluded most of the social basis of the autonomists from direct political participation.

For twenty years, the Constitutional Union had been the spoiled party of Spain's policy in Cuba at the expense of autonomists and reformists. The party sincerely supported the strategy of an uncompromising, harsh war against the insurgency represented by Weyler and Cánovas.[82] Hence, the party regarded the new policy represented by Sagasta and Blanco as simply unacceptable. They were not willing to accept the coming to power of a new regime in which the autonomists held power. The Cuban Autonomist Party had been rather marginalized by Weyler for he distrusted the party's real commitment to the Spanish cause.[83] While *constitucionales* acknowledged that most autonomists remained loyal to Spain during the war, despite their open opposition to Weyler's strict policy, they could not forget that many of their colleagues had joined the revolution from the very beginning.

Among doubts and fears about the future implications of autonomy, on January 1, 1898, the brand-new Insular Government was inaugurated under the presidency of José María Gálvez, leader of the Autonomist Party, which also provided the secretaries of Justice, Treasury, Education, Public Works and Communications, and Agriculture, Commerce and Industry. For the first time in the history of Cuba, the island had its own elected government, and it was all autonomist. And from the very beginning, it had to face unsurmountable pressures. Opposition from *integristas* was taken for granted, but the waters among nationalists had to be tested.

Autonomy was not much welcomed among supporters of a free Cuba either. It failed to grant them the very issue they had been fighting for so long: independence. Leaders of the *Ejército Libertador* staunchly opposed autonomy. Máximo Gómez, its leader, and Calixto García, the man who commanded the insurgent forces in Oriente, the only region where they still were strong, issued several decrees warning that anyone who accepted autonomy would be put to death. However, beneath the leading ranks of the rebel army, there were signs that some of its members, exhausted after years of war, thought otherwise. After all, the war had long entered a state of stalemate, in which the Spanish forces had not crushed the insurgency, but rebel forces were in no position of ousting the Spaniards from Cuba. Consequently, following the November 25, 1897, decree granting autonomy, a window for peace timidly opened, with an increasing number of *mambís* giving up arms and accepting the new regime.[84] For instance, in the eastern town of Manzanillo, one of the cradles of the revolution, its military governor, Lieutenant Colonel Luis Otero y Pimentel, reported to Provincial Government in

---

[82] Roldán de Montaud. *La Restauración en Cuba*, pp. 617–28.
[83] Bizcarrondo & Elorza. *Cuba/España*, pp. 351–401.
[84] AGMM, Ultramar, Capitanía General de Cuba, caja 5791, exp. 25.

Santiago de Cuba that between March 7 and April 6, 1898, 72 *mambises*, 62 women, and 108 children had come to him leaving the insurgency, declaring their loyalty to the Crown and accepting autonomy under Spanish sovereignty.[85] Even some leading *mambí* officers gave up their fight, such as Brigadier Juan Masó Parra, who had embraced autonomy alongside 120 of his men in January 1898. Shortly after, he was appointed colonel in the Spanish Army and created a brigade named *Cuba Española*.[86] He was not the only officer. With him, Lieutenant Colonels Augusto Feria and José del Carmen Hernández; Majors Feliciano Quesada, Saturnino León, and Victoriano Gómez; Captain Santiago Carrera, and five lieutenants took the step. The surrender took place in Sancti Spíritus. They gave in their weapons and ammunition to the Spanish authorities in Manzanillo, accepted Spanish sovereignty, and hailed the regent Queen Maria Christina, Spanish Cuba, and autonomy.

Political leaders of the revolution also had second thoughts between continuing war and embracing autonomy, though not openly, for negotiating with the enemy would have discredited them and put their lives at stake. Domingo Méndez Capote, the vice-president of the Cuban insurgent government, the so-called *República en Armas*, did try to negotiate a peace agreement on the basis of autonomy with Camilo Campos, an informant of Captain General Blanco based in Manzanillo.[87] Although *mambí* commanders fiercely condemned the mere possibility of negotiation, the evidence is that hundreds of insurgents, alongside their families, began to surrender to the Spanish authorities.

For other actors beyond the camps of the *Ejército Libertador*, prospects of an autonomic success were a danger, for it would probably secure longer life to Spanish sovereignty in the island. The US Government, eager to intervene in Cuba, promoted opposition to autonomy among rebel leaders.[88] The pacification of Cuba through home rule would make it much more difficult to justify military intervention in the island, despite the popular support the idea enjoyed among many in the American society. This was one of the main causes of the autonomic experiment's failure. But there were other sources of instability.

In Cuba, *integristas* rejected autonomy from its very inception. Informal conversations on the streets and in cafés, articles in the press, statements by leaders of the Constitutional Union, and discontent among the Volunteers, all conspired against home rule and a more lenient free speech policy which allowed the creation of newspapers criticizing Spanish rule in Cuba. Some of the most radical elements of *integrismo* opted for a plain refusal of all of Blanco's policy, including his efforts aimed at assuaging the appalling living conditions of *reconcentrados*. The US consul in Matanzas reported to the general consul in Havana, John Fitzhugh Lee, that Adolfo

---

[85] AHPSC, Gobierno Provincial, leg. 743, exp. 25.
[86] AHPSC, Gobierno Provincial, leg. 743, exp. 37; *La Unión Constitucional*, 26-04-1898; Enrique Ubieta. *Efemérides de la Revolución Cubana*, vol. I. Havana: La Moderna Poesía, 1911, pp. 129–30.
[87] AGMM, Ultramar, Capitanía General de Cuba, caja 2535, carpeta 14.20, letter from Camilo Campos to Ramón Blanco, 07-04-1898.
[88] Agustín Sánchez Andrés. "Entre la espada y la pared. El régimen autonómico cubano, 1897–1898." *Revista Mexicana del Caribe*, 2003, Año/vol. VIII, No. 16, pp. 7–41.

Porset, the former governor of Matanzas under Weyler, was holding meetings with government officials, army, Civil Guard, Volunteer officers, and local leaders of the *integrista* Constitutional Union party to plot against the captain general, and organize attacks against foreign consulates and nationals, basically US citizens, and to create a state of instability in the city. Such meetings were not only known to the US consul, for the governor of Matanzas confirmed the information in a report sent to Havana on December 6, 1897.[89] The very existence of thousands of Volunteers was the most controversial element of Spanish rule in Cuba and became a tool to be exploited politically at their expense. They were to unwillingly play a key role in the events unfolded before the war between the United States and Spain began.

Although the war was fought in the countryside, the situation in the cities was critical too. The arrival of thousands of *reconcentrados*, coupled with food shortages, spread the idea that Spain was losing the war, and that victory of the insurgency might be likely. In this context, autonomy was interpreted by the most radical elements of *integrismo* as a signal of weakness, hence a step toward the defeat of Spain. Anger at the captain general became evident as early as Christmas Eve 1897. Amid the celebration of that holiday in Havana's Parque Central, groups of young men, among them several Volunteers, began to shout "*Long Live, Spain! Long Live Weyler! Long Live the Volunteers! Down with autonomy!*" in front of the headquarters of *Diario de la Marina*, for this newspaper had accepted the new autonomous regime despite its traditional conservative leaning. The situation became so tense that the demonstrators refused insistently to call the protest off, forcing a mounted Public Order force unit to intervene waving their sabers.[90] The attitude of demonstrators began to dangerously resemble the behavior of Havana's Volunteers in 1869, when they ousted Captain General Dulce for implementing a policy aimed at earning the support of Cuban nationalists through reforms, just as Blanco was trying to do. In Spain, the political spectrum left to the Conservative Party, bitterly criticized Blanco's opponents. Since the days of the Ten Years' War, republicans in the Peninsula had generally been very critical of the Volunteers' staunch rejection of any reforms for Cuba. *La Iberia*, a Madrid republican newspaper, considered the Christmas Eve demonstration "a bothersome protest by a monopoly that will soon go; this is the last convulsion of the *agiotistas* [usurers] who do not want to lose their power."[91] The journalist did not clarify whether that monopoly would be out soon because of autonomy or because of the likely intervention of the United States, which made no efforts to conceal its desire to invade Cuba.

The fact is that tension in Havana ran high during the early days of 1898, coinciding with the start of the autonomic regime and the establishment of more press freedom. A press article triggered a series of dramatic events in Cuba, as a result of Blanco's more lenient stance toward press freedom. He had allowed the creation of newspapers which openly criticized Spanish rule and even supported Cuban independence. One of them, *El Reconcentrado*, published an article entitled "Fuga de granujas" (The Flight

---

[89] AGMM, Ultramar, Capitanía General de Cuba, caja 5791, exp. 40.
[90] *La Lucha*, 25-12-1897, p. 2.
[91] *La Iberia*, 28-12-1897.

of the Rascals) on January 11, 1898. It accused some well-known *integristas* of making money out of the *reconcentrado*'s disgrace and fleeing with it to Spain, for they knew that Cuba would soon be free. The article enraged the *integristas* and triggered violent demonstrations by the Volunteers, who took to the streets of Havana the day after alongside other staunch supporters of Spain. About a hundred *integristas*, including many Volunteers and army officers, paraded central Havana donning their uniforms and shouting, "*Long Live Weyler*" and "*Death to autonomy.*" They broke windows and doors of people suspected of supporting independence on their way and headed to the offices of *El Reconcentrado* and *La Discusión*, another newspaper very critical with Spain. After looting both premises, the demonstrators moved toward *El Diario de la Marina*, which they were close to storm.[92]

The most radical among the Volunteers, usually socially and economically humble, played a leading role in the violent demonstration, just as their colleagues had done in 1869 and 1871. With nearly 19,000 men in their ranks only in Havana, far outnumbering the army and public order forces, and allowed to keep a personal firearm at home, the Volunteers were a fist ready to punch. Despite the looming menace of an US intervention, and the fact that the rebel army was still alive, the Volunteers felt confident enough to reject Blanco's policy of reconciliation by ransacking newspapers and demanding his removal amid such a tense context. While a minority of Volunteer chief officers clearly rejected the violent demonstrations, most of them had an ambiguous attitude as their men ransacked central Havana. Arturo Amblard, a lawyer who witnessed the events, recalled that only two of Havana's nearly twenty Volunteer chief officers went to the palace of the captain general during the riots. The rest, who probably despised Blanco but feared the crowd, only came when the *segundo cabo* called for them, for it became all too evident that their involvement in the riots could have easily ended up with the toppling of the captain general. Power vacuum was not something they could afford considering the circumstances. Only two Volunteer officers, the colonels of the 5th Battalion and the Cavalry Regiment, stood with Blanco. They ordered their men to protect the palace and quash the rioters, not always successfully.[93] Lieutenant Colonel Ricardo Calderón y Pontisi, a Havana councilor and member of the Autonomist Party, resigned the day after the demonstration as some of his men broke into the palace's courtyard and yelled at Blanco.[94] Men like Calderón were certainly committed to the continuity of Spanish sovereignty in the Antilles, but considered that attacking the captain general was not the best way to secure it. They were much likely a minority, however.

The most popular milieu among the Volunteers was decidedly against Blanco, against autonomy, and rejected the end of *reconcentración*. They plotted to oust Blanco because of his plan to dismantle Weyler's policy of harsh measures against the rebels and the autonomists. They were not willing to accept the new political situation, considering that granting autonomy was a step toward independence which would

---

[92] *El Reconcentrado*, 11-01-1898, p. 1; Tone. *War and Genocide*, p. 240.
[93] Amblard. *Notas coloniales*, pp. 291–2.
[94] Cabrera. *Cuba and the Cubans*, p. 192; Weyler. *Mi mando en Cuba*, vol. V, p. 535.

be interpreted by the *mambises* as a sign of Spain's weakness, not generosity. They also considered that autonomy would not shy the United States away from invading Cuba. Hence, *integristas* felt trapped between autonomy, the insurgents, and the likely possibility of a US intervention, in a context which powerfully resembled 1869. The Volunteers' violent reaction stemmed from panic, not confidence. Their position in Cuba was very delicate due to the likely invasion coming from the north of the Straits of Florida, rather than by the ongoing fight posed by the *mambís*. "Fiacre," the pseudonym of a Havana *laborante* who witnessed the demonstrations, wrote to a fellow colleague called "No. 12" on February 8, 1898, that although the demonstrations had been "impressive," the *integristas* feared that the United States would go to war against Spain and that consequently Spain would be ousted from Cuba.[95]

The fact is that rumors began to spread insistently around in Havana and other parts of the island concerning the fate of the Volunteers and the very Spanish rule. In early March 1898, the word was on the street that the captain general was considering disarming the Volunteers to break a deal with the rebels. Though the rumor soon proved to be ungrounded, the existing distrust toward the captain general who had ended the *reconcentración* and had granted autonomy to the Antilles had the Volunteers sending a letter to the Spanish Government demanding that their many years of service to Spain in Cuba be taken into consideration.[96] The fact is they truly feared that the days of Spain in Cuba might be soon over should the United States take part in the war. Mobilizing all loyalists in Cuba was paramount to at least resist the likely invasion, and on March 29, 1898, the colonels of Havana's Volunteer battalions submitted a proposal to the captain general suggesting that all *peninsulares* living in Cuba who were not serving in their ranks ought to be forced to join a militia commanded by army officers.[97]

Their fears were well grounded, for a war between Spain and the United States because of Cuba was becoming increasingly likely. In both countries, the press sustained an inflammatory campaign calling for a military clash, although it is not clear whether the administrations were committed to avoiding or provoking conflict.[98] In fact, there were a few scenarios to be considered, both in Madrid and in Washington DC. Some considered that the war was an unwelcome, yet unavoidable, conflict, whereas among Spanish ministers, some argued that since Spain's continuity in Cuba was untenable, it was preferable to lose the island after a short, but honorable, war to the United States, than losing it to a rebel army made up of peasants and black fighters.[99]

In any case, the reports sent by the US Consul in Havana, Fitzburgh Lee, convinced his government to send a warship to Cuba in order to protect their citizens' lives and

---

[95] BNC, CM Lufriu, No. 49.
[96] *El Correo Gallego*, 04-03-1898, p. 2.
[97] *El Correo Gallego*, 29-03-1898, p. 1.
[98] Sara Núñez de Prado Clavell. "La prensa y la opinión pública española en torno al 'desastre,'" in Fusi & Niño Rodríguez (coord.). *Antes del desastre*, pp. 453–64; Rosario Sevilla Soler. "¿'Opinión pública' frente a 'opinión publicada'? 1898: la cuestión cubana." *Revista de Indias*, 1998, vol. LVIII, No. 212, pp. 255–76.
[99] Offner. *An Unwanted War*, pp. 127–59; Serrano. *Final del Imperio. España 1895–1898*. Madrid: Siglo XXI de España Editores, 1984, pp. 32–7.

interests. Thus, on January 25, 1898, the USS *Maine* entered Havana's port amid much suspicion among supporters of Spain, and scarcely concealed hope among supporters of independence. Though the Spanish authorities accepted its presence in the harbor, it was clearly a first step toward intervention in Cuba. By sending the ship, the White House stated that it had no confidence in Spain's ability to keep the island under control, which was precisely the core argument in favor of US intervention in the island.

Despite the tensions and reciprocal distrust between the two governments, the USS *Maine* crew was well received by Spanish authorities in Havana and became a very popular attraction among *habaneros*. Every day, thousands of them gathered to the port to watch the ship, some resenting its presence, some hoping that more American ships would come to liberate Cuba. Beyond popular reception, its officers were received by the captain general and members of the City Council, who celebrated banquets to honor the visitors. In return, the Spanish Government ordered the *Vizcaya* cruiser to pay a courtesy visit to New York. It was received amid great popular hostility on February 19 because of events which took place four days earlier in Havana harbor.

On February 15 at 21:40, the USS *Maine* blew up killing 256 of its 361 crew. There has been much debate on whether it was caused by an accident or a deliberated attack.[100] Though in a thorough analysis published in 1976 Admiral Rickover of the US Navy proved that the explosion started inside the ship, and not outside, thus discarding the Spanish attack. But in 1898, the US yellow press, led by Hearst's *Journal* and Pulitzer's *Globe*, rushed to blame Spain, pushing the government to assume its narrative and convincing the American people that declaring war on Spain and intervening in Cuba was a moral imperative.[101] "*Remember the Maine!*" became the emotional battle cry to rally volunteers to go to Cuba and fight the Spaniards. Finally, the United States could count on a casus belli to declare war.

The Cuban independence movement did not miss the opportunity to support the hypothesis that Spain had sabotaged the *Maine*, hoping that it would secure an US intervention which would help the *mambís* to oust Spain from the island. The Cuban exile community in the United States spread the word, stemming from alleged reports received from their agents in Havana. For instance, only four days after the explosion, "El Monje," an agent of the revolution based in the city, wrote a letter to a female colleague in New York informing that groups of Volunteers gathered around the port rejoicing for the loss of American lives.[102] Despite this propaganda, the fact is Spanish authorities collaborated with the US Consulate in rescuing the *Maine* survivors, providing them with medical attention, and support for organizing the funeral. The contrast between this reaction and the political manipulation of the explosion in the United States fueled the anti-American feelings which already existed among *integristas* in Cuba. The Spanish press began a campaign accusing the US Government

---

[100] H. G. Rickover. *How the battleship* Maine *was destroyed*. Washington, DC: Naval History Division/Department of the Navy, 1976, pp. 75–91. Agustín Remesal offered a complete revision of the different theories: *El enigma del Maine. 1898. El suceso que provocó la Guerra de Cuba. ¿Accidente o sabotaje?* Barcelona: Plaza & Janés Editores, 1998, pp. 181–223.

[101] Thomas. *The War Lovers*, pp. 209–29.

[102] BNC, CM Arango, No. 59.

of using the *reconcentrados* and the USS *Maine* accident as mere pretexts to justify the long-coveted invasion of Cuba. *Los Voluntarios*, a newspaper founded in 1895 to defend the interests of Havana's Volunteers, blamed both the US and the Cuban exiles for "sacrificing the welfare of Cuban people for the sake of the expulsion of Spain."[103]

Far from Cuba, in Madrid, the Spanish Government provided the press with information assuring that the might of the army and the navy would easily crush the ships and soldiers sent by the *yanquis*. However, the reality was her ruling class was well aware that Spain could not possibly win that war. Spain had a more powerful army, but the fight for Cuba was to take place in the seas. The bulk of the Spanish Navy was too far from Cuba and had less resources than the United States Navy, which was only a few hours away from the island. Thus, the Spanish Government tried to appease the United States by meeting the most important demand of McKinley's government: that Spain put the war against the insurgents to an end. Captain General Blanco was ordered to declare a unilateral ceasefire on April 10, 1898, which was nonetheless disregarded by the insurgents as they had not been consulted and had never accepted any proposal of the kind. Blanco's proposals to Máximo Gómez to unite their forces against the American invader went unheard. Despite the Spanish concessions and intense diplomatic moves, the US Government was determined to fight Spain for Cuba, but also for its remaining territories of Puerto Rico and the Philippines, as we will see.

Despite Spain having met all of the US Government's demands, and that the Spanish hand in the USS *Maine* explosion was less than clear, saber-rattling and anti-Spanish press campaign continued in the United States, which had decidedly taken a course to war. The US Congress declared war on Spain on April 25, 1898, but the war preparations had already begun. On April 20 a naval force had been sent to block the island, and three days later President McKinley called to create an army of 125,000 volunteers. After the Indian Wars had officially ended in 1890, the regular US Army consisted of merely 26,000 men, deemed not enough for the upcoming campaign. But war against Spain was tremendously popular, and soon the ranks were filled. Men from the cities, but also cowboys, whites, and Blacks rushed to Tampa, Florida, where the army was assembled. Lack of discipline and poor health conditions, which took its death toll, made it difficult to forge a proper fighting force, but enthusiasm compensated the shortcomings. Former Confederate soldiers volunteered to fight alongside Union Army veterans, Buffalo Bill offered his men for the war, and the all-Black US Army units known as Buffalo Soldiers recruited young Black men hoping to help fellow black Cubans to get rid of Spanish rule. Even Theodore Roosevelt quit his appointment as assistant secretary of the navy and created his own volunteer cavalry regiment, the Rough Riders.[104]

South of the Florida Straits, the Spaniards were getting ready for war too. By April 1898, the Volunteers were still an impressive force of around 90,000 men who

---

[103] *Los Voluntarios*, 27-03-1898, p. 2.
[104] Trask. *The War with Spain*, pp. 30–59; Julián Companys Monclús. *De la explosión del Maine a la ruptura de relaciones diplomáticas entre Estados Unidos y España (1898)*. Lérida: Estudi General de Lleida, 1989, pp. 46–126.

collaborated with the 115,000-men regular army in preparing the island to receive the invading troops. According to Arturo Amblard, by late 1897 there were 90,214 Volunteers distributed throughout Cuba as follows: 28,616 in Havana province (20,124 in the capital), 12,163 in Pinar del Río, 11,316 in Matanzas, 20,682 in Santa Clara, 1,867 in Camagüey, and 9,889 in Oriente.[105] As early as April 20, 1898, when the United States Navy started blockading Cuba, Captain General Blanco had decreed the mobilization of the Volunteers and ordered the creation of new companies to be embedded into regular infantry battalions. The embedding of the mobilized Volunteers into the regular army was a regular practice, for it was considered that their military performance could be improved under the command of army officers.[106] The blockade soon had the garrison running short of food and ammunition.[107] According to General Luis Manuel Pando, bestowed with preparing the defense of the capital of Cuba, the Armoury of Havana had only 2,000 Remington rifles left with 20 ammunition rounds each to supply an army of 26,000 men in Havana and 14,000 in Pinar del Río. Despite this, new Volunteer units were created, for they could count on their own weaponry which needed not to be standardized. Any disposable weapon and skills were good in such a situation. For instance, 900 retired navy personnel created the Sailors Volunteer's Battalion, and a group of 75 Catalans formed the Catalan Volunteers Company.[108] *Integristas* in Havana and across Cuba mobilized their resources to face the upcoming battle.

Throughout the island, the Volunteers were a key element in the defensive strategy organized by military authorities, as they already had a dense network of sections, companies, and battalions across the island, from big cities to small towns, where *Juntas de Defensa* were created in order to coordinate the defense locally. From east to west, the Volunteers took a leading role in these *Juntas* with financial aid and their physical work by digging trenches and building forts. Thus, during the spring of 1898, whereas the regular troops were generally gathered around the most important cities, the defense of small towns still depended on the Volunteers. In the cities, their role was generally constrained to upholding public order, and protecting official buildings. For instance, on May 15, 1898, the governor of Santiago de Cuba, General José Toral, ordered the Volunteers to protect the seats of the Regional Government and the City Council in case of alarm.[109] In Artemisa, Pinar del Río, men from the army's Vergara Battalion defended the town, while local Volunteers, alongside others from nearby Guanajay, and a section of Havana's Sixth Volunteer Battalion built forts and trenches around the town. In order to fund the construction, the local council established that propertied classes pay higher taxes, and poor ones contribute with their physical work.[110] In Gibara, a loyalist stronghold in Oriente, the local Volunteers and the

---

[105] Amblard. *Notas coloniales*, p. 163.
[106] ANRC, Asuntos Políticos, leg. 240, exp. 21.
[107] Luis M. de Pando. *Documento presentado al Senado por el Excmo. Sr. Senador D. Luis M. de Pando en 22 de octubre de 1898*. Madrid: Imprenta y Fundición de los Hijos de J. A. García, 1899, p. 16.
[108] AGMM, Ultramar, Capitanía General de Cuba, caja 4690, "Voluntarios Marineros General Blanco" and "Voluntarios de La Habana. Voluntarios Catalanes."
[109] AHPSC, Gobierno Provincial, leg. 2875, exp. 25.
[110] AGMM, Ultramar, Capitanía General de Cuba, caja 3223.

Casino Español closely collaborated with Carlos Moreno, the military commander, in the creation of the *Junta de Defensa* on April 30, 1898. Under Moreno's command, 10 Volunteer officers, the harbor captain, the mayor, the priest, and the judge organized the town's defense, raised 9,000 *pesos* to fund the works, and called all able-bodied men to join the Volunteers.[111]

Between late April, May, and June, the United States Navy attacked several important ports, such as Matanzas and Cienfuegos, but avoided Havana, for it had strong coast artillery batteries and was armed to the teeth. The US military knew that the Spaniards were not to give up Havana without a good fight. While the navy conducted diversion attacks, in the meantime the invading army gathered in Tampa to receive military training for the war's next step. Bombing Cuba's harbors was only a preparation for the actual land invasion, which took place in Spain's Achilles' heel: Oriente. Except for its major towns, still under Spanish control, the region was dominated by the rebel division commanded by Calixto García, who would let the doors open for an invasion.

The 17,000-men US Army's V Corps, commanded by General William R. Shafter, began landing on June 22 on Daiquirí Beach, only 26 km east to Santiago de Cuba, the center of Spanish power in Oriente. Shafter was a veteran of the American Civil War and the Indian Wars who before going to Cuba had been commander of the Department of California. Despite heavy casualties caused by tropical diseases, the invading army began its march toward Santiago, encountering on its way help from Cuban rebels and more resistance than expected from Spanish forces, for instance during close fight at Las Guásimas on June 24. After a few-day halt, the *yanquis*, as US people were known among Spaniards, kept landing east to Santiago, reaching a force of around 45,000 men in just a few days. Now backed by strong numbers, the US forces launched the final thrust on 1 July against two key positions defending Santiago's main ways: El Caney to the north and San Juan Hill to the south. Both positions were garrisoned by 500 and 800 men, respectively, including some dozen Volunteers, commanded by Generals Joaquín Vara de Rey and Arsenio Linares. Knowing that reinforcements would not likely arrive, and that they were the last positions before Santiago, the Spanish defending forces held intense fight for over twelve hours against two columns of over 6,000 and 8,000 men.

Alongside the great combat spirit showed by regular Spanish conscripts during those days, the Volunteers put in an outstanding fight. No desertion was recorded, and forty Volunteers died while covering the 3-km retreat of regular troops from Canosa Fort in San Juan Hill to downtown Santiago, including their wounded and dead. However, as the days passed by, the shortages of food, weapons, and ammunition became graver, and the morale of the defenders grew weaker. Despite the many calls for help sent from Santiago, no reinforcements arrived, except for a 1,000-men column commanded by Colonel Federico Escario García, who had fought its way against *mambís* in an exhausting march throughout 180 km from Manzanillo to Santiago. Their arrival, though heroic, only worsened the food shortage in Santiago. The city was still defended by 15,000 men, among whom were 2,000 men from Santiago's First and Second Volunteer Battalions, but they were starving, had barely any ammunition

---

[111] AGMM, Ultramar, Capitanía General de Cuba, caja 3691; *Suplemento a la Legalidad*, 30-04-1898.

left, and little hopes of any relief.[112] At Santiago's harbor, a fleet made up of cruisers *Almirante Oquendo*, *Cristóbal Colón*, *Infanta María Teresa* and *Vizcaya*, plus destroyers *Plutón* and *Furor* and commanded by Admiral Pascual Cervera, gathering around 2,400 sailors, waited for instructions from Havana and Madrid. Outside and around the city, the c. 45,000 US troops were suffering a high death toll due to tropical diseases, but could still rely on food and men supplies, and could pass on the fighting burden to the navy. While US land forces kept the beleaguered Spanish garrison under check, a US fleet commanded by Admiral William T. Sampson, a veteran of the Civil War who had held several appointments at the Naval Academy and the Naval Department, deployed four battleships (USS *Indiana*, USS *Massachusetts*, USS *Iowa*, and USS *Texas*), two armored cruisers (USS *New York* and USS *Brooklyn*), and two armored yachts (USS *Vixen* and *Gloucester*) along the narrow entrance of Santiago Bay on July 3.

After much heated debate in Madrid, Havana, and Santiago, the final decision was to be taken by the far-away Navy Staff in Madrid, which ordered Admiral Cervera to leave the safety of Santiago's harbor. The Bay of Santiago is extremely narrow, only allowing one ship at a time. Thus, leaving the port in line meant that the four armored cruisers and two destroyers under Cervera's command would be facing the entire US fleet one by one. Rather than a battle between two fleets, what ensued was a battle of the US fleet against a Spanish ship at a time. The defeat was taken for granted, but Cervera, a former minister of the navy and veteran of Africa, Cuba, and the Philippines, fulfilled his duty knowing that he and his men were being forced to face an inevitable and useless death. After a quick combat on July 3, 1898, the Spanish fleet lost off Santiago Bay all the ships, 343 men killed, 151 wounded, and nearly 1,900 captured by the US ships, who only lost one man and another injured.[113]

With an enemy running out of food, ammunition, and having just lost their fleet, Major General Shafter announced the bombardment of the city within twenty-four hours on July 4, Independence Day. That very day Governor José Toral allowed the 25,000 civilians who remained within Santiago to leave the city. The invading army controlled all the routes to Santiago, had the city under siege, and counted with the help of around 3,000 *mambises* commanded by Calixto García, men who had by then nearly three years of fighting experience. However, these *mambises* were prevented from taking direct action and were relegated to a mere auxiliary force of the American during the fight. Shafter and the American Staff distrusted men who they generally regarded as inferior, especially since most rebel troops in Oriente were made up of Blacks and mulattoes. Even before having an empire of their own, a highly hierarchical and racist ideology permeated US Army officers, who were not willing to share any credit for the liberation of Cuba with Cuban rebels themselves, especially since many

---

[112] Baldovín Ruiz. *Cuba*, pp. 533–50; Elorza & Hernández Sandoica. *La Guerra de Cuba*, 417–51; Foner. *The Spanish-Cuban-American War*, vol. II, 388–405; Ivan Musicant. *Empire by Default. The Spanish-American War and the Dawn of the American Century*. New York: Henry Holt and Company, 1998, pp. 352–515; G. J. A. O'Toole. *The Spanish War. An American Epic 1898*. New York and London: W. W. Norton & Company, 1984, pp. 254–352; Trask. *The War with Spain*, pp. 194–335.
[113] Ángel Luis Cervera Fantoni. *El desastre del 98 y el fin del imperio español*. Córdoba: Sekotia, 2021, pp. 198–210.

of them were men of African descent and were probably born slaves.[114] This created much unrest among *mambís*, who became suspicious of the real motivation behind the US intervention in Cuba.

On the other side of the trenches, Volunteers had taken part in all the military operations, but their performance was generally considered weak and unreliable by senior army officers. The reason for discredit in this case was not race, but military pride versus the participation of civilian "parvenues." For instance, in a book published shortly after the war, Severo Gómez Núñez, director of *Diario del Ejército*, a Havana military newspaper, wrote that the Volunteers deserted whenever they had a chance and had abandoned Santiago when Governor José Toral allowed evacuation of civilians on July 4, after Shafter announced his artillery would bomb the city. Gómez Núñez wrote that all the Volunteers took their uniforms off, threw them away, and fled the city disguised as civilians. This was a blatant accusation of desertion, for in a warzone, Volunteers were assimilated to regular soldiers in terms of military law. Furthermore, the July 4 permit allowing civilians to leave the city did not include the Volunteers precisely for the same reason.[115]

Contrary to the version of Gómez Núñez, there were Volunteers who remained in Santiago during the siege. A few years after the war, Jaume Sans, a Catalan who had been a Volunteer in Santiago, admitted that when Governor Toral allowed the evacuation of civilians, many of his comrades left for the countryside with their families disguised as civilians, but a few hundred remained in the city. According to Sans, by July 6 there were less than 1,000 civilians in Santiago, plus 13,000 starving and short-of-ammunition defenders, including around 500 Volunteers.[116] Their low morale was not dramatically different from the regular soldiers. Their military efficiency and their commitment to the defense of the city only faded away over subsequent days, when it became clear that the men defending Santiago de Cuba had no chance of lifting the siege.[117]

Despite Spain still having an impressive army in Cuba, over 200,000 men between regular soldiers and militias, including the Volunteers, and the insistence of most army commanding officers, the Spanish Government drafted no plans to come to the rescue of Santiago and continue the war against the United States. By mid-July, the *Ejército Liberador* controlled most of the countryside, especially in Oriente; the US forces controlled the area between Guantánamo and Santiago, but the Spaniards were still in possession of all the cities and the key infrastructures, such as ports and railroads. Spain was exhausted after more than three years of continuous fighting in Cuba and another ongoing war in the Philippines, the rebel army was still operative,

---

[114] Enrique Collazo. *Los americanos en Cuba*. Havana: Editorial de Ciencias Sociales, 1972 (first published by Imprenta y Papelería C. Martínez y Cía., 1905, 2 vols.), pp. 219–36; Pérez, Jr. *Cuba Between Empires*, pp. 211–28.

[115] Severo Gómez Núñez. *La Guerra Hispano-Americana. Santiago de Cuba*. Madrid: Imprenta del Cuerpo de Artillería, 1901, p. 61.

[116] David Jou i Andreu. *El 98 vist pels sitgetans. Memòries de Jaume Sans sobre el setge americà a Santiago de Cuba*. Sitges: Ajuntament de Sitges, 1999, pp. 57–8.

[117] Manuel Montero García. "La moral militar de los soldados españoles durante las guerras coloniales, 1895–1898." *Revista de Historia Militar*, Año LXI, 2017, No. 121, pp. 199–233.

and a US force had invaded a tiny strip of land in eastern of Cuba, but the Spanish forces were still in no position to be kicked out of Cuba. Certainly, Spain could not win the war due to the superiority of the United States Navy, and the seas were the key scenario of a war for an island. However, Spain still had resources enough to continue the fight against the US Army in order to achieve a better position from which to start talks of peace. Thousands of men stationed in Havana, Cienfuegos, or Matanzas were still waiting for the enemy to come. Keeping the war on, however, meant dragging more conscripts and resources from Spain, and this was already testing the resilience of the Crown and the political regime, with a growing popular opposition to sending to war the sons of poor families who could not afford paying the 2,000 *pesetas* for the exemption of serving in the colonies.

Probably preferring to preserve the status quo rather than testing further the regime's limits and preferring to lose the island to the United States than to Cuban rebels, on July 14, 1898, the Spanish Government ordered Governor José Toral to surrender the city to the Americans, on the condition that the insurgents were not allowed to enter the city. Giving up the city to another civilized nation, according to the standards of the day, was less onerous than surrendering it to a force of rebel soldiers, who might also take revenge against them. Toral and the Spanish garrison feared reprisals from the men they had fought for more than three years. Calixto García, still commander of the 3,000 *mambís* surrounding Santiago, did not conceal his outrage before the US command. He rightly considered that, after over three years of war, his men were entitled to enter Santiago, but there was not much he could do against a much superior army. Cuban rebels could just feel terribly frustrated for being deprived the glory of triumph at Santiago by a group of newcomers to the war. As understandably their feelings were, the truth is that without the US intervention, Santiago de Cuba would much likely still be in Spanish hands.

The Spanish and US commissioners met on July 16, 1898, near Santiago de Cuba, under a ceiba which has been known as Peace Tree (*Árbol de la Paz*) ever since. For the Spaniards, on behalf of Governor Toral, the commissioners were Brigadier General Federico Escario and Lieutenant Colonel Ventura Fontán. On behalf of Major General W. Shafter, commander of the US expeditionary force, there were Major General J. Wheeler, Major General W. Lawton, and 1st Lieutenant S. D. Midley. Roberto Mason was the interpreter. According to the capitulation agreement between the Spanish and American commissioners, the Volunteers could stay in Cuba if they gave up their weapons to the US forces and promised not to fight against them during the rest of the war.[118] The day after the capitulation agreement, Governor Toral surrendered Santiago de Cuba to the US Army on July 17, 1898, thus putting an end to almost four centuries of history since Diego Velázquez de Cuéllar founded the city in 1515. It was the first time a foreign power occupied a Spanish city in the Americas since the British took Havana in 1762, but this time it seemed unlikely that Santiago would return to Spanish hands.

---

[118] Bacardí y Moreau. *Crónicas de Santiago de Cuba*, vol. X. Santiago de Cuba: Tipografía Arroyo Hermanos, 1924, pp. 112–13.

Ironically, the men who had landed in Cuba purportedly to aid the Cuban people to free their nation from Spanish rule ended up protecting the lives and properties of Spanish loyalists, including many Cubans who feared a certain death should they fell into the hands of fellow Cubans. Such was the nature of the civil war that was going on in Cuba. There was a general sense of relief among them, especially among Volunteers. Unlike army soldiers, who were generally eager to be sent back to the Peninsula, the Volunteers in Santiago de Cuba, just as in the rest of the island, had their families and jobs well established in the city, and could hardly begin anew in Spain. After the US troops entered Santiago, there were many scenes of confraternization between the Spanish Volunteers and army soldiers with *yanqui* soldiers, whereas the *mambises* were still camped outside Santiago de Cuba.[119] Perhaps they began to think that they had just swapped one old ruler by a new one.

War from the Distance in Puerto Rico

War only came to Puerto Rico with the US invading army in July 1898, but the island had been affected by events in Cuba since the beginning. Being only a few days away by sea from Cuba, the five infantry battalions of the local garrison, Colón No. 23, Valladolid No. 21, Alfonso XIII, No. 24, Patria No. 25, and the Puerto Rico Provisional Battalion were sent to Cuba to reinforce the Spanish Army, alongside much logistic support.[120] The local Volunteers, who had had a relatively quiet existence until then, were mobilized for the first time to patrol the coast. Despite the peaceful situation in Puerto Rico, Captain General Antonio Dabán (1893–5) feared that the *mambí* uprising might replicate in the island in the form of riots, since politically there was a tense calm since the *compontes* of 1887.

In effect, Cuban nationalist rhetoric had always included the liberation of Puerto Rico. In the 1892 original manifesto of José Martí's Cuban Revolutionary Party, it was stated that the aim of the party was to "achieve […] Cuba's total independence, as well as promoting and helping Puerto Rico's."[121] This idea was echoed by some exiled Puerto Rican intellectuals, most notably Eugenio María de Hostos, and Ramón Emeterio Betances, the latter being the foremost promoter of the island's independence since the 1860s.[122] Since the war started in Cuba, a few hundred Puerto Ricans had joined the rebel army, and a "Puerto Rican Section of the Cuban Revolutionary Party" had been established in New York by Julio J. Henna.[123]

---

[119] Pérez, Jr. *Cuba Between Empires*, pp. 212–17.
[120] AGMM, Documentación de Puerto Rico, 5170.1.
[121] José Martí. *Obras completas*, vol. I. Havana: Editorial de Ciencias Sociales, 1975, p. 259.
[122] Paul Estrade. "La nación antillana: sueño y afán de 'El Antillano' (Betances)," in Naranjo Orovio, Puig Samper & García Mora (eds.). *La Nación Soñada*, pp. 23–36; M.ª Dolores González-Ripoll Navarro. "Independencia y antillanismo en la obra de Hostos," in Puig-Samper Naranjo Orovio & García Mora. *La Nación Soñada*, pp. 37–48.
[123] Negroni. *Historia militar de Puerto Rico*, pp. 305–6.

Nonetheless, the independence of Puerto Rico had always been the dream of a minority, and no serious attempt was made to rebel against Spain. This, of course, did not preclude the existence of social and political discontent. The status quo, which usually benefited the propertied class of landowners and merchants, many of whom were *peninsulares*, caused social and political tensions. It kept members of the Unconditional Spanish Party, many of whom were also Volunteers, in a privileged position. Despite this, loyalty to Spain was predominant among Puerto Ricans, although there was a growing disaffection among wide echelons of society.[124] Discontent was especially strong in the southwest of the island, the hinterland of the city of Ponce, the coffee-producing area, only slightly dependent on the Spanish market, which had been the autonomist stronghold since the 1870s.

Captain General Dabán's fears were not all ungrounded. The detection of Cuban revolutionary agents set the alarms ringing in La Fortaleza, seat of the Spanish power in San Juan. In June 1895, the military commander of Ponce, Julio Soto Villanueva, reported to the captain general that a *mambí* agent had been detected in that city, according to reports sent to him by an informant in New York.[125] From that moment, the documents generated by the Spanish authorities reveal a genuine desire to isolate Puerto Rico as much as possible from the Cuban revolutionary influence. Indeed, they feared that the existing tensions could explode into open rebellion against Spain should the insurgents gain a stable presence on the island. To impede the presence of Cuban revolutionary agents, it was vital to seal the coast from unwanted arrivals of men, weapons, and ideas. For that purpose, beyond tight control of the maritime traffic coming in and out Puerto Rico, the Volunteers were mobilized to patrol the coast, alongside the army and the Civil Guard. On September 13, 1895, men from the 2nd, 8th, 9th, and 10th battalions were deployed to patrol the area of Bayamón, Sabana Grande, Ponce, and Coamo, thus covering most of the Southwest and part of the North coasts.[126] They already made up a significant portion of the Spanish forces in Puerto Rico: for 8,200 regular soldiers, there were 7,135 Volunteers.[127] They presented many advantages, too. Contrary to army units, which were stationed only in San Juan, Ponce, and Mayagüez, plus a few small towns, the Volunteers had companies and sections all over the island.[128] As well, the Volunteers were men most familiar with Puerto Rican geography and society, as their ranks were generally made up of Puerto Rican peasants, known as *jíbaros*, and *peninsulares* long established on the island, who usually had married local women and were well integrated into local society.

To be mobilized away from home for a few days, however, posed a problem for these men, who depended on their daily work. Mobilization implied a small allowance,

---

[124] Cubano Iguina. *El hilo en el laberinto*, pp. 145–50.
[125] AGMM, Documentación de Puerto Rico, 5145.38.
[126] AGMM, Documentación de Puerto Rico, 5202.3; AGMM, Documentación de Puerto Rico, 5201.4.
[127] *Provincia de Puerto Rico. Instituto de Voluntarios*, p. 15; Luis González Vales. "La campaña de Puerto Rico. Consideraciones histórico-militares," in *El Ejército y la Armada en 1898: Cuba, Puerto Rico y Filipinas, I Congreso Internacional de Historia Militar*, vol. I. Madrid: Ministerio de Defensa, 1999, p. 262; *Provincia de Puerto Rico. Instituto de Voluntarios*, p. 18.
[128] *Anuario Militar de España*. Madrid: Tipografía e Imprenta del Depósito de la Guerra, 1895, pp. 170–2.

but it rarely arrived. The impression was that the military authorities had a widespread contempt for the Volunteers, if not open distrust for the Puerto Ricans' loyalty to Spain. A Spanish staff officer wrote after the war that "the abyss between creoles and *peninsulares* in the island was as deep as in Cuba, even among Army officers."[129] So far, the attitude of Puerto Ricans serving in the Spanish forces discredited these words, but they were quite symptomatic of the treatment that these men could expect from some members of the military authorities on the island. Throughout the autumn of 1895, Julio Soto Villanueva kept reporting the captain general the problems their men were suffering in the area around Ponce. The rainy season had blocked many roads, thus leaving some of them isolated in remote areas. More importantly, the stipend that was granted to mobilized Volunteers, due since September, only began to arrive by mid-December 1895. This, in its turn, made finding Volunteers for service at the coast rather difficult, especially during the coffee harvest, for many of them were employed in this industry.[130]

With some Volunteers precariously patrolling the coast, and the rest keeping public order in the cities, their military role remained practically unaltered until the United States Navy first attacked San Juan on May 12, 1898. In the meantime, groups of Puerto Rican nationalists exiled in the United States, aided by their Cuban colleagues, continued to plot. On October 20, 1896, the Spanish minister in Caracas (Venezuela) reported to Sabas Marín, who had replaced Captain General Antonio Dabán that very year, confidential information about the plot for an invasion of the island, organized by Cuban, Puerto Rican, and Dominican revolutionaries in Santo Domingo, in which the former president of Venezuela, Juan Pablo Rojas Paúl (1888–90), was also involved.[131] Their main problem was the lack of popular support for a rebellion against Spain. This was the basic reason that a short-lived uprising, known as *Intentona de Yauco*, a town nearby Ponce, failed. In March 24–26, 1897, two gangs of a few dozen men each took up arms but were swiftly quelled by the Civil Guard and the local Volunteers, eight of whom ended up being decorated for their services.[132] Yauco was the center of a thriving coffee-producing industry, mostly controlled by Corsican migrants and their Puerto Rican offspring, who identified only weakly with Spain, if at all.[133] The mastermind of the failed insurrection was Antonio Mattei Lluveras, son to a Corsican father and a Puerto Rican mother. He had recruited Cuban and Dominican agents to organize the armed rebellion but could not convince more than one hundred Puerto Ricans to join the rising. The fact that local Volunteers helped the Civil Guard to quell the attempted insurrection was a symptom that an open rebellion against Spain was still an unlikely outcome in Puerto Rico.

---

[129] Francisco Larrea y Lisa. *El desastre nacional y los vicios de nuestras instituciones militares*. Madrid: Imprenta del Cuerpo de Artillería, 1901, pp. 66–7. The book, however, is signed with Larrea's pseudonym EFEELE.

[130] AGM, Documentación de Puerto Rico, sig. 5202.20.

[131] AGMM, Capitanía General de Puerto Rico, sig. 5146.21.

[132] Negroni. *Historia militar de Puerto Rico*, pp. 306–7; AGMM, Capitanía General de Puerto Rico, sig. 5610.12.

[133] Laird W. Bergad. *Coffee and the Growth of Agrarian Capitalism in Nineteenth-Century Puerto Rico*. Princeton: Princeton University Press, 1983, pp. 145–203.

The biggest threat to Spanish sovereignty in Puerto Rico came from the United States. Alongside Cuba, the McKinley administration also planned to seize Puerto Rico for the absolute control of the Spanish Caribbean. The Volunteers participated in the preparations for conflict as soon as the United States declared war on Spain in April 1898. On paper, they were ready to resist the invasion alongside the army, combining between the two a force of over 15,000 men.[134] In San Juan, the Puerto Rican journalist and former member of the Parliament Vicente Balbás Capó was appointed major in the newly created Puerto Rico Tirailleurs Volunteers Battalion Volunteer, made up of well-known *incondicionales* and Volunteer veterans, on April 23, 1898, two days before the formal US war declaration.[135] Throughout the island, new sections and companies were created, despite the lack of resources in some areas. For instance, a group of humble *jíbaros* set up a force named *Voluntarios Macheteros* named after the machete, the only weapon they could count on, as well as several mounted guerrillas. The first company of *macheteros* was created in Juncos on April 25, being followed by the company of San Juan (May 4) and Maunabo (May 12).[136]

Despite the ingrained distrust that a good deal of army commanding officers from the Peninsula harbored toward them, the Volunteers' early participation in war preparations earned them more consideration and respect. At the same time, sectors who had traditionally challenged the status quo but wanted to remain Spaniards gathered under the Volunteer banner as the US invasion seemed imminent. Ángel Rivero Méndez, a Puerto Rican artillery officer in the Spanish Army, recalled that many autonomists, mostly Puerto Rican but also some *peninsulares*, who had previously held a negative conception of the Volunteers, began to join the militia.[137] From the declaration of war on April 25, 1898, the autonomist press launched a campaign attacking the United States for wanting to sever the centuries-old Spanish presence in Puerto Rico. Unlike Cuba, which had a strong community of African descent, most Puerto Ricans were descendants of *peninsulares* who had settled in the seventeenth and eighteenth centuries. Even the leader of the Autonomous Party, and head of the Insular Government established on January 1, 1898, Luis Muñoz Rivera, published an article in May 1898 entitled *"Long Live Spain!"* in his newspaper *La Democracia*, calling all Puerto Ricans to flock to the Spanish banner and defend their nationality against the "Yankee aggressor."[138] After all, autonomists stood for wider political rights for Puerto Rico, but within Spain. This was constantly reinforced in the autonomist press throughout the war against the United States, whose intervention threatened to put Spanish sovereignty to an end and potentially put the identity of Puerto Ricans at risk. This might explain the growing numbers of Puerto Ricans who joined the Volunteers, who by July amounted to over 9,000 men.[139]

As Puerto Rico was getting ready for a battle, the war came to the island at dawn on May 12, 1898, when an eight-vessel US fleet commanded by Admiral William

---

[134] Rivero Méndez. *Crónica de la Guerra*, pp. 449–55.
[135] AGMM, Documentación de Puerto Rico, 5195.1; Rivero Méndez. *Crónica de la Guerra*, p. 86.
[136] AGMM, Documentación de Puerto Rico, sig. 5146.33.
[137] Rivero Méndez. *Crónica de la Guerra*, p. 450.
[138] *La Democracia*, 13-05-1898, p. 2.
[139] Larrea y Lisa. *El desastre nacional*, p. 73.

T. Sampson was sighted from San Juan. Sampson was chasing the fleet of Admiral Cervera, which had departed from Cape Verde on April 29 for Cuba, but which he reckoned would be harbored in Puerto Rico by then. Not finding Cervera, the US fleet decided to shell the old walls of San Juan anyway. The bombing killed seven people—including five civilians, injured over sixty, and had a tremendous psychological effect, for Puerto Rico had not suffered an attack by a foreign force since the failed British invasion of 1797. San Juan was defended not by a fleet, for the Spanish fleet in the Caribbean had just left for Cuba, but by the strong coastal artillery of the forts of San Felipe del Morro and San Cristóbal. Though the aim of Admiral Sampson was to test the defenses of San Juan, the bombardment provided a good opportunity for the Volunteers to demonstrate their military capacity and reliability for the campaign likely to come. During the attack, the captain general used the Volunteers for the protection of La Fortaleza and several key infrastructures.[140]

The combat lasted for slightly over two hours, but everyone knew that another attack would come. Cuba was the main target for the United States, which would not launch a thrust against Puerto Rico until that scenario was clarified. The capitulation of Santiago de Cuba on July 17 allowed the implementation of the plans of invasion in the smaller of the Spanish Antilles, as if they knew that war would not go on for the rest of Cuba. As in Cuba, the army followed the navy. The US secretary of war Russell A. Alger ordered the experienced General Nelson A. Miles, a veteran of the US Civil War and the Indian Wars, who had also taken part in the Cuban campaign, to leave Guantánamo with 4,000 troopers and assume command of the force that was going to land in Puerto Rico.[141] Other 12,000 men were dispatched from the United States, forming an invading army of 16,000 men in total, slightly outnumbering the 15,000 soldiers and Volunteers who defended Puerto Rico.

While a fleet blockaded San Juan, on July 25, 1898, Saint James' Day, Saint Patron of Spain, General Nelson A. Miles and his 16,000 men landed in Guánica, a small town in the southwest of Puerto Rico. The location for the invasion was strategic because this area was where discontent with Spain was most widespread. The region around Ponce essentially received non-Spanish migrants during the first half of the nineteenth century, whose links with Spain were generally weak. Also, this region of Puerto Rico heavily depended on sugar exports, much more dependent on the US than on the Spanish market.[142] Guánica is only 42 km east to Ponce, the autonomist stronghold, and less than 10 km from Yauco, seat of the short-lived uprising a few months before. According to contemporary American sources, "there was great disaffection toward the Spanish cause among the citizens and the Volunteers" of this region.[143] The fact

---

[140] AGMM, Documentación de Puerto Rico, sig. 5171.13.
[141] See Peter R. De Montravel. *A Hero to His Fighting Men, Nelson A. Miles, 1839–1925*. Kent: The Kent State University Press, 1998.
[142] Francisco A. Scarano. *Sugar and Slavery in Puerto Rico Plantation Economy of Ponce, 1800–1850*. Madison: University of Wisconsin Press, 1984, pp. 79–102.
[143] Fitzhugh Lee, Theodore Roosevelt & Joseph Wheeler. *Cuba's Struggle against Spain with the Causes of American Intervention and a Full Account of the Spanish-American War: Including Final Peace Negotiations*. New York: American Historical Press, 1899, p. 556.

is that, upon Miles's landing, the Spanish defenses quickly collapsed, including the Volunteers. Indeed, there was a contagious wave of desertions among the Volunteers in the wake of Miles's incursion. Some cases were particularly surprising, including rank-and-file Volunteers and officials who held political office for the Unconditional Spanish Party, and thus were supposed to harbor strong Spanish feelings. Florencio Santiago, the *incondicional* mayor of Coamo and a Volunteer colonel, recalled having breakfast at his house with Rafael Martínez Illescas, the Spanish commander of Ponce, and lunch with US Army captain Anderson on August 9, 1898, right before the start of the battle for the Asomante pass, midway between Guánica and the island's capital, San Juan.[144]

Ángel Rivero Méndez argued that the weak Volunteers' response to the invasion was caused by decisions taken by the military authorities in San Juan. For example, the very day of the invasion, July 25, all the conscripts serving in the Volunteers, around 500 men, were ordered to leave the militia and join regular army units. This often meant leaving their towns on their own means and moving to barracks stationed in San Juan, Ponce, and Mayagüez. On top of this, a day later, regular soldiers were ordered to evacuate the southwest for San Juan, while the Volunteers were ordered to gather in the military districts' headquarters, thus leaving most of towns entirely unprotected. Consequently, fearing that their families and properties could fall prey to reprisals from either the US troops or bandits fighting in troubled waters, many of these Volunteers refused to leave their towns and deserted.[145] As a result, the Spanish command decided to destroy their weapons and to dismantle most of the Volunteer units scattered throughout the island, but not all. For instance, the note ordering the destruction of weapons was sent to Colonel Puig in Yauco on July 26, 1898, for the authorities were suspicious of the loyalty of local Volunteers, some of whose relatives might have taken part in the thwarted 1897 uprising.[146]

Actually, Puerto Rican Volunteers were essentially abandoned by the Spanish command, which was not able to put up a good resistance against the US invading army. Miles had taken Ponce on July 27 and kept advancing toward San Juan through the hilly interior of the island, encountering little resistance. Quite ironically, the US troops took advantage of the recently completed Central Road (*Carretera Central*), which connected Ponce to San Juan crossing the Cordillera Central. On their way, the only serious engagement between the two armies took place in Aibonito, 60 km south to San Juan. The fight lasted four days, from August 9 to 13, as the Spanish forces retreating from Ponce tried to stop the US Army on its way to the capital. By then, most of the Volunteers had deserted, and some had joined the invading army as scouts, but about a third of Ponce's Ninth Volunteer Battalion took the stand for Spain alongside the army.[147] Taking advantage of the hilly terrain and showing good fighting

---

[144] I would like to give thanks for this information to Lindy Usera Fernández, great-granddaughter of Florencio Santiago. Also in Rivero Méndez. *Crónica de la Guerra*, pp. 241–2.
[145] Rivero Méndez. *Crónica de la Guerra*, pp. 449–55.
[146] Rivero Méndez. *Crónica de la Guerra*, p. 203.
[147] AGMM, Documentación de Puerto Rico, sig. 5175.14 & 5173.23; Larrea y Lisa. *El desastre nacional*, pp. 195–212; Rivero Méndez. *Crónica de la Guerra*, pp. 427–39.

skills, the Spanish troops were holding the US soldiers at bay when news came that the governments of Spain and the United States had signed an armistice on August 12.

The fact is that in just nineteen days, the US invading army had been able to occupy a third of Puerto Rico's territory, and a city like Ponce had been evacuated without firing a shot. Some embittered and ashamed army officers blamed the Puerto Rican Volunteers for such a quick defeat, rather than assuming their own share of responsibility. For instance, Francisco Larrea y Lisa considered that the Volunteers had not "fulfilled their duty."[148] Shortly after the conflict, Major Julio Cervera Baviera wrote that the Volunteers had only been a source of trouble and disturbance during the war, for they "had never been relied upon for the defence" of the island.[149] These opinions were a blow below the belt for Puerto Ricans who had loyally fought for Spain. One of them, Ángel Rivero Méndez, the army gunner officer, considered these criticisms as a mere pretext to blame Puerto Ricans for the military defeat.[150]

Spanish command could hardly pretend that a few thousand men with barely military training faced a 16,000-men invading army, once regular forces had evacuated the entire southwest of Puerto Rico, where the Americans were expected to find many collaborators.[151] The Volunteers were auxiliary forces, and as such, their performance usually depended on the skills and preparation of regular forces. Unlike Cuba, Puerto Rican Volunteers had not had the chance to take part in a war previously, so they had no combat experience and barely any military training. On top of this, they were left alone in the southwest, and found themselves trapped between 16,000 armed enemies and the disaffection of part of the people they were supposed to defend. Thus, it is hardly surprising that they tended to give up their weapons as *yanqui* soldiers advanced.

As in Cuba, after the armistice, the enemies soon turned not into allies, but protectors, especially after all Spanish regular forces evacuated the island on October 18, 1898. The Volunteers, once their units were dismantled, were given the chance to choose between staying in Puerto Rico and leaving for Spain. Most chose to stay, for a great many were natives of the island and had no other home, and most of the *peninsulares* were probably married to local women and had created their own families in Puerto Rico, or were simply looking for better living prospects in the island. Actually, many officials were confirmed by the new US authorities, like Florencio Santiago, the former Volunteer colonel who continued as mayor of Coamo. In Puerto Rico, the independence movement had barely any substantial popular support, but some anti-Spanish sentiments erupted right after the invasion in the form of attacks on people who had openly sided with Spain, either Puerto Ricans or *peninsulares*, often carried out by *tiznados*, bands of impoverished peasants and outlaws. For instance, on July 29, only two days after the occupation of Yauco, American soldiers prevented

---

[148] Larrea y Lisa. *El desastre nacional*, p. 73.
[149] Julio Cervera Baviera. *La defensa militar de Puerto-Rico*. San Juan: Imprenta de la Capitanía General, 1898, pp. 8–9; VVAA. *Julio Cervera y la telegrafía sin hilos*. Madrid: Ministerio de Defensa y Ministerio de Economía y Competitividad, 2015.
[150] Rivero Méndez. *Crónica de la Guerra*, pp. 452 & 473.
[151] María de los Ángeles Castro Arroyo. "'¿A qué pelear si los de Madrid no quieren?' Una versión criolla de la guerra del 98 en Puerto Rico." *Revista de Indias*, 1997, vol. LVII, No. 211, pp. 657–94.

local Volunteers from being lynched by some of their fellow neighbors.[152] In Ciales, a shop owned by two former Volunteers was attacked on September 29.[153] Events of this kind occurred throughout the island, forcing the authorities to intervene. US Army general Ernst issued a decree prohibiting any reprisals against the Volunteers or *incondicionales*, or any known supporter of Spain, as long as they respected the new situation.[154] From the perspective of the US invading force, the collaboration of Spanish loyalists was vital for ruling a recently conquered territory. Most of the mayors, civil servants, policemen, merchants, and company owners were *incondicionales*, Volunteers, and often *peninsulares*. The success of US occupation greatly depended upon these men, at least initially, when the Americans had no governing structure on the island.[155] Ironically, Spanish loyalists ended up being protected by the very people they were meant to fight.

---

[152] Rivero Méndez. *Crónica de la Guerra*, p. 217.
[153] AGPR, Fondo del Tribunal Superior de Guayama. Serie Criminal. Caja 529, exp. sin título, pieza 1 (sumario 420 de 1898); Fernando Picó *Al filo del poder. Subalternos y dominantes en Puerto Rico, 1739-1910*. Río Piedras: Editorial de la Universidad de Puerto Rico, 1993, pp. 161-71.
[154] Rivero Méndez. *Crónica de la Guerra*, pp. 246-7.
[155] Pérez, Jr. *Cuba between Empires*, pp. 211-28; Picó. *1898. La guerra después de la guerra*, pp. 161-200.

10

The Volunteers in the Philippines

Far from the Antillean scenario, in the far-flung Filipino archipelago, Spain also fought a war against local revolutionaries and the United States to keep its only Asian colony, which had been under Spanish rule since the days of King Philip II, who could claim that, in his vast dominions, the Sun never set. During the final years of the nineteenth century, in the Antillean and Asian relics of the once huge empire, the blood never dried. On August 23, 1896, a group of Filipino nationalists issued the *Grito de Balintawak* (Proclamation of Balintawak), a town just 8 km north to Manila. Following the example of Cuba and Puerto Rico, the tiny community of Spaniards in the Philippines also rallied to create their own Volunteer units to help the Spanish Army in the fight. Until that moment, a few tiny garrisons made up of Spanish officers and native soldiers had been enough to keep the Philippines under Spanish control for centuries, but the colony had never seen anything like the revolution started in 1896.

First visited in 1521 by the Castilian expedition headed by Ferdinand Magellan and continued by Juan Sebastián de Elcano, the first to circumnavigate the globe, the Philippines had come under the Spanish aegis after Miguel López de Legazpi's men landed in Cebú in 1565 and conquered the city of Manila from its Muslim rulers in 1571. Being so far away from the Spanish homeland, only a tiny number of administrators, soldiers, and clergy settled in the archipelago, where Spanish effective control was reduced to a few outposts and their hinterlands, especially in the island groups of Luzón and the Visayas. In the southern islands of Mindanao, a predominantly Islamic population kept the Christian presence at bay. Due to the scant numbers of officials and settlers, the role of the clergy was extremely important in establishing Spanish rule in the Philippines. Augustinians, Discalced Franciscans, Jesuits, Dominicans, and the Augustinian Recollects, bestowed with evangelizing the natives, often acted as the true administrators of the archipelago, instead of Crown officials. The friars learn the native languages and become middlemen between the policies dictated in Madrid and the actual implementation on the ground.[1] This shaped a colony widely Christianized, save for the Muslim south, but generally alien to the Spanish language and law, leaving it to the minority of Spaniards, Filipino mestizos, and local elites closer to Spanish power.

---

[1] María Dolores Elizalde Pérez-Grueso & Xavier Huetz de Lemps. "Un singular modelo colonizador: el papel de las órdenes religiosas en la administración española de Filipinas, siglos XVI al XIX." *Illes i Imperis*, 2015, No. 17, pp.185–222.

Due to the geographical position of the Philippines, between China and the New Spain, for centuries Manila played a key role as a commercial hotspot where the Chinese need of Spanish silver and the Spanish taste for Chinese goods met thanks to the so-called Manila Galleon, the trading route which connected Asia and America for almost three centuries. De facto, the Philippines were administered as a dependency of the Viceroyalty of the New Spain through the *asiento*, the funds with which the cost of keeping the archipelago under Spanish control was paid. The loss of New Spain in 1821 placed the Philippines in a sort of limbo. For a few decades, the Asian colony was more disconnected from Spain than ever before to the point that in 1839 the Spanish Government even considered selling the Philippines to France.[2] Only after the opening of the Suez Canal in 1869, which shortened the six-month-long trip from the Peninsula to Manila to just one, Spain began to increase its presence in the archipelago.[3] New investment opportunities appeared for shipping lines and the production of commodities. The flagship of the renewed Spanish interest for the archipelago was represented by the General Tobacco Company of the Philippines, with headquarters in Barcelona and Manila, established in 1881 by Antonio López, Marquis of Comillas, one of the founders of the *Círculo Hispano-Ultramarino* of Barcelona ten years before.

Growing interest in its far-flung colony also stemmed from challenges to its sovereignty from rival colonial powers. In 1885, Bismarck's Germany threatened to occupy the Caroline Islands, an archipelago in the Pacific Ocean which was part of the Captaincy General of the Philippines that had been under theoretical Spanish control since the seventeenth century.[4] Although war was averted and Spain kept control of the islands, the so-called Crisis of the Carolines sparked a wave of interest in Spain and the Spanish Antilles regarding the country's colonial presence in the Far East. In the Antilles, promoting the idea that Spain had to take care of its colonies was vital. For instance, the *Casino Español* in Havana collected 50,000 golden pesos among its members toward contributing to the military expansion of Spain in the islands recently coveted by the German Empire.[5] In metropolitan Spain, Minister of the Colonies Víctor Balaguer (1886–8), a Catalan writer and representative of the powerful Barcelona colonial lobby, organized the General Exhibition of the Philippines Islands held in 1887 in Madrid, which was aimed at attracting capital for the development of the archipelago.[6]

---

[2] Yllán Calderón, Esperanza. "Un proyecto de cesión a Francia de las islas Filipinas (1839)," in José María Jover Zamora (dir.). *El siglo XIX en España: doce estudios*. Barcelona: Editorial Planeta, 1974, pp. 253–83.
[3] Josep M. Delgado. "'Menos se perdió en Cuba'. La dimensión asiática del 98." *Illes i Imperis*, 1999, No. 2, pp. 49–64; Carmen Gallego Fresnillo. "El sexenio español y el Extremo Oriente: Filipinas," in María Dolores Elizalde Pérez-Grueso (ed.). *Las relaciones internacionales en el Pacífico (siglos XVIII–XX): colonización, descolonización y encuentro cultural*. Madrid: CSIC, 1997, pp. 375–94.
[4] María Dolores Elizalde Pérez-Grueso. *España en el Pacífico. La colonia de las Islas Carolinas, 1885–1899. Un modelo colonial en el contexto internacional del imperialismo*. Madrid: CSIC/Instituto de Cooperación para el Desarrollo, 1992, pp. 29–44; Agustín R. Rodríguez González. "La crisis de las Carolinas." *Cuadernos de historia contemporánea*, 1991, No. 13, pp. 25–46.
[5] AHN, Archivo Antonio Cánovas del Castillo, 2543, exp. 68.
[6] Luis Ángel Sánchez Gómez. *Un imperio en la vitrina. El colonialismo español en el Pacífico y la exposición de Filipinas de 1887*. Madrid: CSIC, 2003, pp. 29–38.

Despite this increased interest in the Philippines, effective Spanish rule was virtually constrained to Manila and a few outposts distributed throughout the archipelago, thus leaving vast areas outside of Spanish control. The Philippines were still populated by dozens of different ethnicities, scarcely Hispanized, mostly Catholic, though with important pockets of Muslims in the recently incorporated archipelagos of southern Mindanao and Joló, who rejected the Spanish presence until 1898 and continued in a state of rebellion until they were crushed by force during the early years of American occupation of the Philippines.[7] In Luzón, the biggest and most important island, where Manila is located, the dominant ethnicity were the Tagalog, who became the bedrock of the Filipino nationalist movement.[8] However, unlike in Cuba, Filipino nationalism was still incipient by the end of the nineteenth century.[9] The archipelago was made up of thousands of islands where a sense of a united anti-Spanish and anti-colonial nationalism could hardly have taken ground. This was the main reason a major military presence had not been necessary before 1896, for Spanish rule was weak but mostly uncontested, save for some sporadically anticolonial outbursts.[10]

In this context, the Spanish sovereignty in the Philippines depended on the collaboration of local Filipino and religious elites, two forces which were not always collaborative. The clash between local power and the Spanish clergy shaped the ways in which the Filipino nationalists sought to overcome their subservient relation with Spain, as native Filipinos were only appointed in the lower echelons of the colonial administration.[11] By the end of the nineteenth century, a group of young educated Tagalogs, often of mix Spanish and Chinese race, who came to be known as *Ilustrados*,

---

[7] W. R. Retana. *Mando del general Weyler en Filipinas. 5 Junio 1888–17 Noviembre 1891. Apuntes y documentos para la historia política, administrativa y militar de dichas islas*. Madrid: Imprenta de la Viuda de M. Minuesa de los Ríos, 1896, pp. 328–35; Luis E. Togores Sánchez. "La última frontera: el establecimiento de la soberanía española en el país moro," in Elizalde, Fradera & Alonso. *Imperios y Naciones en el Pacífico*, vol. II, pp. 675–98; Isaac Donoso Jiménez. "El desarrollo del mundo meridional filipino en el siglo XIX: el difícil encaje de la población musulmana," in María Dolores Elizalde Pérez-Grueso & Xavier Huetz de Lemps (coord.). *Filipinas, siglo XIX: coexistencia e interacción entre comunidades en el Imperio español*. Madrid: Polifemo: 2017, pp. 427–56.

[8] Leonard Y. Andaya. "Ethnicity in the Philippine Revolution," in Florentino Rodao & Felice Noelle Rodríguez (eds.). *The Philippine Revolution of 1896: Ordinary People in Extraordinary Times*. Quezon City: Ateneo de Manila University Press, 2001, pp. 49–82.

[9] María Dolores Elizalde. "El sueño de la nación filipina. 1812–1896," in María Dolores Elizalde Pérez-Grueso (ed.). *Problemas en la construcción nacional de Filipinas, India y Vietnam*. Barcelona: Edicions Bellaterra, 2013, pp. 37–82.

[10] Luis E. Togores Sánchez. "Antecedentes y causas de la revuelta tagala de 1896-1897," in Emilio de Diego García & Demetrio Ramos (dir.). *Cuba, Puerto Rico y Filipinas en la perspectiva del 98*. Madrid: Editorial Complutense, 1997, pp. 127–46.

[11] Juan Antonio Inarejos Muñoz. "Reclutar cacique: la selección de las elites coloniales filipinas a finales del siglo XIX." *Hispania*, 2011, vol. LXXI, No. 239, pp. 741–62; "La *influencia moral* en Asia. Práctica política y corrupción electoral en Filipinas durante la dominación colonial española." *Anuario de Estudios Americanos*, 2012, vol. 69, No. 1, pp. 199–224; "Los procedimientos de elección de los gobernadorcillos de 'igorrotes' en Filipinas a finales del siglo XIX." *Revista Complutense de Historia de América*, 2014, vol. 40, pp. 255–76; *Los (últimos) caciques de Filipinas. Las élites coloniales antes del 98*. Granada: 2015; María Dolores Elizalde Pérez-Grueso & Xavier Huetz de Lemps. "Poder, religión y control en Filipinas. Colaboración y conflicto entre el Estado y las órdenes religiosas, 1868–1898." *Ayer*, 2015, No. 100, pp. 151–76; Luis Ángel Sánchez Gómez. "Élites indígenas y política colonial en Filipinas (1847–1898)," in Naranjo Orovio, Puig-Samper & García

became the spearhead of Filipino nationalism. Most of them had studied at the University of Santo Tomás in Manila, Asia's oldest university established in 1611 by Spanish friars of the Dominic Order, or the Ateneo de Manila, run by the Jesuits since 1859. Some of them had also studied in Europe's top universities thanks to Spanish Government grants. The *Ilustrados* attempted to forge a sense of Filipino nationality, create a political culture based on the European Nation-State model, and prepare the archipelago for a peaceful transition toward independence.[12]

The most notorious of the *ilustrados* was José Rizal, considered the Philippines' national hero. He was a mestizo of native Filipino, Spanish, and Chinese descent and a trained physician who studied in the Philippines, Spain, France, and Germany. In 1884 he joined the freemasons in Madrid and became an ardent opponent of clerical influence in the Philippines. Rizal authored two famous novels in which he criticized the Spanish colonial abuses: *Noli me tangere* (1887) and *El filibusterismo* (1891). In 1892, he created the *Liga Filipina*, a clandestine organization aimed at structuring a peaceful political movement for the emancipation of the Philippines.[13] However, the purely colonial regime that existed in the archipelago, which denied the Filipinos political rights that had been granted to Cubans and Puerto Ricans, eventually convinced many Filipinos of the impossibility of getting any reform under Spanish rule. After the colonial authorities shut down the *Liga Filipina* in 1893, some of its members, led by Emilio Aguinaldo, created the *Katipunan*, a secret organization with which to prepare an armed uprising against Spain.[14] Thanks to the network of Filipino freemasonry in the archipelago, intensely implicated in the emancipation of the colony, the *Katipunan* began to grow in the provinces around the city of Manila from its headquarters in the city of Cavite, the seat of the Spanish fleet in the Philippine and South China Seas.[15] Since the paramountcy of the Catholic Church in the Philippines was a major source

---

Mora. *La Nación Soñada*, pp. 417-28; Benedict Anderson. *The Age of Globalization. Anarchists and the anticolonial imagination*. London and New York: Verso, 2013 (first published as *Under Three Flags*, 2005), pp. 123-67. For the commercial aspect of the colonial relation see J. A. Larkin. *Sugar and the Origins of modern Philippine Society*. Berkeley: University of California Press, 1993, pp. 46-53; Filomeno V. Aguilar. *Clash of Spirits: The History of Power and Sugar Planter Hegemony on a Visayan Island*. Honolulu: The University of Hawaii Press, 1998, pp. 156-88.

[12] See Wenceslao E. Retana. *Vida y escritos del Dr. José Rizal*. Madrid: Librería General de Victoriano Suárez, 1907.

[13] Hélène Godet-Goujat. "La Liga Filipina, creada por José Rizal en 1892, como balance político y base de un programa nacional para Filipinas," in Naranjo Orovio, Puig-Samper & García Mora. *La Nación Soñada*, pp. 79-84; Lourdes Díaz-Trechuelo. *Filipinas. La gran desconocida (1565-1898)*. Pamplona: Editorial de la Universidad de Navarra, 2001, pp. 318-20; Anderson. *The Age of Globalization*, pp. 129-33; Martín Rodrigo y Alharilla. "La 'cuestión Rizal': memoria del gobernador general Despujol (1892)." *Revista de Indias*, 1998, vol. 58, No. 213, pp. 365-84.

[14] Susana Cuartero Escobés. "El nacionalismo independentista del Katipunan," in Fusi & Niño Rodríguez (eds.). *Antes del desastre*, pp. 225-34; Díaz-Trechuelo. *Filipinas*, pp. 320-2; Carmen Molina Gómez-Arnau. "Apuntes sobre el Katipunan." *Revista española del Pacífico*, 1996, No. 6, pp.47-70.

[15] Díaz-Trechuelo. *Filipinas*, pp. 316-18; Hermenegildo Franco Castañón. "El apostadero de Filipinas: sus años finales." *El Ejército y la Armada en 1898: Cuba, Puerto Rico y Filipinas*, 1999, vol. I, pp. 345-74.

of discontent among Filipino nationalists, it is hardly surprising that local freemasonry acted as a vehicle for propagating the idea of ending colonial rule. Quite conveniently, this sect also allowed for a network of secret lodges, which were to duly prepare the insurrection against Spain.[16]

This was the context when the insurrection began in August 1896. To cover an archipelago of 7,000 islands and more than seven million inhabitants, Captain General Ramón Blanco only had 18,000 men at his disposal.[17] Manila, the main target of the 20,000-men insurgent army, had a garrison of just 1,500 regular soldiers, of whom 1,000 were native Filipinos.[18] The high percentage of native soldiers was a source of alarm for their leaders rather than of confidence, for the memories of the Cavite mutiny in 1872 were still fresh among the Spanish community. In that year, a group of Filipino soldiers in the Spanish Army, in connivance with local priests, attempted to raise the native population against the Spanish community.[19] Although the mutiny was rapidly quelled, it claimed a high death toll, and was a serious admonition of the precarious position of the Spain in the Philippines.

For Spaniards in the archipelago, being so far from Spain, and being so few, creating militia units was a sensible measure to reinforce their position. Back in 1876, during the campaign to conquer the Sultanate of Sulu, there had been a few hundred Filipino Volunteers from Misamis who were mobilized by a local priest but were rapidly dismantled after the campaign.[20] This time, in 1896, no territory annexation was on the table, but the very survival of Spaniards in the Philippines. The *Casino Español* of Manila, established in 1893 following the example of Havana and Puerto Rico, was the informal headquarters of Spanish supporters. In its rooms, the creation of a volunteer unit had been already discussed in March 1896 amid rumors of an imminent uprising due to the constant visits of Filipino nationalists to the US Consulate in the city.[21] But Captain General Blanco, a liberal who often clashed with the generally conservative local Spanish community, was very reluctant to hand them weapons, for he feared they could end up being used against him. According to contemporary journalists, he feared being ousted like Domingo Dulce in 1869.[22] Even the Church openly showed its discontent with Blanco's bland position. Archbishop Bernardino Nozaleda (1890–1902), who had been one of the main promoters of creating a Volunteers battalion, surreptitiously accused the captain general of being a freemason and a collaborator of the *katipuneros* who wanted to end Spanish rule.[23]

[16] Leoncio Cabrero. "Las interferencias de la masonería extranjera en Filipinas en la segunda mitad del siglo XIX." *Revista de Indias*, 1998, vol. LVIII, No. 213, pp. 519–27.
[17] Mas Chao. *La guerra olvidada de Filipinas*. Madrid: Editorial San Martín, 1997, pp. 29–44.
[18] Ramón Blanco. *Memoria que dirige al Senado dirige el general Blanco acerca de los últimos sucesos ocurridos en la isla de Luzón*. Madrid: Establecimiento Tipográfico de "El Liberal," 1897, pp. 88–9.
[19] Manuel Rolandi Sánchez-Solís. "La algarada de Cavite de enero de 1872: El primer intento independentista filipino fracasa en el Fuerte de San Felipe y en el Arsenal de Cavite." *Revista de Historia Militar*, 2008, No. 104, pp.201–56.
[20] Miguel A. Espina. *Un libro sobre Joló*. Manila: Imprenta y Litografía de M. Pérez, Hijo, 1888, p. 250.
[21] *La Dinastía*, 03-09-1896, p. 3.
[22] Rafael Guerrero. *Crónica de la guerra de Cuba y de la rebelión de Filipinas*, vol. IV. Barcelona: Tip. Hispano-Americana, 1898, p. 32.
[23] Díaz-Trechuelo. *Filipinas*, p. 322; *El Siglo Futuro*, 20-02-1904, p. 2.

Messages between the *Casino Español* and the Malacañang Palace, seat of the captain general, were very intense, but as Filipino rebels advanced almost unchecked at Manila's gates, Blanco finally agreed to call for the establishment of a Volunteer battalion on August 31, 1896.[24] The newly created Loyal Volunteers' Battalion was mostly formed by merchants, officials, and retired army personnel.[25] Unlike Havana or San Juan, there was no big community of working-class *peninsulares* in Manila. Most of the Spaniards were officials, soldiers, and priests. Hence, recruiting options were much more reduced for Manila's Volunteers.

Alike their colleagues in Cuba and Puerto Rico, the Loyal Volunteers were sent to protect key infrastructures such as military hospitals, jails, fortresses, and other official buildings, roads, and telegraph lines. Apparently, their performance was satisfactory, and in November 1896 two more units were created, the Guerrilla de San Rafael and the Guerrilla del Casino Español, which were used to patrol Manila Bay and keep a permanent connection between Malacañang Palace and the Cavite Naval Base.[26] The men who joined the Volunteers were directly interested in the continuity of Spanish rule, and in some cases had military training. This was the case, among others, of José Moreno Bueso, a native of Valencia who volunteered for the army at 18 in 1879, served in Puerto Rico and later joined the Civil Guard for four years in Manila, where he studied two degrees after retiring and married a Filipino woman with whom he fathered six children. In 1896, at 36, he took up arms again and joined the Guerrilla de San Rafael, in order to keep the Philippines Spanish and to fight for the life he had built there.[27]

The success of the Volunteers, amounting to around 1,500 men, was soon known in other parts of the archipelago. Though there were only tiny communities of *peninsulares* outside Manila, new units were created in Iloilo and the island of Mindoro, and in several towns across the countryside in which Spaniards and native Filipinos filled the ranks together.[28] The model was also extended to regions where Spanish presence was not only weak, but recent, like Mindanao and Joló, to keep held local Muslim population at bay.[29]

Despite the many Volunteer companies created throughout the Philippines, the situation in Manila was still desperate. A state of war was declared in the provinces of Manila, Bulacán, Pampanga and Nueva Écija on August 30, 1896, Morong on October 23, and Zambales, and Bataan on December, 30. By early 1897 the provinces surrounding the city had mostly fallen into the hands of the rebels, who had agents within the city walls. On top of this, reinforcements were unlikely to arrive from Spain in the short term.[30] The Cuban war was Spain's main concern, leaving the Filipino

---

[24] Blanco. *Memoria que dirige al Senado*, pp. 40–2.
[25] See, for instance, AHN, Ultramar, 5304, exps. 14, 73, 129.
[26] Blanco. *Memoria que dirige al Senado*, p. 33; AGMM, Ultramar, CGF, caja 5305, *Guerrilla de San Rafael*.
[27] I owe this information to Antonio Moreno, great-grandson of José Moreno Bueso.
[28] AHN, Ultramar, 5330, exp. 11; AGMM, Ultramar, CGF, caja 5305, *Sección de Voluntarios de Mindoro*.
[29] Blanco. *Memoria que dirige al Senado*, p. 33.
[30] AHN, Ultramar, 5356, exp. 4; Mas Chao. *La guerra olvidada de Filipinas*, pp. 29–57.

uprising not a priority. In any case, reinforcements could not be expected to arrive before a month. This nurtured a sort of permanent state of fear among *peninsulares*, who began to be seen on the streets of Manila and other major cities carrying pistols at all times.[31] Confidence in Blanco's capacity to revert the situation ran weak as days passed by. Blanco had taken harsh measures against the rebels, but despite ordering dozens of executions, he was unable to quell the rebellion and to control the area around Manila. Looking for a new governor who could raise the spirit in Manila, the Spanish Government appointed General Camilo García de Polavieja as the new captain general on December 13, 1896.[32]

The *peninsulares* of Manila, including the Volunteers, hoped that Polavieja would be implacable with the rebels, and pressed him to carry on with the legal process against José Rizal, who had been falsely accused of being involved in the Katipunan armed struggle.[33] Actually, Rizal had been arrested in Barcelona in October 1896, while he was on his way from Manila to Havana, as he had volunteered to serve as an army doctor in Cuba. After he was sent back to Manila to face the courts, *integristas* insistently demanded his execution, for he had become a symbol of Filipino nationalism. Due to his previous experience as provincial governor and captain general in Cuba, Polavieja distrusted arming the Volunteers for he thought it a secure recipe for trouble. The Philippines was different from Cuba, but the Manila Volunteers were beginning to act similarly to their Havana colleagues. According to the Manila-based Spanish journalist W. E. Retana, the Volunteers publicly declared that should Polavieja impede Rizal's execution, they would send him back to Spain and kill Rizal themselves.[34] Considering that Manila was a town under siege, and in order to avoid any internal divisions, Polavieja finally yielded to the Volunteers' pressures, allowing them to sacrifice a scapegoat. José Rizal was executed on December 30, 1896, in Luneta, a park off the old walled city of Manila. On the field, a company of the Loyal Volunteers was formed alongside two companies of the Chasseurs Expeditionary Battalion No. 7, one from the No. 8, a company of indigenous soldiers from the Line Infantry Regiment "Magallanes" No. 70, and a military music band, which paraded before the execution. Hundreds of *manileños* surrounded the scene as they witnessed eight natives from the "Magallanes," closely watched by eight Spanish chasseurs, firing at Rizal.[35]

Despite the many differences between the Philippines and the Antilles, the Manila Volunteers had shown an attitude notably resembling their colleagues in Havana. They were a necessary defensive tool for captains general, but a threat as well. In political terms, their opposition to any movement deemed to undermine Spanish rule was just as radical as it had been in Havana. Their role in the process and execution of José Rizal powerfully recalls the assassination of the medical students in Havana in

---

[31] Ricardo Burguete. *¡La Guerra! Filipinas (memorias de un herido)*. Barcelona: Casa Editorial Maucci, 1902, p. 70.
[32] Pilar Lozano Guirao. "Filipinas durante el mandato del General Camilo García de Polavieja." *Anales de la Universidad de Murcia. Letras*, 1983, vol. 41, No. 3–4, pp. 95–131.
[33] Anderson. *The Age of Globalization*, pp. 160–4.
[34] Retana. *Vida y escritos del Dr. José Rizal*, p. 447.
[35] Ibid., p. 430; *La Voz Española*, 30-12-1896.

November 1871. In both cases, the authorities sacrificed a scapegoat to assuage the Volunteers' rage against the elements they regarded as enemies of Spain. In Manila, as in Havana, the Volunteers had the capacity to condition the policy of the authorities regarding the repression of the movements aiming to alter the colonial status quo. It is remarkable to note the many similarities between the Volunteers in the Philippines and their colleagues in the Caribbean, especially considering the completely different context of the Asian colony in terms of society or economy. As in Cuba and Puerto Rico, the Manila Volunteers were the armed wing of Spanish *integrismo*. Also, in terms of organization, the *Casino Español* functioned as the dynamizing center of the Volunteers, as well as a social center for the *peninsulares* capable of exerting a certain political pressure on the Spanish authorities.

The execution of Rizal had been a tragic injustice which did not help to improve Spain's position in the Philippines. Manila, as the other Spanish outposts scattered throughout the vast archipelago, continued under a continuous harassment by Filipino revolutionaries. Despite the many demands for troops and weapons by Polavieja, the government denied resources which were instead sent to Cuba. Unwilling to cope with the situation, and fearing a major defeat, Polavieja resigned in March 1897.

Fernando Primo de Rivera was appointed as new captain general of the Philippines (1897–8). A man born into a family with a long military tradition, Primo de Rivera knew well the archipelago, for he had been captain general of the Philippines in 1880–3. At age 66, he was sent to Manila with the idea of waging the war with the scant resources he had at his disposal. He knew he could not expect many reinforcements to arrive from Spain. Instead, he planned to conquer the country with the country. Since his arrival to Manila in April 1897, Primo de Rivera allowed the creation of a series of Volunteer companies recruited among Filipino natives in areas where virtually no *peninsulares* were to be found.[36]

Due to the good performance of these units, the captain general wanted to take a step further and organize them in a more stable manner without merging them with the Volunteer units made up of *peninsulares* and Filipinos of Spanish descent. He might have considered the cultural and social differences between the two groups too wide to place them under the same fighting units. Hence, in October 1897 the captain general began to promote the creation of the Volunteer Native Companies, aimed at attracting native Filipinos to the Spanish cause. This separated native militia was a unique case in the history of the Volunteers in the wider Spanish colonial context. It was the result of the deep ethnic differences that existed between the Philippines and the Spanish Caribbean. This represented a rather late project to engage the local population with the defense of the Spanish Philippines that was thwarted by US intervention.

These native companies were created at a time when peace seemed reachable in the Philippines. Their creation was part of the Spanish strategy envisioned to end the war. Primo de Rivera had been working to change the conduct of the war since his arrival to Manila. He wanted to increase the participation of native Filipinos in the

---

[36] Fernando Primo de Rivera Y Sobremonte. *Memoria dirigida al Senado por el Capitán General D. Fernando Primo de Rivera y Sobremonte acerca de su gestión en Filipinas*. Madrid: Imprenta y Litografía del Depósito de la Guerra, 1898, pp. 111–18.

Spanish military control of the archipelago. In a report sent to the Premier Sagasta on October 13, 1897, Primo de Rivera wrote that he wanted to "conquer the country with the country." He also considered the native Volunteers a solution to save resources for the treasury, as it was much cheaper to organize them than to prepare regular army units in the Peninsula and send them to the Philippines. He reckoned that a force of 20,000 Filipino Volunteers would only cost 600,000 pesos, which was the cost of sending several regular army battalions from Spain.[37] The use of Filipino troops became the backbone of this new strategy.

Only three days after sending the report to the prime minister, on October 16, 1897, Primo de Rivera submitted the *reglamento* to the Ministry of War, which approved it, officially creating the Native Volunteer Companies thirteen days later on October 29.[38] Although it was not explicitly mentioned in the *reglamento*, the Antillean Volunteers had been a clear inspiration. The organization was almost identical. The idea was to integrate men with influence over their communities, while at the same time avoiding the costly organization and expedition of battalions made up of Spanish conscripts in the Peninsula.[39] However, in order to train these new units and to keep them under control, the native Volunteers were attached to regular army battalions as auxiliary companies.[40] Most Filipinos, especially in the countryside, spoke no Spanish, and their attachment for Spanish culture and identity was only superficial, if they had any at all. In any case, between the end of 1897 and the arrival of US invading forces in May 1898, these native companies generally remained loyal to Spain, devoting most of their time to military training and basic drilling, as well as making Spanish rule present in their communities.

Though the revolution was latent, not extinguished, Primo de Rivera's strategy seemed to be working eight months after his arrival to the Philippines. After intense negotiations with delegates of the Filipino rebel commanders, both parties signed the Pact of Biak-na-Bato on December 14, 1897.[41] The leader of the revolution Emilio Aguinaldo agreed to stop the armed struggle in exchange for a generous sum of money and being sent to exile in Hong Kong.[42] For him, the stay in the British colony was only an excuse to reorganize the rebellion far from the control of the Spanish authorities. Getting in touch with US agents in the region was vital for his plans. As war loomed in Cuba, opening a second front in the Philippines was a very attractive scenario for the United States, and a great opportunity for Filipino independence, or so Aguinaldo reckoned. Since March 1898, the US consuls in Hong Kong and Singapore began to negotiate with Emilio Aguinaldo the recommencement of the revolution. The agreement to collaborate against the Spaniards had been already sealed by the time the US Congress declared war on Spain in April 1898.

[37] AGMM, Documentación de Filipinas, sig. 5324.42.
[38] AGMM, Documentación de Filipinas, sig. 5322.44.
[39] AGMM, Capitanía General de Filipinas, caja 5306, "Minuta del capitán general al ministro de la Guerra," 07-11-1897.
[40] The complete list of the native Volunteers and the army battalions they were attached to in AGMM, Capitanía General de Filipinas, caja 5306 & 5308.
[41] See Primo de Rivera y Sobremonte. *Memoria dirigida al Senado*, pp. 121–58.
[42] Mas Chao. *La guerra olvidada de Filipinas*, pp. 146–61.

Due to the failure of the peace agreement reached with the rebels at Biak-na-Bató, and prospects of a war against the United States that seemed unavoidable, Primo de Rivera was replaced, and a new captain general was appointed, Basilio Augustín. His task was not certainly an easy one. Only a week after the US declaration of war, the main Spanish fleet defending the Philippines suffered a crushing defeat at Manila Bay on May 1, 1898. Having set sail from Hong Kong, a six-vessel fleet commanded by Admiral George Dewey defeated the fleet of Admiral Patricio Montojo, who commanded ten vessels only partially armed, which for the most part was in dire need of reparations. Foreseeing an inevitable defeat, Montojo ordered to burn most of his vessels after a few hours, in order to avoid their capture by the enemy. Manila Bay was the first American victory of the war against Spain, but for the Spaniards it was a major blow. In just a few hours, the entire fleet of the Philippines had been lost and the Cavite Arsenal taken, rendering the archipelago virtually defenseless from foreign invasion and isolated from Spain.[43] This was the scenario coveted by the revolution. Fearing a defeat, and probably reprisals, most of the native Volunteers deserted to the insurgency, thus shattering the Spanish strategy of "conquering the country with the country." Only a minority of them, most notably the Macabebes commanded by the mestizo Eugenio Blanco, joined the remaining Spanish troops on their way to Manila. By June 17, when the siege to Manila began the city was completely isolated from the rest of the archipelago.

The loyalty of some native troops within Manila was doubtful at the very least, except for the Civil Guard. José Toral, a *peninsular* Volunteer who witnessed the siege from inside, recalled that the Carabineros, the police force of around 400 men in charge of fighting smuggling, was "undermined by separatism."[44] With some exceptions, anti-colonial sentiment was widespread among Filipino population, even among those whose salary depended on the Spanish presence in the archipelago. Coercion might have also been a reason for these troops to join the insurrection. As in Cuba, native Filipinos who stood loyal to Spain could expect no mercy from insurgents. Outright execution was the common fate of these men in cases of being captured.[45]

Meanwhile, the revolution pushed forward its ideal. On June 12, 1898, a rebel congress held at the Barasoain Church at Malolos, a town just 37 km north to Manila, proclaimed the Republic of the Philippines under the leadership of Emilio Aguinaldo. That very day, probably instructed by the rebel authorities, the Carabineros and the Pampanga Volunteers stationed in Manila rioted against the Spaniards, with fellow native Volunteer units following throughout the archipelago. The riot was aimed at provoking a popular uprising in favor of independence.[46] It succeeded in most of the

---

[43] Reynaldo C. Ileto. "The Birth of the Filipino Revolutionary Army in Southern Tagalog, Luzón, 1898," in *El Ejército y la Armada en 1898: Cuba, Puerto Rico y Filipinas. I Congreso Internacional de Historia Militar*, vol. I. Madrid: Ministerio de Defensa, 1999, pp. 281–306.

[44] Juan & José Toral. *El sitio de Manila. 1898. Memorias de un Voluntario*. Manila: Imprenta Litográfica Partier, 1898, p. 188.

[45] Ulpiano Herrero y Sampedro. *Nuestra prisión en poder de los revolucionarios filipinos. Crónica de dieciocho meses de cautiverio de más de cien religiosos del centro de Luzón, empleados en el ministerio de las almas*. Manila: Imprenta del Colegio de Santo Tomás, 1900, p. 61.

[46] Burguete. *¡La guerra!*, p. 195.

Philippines, but in Manila it was rapidly quelled by the Loyal Volunteers. However, it could not conceal the fact that the Spanish military position even within Manila, the seat of colonial power, was extremely weak. After the siege began, the situation of the defenders, soldiers and Volunteers alike, was desperate. They were trapped between the besieging forces, unreliable native allies, and US troops commanded by General Wesley Merritt, which grew by the day. Between May and July, the United States had dispatched from the port of San Francisco over 16,000 troops to the Philippines.[47]

The 2,000 Volunteers left in Manila, mostly Spaniards, were ready to take part in the defense of a city that still had a 13,000-strong garrison and impressive network of old fortresses surrounding the old city, known as Intramuros, the heart of Spanish Manila. By 29 July, the Guerrilla del Casino Español reported having 213 men, the cavalry Manila Volunteers Squadron 87, the Guerrilla de San Miguel 488, and the Loyal Volunteers Battalion 1,279.[48] However, no relief force could be expected to arrive from far-flung Spain. Most of its Atlantic fleet had been destroyed at the battle of Santiago de Cuba on July 1, and a thirteen-vessel fleet commanded by Admiral Cámara bound for Manila was ordered to sail back to Spain on July 11, after it had crossed the Suez Canal despite British attempts to block it. The Spanish Government feared that the United States Navy might go on to attack the Canary Islands or Peninsular Spain's Atlantic coast.[49] The Philippines was too far away to become a priority for Spain. Thus, to carry on the fight to the very end would have caused unnecessary bloodshed in Manila. Peace talks secretly began between Malacañang Palace and the besieging forces. During the siege, on July 24 Fermín Jáudenes was appointed the new captain general, whose main task was to prepare the city for surrender. On August 5 he addressed a message to the men defending Manila which seems to indicate that he had already been negotiating the terms of surrender with the Americans. He reminded soldiers, sailors, and Volunteers that the siege had already been going on for two months, and that in the future they could proudly claim to have taken part in the defense of Manila. In a way, Jáudenes was telling the defenders that they had bravely fought, but that the fight was over.[50]

In order to show the world a less onerous defeat, it seems that Jáudenes and Merritt agreed to represent a sort of final mock battle before surrendering the city.[51] In fact, the final stages of the siege consisted of small-scale skirmishes and the progressive withdrawal of the Spanish forces from their outer defensive lines. Manila finally

---

[47] Mas Chao. *La guerra olvidada de Filipinas*, pp. 206–20; Stan Cohen. *Images of the Spanish-American War*. Missoula: Pictorial Histories Publishing Co., Inc., 1997, p. 250.
[48] AGMM, Documentación de Filipinas, sig. 5342.65; sig. 5342.71; sig. 5342.67; sig. 5342.66.
[49] Agustín R. Rodríguez. *Tramas ocultas de la guerra del 98*. Madrid: Editorial Actas, 2016, pp. 241–53.
[50] AGMM, Documentación de Filipinas, sig. 5344.18; Ignacio Salinas y Angulo. *Defensa del general Jáudenes*. Madrid: Imprenta y Litografía del Depósito de la Guerra, 1899, pp. 61–5.
[51] Jesús Dávila Wesolovsky. "Las operaciones en Luzón. Asedio y defensa de Manila. Mayo-agosto 1898." *El Ejército y la Armada en 1898* ..., 1999, vol. I, pp. 307–44; Musicant. *Empire by Default*, pp. 541–85; Pedro Ortiz Armengol. "La campaña militar en Filipinas: año 1898," in *El Ejército y la Armada en 1898: Cuba, Puerto Rico y Filipinas. I Congreso Internacional de Historia Militar*, vol. I. Madrid: Ministerio de Defensa, 1999, pp. 375–84; Luis E. Togores Sánchez. "El asedio de Manila (mayo-agosto 1898). 'Diario de los sucesos ocurridos durante la guerra de España con los Estados Unidos, 1898.'" *Revista de Indias*, 1998, vol. LVIII, No. 213, pp. 449–98; Trask. *The War with Spain*, pp. 417–22.

capitulated on August 13, 1898, just a day after the armistice between Spain and the United States was agreed. Alike what had happened in Santiago de Cuba a month before, the US and Spanish forces agreed not to give the rebels a triumph. Manila was surrendered to US troops, not to Filipino revolutionaries. This was an agreement between Jáudenes and Merritt, who wanted at all costs to have the old Spanish colonial city in the hands of Emilio Aguinaldo. They both feared the looting of property and retaliation against Spaniards and their Filipino allies, but also wanted to avoid the shame of having to surrender the city to the very people to whom Spain had claimed to be bringing a civilizing mission upon.[52] Indeed, colonial prejudice shaped the way Spaniards and Americans handled the transfer of power. Rather than handing Manila, which had been the seat of Spanish power in the Philippines since 1571, to Filipino insurgents, who they considered barbarous and uncivilized, Jáudenes surrendered the city to the US forces, representatives of a civilized nation, according to the standards of the day. Merritt also wanted to avoid giving Filipinos a victory which they could use to claim independence, which was not contemplated by the Government of the United States.

US troops entered Manila on August 13, 1898, and the following day Jáudenes and Merritt issued a joint decree whereby all the Spanish forces, including the Volunteers, had to return to their barracks and be put under the direct command of US Army officers, whereas civilians were allowed to leave Manila.[53] Giving up weapons and power to US troops and not to the rebels they had been fighting for two years was probably a relief for Spaniards in Manila. With the presence of what they regarded as a civilized enemy, their lives and properties were secured.

Despite this temporary relief, surrendering Manila must have been a bitter experience for the men who had fought to keep the Philippines Spanish. José Toral, who had joined the Volunteers since they were established and wrote about his war experience, recalled that after seeing the US flag waving over the Fort of Santiago, the old stone castle which had guarded the city since the sixteenth century, he thought "the sacrifice is consummated. The flag that the strong arm of Legazpi nailed into this soil, has now fallen from the weak arms of our authorities."[54]

Wide areas of the Philippines, especially in the southern archipelagos of Visayas and Mindanao, remained under Spanish control until the end of 1898, at least de jure, but fighting against Filipino rebels continued, since they did not want to see Spanish rule replaced by the US colonial power. Even the garrison on Baler, a coastal town in Luzón, unaware of the Spanish defeat, resisted entrenched in the local church until June 2, 1899, and came to be known as *Los últimos de Filipinas*, the last ones of the Philippines. But the fact is that, with the capitulation of Manila, more than three and a half centuries of Spanish history in the Philippines had come to an end.

---

[52] Trask. *The War with Spain*, pp. 412–22.
[53] AGMM, Documentación de Filipinas, sig. 5344.60.
[54] Toral. *Memorias de un Voluntario*, pp. 190–1.

11

Dismantling the Volunteers

The armistice of August 12, 1898, ended military actions between Spain and the United States and marked the beginning of political negotiations for the future of the Antilles and the Philippines. Spanish and US delegations held intense negotiations between October and December 1898 at the Quai d'Orsay in Paris, seat of the French Ministry of Foreign Affairs, which had intermediated between the two countries after diplomatic relations broke up. Both parties agreed to exclude any representatives from the Cuban and Filipino revolutionary governments. This caused much frustration in Cuba and the Philippines, leaving lingering scars in both countries regarding their political sovereignty and their relations with the United States which fall out of the remit of the history of the Volunteers.

In the meantime, during the second half of 1898, Volunteer units were dismantled in Cuba, Puerto Rico, and the Philippines, for even before negotiations in Paris came to a conclusive end, it was clear that Spanish sovereignty in most of the colonies was soon to be over. And once it was gone, the Volunteers would be gone too.

In the Philippines, the dissolution of the Volunteers seems to have taken place in a disorderly fashion, as no evidence of a formal order of dissolution by the Spanish authorities was found. This was probably caused by the fact that neither the Spanish nor the Americans entirely controlled the archipelago after the capitulation of Manila. In fact, wide areas of Mindanao and the Visayas were still under nominal Spanish sovereignty, while vast regions of the country were controlled by Filipino revolutionaries who had proclaimed the Republic of the Philippines, and who would soon begin to wage a long and bitter war against the United States for the archipelago's independence. The Manila Volunteers probably dissolved after the decree of August 14 ordering all the Spanish forces to obey the new rulers. By then, most of the native Volunteers had already defected to the insurgency, except for the Macabebe Volunteers, who were sent to the Caroline and Marianas, a chain of Spanish islands in Oceania which were sold to the German Empire in February 1899. After the islands were handed over to Germany in November 1899, some of these Macabebe Volunteers voluntarily settled in Madrid, while some others joined the US Army in the Philippines as scouts in its fight against Filipino revolutionaries.

In Puerto Rico, the dismantlement took an orderly fashion. Amid a smooth transition of sovereignties, Captain General Ricardo Ortega ordered the Volunteer units to be dismantled on September 5, 1898. The fact that there was no strong movement for independence in the island made things easier from replacing a centuries-old rule by another. Most of Puerto Rico's Volunteers gave up their uniform and weapon and resumed their normal lives in the island, while some of them asked to "follow the fate of the [Spanish] Army," and even settled in Spain after the United States took formal possession of Puerto Rico on October 18, 1898.[1]

In Cuba, the legacy of three wars for independence, the burden of thousands of people killed, and a major political problem over the island's future made the Volunteers' dismantlement more complicated. The Volunteers themselves had taken a heavy death toll during the war. Between 1895 and 1898, around 2,400 of them were killed, mostly by tropical diseases. At least a third of them, probably more, were Cuban.[2] When the armistice was signed on August 12 Spanish forces still controlled all the cities, most of the countryside was in the hands of the *Ejército Libertador*, and the US Army was firmly established in the area connecting Santiago de Cuba to Guantánamo Bay, where it had established a major camp. Beyond the political and logistical problem of having three forces in an island, fears of retaliation from the *mambís* made an orderly dissolution of the Volunteers practically impossible, especially in the areas where they had been the only Spanish force for a long time. They generally rejected to give up their weapons, especially since the *mambís* still hold theirs. After all, regular soldiers would be repatriated to Spain, whereas the Volunteers were reluctant to leave their hometowns where they had family and often property. Most of them were forced by circumstances to stay in Cuba, but under what conditions? Recognizing these fears, Captain General Blanco opted for an indirect way to dismantle the Volunteers. On August 26, 1898, he ordered that the vacancies in Volunteer units would not be replaced.[3] Defections would not be prosecuted, either.

Legal troubles as to their military performance from the Spanish authorities seemed not to be expected, but the Volunteers had many reasons to feel deeply anxious about their own personal future. Even before any peace treaty between Spain and the United States, the sovereignty of Spain was soon to be gone. The reality was that either the Cuban rebels or the United States were to take control of the island, any openly supporter of Spain was to be placed in the position of the defeated enemy. In the case of the Volunteers, men who had generally created a family in Cuba, would they be allowed to stay? Were there to be reprisals against them? Would they have any stake in the future of Cuba?

Fears about the imminent future were most likely felt by Volunteers of all means, but it was for their commanding officers to articulate a series of demands and defense. In September 1898, the chief officers of the Volunteer battalions of Havana held a meeting to discuss a series of demands they would submit to the authorities. Juan Antonio

---

[1] González Cuevas. *¿Defendiendo el honor?*, pp. 161–9.
[2] Francisco Javier Navarro Chueca has identified a total of 2,434 Volunteers killed during the war, of whom 814 were born in Cuba, 1,325 in the Peninsula, 16 elsewhere, and 279 with no disclosed birthplace. Among them, there were much likely a good deal of Cubans. Francisco Javier Navarro Chueca. *La mortalidad de las tropas españolas en la guerra de Cuba (1895–1898)*. Ph.D. Thesis. Valencia: Universidad Católica de Valencia San Vicente Mártir, 2021, p. 504.
[3] ANRC, Asuntos Políticos, leg. 240, exp. 21.

Soler y Morell, Count of La Diana, a Catalan landowner and merchant who had been mayor of Matanzas and member of the Senate in the early 1880s, on behalf of his colleagues, submitted a request to the captain general asking for the following points:[4]

1. All conscripts serving their military service in the Volunteers be fully licensed.
2. All Volunteers who wished to leave Cuba but could not afford the trip be shipped back to Spain in the same terms as regular soldiers.
3. That the captain general set a date to start licensing the Volunteers.
4. The Volunteer battalions' flags to be transported to Spain by a special committee.
5. To offer the captain general all due respect and consideration the Volunteers always had until he leaves Cuba.
6. To stress to all Volunteers the importance of being prudent in the current situation.[5]

Stemming from these points, being prudent, keeping their honor intact, and granting that no one would be left behind in Cuba against his will seemed to be the main concerns of the Volunteers, who had accepted the defeat of the cause they had defended with arms for over forty years. With this spirit, the Volunteers began a slow process of dissolution over the autumn of 1898. Volunteers began to quit the uniform all over the island, while some still fulfilled their ordinary duties. On December 1, 1898, a powerful symbolic event took place in Havana, when a squad of Volunteers was relieved by regular soldiers in what was their last sentry guard at the palace of the Captains Generals.[6]

The formal end of the over four-centuries-old Spanish rule in Cuba took place on January 1, 1899, at noon, when Adolfo Jiménez Castellanos, Cuba's last captain general, handed the control of the island to the US Army general Leonard Wood, Cuba's new governor. At that very moment, the Spanish flag was lowered from El Morro Castle, and the bars-and-striped flag of the United States was raised. Narciso Maciá, a Catalan businessman who had settled in Cuba at 17 in 1872 and had been a Volunteer ever since, witnessed with deep sorrow the ceremony from the rooftop of his house in Old Havana. Surrounded by his Cuban wife, children, and servants, who watched behind him and restrained from expressing any joy out of consideration for him, Maciá saw that many other Spaniards were contemplating the scene from the terraces and balconies nearby, and weeping. "My feelings had no limits."[7] As the new flag waved over the fort that had protected Havana's Bay since the seventeenth century, four centuries of Spanish history in Cuba came to an end. And with them, the history of the Volunteers.

The end of Spanish sovereignty in Cuba, Puerto Rico, and the Philippines, and consequently the dismantlement of the Volunteers, were the foreseeable result of the

---

[4] Carlos Nieto Sánchez. "Los procesos de ennoblecimiento en la Cuba colonial," in Javier Alvarado Planas (coord.). *La Administración de Cuba en los siglos XVIII y XIX*. Madrid: Centro de Estudios Políticos y Constitucionales, 2017, p. 217.
[5] *El Imparcial*, 24-09-1898, p. 2.
[6] *El Regional: Diario de Lugo*, 10-01-1899, p. 1.
[7] Maciá, *Vida y obra*, p. 27.

negotiations held in Paris, which were concluded with the Treaty of Peace signed by the representatives of Spain and the United States on December 10, 1898. The two-month-long negotiations soon frustrated Spanish vague hopes to retain some of its colonial possessions. Hopes were not posed in Cuba, for it had historically been coveted by the United States, and Spain could not face another costly war in case it retained part of its territory. The United States would not renounce Puerto Rico either, for controlling both Antilles meant keeping the gates of the Panama Canal and the entire Caribbean. In the Philippines, however, Spain still controlled the southern archipelagos of Mindanao and Visayas, although its scattered positions were held at bay by Filipino revolutionaries, who were also fighting the US forces in the rest of the country. These hopes soon faded away, especially since the US delegation mentioned the possibility of resuming war operations by attacking the Canary Islands or Spain's Atlantic coast. Spain had lost most of its naval power in Santiago and Cavite and was forced to accept its military inferiority and exhaustion after three years of war.

Finally, the treaty signed on December 10 stated that Spain renounced its sovereignty on Cuba, which was put under US temporary rule, and assumed its 400 million pesetas debt; Puerto Rico and Guam, a tiny island in the Marianas Archipelago, was ceded to the United States; and the United States agreed to compensate Spain with 20 million US dollars for the cession of the Philippines.

After much debate over the imperial nature of the United States and its rights and duties toward the recently conquered territories, the US Senate ratified the treaty on February 6, 1899. For Spain, the treaty was a huge blow which could not be avoided. Losing the Philippines was the loss of a colony which had been under Spanish rule for almost four centuries, a reminder of the globe's first circumnavigation by Magellan and Elcano in the 1520s and a major work of Catholic propagation in Asia. The loss of Cuba and Puerto Rico meant losing part of the national territory, for the Antilles were Spanish provinces with representatives in the Spanish Parliament, reminders of Columbus's first voyages, two hugely important markets for some industries, and two parts of the overseas territories where thousands of *peninsulares* had established their homes and planted the seeds of Cuban society alongside enslaved Africans.

In order to avert major political consequences in Spain, the very representative institutions of the Spanish nation were excluded from the negotiating process in Paris. Between September 1898 and February 1899, the Congress and the Senate were locked down, although according to the 1876 Constitution, both chambers had to vote on the ratification of the peace treaty. They never did. Instead, the Regent Queen Maria Christina was demanded by the government to ratify the treaty, which she did in May 1899, in a clear violation of the Constitution, which did not allow the monarch to alienate any part of Spain's national territory. The irregular end of the old Spanish colonial empire, of parts of its own national territory, did not spur riots or protests in Spain. Three years of war in Cuba and the Philippines had claimed a heavy toll of men and money. The country was exhausted and willing to end the colonial chapter, at least to lick its open and bleeding wounds. The Volunteers had been firsthand witnesses and participants to this process. With the end of the colonies, they too had to start anew.

12

After the War

The Volunteers ceased to exist with the end of the empire. The prominent role they had played in Cuba and Puerto Rico for almost half a century, and for a short time in the Philippines, was only comparable to the swiftness with which they disappeared along the autumn of 1898. Their fate was signaled by the end of Spanish sovereignty in the Caribbean and Asia. Volunteer veterans did not create any association to recall their days of service, neither in Spain nor in Cuba, Puerto Rico, or the Philippines. The reason for this is unclear. The ones who settled in Spain after 1898 could have shared many memories of the long years spent overseas and war stories to keep the memory of the Volunteers alive, at least for a while. As to Cuba, Puerto Rico, and the Philippines, the reasons for not creating such an association seem rather evident. As the very incarnation of *integrismo*, to keep the Volunteers' memory alive would not be very well welcomed in societies which had just underwent the trauma of war precisely over the very issue of Spanish sovereignty, such as Cuba or the Philippines. Neither would it be welcomed in Puerto Rico, where the new American colonial ruler had to build its legitimacy in opposition to the former one.

The fate of the Volunteers after 1898 was as varied as the paths taken by these men individually. They did not act as a group but rather sought to protect their own personal interests. To track their lives after 1898 would require following the evolution of thousands of them after the war. It is not known exactly how many Volunteers settled in Spain after 1898 or remained in the former colonies, but it is quite likely that not just a few of them, both *peninsulares* and creoles, left for the Peninsula during the autumn of 1898 out of fear of reprisals, though most of them probably were back home in the Caribbean of the Philippines after a while.[1]

Much likely, most of the Volunteers much probably remained in Cuba, Puerto Rico, or the Philippines. José Joaquín Hernández y Mancebo, a Cuban separatist who lived in Santiago de Cuba throughout the war, recalled that after the city's capitulation to the US forces, the Spanish Government offered a free repatriation to all the Volunteers who wished to do so, but that only "some of them took that opportunity."[2] Certainly, Spanish newspapers published stories about the arrival of Volunteers to the Peninsula between late 1898 and early 1899, but nothing indicates a massive resettlement. Images

---

[1] De Miguel Fernández. "Las tropas españolas en la guerra de Cuba," p. 257.
[2] Emilio Bacardí y Moreau. *Crónicas de Santiago de Cuba*, vol. X, p. 369.

of a massive exodus, which have been seen at the end of colonial empires before and after 1898, were not to be seen in the old Spanish overseas territories. As it seems, most of the former Volunteers kept on with their lives. Creoles adopted to the new political reality, either as citizens of the Cuban republic after 1902 or as colonial subjects of the United States in Puerto Rico and the Philippines. As to *peninsulares*, the influx of migrants from Spain kept arriving after 1898. In fact, around 470,000 of them settled in Cuba until the outbreak of the First World War.[3]

Considering that between Cuba, Puerto Rico, and the Philippines there might have been over 100,000 former Volunteers, most of them continued their modest lives, while a few of them rose to become relevant members of their societies. For instance, Narciso Maciá y Doménech, a Catalan tradesman who had been a lieutenant in the Artillery Volunteer Battalion, remained in Havana with his Cuban wife and children, where he became a successful businessman and presided over the *Casino Español* in the 1920s.[4] The Puerto Rican Vicente Balbás Capó, the journalist and former member of the Spanish Parliament and former major of the Tirailleurs Volunteers Battalion, devoted his life after 1898 to the cause of Spanish language, Catholic faith, Roman Law, and independence for Puerto Rico from the United States as a way to preserve the Spanish identity of the island. In 1899 he created the Opportunist Party to fight politically for the island's independence, since reincorporation into Spain was unfeasible. As editor of the *Heraldo de las Antillas*, the newspaper which succeeded the *Heraldo Español*, he firmly opposed the US military occupation of Puerto Rico. A staunch opponent of Americanization, Balbás Capó wrote *Puerto Rico a los diez años de americanización* in 1910 to denounce this process. Due to his campaigns in defense of the Spanish legacy against the US cultural influence, he was awarded several civilian decorations by the Spanish Government and even regained Spanish citizenship in 1923.[5] This was an exception, since only *peninsulares* kept their Spanish citizenship in the former colonies after 1898. Some others proudly highlighted their past as Volunteers. As late as May 1931, only a few weeks after the proclamation of the Second Spanish Republic on April 14, the *peninsular* Isidoro Yboleón, who had arrived in the Philippines in 1883 as a conscript, signed a document in favor of the recently abdicated King Alphonse XIII issued by the most conservative elements of the local Spanish colony. Yboleón stressed that he had been a Volunteer captain as a proof of loyalty toward Spain and the Bourbon dynasty.[6]

There was no generalized retaliation against the Volunteers in the former colonies but living side by side with those who had fought against them was not always easy, at least for a short period after the war. Their prospects after the end of Spanish sovereignty were certainly a concern for the Volunteers. In September 1898 the chief officers of Havana's Volunteer units held a meeting to discuss this. They agreed,

---

[3] Pérez, Jr. *Cuba*, p. 202.
[4] Maciá y Doménech. *Vida y obra*, pp. 28–61.
[5] *Unión Ibero-Americana*, February 1923, p. 24; Ana Isabel Benito Sánchez. "Determinantes instituciones de la reivindicación autonomista en Puerto Rico." *Revista de Humanidades Tecnológico de Monterrey*, 2008, No. 24, p. 114.
[6] *Voz española*, 09-05-1931, p. 8; *Diario oficial de avisos de Madrid*, 23-04-1883, p. 1.

among other points, to ask the Spanish Government that all Volunteers who wished so should be repatriated to Spain for free and advised the Volunteers to be cautious.[7] It was sensible advice. In December 1899 Enrique Fournier, mayor of El Cristo, a small town in Oriente, reported to the American military governor of Santiago de Cuba that two former *guerrilleros*, "Chucho" Guerra and Higinio Pérez, had stormed into the house of Josefa Suárez shouting, "*Long Live Spain, the Spanish guerrilleros and Weyler!*" Subsequently, they were threatened by their neighbors, mostly Cuban nationalists. Since the mayor could not secure these men's lives, he asked the US governor to remove them from the town.[8] This episode illustrates the atmosphere in a rural community of eastern Cuba shortly after 1898. However, as years passed by, reconciliation between Cubans and Spaniards, tied by blood and culture, helped to forge a new Cuba. After all, Cuba had undergone a civil war.

As much as the Volunteers had embodied the worse radical forms of Spanish rule for Cuban nationalists, they could also represent a symbol of reconciliation as the fog of war was fading away. In 1905, the *Diario de la Marina* published a note from Placetas, in the province of Santa Clara, on the third anniversary of the local Spanish Colony, a social club open to Spaniards as well as Cubans. As part of the celebrations, a children's costume party was held at the Colony, each couple being introduced to the crowd. Among costumes of geishas, Pierrots, Andalusian dancers, and generals, a couple attracted the attention of the public. He was dressed as a sergeant of the Rural Guard, the republican militia fighting banditry, and she donned the uniform of Havana's 1st Volunteer Battalion cantinière. As the couple hugged in the scenario, the ball room was instantly filled with applauses and tears.[9] A new era was dawning in Cuba.

Ironically enough, former Volunteers underwent a wave of reprisals in Puerto Rico, where no major independence struggle took place. In fact, between 1868 and 1898 the military participation of Puerto Ricans was essentially devoted to the defense of Spanish sovereignty, except for the few men who joined the Cuban insurgent armies. Between late 1898 and early 1899, bandit groups from the rural areas assaulted peninsular-owned shops, many of whom were former Volunteers. These attacks might have been a popular reaction against the unwanted result of the Spanish–American war by which Puerto Rico became a colony of the United States, and against the previous social and economic system of Spanish dominance represented by the Volunteers. In fact, since the 1890s there had been a growing resentment among Puerto Rican autonomists against *peninsulares* for their dominant position in commerce, and against the Volunteers for their ferocious repression of the autonomists during the *compontes* of 1887. The crisis of 1898–9 only provided the context that unleashed the accumulated tension. Ironically, the US troops that had come to Puerto Rico to expel the Spaniards ended up protecting their lives and properties. After all, a great deal of the US administration still depended on many Spaniards who held key positions in the administration and the economy. Thus, tranquility soon returned to the island.[10]

---

[7] *El Correo Español*, 24-09-1898, p. 2.
[8] AHPSC, Gobierno Provincial, leg. 514, exp. 17.
[9] *Diario de la Marina*, 9-2-1905.
[10] Picó. *1898*, pp. 201–7.

Some Volunteers decided to start afresh in Spain for different reasons, political, economic, or both. Perhaps no less than 5,000 Volunteers left Cuba after the Spanish defeat.[11] Captain Melitón Castelló Anglada, who had served in Puerto Príncipe's Volunteer Battalion for thirty years and owned a hardware store in that city, was well integrated into Cuban society through marriage to a local woman. Despite this, this Catalan left the island in December 1898 for he "would not stay in a country where the Spanish flag is not respected." Shortly afterward, in April 1900, Melitón Castelló died in Barcelona. His wife and children returned to Cuba, but she rejected an appointment as a teacher offered by the Cuban Ministry of Education for the sake of his husband's memory.[12] Some creole Volunteers also decided to settle in Spain, probably out of fear of being regarded as traitors in their own land. For instance, Sixto Bravo, a native of Santiago de Cuba, arrived in La Corunna in September 1898, after having taken part in the defense of his native city against the US and *mambí* troops in July of that very year. Since his *hacienda* had been destroyed by the insurgents and his Spanish sentiments were well known in an area dominated by Cuban nationalism, he considered that staying in the island was not an option. His situation was so desperate upon arriving in Spain that La Corunna's military governor bought him a ticket for Madrid so that he could look for employment there.[13]

A curious case was represented by the Macabebes, members of a warrior ethnicity in the Filipino island of Luzón. Commanded by the *mestizo* Eugenio Blanco, they were among the few native Volunteers who remained loyal to Spain to the very last. After the loss of the Philippines, the Macabebes were sent to the Marianas Islands in the Pacific Ocean since Blanco had been appointed governor by the Spanish Government. For a few months, these natives of Luzón were the last representatives of the Spanish Empire in the Marianas, until the islands were handed over to Germany in November 1899.[14] Once back in the Philippines, some Macabebes collaborated with the US Army during the Philippine–American War (1899–1902).[15] Some others rejected serving the country that had ousted Spain from the Philippines. Eugenio Blanco turned down a position in the army offered by the US colonial government, and instead decided to sail to Spain with a few hundred of his former Macabebe Volunteers, arriving in Barcelona in June 1900 hoping to rebuild their lives.[16] It is unclear whether they stayed in Spain or returned to the Philippines, but to this day they are remembered by a street

---

[11] Enrique de Miguel Fernández. *Azcárraga, Weyler y la conducción de la guerra de Cuba*. Ph.D. Thesis. Castellón de La Plana: Universitat Jaume I, 2011, p. 221, footnote No. 372.

[12] I am indebted to Melitón Castelló's Cuban great-grandson, Osvaldo Betancourt Sanz, for this information. Like his Volunteer forebear, Osvaldo also left Cuba for political reasons almost a century after his great-grandfather.

[13] *La Correspondencia de España*, 20-09-1898, p. 2.

[14] *La Ilustración Artística*, 03-09-1900, pp. 571–3; Belén Pozuelo Mascaraque. "Los Estados Unidos, Alemania y el desmantelamiento colonial español en el Pacífico: el caso de las islas Marianas." *Anales de Historia Contemporánea*, 1998, No. 14, pp. 147–68.

[15] Dennis Edward Flake. *Loyal Macabebes. How the Americans Used the Macabebe Scouts in the Annexation of the Philippines*. San Fernando: Holy Angel University Press, 2009, pp. 33–68.

[16] *La Ilustración Artística*, 18-06-1900, p. 402.

name in Madrid: the *calle de los Voluntarios Macabebes* in the popular neighborhood of La Chopera. To this day, it is Spain's only public space that remembers the Volunteers.

As to the treatment received by the Volunteers from the Spanish authorities after 1898, it was generally marked by neglect, abandonment, and disdain. As to the men who remained in Cuba, Puerto Rico, or the Philippines, both *peninsulares* and creoles, they were not granted any compensation. The contempt suffered by the Volunteers born outside metropolitan Spain was even deeper, for they lost their Spanish citizenship in accordance with the Treaty of Paris (December 10, 1898), by which the representatives of Spain and the United States negotiated the aftermath of the war. Only in 1901, the Cubans, Puerto Ricans, and Filipinos who had lost the citizenship in 1898 could regain it if they had been appointed in any administrative or military position by the Spanish Government before the Treaty of Paris.[17] The *peninsulares* that remained in Cuba, Puerto Rico, or the Philippines, however, were given the option of keeping their citizenship. Thus, the *peninsulares* were denied any compensation, but the creoles also lost the citizenship they had fought for.

The situation of the Volunteers that decided to leave for Spain did not greatly vary from the fate suffered by the regular Spanish soldiers and sailors after 1898. The Spanish press reflected the miserable conditions of their repatriation which lasted from September 1898 to February 1899.[18] Back in Spain, due to their generally poor health conditions, many of the men who fought in the colonies were compelled to beg on the streets or claim a pension that would never arrive.[19] In this sense, the rank-and-file Volunteers were deprived of any financial aid or compensation by the State. Since they were not members of the regular army or navy, they were not included in the share of the budget devoted to giving meagre allowances to the veterans of Cuba, Puerto Rico, and the Philippines. The only financial aid given by the State to the rank-and-file Volunteers was the right to a free ticket back to Cuba, Puerto Rico, or the Philippines, granted by a law in April 1900.[20] However, those who joined the Volunteers to comply with their military service, and had not extinguished this, were relocated in army units until its completion. Thus, it may be inferred that the Spanish State would rather promote the migration of the young veterans than having to financially support thousands of men likely deemed a burden for a bankrupt nation.

Only the Volunteer chiefs and officers who settled in Spain after 1898 from Cuba and Puerto Rico received some compensation. They were the only Volunteers that coordinated their efforts to defend their interests. On March 19, 1899, they created a committee in Madrid aimed at lobbying before the Ministry of War. It was supported

---

[17] *Gaceta de Madrid*, 12-05-1901, Año CCXL, No. 132, T. II, p. 563.
[18] María Antonia Fernández Jiménez. "La repatriación de los soldados españoles en la prensa del momento. Imágenes de una tragedia del 98," in Mirta Núñez Díaz-Balart (dir.) & Antonio Rojas Friend (Coord.). *El día después. España y sus excolonias tras el* Desastre *del 98*. Madrid: Editorial Argés, 1998, pp. 153–69.
[19] Patricio Hidalgo Nuchera. "'Cuando pintan bastos'. De la derrota naval al drama de los repatriados en la Córdoba de 1898," in Patricio Hidalgo Nuchera (coord.). *Andalucía y la repatriación de los soldados en la guerra del 98*. Seville: Fundación Pública Andaluza Centro de Estudios Andaluces, 2010, pp. 37–82.
[20] *Diario Oficial del Ministerio de la Guerra*, 12-04-1900, pp. 157–8.

by the former captains general Arsenio Martínez de Campos and Ramón Blanco, who were appointed honorary presidents. The members of the committee were Colonel Luis Ramos Izquierdo (president), Colonel Juan Malo Parra (vice-president), Captain Juan Bravo (first secretary), 2nd Lieutenant Julio A. Domínguez (second secretary), Major Guillermo Castelví, Captains Vicente Díez and Juan de Urquía (members of the board), and Captain Juan Mateo (deputy member of the board).[21] Due to their pressure, the Volunteer chiefs and officers were somehow equated to the regular army and navy officers and were recognized the right to a pension on a law sanctioned by the Queen Regent on April 11, 1900, more than a year and a half after the end of the war.[22] Nonetheless, a series of requisites included in the law left many Volunteers ineligible for the pension. This caused hundreds of them to demand their pension from the Ministry of War, with uneven success, at least until 1910, when Antonio Asensio Pérez, who had been a member of the Puerto Rican Volunteers between 1897 and 1898 after a long career in the army medical corps, filed the last reported claim for a pension as a former Volunteer.[23] In 1903 Elías Martínez Nubla, a magistrate and former cavalry Volunteer major in Manila, denounced the fact that out of the c. 15,000 Volunteer chief officers and officers that had served in Cuba, Puerto Rico, and the Philippines during 1895–8, only 320 were eligible for a pension according to the law of April 11, 1900. Also, their pension represented 70 percent of the allowance given to their army and navy colleagues. In this respect, Martínez Nubla recalled that although the Volunteers did not join the militia for money, the bullets of the enemy did not distinguish regular soldiers from Volunteers either.[24] It is known that Martínez Nubla met in December 1903 with the minister of War, Vicente Martitegui, to negotiate better conditions for his comrades-at-arms to no avail on behalf of the *Comisión de Jefes y Oficiales movilizados*.[25] The compensation by the state remained unaltered after the law of April 1900.

In another area, political participation proved to be a controversial activity for the Volunteers who remained in the former colonies. As a collectivity, they had no voice. More widely, the creation of political parties that might defend a return to Spanish sovereignty or that would represent the interest of the *integristas* was not even considered. The integration of the people that had supported Spanish rule into the new regimes, in the form of either new sovereign states (Cuba) or US colonies (Puerto Rico and the Philippines), came at the price of renouncing any form of collective political identity. The integration of those who wanted to actively participate in politics was thus made individually through the new political parties that represented the social and ideological divisions of any given society. The individual right of former Volunteers to participate in politics was nonetheless not accepted by all actors. In Puerto Rico, some elements of the Republican Party, mostly former radical autonomists who advocated for the island to become a new US state, considered that former *integristas* should not

---

[21] *El Día*, 20-03-1899, p. 2.
[22] *Diario Oficial del Ministerio de la Guerra*, 12-04-1900, pp. 157–58.
[23] *Diario Oficial del Ministerio de la Guerra*, 09-07-1910, p. 121.
[24] Martínez Nubla. *Los Voluntarios de Ultramar*, p. 20.
[25] *El Heraldo de Madrid*, 21-09-1903, p. 2.

be allowed to participate in politics under the US regime, fortunately to no avail. Thus, former Volunteers and members of the Spanish Unconditional Party participated in the different political parties created after 1898, although they tended to support options that fought for wide autonomy or outright independence from the United States.[26]

As a military concept, however, the Volunteers outlived 1898. The creation of a militia of civilians-at-arms might also have served the needs of the Republic of Cuba. The creation of a militia of civilians-at-arms might also have served the needs of the Republic of Cuba, like during the uprising of Black *mambí* veterans known as *Guerrita de los Independientes de Color* that took place in eastern Cuba between May and July 1912. It was caused by the illegalization of the *Partido de los Independientes de Color*, a political party which stood for the rights of the Cubans of African descent, as the Cuban electoral law of 1910 prohibited the participation of racially based political parties. The war caused between 2,000 and 6,000 victims, mostly rebels. In order to quash the uprising, the Cuban Government created a Volunteer Battalion in Guantánamo to fight the Black rebels, as well as a *Voluntarios de Occidente* battalion sent from Havana, and Volunteer units in several small towns of the area.[27] It is significant that the Cuban Government chose the very name of Volunteers, profoundly identified with Spanish *integrismo*, to name these militias. The name was not the only resemblance. The members of the Volunteers created in 1912 were young men that had to combine their regular jobs with unpaid military service chasing the rebels.[28] The creation of this militia in 1912, during the first years of a Republic that was still forging its national identity, may indicate that the Volunteers were not considered an entirely alien Spanish concept, but a model deeply rooted in Cuban history.

These Volunteers were dissolved in 1912 after having quashed the rebellion, but a new project to revive them was presented to the authorities three decades later. The years around the Second World War were not very amiable for the Spanish community in Cuba, let alone the memory of the Volunteers. The push by President Fulgencio Batista (1940–4) to displace Spaniards from their dominant position in Cuban economy was accompanied by a cultural policy which cast a dark shadow over the memories of Spanish rule, let alone the Volunteers. In 1942, in a fine example of anachronic parallelism only understandable by the context, Juan Luis Martín delivered a series of conferences to his brothers of the Fraternity and Constance masonic lodge in Havana calling the Volunteers "a most genuine Fascist party of 19th century Cuba."[29] Despite this atmosphere, that very year, 1942, a group of army officers considered that Cuba's defensive capacities must be strengthened in the context of the Second World War. Cuba's position as an ally of the United States might make the island a target for the German U-boats that patrolled the Atlantic. The officers suggested President Batista

---

[26] Vicente Balbás Capó. *Puerto Rico a los diez años de americanización*. San Juan: Tip. Heraldo Español, 1910, pp. 397–400 & 415–19.

[27] Rolando Rodríguez. *La conspiración de los iguales. La protesta de los Independientes de Color en 1912*. Havana: Imagen Contemporánea, 2010.

[28] Carlos Forment Rovira. *Crónicas de Santiago de Cuba*, vol. II. Santiago de Cuba: Ediciones Alqueza, 2005, pp. 27–35; Aline Helg. *Our Rightful Share: The Afro-Cuban Struggle for Equality, 1886-1912*. Chapel Hill: The University of North Carolina Press, 1995, pp. 204–25.

[29] Juan Luis Martín. *Los Voluntarios de 1871. Un partido fascista en Cuba en el siglo XIX*, 1942, p. 4.

the need to create a Volunteer Corps of the Republic of Cuba.[30] The project was not finally approved, but it is quite telling of the lingering memory of the Volunteers as a model militia almost half a century after their formal dissolution.

In Puerto Rico, the legacy of the Volunteers as a militia also outlived 1898. In 1906 a group of Puerto Ricans who favored the Americanization of the island tried to create a militia made up of young volunteers who would have needed to afford their own uniforms and weapons and would combine their regular jobs with unpaid military service in a force meant to be the reserves for the US Army in Puerto Rico. This militia was not finally created because of the US military authorities' dislike of the idea of arming Puerto Ricans. However, amid the necessity of reinforcing the defenses of its Caribbean colony in the context of the First World War, the Puerto Rican branch of the National Guard of the United States was created in 1917. This was possible only after the implementation of the Jones Act (1917), which granted Puerto Ricans US citizenship, thus allowing them to serve in the US armed forces, which included the National Guard, or to be conscripted if necessary.[31]

Due to the politically charged background of the Volunteers, which had been considered the armed wing of Spanish *integrismo*, the US authorities wanted to consider Puerto Rico's National Guard as heir of the Disciplined Militias. Despite these militias having been dismantled in the 1870s, their historical association with creoles was more convenient for the policy of erasing Puerto Rico's Spanish identity conducted by the United States after the invasion of 1898.[32] However, the Volunteers and the National Guard are similar in certain ways. Both were used by the regular army as a reserve force, and both play a political role. The Volunteers embodied the support for Spanish rule among a part of Puerto Rican society. The National Guard is an example of the support by part of the Puerto Rican people for ever-closer ties between the island and the United States amid a context where the status of Puerto Rico has been contested since the US military conquest of 1898.

Thus, although the Spanish Volunteers vanished from history in 1898, the idea of a militia of civilians-at-arms to serve as the regular army reserve and to defend a political cause outlived in the Antilles after the end of Spanish sovereignty. In this regard, exploring the links between the men who donned the Volunteers uniform before 1898 and the creation of the new Volunteers in Cuba in 1912, and the US National Guard in Puerto Rico in 1917, might reveal new paths and suggest new interpretations of the history of the Antilles after the end of the Spanish Empire, through the persistence of some of its imperial legacies. The idea of the Volunteers as a militia might have survived the collapse of the Spanish Empire after all.

---

[30] ANRC, Secretaría de la Presidencia, leg. 6, exp. 46.
[31] Rogers M. Smith. "The Bitter Roots of Puerto Rican Citizenship," in Christina Duffy Burnett & Burke Marshall (eds.). *Foreign in a Domestic Sense. Puerto Rico, American Expansion, and the Constitution*. Durham & London: Duke University Press, 2001, pp. 373–88; Trías Monge. *Puerto Rico*, pp. 67–76.
[32] Negroni. *Historia militar de Puerto Rico*, pp. 387–8.

Sources Consulted

Archival Manuscripts

Cuba

AHPSC	Archivo Histórico Provincial (Santiago de Cuba)
ANRC	Archivo Nacional de la República de Cuba (Havana)
BNC	Biblioteca Nacional de Cuba "José Martí" (Havana)

Mexico

AGN	Archivo General de la Nación (Mexico City)

Puerto Rico

AGPR	Archivo General de Puerto Rico (San Juan)
BUPR	Biblioteca de la Universidad de Puerto Rico (Río Piedras)
CIH-UPR	Centro de Investigaciones Históricas-Universidad de Puerto Rico (Río Piedras)

Spain

ACD	Archivo del Congreso de los Diputados (Madrid)
AFAM	Archivo de la Fundación Antonio Maura (Madrid)
AGI	Archivo General de Indias (Seville)
AGMM	Archivo General Militar (Madrid)
AGMS	Archivo General Militar (Segovia)
AGP	Archivo General de Palacio (Madrid)
AHMS	Arxiu Històric Municipal (Sitges)
AHN	Archivo Histórico Nacional (Madrid)
ANC	Arxiu Nacional de Catalunya (Sant Cugat del Vallès)
AS	Archivo del Senado (Madrid)

BNE   Biblioteca Nacional de España (Madrid)

BVB   Biblioteca Víctor Balaguer (Vilanova i La Geltrú)

RAH   Real Academia de la Historia (Madrid)

Periodicals and Gazettes

Altar y Trono, Burgos
Boletín de loterías y de toros, Madrid
Boletín de procedimientos, Madrid
Boletín Mercantil de Puerto-Rico, San Juan
Diario de la Marina, Havana
Diario de Tenerife, Santa Cruz de Tenerife
Diario Oficial de Avisos de Madrid, Madrid
Diario Oficial del Ministerio de la Guerra, Madrid
El Correo Español, Madrid
El Correo Militar, Madrid
El Deporte Velocipédico, Madrid
El Día, Madrid
El Eco de los Voluntarios, Havana
El Eco de Sitges, Sitges
El Globo, Madrid
El Imparcial, Madrid
El León Español, Havana
El Moro Muza, Havana
El Noticiero Balear, Palma de Mallorca
El Pensamiento Español, Madrid
El Reconcentrado, Havana
El Resumen, Madrid
El Voluntario de Cuba, Madrid
Gaceta de La Habana, Havana
Gaceta de Madrid, Madrid
Gaceta de Puerto Rico, San Juan
La América, Madrid
La Convicción, Barcelona
La Correspondencia de España, Madrid
La Correspondencia Militar, Madrid
La Democracia, Ponce
La Dinastía, Barcelona
La Discusión, Madrid
La Época, Madrid
La Ilustración artística, Barcelona
La Ilustración española y americana, Madrid
La Ilustración ibérica, Barcelona
La Independencia Española, Madrid
La Integridad Nacional, San Juan
La Legalidad, Gibara

La Lucha, Havana
La Nación, Madrid
La Regeneración, Madrid
La Unión Constitucional, Havana
La Voz de Cuba, Havana
La Voz española, Manila
Los Voluntarios, Havana
Revista de Puerto Rico, San Juan
Unión Ibero-Americana, Madrid

Bibliography

Primary Works

A+B. *Apuntes en defensa del honor del Ejército*. Madrid: Est. Tipográfico de Ricardo Fe, 1898.
Acosta y Albear, Francisco. *Compendio histórico del pasado y presente de Cuba y de su guerra insurreccional hasta el 11 de marzo de 1875, con algunas apreciaciones relativas á su porvenir*. Madrid: Imprenta á cargo de Juan José de Las Heras, 1875 (2nd ed.).
Acosta, José Julián. *Los partidos políticos. Artículos publicados en "El Progreso."* San Juan: Imprenta y Librería de Sancérrit, 1875.
Aenlle, César. *De todo un poco*. Havana: Imprenta Mercantil de los Herederos de Spencer, 1889.
Álvarez Chacón, Julio. *España gran potencia por su organización militar*. Santiago de Cuba: Sección Tipográfica del E.M. de la Comandancia General, 1882.
Amblard, Arturo. *Notas coloniales*. Madrid: Ambrosio Pérez y Compañía, 1904.
Andrés, S. *La reforma electoral en nuestras Antillas*. Madrid: Imprenta de la "Revista de España," 1889.
Anuario Militar de España. Madrid: Tipografía e Imprenta del Depósito de la Guerra, 1895.
Armas y Céspedes, Juan Ignacio de. *Combate de Russell House o muerte de Castañón en Key West el 31 de enero de 1870*. New Providence: Im. del Nassau Times, 1870.
Arrillaga Roqué, Juan. *Memorias de antaño*. Ponce: Tip. Baldorioty, 1910.
Bacardí y Moreau, Emilio. *Crónicas de Santiago de Cuba*, vol. X. Santiago de Cuba: Tipografía Arroyo Hermanos, 1924.
Balaguer, Víctor. *Memoria que precede á los dos volúmenes de documentos que publica el Excmo. Sr. D. Víctor Balaguer acerca de su gestión en el Ministerio de Ultramar durante el desempeño de su cargo como ministro del ramo desde 11 de octubre de 1886 hasta 14 de junio de 1888*. Madrid: Imprenta y Fundición de Manuel Tello, 1888.
Balbás Capó, Vicente. *Puerto Rico a los diez años de americanización*. San Juan: Tip. Heraldo Español, 1910.
Barras y Prado, Antonio de las. *La Habana a mediados del siglo XIX*. Madrid: Imprenta de la Ciudad Lineal, 1926.
Betancourt, J. R. *Las dos banderas. Apuntes históricos sobre la insurrección de Cuba. Cartas al Excmo. Sr. Ministro de Ultramar. Soluciones para Cuba*. Seville: Establecimiento Tipográfico del Círculo Liberal, 1870.

Blanco, Ramón. *Memoria que dirige al Senado el general Blanco acerca de los últimos sucesos ocurridos en la isla de Luzón.* Madrid: Establecimiento tipográfico de "El Liberal," 1897.

Brau, Salvador. *Historia de Puerto Rico.* San Juan: Editorial Coquí, 1966 (first published in New York: Appleton & Company, 1904).

Burguete, Ricardo. *¡La guerra! Filipinas (memorias de un herido).* Barcelona: Casa Editorial Maucci, 1902.

Cabrera, Raimundo. *Cuba and the Cubans.* Philadelphia: The Levytype Company, 1896.

Camps y Feliú, Francisco de. *Españoles é insurrectos. Recuerdos de la guerra de Cuba.* Havana: Imprenta de A. Álvarez y Comp., 1890.

Cervera Baviera, Julio. *La defensa militar de Puerto-Rico.* San Juan: Imprenta de la Capitanía General, 1898.

Collazo, Enrique. *Desde Yara hasta el Zanjón. Apuntaciones históricas.* Havana: Tipografía de "La Lucha," 1893.

Collazo, Enrique. *Los americanos en Cuba.* Havana: Editorial de Ciencias Sociales, 1972 (first published by Imprenta y Papelería C. Martínez y Cía., 1905, 2 vols.).

Conangla, Josep. *Memorias de mi juventud en Cuba. Un soldado del ejército español en la guerra separatista (1895–1898).* Barcelona: Ediciones Península, 1998.

Constitución democrática de la Nación española. Madrid: Imprenta de "El Imparcial," 1869.

Cuerpos de Voluntarios de la Isla de Cuba. Escalafón general de señores jefes, oficiales y sargentos por el orden de antigüedad en 1º de enero de 1860. Havana: Imprenta del Gobierno y Capitanía General, 1860.

Disposiciones relativas a bienes embargados e incautados a los infidentes. Havana: Almacén de papel y efectos de escritorio de Castro Hermanos y Compañía, 1874.

Ejército de Puerto-Rico. Estado militar de todas las armas é institutos y escalafón general de los jefes, oficiales, sargentos 1º de Infantería en 1º de enero de 1884. San Juan: Imprenta de la Capitanía General, 1884.

Ejército de Puerto-Rico. Estado militar de todas las armas e institutos y Escalafón General de todos los Jefes y Oficiales de Infantería. San Juan: Imprenta de la Capitanía General, 1888.

Españoles residentes en la República Argentina. Álbum dedicado a los heroicos Voluntarios de Cuba. Buenos Aires: Establecimiento tipográfico de *El Correo Español*, 1874.

Estévanez, Nicolás. *Mis memorias.* Madrid: Tebas, 1975 (first published in 1899).

Estévez y Romero, Luis. *Desde el Zanjón hasta Baire. Datos para la historia política de Cuba.* Havana: "La Propaganda Literaria," 1899.

Estorch, M. *Apuntes para la historia sobre la administración del Marqués de la Pezuela en la isla de Cuba, desde el 3 de diciembre de 1853 hasta 21 de setiembre de 1854.* Madrid: Imprenta de Manuel Galiano, 1856.

Ferrer de Couto, José. *Cuba puede ser independiente: folleto político de actualidad.* New York: Imprenta de "El Cronista," 1872.

Fité, Vital. *Las desdichas de la Patria. Políticos y frailes.* Madrid: Imprenta de Enrique Rojas, 1899.

Flores, Eugenio Antonio. *La guerra de Cuba (apuntes para la Historia).* Madrid: Tipografía de los Hijos de M. G. Hernández, 1895.

Forment Rovira, Carlos. *Crónicas de Santiago de Cuba*, vol. II. Santiago de Cuba: Ediciones Alqueza, 2005.

Fórmula o minuta de la escritura que habrá de otorgarse y bases bajo las cuales ha de constituirse la sociedad El Casino tan pronto como se halle suscrita la mitad de las acciones fijadas en el artículo tercero. Havana: Imprenta del Avisador Comercial, 1872.

G., M. & M-C. *Novísimo Reglamento del Instituto de Voluntarios de la Isla de Cuba aprobado por Real Decreto de 7 de julio de 1892; Comentado y anotado con numerosas disposiciones, formularios y apéndices conteniendo la parte de las Ordenanzas del Ejército aplicable a los mismos; el Tratado 2° del Código de Justicia Militar y el Reglamento de Voluntarios de Puerto Rico, é índices cronológico y alfabético.* Havana: P. Fernández y Compañía, 1892.

Gallego y García, Tesifonte. *Cuba por fuera (apuntes al natural).* Havana: La Propaganda Literaria, 1890.

Gándara, José de la. *Anexión y guerra de Santo Domingo,* 2 vols. Madrid: Imp. de "El Correo Militar," 1884.

García Camba, Andrés. *Memorias del general García Camba para la historia de las armas españolas en el Perú, 1809–1821.* Madrid: Editorial América, 1916.

García de Arboleya, José María. *Tres cuestiones sobre la isla de Cuba. ¿De dónde venimos? ¿Dónde estamos? ¿Adónde vamos?* Havana: Imprenta del Tiempo, 1869.

García de Polavieja, Camilo. *Relación documentada de mi política en Cuba: lo que vi, lo que hice, lo que anuncié.* Madrid: Imprenta de Emilio Minuesa, 1898.

Gelpí y Ferro, Gil. *Álbum histórico fotográfico de la guerra de Cuba desde su principio hasta el reinado de Amadeo I.* Havana: Imprenta "La Antilla" de Cacho-Negrete, 1872.

Gelpí y Ferro, Gil. *Historia de la revolución y guerra de Cuba.* Havana: Tipografía de la Gaceta Oficial, 1887.

Gómez Núñez, Severo. *La Guerra Hispano-Americana. Santiago de Cuba.* Madrid: Imprenta del Cuerpo de Artillería, 1901.

Gómez, Juan Gualberto & Sendras y Burín, Antonio. *La isla de Puerto-Rico. Bosquejo Histórico (desde la conquista hasta principios de 1891).* Madrid: Imprenta de José Gil y Navarro, 1891.

González Barrios, René. *Apuntes autobiográficos de la vida de Ricardo Batrell Oviedo.* Havana: Editorial de Ciencias Sociales, 2014.

González del Tánago, Benito. *Estadística de los Voluntarios existentes en 31 de julio de 1869 en Matanzas, Cabezas, Ceiba-Mocha, Corral-Nuevo, Canasí, Guanábana, Sabanilla del Encomendador, Bolondrón, Unión de Reyes, Madruga, Güira de Macuriges y Alacranes, con expresión de las clases, nombres y apellidos, edad, pueblos y provincias de donde son naturales.* Havana: Imprenta La Intrépida, 1869.

Gremio Central del Tabaco en La Habana. *Informe del Comité permanente del Gremio Central del Tabaco en La Habana al Congreso solicitando la exención del pago de contribución municipal a las fábricas de tabacos puros y de cigarros.* Havana, 1871.

Guerrero, Rafael. *Crónica de la guerra de Cuba y de la rebelión de Filipinas,* vol. IV. Barcelona: Tip. Hispano-Americana, 1898.

Gutiérrez de la Concha, José. *Memorias sobre el estado político, Gobierno y administración de la isla de Cuba.* Madrid: Establecimiento Tipográfico de D. José Trujillo, 1853.

Heredia, J. F. *Memorias del regente Heredia (de las Reales Audiencias de Caracas y México).* Madrid: Editorial América, 1916.

Herrero y Sampedro, Ulpiano. *Nuestra prisión en poder de los revolucionarios filipinos. Crónica de dieciocho meses de cautiverio de más de cien religiosos del centro de Luzón, empleados en el ministerio de las almas.* Manila: Imprenta del Colegio de Santo Tomás, 1900.

Ibáñez, Francisco Feliciano. *Observaciones sobre la utilidad y conveniencia del establecimiento en esta isla de grandes ingenios centrales para salvar nuestra agricultura é industria azucarera, por el aumento de producción y disminución de gastos y bases para la formación de una compañía para la fácil realización de este objeto.* Havana: Imp. y Lit. Obispo, 1880.

Isla de Puerto-Rico. Reglamento para los cuerpos de Voluntarios de la misma, aprobado por Real Orden de 10 de julio de 1888. San Juan: Imp. de la Capitanía General, 1888.

Jou i Andreu, David. *El 98 vist pels sitgetans. Memòries de Jaume Sans sobre el setge americà a Santiago de Cuba.* Sitges: Ajuntament de Sitges, 1999.

Larrea y Lisa, Francisco. *El desastre nacional y los vicios de nuestras instituciones militares.* Madrid: Imprenta del Cuerpo de Artillería, 1901.

Lee, Fitzhugh, Roosevelt, Theodore & Wheeler, Joseph. *Cuba's Struggle Against Spain with the causes of American intervention and a full account of the Spanish-American War: including final peace negotiations.* New York: American Historical Press, 1899.

Llofriu y Sagrera, Eleuterio. *Historia de la insurrección y guerra de la isla de Cuba,* 3 vols. Madrid: Imprenta de la Galería Literaria, 1871.

Loynaz del Castillo, Enrique. *Memorias de la guerra.* Havana: Editorial de Ciencias Sociales, 1989.

Maciá y Doménech, Narciso. *Vida y obra (1855–1933).* Havana: 1954.

Manifestaciones del elemento español de Puerto-Rico con motivo de los sucesos de Juana Díaz. Puerto Rico: 1887.

Manual de Instrucción Militar y Reglamento comentado para el Instituto de Voluntarios de la Isla de Cuba. Havana: Imprenta del Diario del Ejército, 1892.

Mañé Flaquer, Juan. *La revolución de 1868 juzgada por sus autores.* Barcelona: Imprenta de Jaime Jepús, Editor, 1876.

Martí, José. *Obras completas,* vol. I. Havana: Editorial de Ciencias Sociales, 1975.

Martín Contreras, Evaristo. *Los Voluntarios de la Isla de Cuba. Reconocimiento de su heroísmo y vindicación a su honor.* Valladolid: Imprenta, Librería, Estéreo-galvanoplastia y Taller de Grabado de Gaviria y Zapatero, 1876.

Martínez Nubla, Elías. *Los voluntarios de Ultramar. El Libro Azul. Apuntes para la Historia.* Madrid: Imprenta del Fomento Naval, 1903.

Martínez, Jacinto María. *Los Voluntarios de Cuba y el Obispo de La Habana, ó historia de ciertos sucesos que deben referirse ahora, y no después, y los refiere el mismo Obispo, Senador del Reino.* Madrid: Imprenta á cargo de D. A. Pérez Dubrull, 1871.

Memoria que presenta á los señores socios del Centro Hispano-Ultramarino de Madrid el Presidente Excmo. Sr. Marqués de Manzanedo. 20 de enero de 1873. Madrid: Imprenta de Andrés Orejas, 1873.

Menéndez Acebal, Alejandro. *Cartilla del Voluntario.* Cárdenas: Establecimiento Tipográfico, 1895 (first published in 1890).

Moreno Solano, Fernando C. *Álbum de los Voluntarios.* Cárdenas: Imprenta "El Comercio" de E. Trujillo, 1874.

Moreno, Francisco. *El país del chocolate (la inmoralidad en Cuba).* Madrid: Imp. de F. García Herrero, 1887.

Moure Saco, José. *1102 días en el Ejército español. Recuerdos de un soldado en la guerra de Cuba.* Havana: Ediciones Boloña, 2001.

Otero Pimentel, Luis. *Memoria sobre los Voluntarios de la isla de Cuba. Consideraciones relativas a su pasad, su presente y su porvenir.* Havana: La Propaganda Literaria, 1876.

Palomino, Joaquín de. *Merecido ramillete que dedican los Voluntarios de la isla de Cuba al mal aconsejado diputado a Cortes Díaz Quintero, formado con las protestas, manifestaciones y composiciones poéticas publicadas en los periódicos de esta capital y precedido de varias dedicatorias en prosa y verso.* Havana: Imprenta y Encuadernación "Sociedad de Operarios," 1870.

Pando, Luis M. de. *Documento presentado al Senado por el Excmo. Sr. Senador D. Luis M. de Pando en 22 de octubre de 1898.* Madrid: Imprenta y Fundición de los Hijos de J. A. García, 1899.

Pastor Díaz, Nicomedes & Cárdenas, Francisco de. *Galería de españoles célebres contemporáneos, ó biografías y retratos de todos los personajes distinguidos de nuestros días en las ciencias, en la política, en las armas, en las letras y en las artes*, vol. III. Madrid: Boix, Editor, 1843.

Peláez, Miguel. *Contestación del general D. Antonio Peláez á las groseras calumnias que contiene el manifiesto á la nación por los Voluntarios de la isla de Cuba.* Madrid: Imprenta de D. Cárlos Frontaura, 1869.

Pérez Morís, José & Cueto y González Quijano, Luis. *Historia de la insurrección de Lares, precedida de una reseña de los trabajos separatistas que se vienen haciendo en la Isla de Puerto-Rico desde la emancipación de las demás posesiones hispano-ultramarinas, y seguida de todos los documentos á ella referentes.* Barcelona: Establecimiento Tipográfico de Narciso Ramírez y Cº, 1872.

Pérez, Jr. & Louis A. (ed.). *Slaves, Sugar, & Colonial Society. Travel Accounts of Cuba, 1801–1899.* Wilmington: Scholarly Resources Inc., 1992.

Pezuela, Jacobo de la. *Crónica de las Antillas.* Madrid: Rubio, Grilo y Vitturi, 1871.

Pi y Margall, Francisco. *Historia de España en el siglo XIX: sucesos políticos, económicos, sociales y artísticos, acaecidos durante el mismo, detallada narración de sus acontecimientos y extenso juicio crítico de sus hombres*, vol. IV. Madrid: Miguel Seguí Editor, 1902.

Piedra Martel, Manuel. *Mis primeros 30 años.* Havana: Editorial de Ciencias Sociales, 2001 (first published by Minerva, 1943).

Pirala, Antonio. *Historia contemporánea. Anales desde 1843 hasta la conclusión de la última guerra civil*, vol. III. Madrid: Imprenta y Fundición de Manuel Tello, 1876.

Pirala, Antonio. *Anales de la Guerra de Cuba*, 2 vols. Madrid: Felipe González Rojas Editor, 1895.

Primo de Rivera y Sobremonte, Fernando. *Memoria dirigida al Senado por el Capitán General D. Fernando Primo de Rivera y Sobremonte acerca de su gestión en Filipinas.* Madrid: Imprenta y Litografía del Depósito de la Guerra, 1898.

Prince, J. C. *Cuba illustrated with the biography and portrait of Christopher Columbus containing also general information relating to Havana, Matanzas, Cienfuegos, and the island of Cuba with illustrations and maps together with an Anglo-Spanish vocabulary.* New York: Napoléon Thompson & Co., 1893–1894.

Provincia de Puerto Rico. Instituto de Voluntarios de la Isla de Puerto Rico. Estado militar y escalafón general de los Sres. Jefes, oficiales, médicos, capellanes, músicos mayores, sanitarios en activo, supernumerarios, honorarios y exentos de servicio en 1º de marzo de 1896. San Juan: Est. Tip. de Francisco J. Marxuach, 1896.

Puerto-Rico por dentro. Cartas abiertas, por XXX. Julio y agosto de 1888, con la sentencia dictada por la Audiencia de Puerto-Rico en 2 de junio de 1888. Madrid: Imprenta de José Gil y Navarro, 1888.

Quiñones, Francisco Mariano. *Apuntes para la historia de Puerto Rico.* Mayagüez: Tipografía Comercial Aduana, 1888.

Quiñones, Francisco Mariano. *Historia de los partidos reformista y conservador de Puerto-Rico.* Mayagüez: Tipografía Comercial, 1889.

Reglamento de las Compañías de Voluntarios Indígenas creadas por Decreto de 16 de Octubre de 1897. Manila: Tipo-Litografía de Chofré y Comp.ª, 1897.

Reglamento para los cuerpos de Voluntarios de la isla de Cuba. Havana: Imprenta del Gobierno y Capitanía General, 1869.

Reglamento para los cuerpos de Voluntarios de la isla de Puerto Rico. San Juan: Imprenta del Gobierno y Capitanía General, 1870.

Retana, W. E. *Mando del general Weyler en Filipinas. 5 Junio 1888–17 Noviembre 1891. Apuntes y documentos para la historia política, administrativa y militar de dichas islas.* Madrid: Imprenta de la Viuda de M. Minuesa de los Ríos, 1896.

Retana, W. E. *Vida y escritos del Dr. José Rizal.* Madrid: Librería General de Victoriano Suárez, 1907.

Ribó, José Joaquín. *Historia de los Voluntarios cubanos,* 2 vols. Madrid: Imprenta y Litografía de Nicolás González, 1872–7.

Rigal, Segundo. *A nuestros hermanos de la península.* Havana: 1871.

Rivero Méndez, Ángel. *Crónica de la Guerra Hispano-Americana en Puerto Rico.* Madrid: Sucesores de Rivadeneyra, 1922.

Rodríguez, José Ignacio. *Estudio histórico sobre el origen, desenvolvimiento y manifestaciones prácticas de la idea de la anexión de la isla de Cuba á los Estados Unidos de América.* Havana: Imprenta La Propaganda Literaria, 1900.

Rosado y Brincau, Rafael. *Bosquejo histórico de la institución de Voluntarios en Puerto-Rico.* San Juan: Imprenta de la Capitanía General, 1888.

Ruiz y López, Francisco Matías. *Cuba y sus enemigos. Defensa de los Voluntarios de la isla de Cuba contra los ultrajes proferidos en las Cortes españolas en detrimento de su honra publicada en la prensa de la Corte y de provincias.* Madrid: Imprenta de Lázaro Maroto, 1872.

Salinas y Angulo, Ignacio. *Defensa del general Jáudenes.* Madrid: Imprenta y Litografía del Depósito de la Guerra, 1899.

Sedano y Cruzat, Carlos de. *Cuba desde 1850 á 1873. Colección de informes, memorias, proyectos y antecedentes sobre el Gobierno de la Isla de Cuba, relativos al citado periodo y un apéndice con las Conferencias de la Junta Informativa de Ultramar, celebradas en esta capital en los años de 1866 y 1867.* Madrid: Imprenta Nacional, 1873.

Toral, Juan & Toral, José. *El sitio de Manila. 1898. Memorias de un Voluntario.* Manila: Imprenta Litográfica Partier, 1898.

Torres-Pardo, Rafael. *Discurso en defensa de los Voluntarios de Cuba, leído en la Junta General del Círculo Hispano-Ultramarino de Sevilla y su provincia, celebrada el 14 de abril de 1872, por D. Rafael Torres-Pardo, socio del mismo.* Seville: Imprenta de Salvador Acuña y compañía, 1872.

Triay, José E. *Las Glorias del Voluntario. Ecos nacionales.* Havana: Imprenta La Intrépida, 1869.

Ubieta, Enrique. *Efemérides de la Revolución Cubana,* vol. I. Havana: La Moderna Poesía, 1911.

Valdés Domínguez, Fermín. *El 27 de noviembre de 1871.* Havana: Imprenta "La Correspondencia de Cuba," 1887.

Vandama y Calderón, Eugenio. *Colección de artículos sobre el Instituto de Voluntarios de la Isla de Cuba.* Havana: Imp. Militar, 1897.

Villa, Rafael. *Álbum biográfico de jefes de Voluntarios.* Havana: Tipografía "La Universal" de Ruiz y Hermanos, 1888.

Vivanco y Argüelles, Domingo. *La reforma electoral. Ley electoral para diputados á Cortes en la península de 26 de junio de 1890 aplicable á las elecciones de concejales y de diputados provinciales, precedida de un Índice de sus títulos y capítulos y seguida de un Repertorio alfabético con notas y observaciones.* Madrid: Imprenta de los Hijos de J. A. García, 1890.

Weyler y Nicolau, Valeriano. *Mi mando en Cuba (10 Febrero 1896 a 31 Octubre 1897). Historia militar y política de la última guerra separatista durante dicho mando*, 5 vols. Madrid: Imprenta, Litografía y Casa Editorial de Felipe González Rojas, 1910.

Ynfiesta, Alejandro. *El marqués de la Esperanza, jefe del partido español de Puerto Rico*. San Juan: Tipografía de González, 1875.

Zaragoza, Justo. *Las insurrecciones de Cuba. Apuntes para la historia política de esta isla en el presente siglo*, 2 vols. Madrid: Imprenta de Manuel G. Hernández, 1872–1873.

Secondary Works

Abreu Cardet, José & Tartaglia Redondo, Juan José. "La Guerra del 1895 en el Oriente de Cuba." Sánchez Mantero, Rafael (coord.). *En torno al "98": España en el tránsito del siglo XIX y XX: actas del IV Congreso de la Asociación de Historia Contemporánea*. Huelva: Universidad de Huelva, Servicio de Publicaciones, 2000, pp. 435–48.

Abreu Cardet, José. "La defensa del Imperio: Cuba 1868–1870." *Tebeto: Anuario del Archivo Histórico Insular de Fuerteventura*, 1994, No. 7, pp. 159–74.

Abreu Cardet, José. *Apuntes sobre el integrismo en Cuba, 1868–1878*. Santiago de Cuba: Editorial Oriente, 2012.

Aguilar, Filomeno V. *Clash of Spirits: The History of Power and Sugar Planter Hegemony on a Visayan Island*. Honolulu: The University of Hawaii Press, 1998.

Albi de la Cuesta, Julio. *Banderas olvidadas. El Ejército español en las guerras de Emancipación de América*. Madrid: Desperta Ferro Ediciones, 2019.

Alonso Romero, Mª Paz. *Cuba en la España liberal (1837–1898)*. Madrid: Centro de Estudios Políticos y Constitucionales, 2002.

Alvarado Planas, Javier. *La Administración Colonial española en el siglo XIX*. Madrid: Agencia Estatal Boletín Oficial del Estado / Centro de Estudios Políticos y Constitucionales, 2013.

Andaya, Leonard Y. "Ethnicity in the Philippine Revolution," in Rodao, Florentino & Rodríguez, Felice Noelle (eds.). *The Philippine revolution of 1896: ordinary people in extraordinary times*. Quezon City: Ateneo de Manila University Press, 2001, pp. 49–82.

Anderson, Benedict. *The Age of Globalization. Anarchists and the anticolonial imagination*. London and New York: Verso Books, 2013 (first published as *Under Three Flags*, 2005).

Andreu Miralles, Xavier. "El pueblo y sus opresores: populismo y nacionalismo en la cultura política del radicalismo democrático, 1844–1848." *Historia y política: ideas, procesos y movimientos sociales*, 2011, No. 25, pp. 65–91.

Arias Castañón, Eloy. "El Centro Hispano-Ultramarino de Sevilla y la Guerra de Cuba (1872–1881)," in *Actas del II Congreso Internacional de Historia Militar*, vol. III. Zaragoza: Servicio de Publicaciones del EME, 1988, pp. 213–29.

Armiñán, Luis de. *Weyler*. Madrid: Editorial "El Gran Capitán," 1946.

Aróstegui, Julio, Canal, Jordi & González Calleja, Eduardo. *El carlismo y las guerras carlistas*. Madrid: La Esfera de los Libros, 2003.

Bahamonde Magro, Ángel & Cayuela Fernández, José G. "Trasvase de capitales antillanos y estrategias inversoras. La fortuna del Marqués de Manzanedo (1823–1882)." *Revista Internacional de Sociología*, 1987, No. 1, pp. 125–48.

Bahamonde Magro, Ángel & Cayuela Fernández, José G. "La creación de nobleza en Cuba durante el siglo XIX." *Historia Social*, 1991, No. 11, pp. 56–82.

Bahamonde Magro, Ángel & Cayuela Fernández, José G. *Hacer las Américas. Las elites coloniales españolas en el siglo XIX*. Madrid: Alianza Editorial, 1992.

Balboa Navarro, Imilcy. "Colonización e inmigración. Dos realidades enfrentadas en la Cuba de fin de siglo," in Morales Padrón, Francisco (ed.). *III Coloquio de Historia Canario-Americana, VIII Congreso Internacional de Historia de América (AEA) (1998)*. Las Palmas de Gran Canaria: Cabildo de Gran Canaria, 2000, pp. 452–70.

Balboa Navarro, Imilcy. "Asentar para dominar. Salamanca y la colonización militar. Cuba, 1889–1890." *Tiempos de América*, 2001, No. 8, pp. 29–46.

Balboa Navarro, Imilcy. "Tierras y brazos. Inmigración, colonización y fuerza de trabajo. Cuba, 1878–1898." *Illes i Imperis*, 2002, No. 6, pp. 67–76.

Balboa Navarro, Imilcy. "La inmigración como forma de presión política: Polavieja, los hacendados y la colonización por la vía militar. Cuba, 1878–1892," *Illes i Imperis*, 2004, No. 7, pp. 133–55.

Baldovín Ruiz, Eladio. *Cuba. El desastre español del siglo XIX*. Astorga: Akrón, 2010.

Barcia Zequeira, María del Carmen. "Los batallones de pardos y morenos en Cuba (1600–1868)." *Anales de Desclasificación*, 2004, vol. 1, No. 2, pp. 1–16.

Barcia, Manuel. "'Un coloso sobre la arena': definiendo el camino hacia la plantación esclavista en Cuba, 1792–1825." *Revista de Indias*, 2011, vol. LXXI, No. 251, pp. 53–76.

Bayón Toro, Fernando. *Elecciones y partidos políticos de Puerto Rico (1809–1976)*. Madrid: Instituto de Cultura Hispánica de Madrid, 1977.

Benavides Martínez, Juan José. *De milicianos del Rey a soldados mexicanos. Milicias y sociedad en San Luis Potosí (1767–1824)*. Madrid: CSIC, 2014.

Benito Sánchez, Ana Isabel. "Determinantes instituciones de la reivindicación autonomista en Puerto Rico." *Revista de Humanidades Tecnológico de Monterrey*, 2008, No. 24, pp. 83–120.

Bergad, Laird W. *Coffee and the Growth of Agrarian Capitalism in Nineteenth-Century Puerto Rico*. Princeton: Princeton University Press, 1983.

Bergad, Laird W. *Cuban Rural Society in the Nineteenth Century: The Social and Economic History of Monoculture in Matanzas*. Princeton: Princeton University Press, 1990.

Bernades, Vicenç. *Ramon Pintó. Una conspiració a la Cuba colonial*. Barcelona: Edicions La Paraula Viva, 1975.

Bizcarrondo, Marta & Elorza, Antonio. *Cuba/España. El dilema autonomista, 1878–1898*. Madrid: Editorial Colibrí, 2001.

Bizcarrondo, Marta. "El autonomismo cubano. Las ideas y los hechos (1878–1898)." *Historia Contemporánea*, 1999, No. 19, pp. 69–94.

Black, Jeremy. *Slavery. A New Global History*. London: Constable & Robinson, 2011.

Bothwell, Reece B. *Orígenes y desarrollo de los partidos políticos en Puerto Rico*. San Juan: Editorial Edil, 1987.

Brown, Matthew. *The Struggle for Power in Post-Independence Colombia and Venezuela*. London: Palgrave Macmillan, 2012.

Buxó de Abaigar, Joaquín. *Domingo Dulce. General isabelino*. Barcelona: Editorial Planeta, 1962.

Cabrero, Leoncio. "Las interferencias de la masonería extranjera en Filipinas en la segunda mitad del siglo XIX." *Revista de Indias*, 1998, vol. LVIII, No. 213, pp. 519–27.

Cardona, Gabriel & Losada, Juan Carlos. *Weyler. Nuestro hombre en La Habana*. Barcelona: Editorial Planeta, 1997.

Carr, Raymond. *Spain, 1808–1975*. Oxford: Oxford University Press, 1982.

Casanovas, Joan. *Bread, or Bullets! Urban Labor and Spanish Colonialism in Cuba, 1858–1898*. Pittsburgh: University of Pittsburgh Press, 1998.

Castro Arroyo, María de los Ángeles. "'¿A qué pelear si los de Madrid no quieren?' Una versión criolla de la guerra del 98 en Puerto Rico." *Revista de Indias*, 1997, vol. LVII, No. 211, pp. 657-94.

Catton, Bruce. *The Civil War*. Boston and New York: Mariner Books, 2004 (first published as *The American Heritage Short History of the Civil War*. New York: American Heritage Publishing, 1960).

Cayuela Fernández, José G. *Bahía de Ultramar. España y Cuba en el siglo XIX. El control de las relaciones coloniales*. Madrid: Siglo XXI de España Editores, 1993.

Cayuela Fernández, José G. "Los capitanes generales de Cuba: élites coloniales y élites metropolitanas (1823-1898)." *Historia contemporánea*, 1996, No. 13-14, pp. 197-222.

Chaffin, Tom. *Fatal Glory. Narciso López and the First Clandestine U.S. War against Cuba*. Charlottesville and London: University Press of Virginia, 1996.

Clemente, Josep C. *Las guerras carlistas*. Madrid: Sarpe, 1986.

Comellas, José Luis. *Cánovas*. Madrid: Ediciones Cid, 1965.

Companys Monclús, Julián. *De la explosión del Maine a la ruptura de relaciones diplomáticas entre Estados Unidos y España (1898)*. Lérida: Estudi General de Lleida, 1989.

Corte Caballero, Gabriela dalla & Luzón, José Luis. "Espacio criollo y espacio colonial: los voluntarios y la batalla de La Habana en la Guerra de los Diez Años," in Centro de Investigaciones de América Latina (comp.). *De súbditos del rey a ciudadanos de la nación (Actas del I Congreso Internacional Nueva España y las Antillas)*. Castellón de La Plana: Univeristat Jaume I, Servicio de Publicaciones, 2000, pp. 339-68.

Costas Comesaña, Antón. "El viraje del pensamiento político-económico español a mediados del siglo XIX: la 'conversión' de Laureano Figuerola y la formulación del librecambismo industrialista." *Moneda y Crédito*, 1983, No. 167, pp. 47-70.

Cruz Monclova, Lidio. *Historia de Puerto Rico (siglo XIX)*, 3 t., 6 vols. Río Piedras: Ediciones Universitarias, 1952-64.

Cruz Monclova, Lidio. *Historia del año de 1887*. Río Piedras: Ed. Universitaria, 1958.

Cuartero Escobés, Susana. "El nacionalismo independentista del Katipunan," in Fusi, Juan Pablo & Niño Rodríguez, Antonio (eds.). *Antes del desastre: orígenes y antecedentes de la crisis del 98*. Madrid: Universidad Complutense, 1996, pp. 225-34.

Cubano Iguina, Astrid. *El hilo en el laberinto. Claves de la lucha política en Puerto Rico (siglo XIX)*. San Juan: Ediciones Huracán, 1990.

Cubano Iguina, Astrid. "Política radical y autonomismo en Puerto Rico: conflictos de intereses en la formación del Partido Autonomista Portorriqueño (1887)." *Anuario de estudios americanos*, 1994, vol. 51, No. 2, pp. 155-73.

Cubano Iguina, Astrid. "El autonomismo en Puerto Rico, 1887-1898: notas para la definición de un modelo de política radical," in Naranjo Orovio, Consuelo, Puig-Samper, Miguel Á. & García Mora, Luis Miguel (eds.). *La nación soñada, Cuba, Puerto Rico y Filipinas ante el 98: actas del Congreso Internacional celebrado en Aranjuez del 2 al 28 de abril de 1995*. Madrid: Ediciones Doce Calles, 1996, pp. 405-16.

Cubano Iguina, Astrid. "Puerto Rico," in Varela Ortega, José (dir.). *El poder de la influencia: geografía del caciquismo en España (1875-1923)*. Madrid: Marcial Pons, 2001, pp. 541-58.

Davies, Catherine & Sánchez, Sarah. "Rafael María de Labra and *La Revista Hispano-Americana* 1864-1867: Revolutionary Liberalism and Colonial Reform." *Bulletin of Spanish Studies: Hispanic Studies and Researches on Spain, Portugal and Latin America*, 2010, vol. 7, No. 87, pp. 915-38.

Dávila Wesolovsky, Jesús. "Las operaciones en Luzón. Asedio y defensa de Manila. Mayo-Agosto 1898," in *El Ejército y la Armada en 1898: Cuba, Puerto Rico y Filipinas. I Congreso Internacional de Historia Militar*, vol. I. Madrid: Ministerio de Defensa, 1999, pp. 307–44.

Delgado, Josep M. "'Menos se perdió en Cuba'. La dimensión asiática del 98." *Illes i Imperis*, 1999, No. 2, pp. 49–64.

Díaz Soler, Luis M. *Historia de la esclavitud negra en Puerto Rico*. San Juan: Editorial de la Universidad de Puerto Rico, 1953.

Díaz-Trechuelo, Lourdes. *Filipinas. La gran desconocida (1565–1898)*. Pamplona: Editorial de la Universidad de Navarra, 2001.

Diego García, Emilio de. "¿La última oportunidad política en las Antillas?" in Diego García, Emilio de (dir.). *1895, la guerra en Cuba y la España de la Restauración*. Madrid: Editorial Complutense, 1996, pp. 99–118.

Domingo Acebrón, María Dolores. "El tráfico de armas durante la guerra de los Diez Años (1868–1878)." *Tebeto: Anuario del Archivo Histórico Insular de Fuerteventura*, 1990, No. 3, pp. 91–132.

Domingo Acebrón, María Dolores. *Los Voluntarios y su papel contrarrevolucionario en la Guerra de los Diez Años en Cuba, 1868–1878*. Paris: L'Harmattan, 1996.

Donoso Jiménez, Isaac. "El desarrollo del mundo meridional filipino en el siglo XIX: el difícil encaje de la población musulmana," in Elizalde Pérez-Grueso, María Dolores & Huetz de Lemps, Xavier (coord.). *Filipinas, siglo XIX: coexistencia e interacción entre comunidades en el Imperio español*." Madrid: Polifemo: 2017, pp. 427–56.

Durán, Nelson. *La Unión Liberal y la modernización de la España isabelina. Una convivencia frustrada 1854–1868*. Madrid: Akal Editor, 1979.

Elizalde Pérez-Grueso, María Dolores & Huetz de Lemps, Xavier. "Poder, religión y control en Filipinas. Colaboración y conflicto entre el Estado y las órdenes religiosas, 1868–1898." *Ayer*, 2015, No. 100, pp. 151–76.

Elizalde Pérez-Grueso, María Dolores & Huetz de Lemps, Xavier. "Un singular modelo colonizador: el papel de las órdenes religiosas en la administración española de Filipinas, siglos XVI al XIX." *Illes i Imperis*, 2015, No. 17, pp. 185–222.

Escolano Jiménez, Luis Alfonso. "El comienzo de las relaciones diplomáticas entre España y la República Dominicana en 1855." *Revista Complutense de Historia de América*, 2011, vol. 37, pp. 277–99.

Elizalde Pérez-Grueso, María Dolores. *España en el Pacífico. La colonia de las Islas Carolinas, 1885–1899. Un modelo colonial en el contexto internacional del imperialismo*. Madrid: CSIC/Instituto de Cooperación para el Desarrollo, 1992.

Elizalde Pérez-Grueso, María Dolores. "El sueño de la nación filipina. 1812–1896," in Elizalde Pérez-Grueso, María Dolores (ed.). *Problemas en la construcción nacional de Filipinas, India y Vietnam*. Barcelona: Edicions Bellaterra, 2013, pp. 37–82.

Escolano Jiménez, Luis Alfonso. *La rivalidad internacional por la República Dominicana y el complejo procesal de su anexión a España (1858–1865)*. Santo Domingo: Archivo General de la Nación, 2013.

Espadas Burgos, Manuel. *Alfonso XII y los orígenes de la Restauración*. Madrid: CSIC, 1990.

Estrade, Paul. "La nación antillana: sueño y afán de 'El Antillano' (Betances)," in Naranjo Orovio, Consuelo, Puig-Samper, Miguel Á. & García Mora, Luis Miguel (eds.). *La Nación Soñada: Cuba, Puerto Rico y Filipinas ante el 98*. Aranjuez: Ediciones Doce Calles, 1996, pp. 23–36.

Estrade, Paul. "El papel de la emigración patriótica en las Guerras de Independencia de Cuba (1868-1898)." *Tebeto: Anuario del Archivo Histórico Insular de Fuerteventura*, 1998, No. 11, pp. 83-102.

Fernández Almagro, Melchor. *Historia política de la España contemporánea*, 3 vols. Madrid: Alianza Editorial, 1968.

Fernández Jiménez, María Antonia. "La repatriación de los soldados españoles en la prensa del momento. Imágenes de una tragedia del 98," in Núñez Díaz-Balart, Mirta (dir.) & Rojas Friend, Antonio (Coord.). *El día después. España y sus excolonias tras el Desastre del 98*. Madrid: Editorial Argés, 1998, pp. 153-69.

Fernández Muñiz, Áurea Matilde. *España y Cuba, 1868-1898. Revolución burguesa y relaciones coloniales*. Havana: Editorial de Ciencias Sociales, 1988.

Fernández Muñiz, Áurea Matilde. "Los indianos: su incidencia en la economía peninsular y en la política colonial." *Trocadero: Revista de historia moderna y contemporánea*, 1992, No. 4, pp. 21-36.

Fernández Prieto, Leida. *Espacio de poder, ciencia y agricultura en Cuba: el Círculo de Hacendados, 1878-1917*. Madrid: CSIC / Universidad de Sevilla / Diputación de Sevilla, 2008.

Fernández, Frank. *El anarquismo en Cuba*. Madrid: Fundación de Estudios Libertarios Anselmo Lorenzo, 2000.

Ferrer, Ada, *Insurgent Cuba. Race, Nation, and Revolution, 1868-1898*. Chapel Hill and London: University of North Carolina Press, 1999.

Ferrer, Ada, "Noticias de Haití en Cuba." *Revista de Indias*, 2003, vol. LXIII, No. 229, pp. 675-94.

Ferrer, Ada, *Freedom's Mirror. Cuba and Haiti in the Age of Revolution*, Cambridge, Cambridge University Press, 2014.

Figueroa, Luis A. *Sugar, Slavery, and Freedom in Nineteenth-Century Puerto Rico*. Chapel Hill: The University of North Carolina Press, 2005.

Flake, Dennis Edward. *Loyal Macabebes. How the Americans Used the Macabebe Scouts in the Annexation of the Philippines*. San Fernando: Holy Angel University Press, 2009.

Flores Onofre, Herminio. *Donaciones y voluntarios a las guerras de Marruecos durante la segunda mitad del siglo XIX*. MA Thesis, #260. San Juan: Centro de Estudios Avanzados de Puerto Rico y el Caribe, 2008.

Foner, Philip S. *The Spanish-Cuban-American War and the Birth of American Imperialism*, 2 vols. New York and London: Monthly Review Press, 1972.

Fontana, Josep. *La época del liberalismo*, in Fontana, Josep & Villares, Ramón (dir.). *Historia de España*, vol. VI. Barcelona and Madrid: Crítica / Marcial Pons, 2007.

Ford, Roger. *The World's Great Rifles*. London: Brown Books, 1998.

Fradera, Josep M. *Gobernar colonias*. Barcelona: Ediciones Península, 1999.

Fradera, Josep M. *Colonias para después de un imperio*. Barcelona: Edicions Bellaterra, 2005.

Fradera, Josep M. "Include and Rule: The Limits of Colonial Policy, 1810-1837," in Brown, Matthew & Paquette, Gabriel (eds.). *Connections after Colonialism. Europe and Latin America in the 1820s*. Tuscaloosa: The University of Alabama Press, 2013, pp. 64-86.

Fradera, Josep M. *La Nación Imperial. Derechos, representación y ciudadanía en los imperios de Gran Bretaña, Francia, España y Estados Unidos (1750-1918)*, vol. I. Barcelona: Edhasa, 2015.

Franco Castañón, Hermenegildo. "El apostadero de Filipinas: sus años finales," in *El Ejército y la Armada en 1898: Cuba, Puerto Rico y Filipinas. I Congreso Internacional de Historia Militar*, vol. I. Madrid: Ministerio de Defensa, 1999, pp. 345-74.

Franklin, John Hope. *Reconstruction after the Civil War*. Chicago and London: Chicago University Press, 1961.
Gallego Fresnillo, Carmen. "El sexenio español y el Extremo Oriente: Filipinas," in Elizalde Pérez-Grueso, María Dolores (ed.). *Las relaciones internacionales en el Pacífico (siglos XVIII-XX): colonización, descolonización y encuentro cultural*. Madrid: CSIC, 1997, pp. 375–94.
Gallego Jiménez, José Joaquín. "La protesta rural y los mecanismos para su represión por parte del Gobierno del Capitán General Camilo García de Polavieja en Cuba: (1890–1892)." *Americanía: revista de estudios latinoamericanos de la Universidad Pablo de Olavide de Sevilla*, 2011, No. 1, pp. 219–34.
Galván Rodríguez, Eduardo. *La abolición de la esclavitud en España. Debates parlamentarios, 1810–1886*. Madrid: Dykinson, 2014.
García Balañá, Albert. "Patria, plebe y política en la España isabelina: la guerra de África en Cataluña (1859–1860)," in Martín Corrales, Eloy (coord.). *Marruecos y el colonialismo español (1859–1912): de la guerra de África a la "penetración pacífica."* Barcelona: Edicions Bellaterra, 2002, pp. 13–78.
García Balañá, Albert. "Clase, Pueblo y Patria en la España liberal: comunidades polisémicas y experiencias plebeyas en la Cataluña urbana, 1840–1870," in Molina Aparicio, Fernando (coord.). *Extranjeros en el pasado. Nuevos historiadores de la España contemporánea*. Vitoria: Servicio de Publicaciones de la Universidad del País Vasco, 2009, pp. 97–128.
García Balañá, Albert. "'The Empire is no longer a social unit': declining imperial expectations and transatlantic crisis in metropolitan Spain, 1859–1909," in McCoy, Alfred W., Fradera, Josep M. & Jacobson, Stephen (eds.). *Endless Empire. Spain's Retreat, Europe's Eclipse, America's Decline*. Madison: The University of Wisconsin Press, 2012, pp. 92–103.
García Balañá, Albert. "Patriotismos trasatlánticos. Raza y nación en el impacto de la Guerra de África en el Caribe español de 1860." *Ayer*, 2017, No. 106, pp. 207–37.
García Figueres, Tomás. *Marruecos (la acción de España en el norte de África)*. Madrid: Ediciones Fe, 1941 (1st ed. 1940).
García Mora, Luis Miguel. "La fuerza de la palabra. El autonomismo en Cuba en el último tercio del siglo XIX." *Revista de Indias*, 2001, vol. LXI, No. 223, pp. 715–48.
García Rodríguez, Mercedes. *Con un ojo en Yara y otro en Madrid. Cuba entre dos revoluciones*. Havana: Editorial de Ciencias Sociales, 2012.
García, Gervasio Luis & Quintero Rivera, A. G. *Desafío y solidaridad. Breve historia del movimiento obrero puertorriqueño*. San Juan: Ediciones Huracán, 1982.
García, Gervasio Luis & Quintero Rivera, A. G. *Historia bajo sospecha*. San Juan: Publicaciones Gaviota, 2015.
Gibson, Carrie. "'There is no doubt that we are under threat by the Negroes of Santo Domingo': the spectre of Haiti in the Spanish Caribbean in the 1820s," in Brown, Matthew & Paquette, Gabriel (eds.). *Connections after Colonialism. Europe and Latin America in the 1820s*. Tuscaloosa: The University of Alabama Press, 2013, pp. 223–35.
Godet-Goujat, Hélène. "La Liga Filipina, creada por José Rizal en 1892, como balance político y base de un programa nacional para Filipinas," in Naranjo Orovio, Consuelo, Puig-Samper, Miguel Á. & García Mora, Luis Miguel (eds.). *La Nación Soñada: Cuba, Puerto Rico y Filipinas ante el 98*. Aranjuez: Ediciones Doce Calles, 1996, pp. 79–84.
Godicheau, François. "La Guardia Civil en Cuba, del control del territorio a la guerra permanente (1851–1898)." *Nuevo Mundo Mundos Nuevos*, 2014 (online): https://nuevomundo.revues.org/67109 [consulted 05-25-2017].

Gómez Acevedo, Labor. *Sanz, promotor de la conciencia separatista en Puerto Rico.* Río Piedras: Editorial Universitaria, 1974.
González Cuevas, Luis. *¿Defendiendo el honor? La institución de voluntarios en Puerto Rico durante la guerra hispanoamericana.* San Juan: Ediciones Puerto, 2014.
González de la Flor, Helios. *Los Voluntarios de Cádiz (1808-1814).* Cádiz: Servicio de Publicaciones de la Universidad de Cádiz, 2018.
González Mercado, Nelson R. *Auge y decadencia de las Milicias Disciplinadas.* PhD Thesis #37. San Juan: Centro de Estudios Avanzados de Puerto Rico y el Caribe, 2005.
González Vales, Luis. "The Challenge to Colonialism (1866-1897)," in Arturo Morales Carrión (dir.). *Puerto Rico. A Political and Cultural History.* New York: W. W. Norton & Company, Inc., 1983, pp. 108-25.
González Vales, Luis. "La campaña de Puerto Rico. Consideraciones histórico-militares," in *El Ejército y la Armada en 1898: Cuba, Puerto Rico y Filipinas. I Congreso Internacional de Historia Militar*, vol. I. Madrid: Ministerio de Defensa, 1999. pp. 257-70.
González Vales, Luis. "Las milicias disciplinadas. Guardianes de la soberanía española en Puerto Rico," in Pino y Moreno, Rafael del & Anes y Álvarez de Castrillón, Gonzalo (coord.). *La América hispana en los albores de la emancipación: actas del IX Congreso de Academias Iberoamericanas de la Historia.* Madrid: Marcial Pons, 2005, pp. 433-52.
González-Ripoll Navarro, M.ª Dolores. "Independencia y antillanismo en la obra de Hostos," in Naranjo Orovio, Consuelo, Puig-Samper, Miguel A. & García Mora, Luis Miguel (eds.). *La Nación Soñada: Cuba, Puerto Rico y Filipinas ante el 98.* Aranjuez: Ediciones Doce Calles, 1996, pp. 37-48.
Guerra y Sánchez, Ramiro. *La expansión territorial de los Estados Unidos a expensas de España y de los países hispanoamericanos.* Havana: Editorial Nacional de Cuba, 1935.
Guerra y Sánchez, Ramiro. *La guerra de los 10 años*, 2 vols. Havana: Editorial Cultural, 1950.
Hamilton, Richard F. *President McKinley, War and Empire*, 2 vols. New Brunswick and London: Transaction Publishers, 2006.
Helg, Aline. *Our Rightful Share: The Afro-Cuban Struggle for Equality, 1886-1912.* Chapel Hill: The University of North Carolina Press, 1995.
Hidalgo Nuchera, Patricio. "'Cuando pintan bastos'. De la derrota naval al drama de los repatriados en la Córdoba de 1898," in Hidalgo Nuchera, Patricio (coord.). *Andalucía y la repatriación de los soldados en la guerra del 98.* Seville: Fundación Pública Andaluza Centro de Estudios Andaluces, 2010, pp. 37-82.
Hilton, Sylvia L. "The Spanish-American War of 1898: Queries into the Relationship Between the Press, Public Opinion and Politics." *REDEN: Revista Española de Estudios Norteamericanos*, 1994, No. 7, pp. 71-87.
Hobsbawm, Eric. *Bandits.* New York: Pantheon Books, 1981 (first published in 1969).
Huetz de Lemps, Xavier. "La faible émigration des espagnols vers les Philippines: vastes projets et maigres réalisations des dernières années de la colonisation espagnole, 1881-1898," in Elizalde Pérez-Grueso, María Dolores (ed.). *Las relaciones internacionales en el Pacífico (siglos XVIII-XX): colonización, descolonización y encuentro cultural.* Madrid: CSIC, 1997, pp. 201-14.
Huetz de Lemps, Xavier. "Un cas colonial de corruption systémique : les Philippines à la fin du XIXe Siècle." *Illes i Imperis*, 2014, No. 16, pp. 135-46.
Ibarra, Jorge. *Ideología mambisa.* Havana: Instituto del Libro, 1967.
Iglesias, Fe. "El censo cubano de 1877 y sus diferentes versiones." *Santiago*, 1979, No. 34, pp. 167-214.

Ileto, Reynaldo C. "The Birth of the Filipino Revolutionary Army in Southern Tagalog, Luzón, 1898," in *El Ejército y la Armada en 1898: Cuba, Puerto Rico y Filipinas. I Congreso Internacional de Historia Militar*, vol. I. Madrid: Ministerio de Defensa, 1999, pp. 281–306.

Inarejos Muñoz, Juan Antonio. *Intervenciones coloniales y nacionalismo español. La política exterior de la Unión Liberal y sus vínculos con la Francia de Napoleón III (1856–1868)*. Madrid: Sílex, 2007.

Inarejos Muñoz, Juan Antonio. "Reclutar cacique: la selección de las elites coloniales filipinas a finales del siglo XIX." *Hispania*, 2011, vol. LXXI, No. 239, pp. 741–62.

Inarejos Muñoz, Juan Antonio. "La *influencia moral* en Asia. Práctica política y corrupción electoral en Filipinas durante la dominación colonial española." *Anuario de Estudios Americanos*, 2012, vol. 69, No. 1, pp. 199–224.

Inarejos Muñoz, Juan Antonio. "Los procedimientos de elección de los gobernadorcillos de 'igorrotes' en Filipinas a finales del siglo XIX." *Revista Complutense de Historia de América*, 2014, vol. 40, pp. 255–76.

Inarejos Muñoz, Juan Antonio. *Los (últimos) caciques de Filipinas. Las élites coloniales antes del 98*. Granada: Comares, 2015.

Jiménez de Wagenheim, Olga. *Puerto Rico. An Interpretive History from pre-Columbian Times to 1900*. Princeton: Markus Wiener Publishers, 1998.

Jou I Andreu, David. *Els sitgetans a Amèrica i diccionari d'"Americanos."* Sitges: Grup d'Estudis Sitgetans, 2008.

Kiernan, V. G. *European Empires from Conquest to Collapse, 1815–1960*. Leicester University Press in association with Fontana Paperbacks, 1982.

Klein, Herbert. "The Colored Militia of Cuba: 1568–1868." *Caribbean Studies*, 1966, vol. 6, No. 2, pp. 17–27.

Knight, Franklin W. *Slave Society in Cuba during the nineteenth century*. Madison: The University of Wisconsin Press, 1970.

Kuethe, Allan J. "Las Milicias Disciplinadas en América," in Kuethe, Allan J. & Marchena Fernández, Juan (eds.). *Soldados del Rey: el ejército borbónico en América colonial en vísperas de la independencia*. Castellón de La Plana: Publicacions de la Universitat Jaume I, 2005, pp. 101–26.

Lahullier Chaviano, Rubén. "La transformación de los espacios de sociabilidad en la Cuba finisecular: el caso de la Asociación de Dependientes del Comercio de La Habana (1880–1898)." *Minius: Revista do Departamento de Historia, Arte e Xeografía*, 2006, No. 14, pp. 171–90.

Lalinde Abadía, Jesús. *La administración española en el siglo XIX puertorriqueño*. Seville: Escuela de Estudios Hispano-Americanos de Sevilla, 1980.

Larkin, J. A. *Sugar and the Origins of modern Philippine Society*. Berkeley: University of California Press, 1993.

Laviña, Javier. "Santiago de Cuba, 1860: esclavitud, color y población." *Boletín de la Asociación de Geógrafos Españoles*, 1992–3, No. 15–16, pp. 17–32.

Le Riverend, Julio. *Historia económica de Cuba*. Barcelona: Ariel, 1972.

Leary, John Patrick. "America's Other Half: Slum Journalism and the War of 1898." *Journal of Transnational American Studies*, 2009, No. 1, pp. 1–33.

López Casimiro, Francisco. "Ramón Blanco Erenas, capitán general de Cuba y la masonería." *Boletín de la Real Academia de Extremadura de las Letras y las Ares*, 2009, t. 17, pp. 109–22.

López-Cordón, María Victoria. *La revolución de 1868 y la I República*. Madrid: Siglo XXI de España Editores, 1976.

Lozano Guirao, Pilar. "Filipinas durante el mandato del General Camilo García de Polavieja." *Anales de la Universidad de Murcia. Letras*, 1983, vol. 41, No. 3-4, pp. 95-131.

Luis, Jean-Philippe. "Les employés : une horde prédatrice ?" in Jean-Philippe, Luis (ed.). *L'État dans ses colonies. Les administrateurs de l'empire espagnol au XIXe siècle*. Madrid: Casa de Velázquez, 2015, pp. 227-52.

Luzón, José Luis. "Estado, etnias y espacio urbano: La Habana 1878." *Boletín americanista*, 1991, No. 41, pp. 137-50.

Maluquer de Motes, Jordi. "La burgesia catalana i l'esclavitud colonial: modes de producció i pràctica política." *Recerques: Història, economía i cultura*, 1974, No. 3, pp. 83-136.

Maluquer de Motes, Jordi. *España en la crisis de 1898: de la Gran Depresión a la modernización económica del siglo XX*. Barcelona: Península, 1999.

Mañach, Jorge. *Martí el apóstol*. Madrid: Espasa-Calpe, 1968 (first published in 1942).

Marchena Fernández, Juan. *Ejército y milicias en el mundo colonial americano*. Madrid: Editorial MAPFRE, 1992.

Mármol, José. *Antonio Maceo Grajales. El Titán de Bronce*. Miami: Ediciones Universal, 1998.

Márquez Macías, Rosario. "La Habana en el siglo XIX. Una visión a través de la emigración." *Ubi Sunt? Revista de Historia*, 2008, No. 23, pp. 13-21.

Martí Gilabert, Francisco. *La Primera República Española, 1873-1874*. Madrid: Ediciones Rialp, 2007.

Martín Corrales, Eloy. "La emigración española en Argelia." *Awraq: Estudios sobre el mundo árabe e islámico contemporáneo*, 2012, No. 5-6, pp. 47-63.

Martín Ramos, Jesús. "Bosquejo histórico-biográfico de Pablo Ubarri y Capetillo, Conde de San José de Santurce," in Ruiz-Manjón Cabeza, Octavio & Langa Laorga, María Alicia (eds.). *Los significados del 98: la sociedad española en la génesis del siglo XX*. Madrid: Biblioteca Nueva, 1999, pp. 201-12.

Martínez Shaw, Carlos. "Los orígenes de la industria algodonera catalana y el comercio colonial," in Gabriel Tortellà & Jordi Nadal Lorenzo (coord.). *Agricultura, comercio colonial y crecimiento económico en la España contemporánea: actas del Primer Coloquio de Historia Económica de España, Barcelona, 11-12 Mayo 1972*. Barcelona: Ariel, 1974, pp. 243-67.

Martínez-Fernández, Luis. *Torn between Empires. Economy, Society, and Patterns of Political Thought in the Hispanic Caribbean, 1840-1878*. Athens and London: The University of Georgia Press.

Mas Chao, Andrés. *Evolución de la infantería en el reinado de Alfonso XII*. Madrid: Servicio de Publicaciones del EME, 1989.

Mas Chao, Andrés. *La guerra olvidada de Filipinas, 1896-1898*. Madrid: Editorial San Martín, 1997.

Mas Gibert, Xavier. *Cartes de L'Havana, 1872*. Canet de Mar: Els 2 Pins, 2013.

Maura, Fernando. "Autonomía para Cuba: el proyecto Maura (1893)." *Razón española: Revista bimestral de pensamiento*, 2014, No. 184, pp. 169-84.

McPherson, James M. *Battle Cry of Freedom. The American Civil War*. London: Penguin Books in association with Oxford University Press, 2013 (first published in 1988).

Miguel Fernández, Enrique de. "Discurso de apertura del XXXI curso de Historia y Cultura valenciana: las tropas españolas en la guerra de Cuba. De las estimaciones especulativas a la cuantificación." *Anals de la Real Acàdemia de Cultura Valenciana*, 2010, No. 85, pp. 243-71.

Miguel Fernández, Enrique de. *Azcárraga, Weyler y la conducción de la guerra de Cuba*. PhD Thesis. Castellón de La Plana: Universitat Jaume I, 2011.

Molina Gómez-Arnau, Carmen. "Apuntes sobre el Katipunan." *Revista española del Pacífico*, 1996, No. 6, pp. 47–70.

Montero García, Manuel. "La moral militar de los soldados españoles durante las guerras coloniales, 1895-1898," in *Revista de Historia Militar*, 2017, Año LXI, No. 121, pp. 199–233.

Moreno Fraginals, Manuel & Moreno Masó, José J. *Guerra, migración y muerte (El ejército español en Cuba como vía migratoria)*. Colombres: Ediciones Júcar, 1993.

Moreno Fraginals, Manuel. *Cuba/España, España/Cuba. Historia común*. Barcelona: Crítica, 1995.

Moreno Fraginals, Manuel. *El ingenio. Complejo económico social cubano del azúcar*. Barcelona: Crítica, 2001 (first published in Havana: Editorial de Ciencias Sociales, 3 vols., 1964).

Moya Pons, Frank. *The Dominican Republic. A National History*. Princeton: Markus Wiener Publishers, 2010 (first published in 1998).

Murray, David. *Odious Commerce. Britain, Spain and the Abolition of the Slave Trade*. Cambridge: Cambridge University Press, 1980.

Musicant, Ivan. *Empire by Default. The Spanish-American War and the Dawn of the American Century*. New York: Henry Holt and Company, 1998.

Nadal, Jordi. *El fracaso de la revolución industrial en España, 1814-1913*. Barcelona: Ariel, 1975.

Naranjo Orovio, Consuelo & García González, Armando. *Racismo e inmigración en Cuba en el siglo XIX*. Aranjuez: Ediciones Doce Calles / FIM, 1996.

Naranjo Orovio, Consuelo. "Trabajo libre e inmigración española en Cuba, 1880-1930." *Revista de Indias*, 1992, No. 195-196, pp. 749–94.

Naranjo Orovio, Consuelo. "Hispanización y defensa de la integridad nacional en Cuba, 1868-1898." *Tiempos de América. Revista de Historia, Cultura y Territorio*, 1998, No. 2, pp. 71–91.

Navarro Azcúe, Concepción. *La abolición de la esclavitud negra en la legislación española, 1870-1887*. Madrid: Ediciones Cultura Hispánica/Instituto de Cooperación Iberoamericana, 1987.

Navarro Chueca, Francisco Javier. *La mortalidad de las tropas españolas en la guerra de Cuba (1895-1898)*. PhD Thesis. Valencia: Universidad Católica de Valencia San Vicente Mártir, 2021.

Navarro, Luis. *Las guerras de España en Cuba*. Madrid: Ediciones Encuentro, 1998.

Negroni, Héctor Andrés. *Historia militar de Puerto Rico*. Madrid: Ediciones Siruela, 1992.

Neira, Jesús. "El régimen político de la Restauración," in *Cánovas y la vertebración de España*. Madrid: Fundación Cánovas del Castillo, 1998, pp. 35–78.

Nord, Philip G. *The Politics of Resentment. Shopkeeper Protest in Nineteenth-Century Paris*. New Brunswick and London: Transaction Publishers, 2009.

Núñez de Prado Clavell, Sara. "La prensa y la opinión pública española en torno al 'desastre,'" in Fusi, Juan Pablo & Niño Rodríguez, Antonio (coord.). *Antes del desastre: orígenes y antecedentes de la crisis del 98*. Madrid: Editorial Complutense, 1996, pp. 453–64.

O'Toole, G. J. A. *The Spanish War. An American Epic 1898*. New York and London: W. W. Norton & Company, 1984.

Offner, John L. *An Unwanted War: the diplomacy of the United States and Spain over Cuba, 1895-1898*. Chapel Hill: University of North Carolina Press, 1992.

Olivar Bertrand. Rafael. *Prim*: Madrid, Tebas, 1975.
Ortiz Armengol, Pedro. "La campaña militar en Filipinas: año 1898," in *El Ejército y la Armada en 1898: Cuba, Puerto Rico y Filipinas. I Congreso Internacional de Historia Militar*, vol. I. Madrid: Ministerio de Defensa, 1999, pp. 375–84.
Padilla Angulo, Fernando J. "El carlismo en Ultramar," in Montañà, Daniel & Rafart, Josep (eds.). *Fronteres del carlisme: del Berguedà a Ultramar. IV Simposi d'Història del Carlisme. Avià, 7 de maig de 2016*. Avià: Centre d'Estudis d'Avià, 2016, pp. 209–29.
Padilla Angulo, Fernando J. "La reconcentración en Cuba (1895–1898): un pasado incómodo," in Puell de la Villa, Fernando & García Hernán, David (eds.). *Los efectos de la guerra. Desplazamientos de población a lo largo de la Historia*. Madrid: Instituto Universitario General Gutiérrez Mellado-UNED, 2017, pp. 295–317.
Pagán, Bolívar. *Historia de los partidos políticos puertorriqueños, 1898–1956*, vol. I. San Juan: Librería Campos, 1959.
Pakenham, Thomas. "The Contribution of the Colonial Forces," in Crawford, John & McGibbon, Ian (eds.). *One Flag, One Queen, One Tongue. New Zealand, the British Empire and the South African War, 1899–1902*. Auckland: Auckland University Press, 2003, pp. 58–73.
Paz Sánchez, Manuel de, Fernández Fernández, José & López Novegil, Nelson. *El bandolerismo en Cuba (1800–1933). Presencia canaria y protesta rural*, vol. I. Santa Cruz de Tenerife: Centro de la Cultura Popular Canaria, 1994.
Paz Sánchez, Manuel de. "Julio Sanguily y Garritte (1846–1906) y los alzamientos de febrero de 1895 en el Occidente de Cuba." *Revista de Indias*, 1996, vol. LVI, No. 207, pp. 387–428.
Pedreira, Antonio S. *El año terrible del 87. Sus antecedentes y sus consecuencias*. San Juan: Biblioteca de Autores Puertorriqueños, 1937.
Pérez Abellán, Francisco. *Matar a Prim*. Barcelona: Editorial Planeta, 2015.
Pérez Cisneros, Enrique. *El reformismo español en Cuba*. Madrid: Editorial Verbum, 2002.
Pérez Dionisio, Maritza. "La inmigración hispana en Santiago de Cuba (1868–1898)." *Estudios de historia social y económica de América*, 1996, No. 13, pp. 427–48.
Pérez Garzón, Juan Sisinio. "La Milicia Nacional," in VVAA. *Sagasta y el liberalismo español*. Madrid: Fundación BBVA, 2000, pp. 137–48.
Pérez Guzmán, Francisco & Sarracino, Rodolfo. *La Guerra Chiquita: una experiencia necesaria*. Havana: Editorial Letras Cubanas, 1982.
Pérez Guzmán, Francisco. *Herida profunda*. Havana: Ediciones Unión, 1998.
Pérez Nápoles, Rubén. *Martí. El poeta armado*. Madrid: Algaba Ediciones, 2004.
Pérez Rivera, Jaime M. *Asociacionismo, prensa y cultura entre los inmigrantes españoles de San Juan, 1871–1913*. PhD Thesis. San Juan: Universidad de Puerto Rico, Recinto de Río Piedras, 2002.
Pérez Vejo, Tomás. *Elegía criolla. Una reinterpretación de las guerras de independencia hispanoamericanas*. Ciudad de México: Tusquets Editores, 2010.
Pérez, Jr., Louis A. *Cuba Between Empires, 1878–1902*. Pittsburgh: University of Pittsburgh Press, 1983.
Pérez, Jr., Louis A. "Vagrants, Beggars, and Bandits: Social Origins of Cuban Separatism, 1878–1895." *The American Historical Review*, 1985, vol. 90, No. 5, pp. 1092–121.
Pérez, Jr., Louis A. *Lords of the Mountain: Social Banditry and Peasant Protest in Cuba, 1878–1918*. Pittsburgh: University of Pittsburgh Press, 1989.
Pérez, Jr., Louis A. "Between Baseball and Bullfighting: The Quest for Nationality in Cuba, 1868–1898." *The Journal of American History*, 1994, vol. 81, No. 2, pp. 493–517.

Pérez, Jr., Louis A. *Cuba: Between Reform & Revolution*. Oxford and New York: Oxford University Press, 1995 (first published in 1988).

Picó, Fernando. *Al filo del poder. Subalternos y dominantes en Puerto Rico, 1739-1910*. Río Piedras: Editorial de la Universidad de Puerto Rico, 1993.

Picó, Fernando. "Genealogía del sudor: la procedencia de algunos jornaleros agrícolas del café en el Puerto Rico del siglo XIX." *Iberoamericana. América Latina, España, Portugal: Ensayos sobre letras, historia y sociedad. Notas. Reseñas iberoamericanas*, 1997, vol. 21, No. 67-68, pp. 20-8.

Picó, Fernando. *1898. La guerra después de la guerra*. San Juan: Ediciones Huracán, 2013 (first published in 1987).

Piqueras Arenas, José Antonio. *La revolución democrática (1868-1874). Cuestión social, colonialismo y grupos de presión*. Madrid: Ministerio de Trabajo y Seguridad Social, 1992.

Piqueras Arenas, José Antonio. *Cuba, emporio y colonia. La disputa de un mercado interferido (1878-1895)*. Madrid: Fondo de Cultura Económica de España, 2003.

Piqueras Arenas, José Antonio. *Sociedad civil y poder en Cuba. Colonia y poscolonia*. Madrid: Editorial Siglo XXI, 2005.

Piqueras Arenas, José Antonio. *La esclavitud en las Españas. Un lazo transatlántico*. Madrid: Los Libros de la Catarata, 2012.

Portela Miguélez, María José. *Redes de poder en Cuba en torno al partido Unión Constitucional, 1878-1998*. Cádiz: Servicio de Publicaciones Universidad de Cádiz, 2004.

Portell de Pasamonte, Rafael. "Don Juan Manuel Manzanedo y González, I Duque de Santoña, I Marqués de Manzanedo." *Monte Buciero*, 2004, No. 10, pp. 87-102.

Portell Vilá, Herminio. *Historia de Cárdenas (edición del centenario)*. Havana: Talleres Gráficos "Cuba Intelectual," 1928.

Portell Vilá, Herminio. *Céspedes, el padre de la Patria cubana*. Madrid: Espasa-Calpe, 1931.

Portell Vilá, Herminio. *Narciso López y su época*, 3 vols. Havana: Cultural / Compañía Editora de Libros y Folletos, 1930-1952-1958.

Pozuelo Mascaraque, Belén. "Los Estados Unidos, Alemania y el desmantelamiento colonial español en el Pacífico: el caso de las islas Marianas." *Anales de Historia Contemporánea*, 1998, No. 14, pp. 147-68.

Prieto Benavent, José Luis. "La guerra larga y las consecuencias de la Paz del Zanjón," in Moreno Fraginals, Manuel (coord.). *Cien años de historia de Cuba (1898-1998)*. Madrid: Editorial Verbum, 2000, pp. 11-34.

Puell de la Villa, Fernando. *El soldado desconocido. De la leva a la "mili" (1700-2012)*. Madrid: Biblioteca Nueva, 2012.

Puell de la Villa, Fernando. *Historia del Ejército en España*. Madrid: Alianza Editorial, 2017 (1st ed. 2000).

Quiroz, Alfonso W. "*Integrista* overkill: The Socioeconomic Costs of 'Repressing' the Separatist Insurrection in Cuba, 1868-1878." *Hispanic American Historical Review*, 1998, No. 78, pp. 261-305.

Quiroz, Alfonso W. "Corrupción, burocracia colonial y veteranos separatistas en Cuba, 1868-1910." *Revista de Indias*, 2001, vol. LXI, No. 221, pp. 91-111.

Ramos, Demetrio. "El antillanismo extremista: Betances y los 'velos' que cubrieron la muerte de Cánovas," in Diego García, Emilio de & Ramos, Demetrio (dir.). *Cuba, Puerto Rico y Filipinas en la perspectiva del 98*. Madrid: Editorial Complutense, 1997, pp. 73-110.

Redondo Díaz, Fernando. "La Guerra de los Diez Años (1868–1878)," in *La presencia militar española en Cuba (1868–1895)*. Madrid: Centro de Estudios Superiores de la Defensa, 1996, pp. 33–65.
Reid-Vázquez, Michele. *The Year of the Lash. Free People of Color in Cuba and the Nineteenth-Century Atlantic World*. Athens and London: The University of Georgia Press, 2011.
Remesal, Agustín. *El enigma del Maine. 1898. El suceso que provocó la Guerra de Cuba. ¿Accidente o sabotaje?* Barcelona: Plaza & Janés Editores, 1998.
Rickover, H. G. *How the Battleship* Maine *Was Destroyed*. Washington, DC: Naval History Division/Department of the Navy, 1976.
Roberts, Andrew. *Salisbury. Victorian Titan*. London: Phoenix, 2000 (or ed. Weidenfeld & Nicolson, 1999).
Robles Muñoz, Cristóbal. *Paz en Santo Domingo (1854–1865). El fracaso de la anexión a España*. Madrid: CSIC, 1987.
Rodrigo y Alharilla, Martín. "La 'cuestión Rizal': memoria del gobernador general Despujol (1892)." *Revista de Indias*, 1998, vol. 58, No. 213, pp. 365–84.
Rodrigo y Alharilla, Martín. "Hacendados versus comerciantes. Negocios y práctica política en el integrismo cubano," in Morales Padrón, Francisco (coord.). *III Coloquio de Historia Canario-Americana; VIII Congreso Internacional de Historia de América (AEA), 1998*. Las Palmas de Gran Canaria: Cabildo de Gran Canaria, 2000, pp. 647–63.
Rodrigo y Alharilla, Martín. *Indians a Catalunya: capitals cubans en l'economia catalana*. Barcelona: Fundació Noguera, 2007.
Rodrigo y Alharilla, Martín. "Cataluña y el colonialismo español (1868–1899)," in Cal Giner, Salvador (coord.). *Estado y periferias en la España del siglo XIX. Nuevos enfoquesjustisoe*. Valencia: Universitat de València, 2009, pp. 315–56.
Rodrigo y Alharilla, Martín. "Spanish Merchants and the Slave Trade: From Legality to Illegality, 1814–1870," in Fradera, Josep M. & Schmidt-Nowara, Christopher (eds.). *Slavery and Antislavery in Spain's Atlantic Empire*. New York and Oxford: Berghahn, 2013, pp. 176–99.
Rodrigo y Alharilla, Martín. *Los Goytisolo. Una próspera familia de indianos*. Madrid: Marcial Pons Historia, 2016.
Rodrigo y Alharilla, Martín. "Los marqueses de Comillas, 1817–1925," in Almodóvar Muñoz, Carmen (ed.). *Presencia de Cuba en la historiografía española actual*. Madrid: Ediciones Doce Calles, pp. 141–54.
Rodríguez Aldave, Alfonso. *La política ultramarina de la República del 73*. Havana: Nuestra España, 1940.
Rodríguez González, Agustín R. "La crisis de las Carolinas." *Cuadernos de historia contemporánea*, 1991, No. 13, pp. 25–46.
Rodríguez González, Agustín R. *Tramas ocultas de la Guerra del 98*. Madrid: Editorial Actas, 2016.
Rodríguez Serrano, Casildo. "Adelardo López de Ayala y el Ministerio de Ultramar," in Lorenzana de la Puente, Felipe (coord.). *España, el Atlántico y el Pacífico y otros estudios sobre Extremadura*. Llerena: Sociedad Extremeña de Historia, 2013, pp. 237–50.
Rodríguez, Pedro Pablo. *La primera invasión*. Havana: Editorial de Ciencias Sociales, 2012.
Rolandi Sánchez-Solís, Manuel. "La algarada de Cavite de enero de 1872: El primer intento independentista filipino fracasa en el Fuerte de San Felipe y en el Arsenal de Cavite." *Revista de Historia Militar*, 2008, No. 104, pp. 201–56.

Roldán de Montaud, Inés. *La Unión Constitucional y la política colonial de España en Cuba (1868–1898)*. PhD Thesis 91/296. Madrid: Universidad Complutense de Madrid, 1991.

Roldán de Montaud, Inés. "Política y elecciones en Cuba durante la Restauración." *Revista de Estudios Políticos*, 1999, No. 104, pp. 245–87.

Roldán de Montaud, Inés. *La Restauración en Cuba. El fracaso de un proceso reformista*. Madrid: CSIC, 2000.

Roldán de Montaud, Inés. *La banca de emisión en Cuba (1856–1898). Estudios de Historia Económica*, No. 44. Madrid: Banco de España, 2004.

Romero Salvadó, Francisco J. "Antonio Maura: From Messiah to Fireman," in Quiroga, Alejandro & Del Arco, Miguel Ángel (eds.). *Right-Wing Spain in the Civil War Era: Soldiers of God and Apostles of the Fatherland, 1914–1945*. London: Bloomsbury Publishing, 2012, pp. 1–26.

Rubio, Javier. "Cánovas ante el gran reto antillano," in Diego García, Emilio de et al. *Cánovas y la vertebración de España*. Madrid: Fundación Cánovas del Castillo, 1999, pp. 199–232.

Ruiz de Gordejuela Urquijo, Jesús. "Los Voluntarios de Fernando VII de Ciudad de México. ¿Baluarte de la capital y confianza del reino?" *Revista de Indias*, 2014, vol. LXXIV, No. 262, pp. 751–82.

Sánchez Andrés, Agustín. *El Ministerio de Ultramar. Una institución liberal para el gobierno de las colonias, 1863–1899*. La Laguna: Centro de la Cultura Popular Canaria, 2007.

Sánchez Gómez, Luis Ángel. "Élites indígenas y política colonial en Filipinas (1847–1898)," in Naranjo Orovio, Consuelo, Puig-Samper, Miguel A. & García Mora, Luis Miguel (eds.). *La Nación Soñada: Cuba, Puerto Rico y Filipinas ante el 98*. Aranjuez: Ediciones Doce Calles, 1996, pp. 417–28.

Sánchez Andrés, Agustín. "Entre la espada y la pared. El régimen autonómico cubano, 1897–1898." *Revista Mexicana del Caribe*, 2003, Año/Vol. VIII, No. 16, pp. 7–41.

Sánchez Gómez, Luis Ángel. *Un imperio en la vitrina. El colonialismo español en el Pacífico y la exposición de Filipinas de 1887*. Madrid: CSIC, 2003.

Sánchez-Albornoz, Nicolás. "La emigración española a América en medio milenio: pautas sociales." *Historia Social*, 2002, No. 42, pp. 40–57.

Sanjuan, José Miguel. "El tráfico de esclavos y la élite barcelonesa. Los negocios de la Casa Vidal Ribas," in Chaviano Pérez, Lizbeth J. & Rodrigo y Alharilla, Martín (eds.). *Negreros y esclavos. Barcelona y la esclavitud atlántica (siglos XVI–XIX)*. Barcelona: Icaria, 2017, pp. 131–58.

Sartorius, David. *Ever Faithful. Race, Loyalty, and the Ends of Empire in Spanish Cuba*. Durham and London: Duke University Press, 2013.

Scarano, Francisco A. *Sugar and Slavery in Puerto Rico Plantation Economy of Ponce, 1800–1850*. Madison: University of Wisconsin Press, 1984.

Scarano, Francisco A. *Puerto Rico. Cinco siglos de historia*. Bogotá: McGraw-Hill Interamericana, 1993.

Schmidt-Nowara, Christopher. *Empire, and Antislavery. Spain, Cuba, and Puerto Rico, 1833–1874*. Pittsburgh: University of Pittsburgh Press, 1999.

Schmidt-Nowara, Christopher. "After 'Spain': A Dialogue with Josep M. Fradera on Spanish Colonial Historiography," in Burton, Antoinette (ed.). *After the Imperial Turn. Thinking with and through the Nation*. Durham and London: Duke University Press, 2003, pp. 157–69.

Schmidt-Nowara, Christopher. "Bartolomé de las Casas and the Slave Trade to Cuba circa 1820s," in Brown, Matthew & Paquette, Gabriel (eds.). *Connections after Colonialism*.

Europe and Latin America in the 1820s. Tuscaloosa: The University of Alabama Press, 2013, pp. 236-49.

Schwartz, Rosalie. *Lawless Liberators: Political Banditry and Cuban Independence*. Durham and London: Duke University Press, 1989.

Scott, Rebecca J. *Slave emancipation in Cuba. The Transition to Free Labor, 1860-1899*. Pittsburgh: University of Pittsburgh Press, 2000 (first published in 1985).

Segreo Ricardo, Rigoberto. *Iglesia y nación en Cuba (1868-1898)*. Santiago de Cuba: Editorial Oriente, 2010.

Sequera Martínez, Luis de. "Las trochas militares en las campañas de Cuba (1868-1898)." *Revista de Historia Militar*, 1996, Año XL, No. 81, pp. 107-46.

Serrallonga Urquidi, Joan. "La Guerra de África y el cólera (1859-60)." *Hispania*, 1998, vol. LVIII, No. 198, pp. 233-60.

Serrano, Carlos. *Final del Imperio. España 1895-1898*. Madrid: Siglo XXI de España Editores, 1984.

Serrano, Carlos. "Conciencia de la crisis, conciencias en crisis," in Pan-Montojo, Juan (coord.). *Más se perdió en Cuba. España, 1898 y la crisis de fin de siglo*. Madrid: Alianza Editorial, 1998, pp. 35-403.

Serulle Ramia, José & Boin, Jacqueline. "Evolución económica de la República Dominicana, 1844-1930," in Moya Pons, Frank. *Historia de la República Dominicana*. Madrid: CSIC/Academia Dominicana de la Historia/Ediciones Doce Calles, 2010.

Sevilla López, José Manuel. "Cuba 1873. La captura del 'Virginius'. El incidente Burriel-Lorraine." *Revista de Historia Militar*, 2017, Año LXI, No. 122, pp. 185-247.

Sevilla Soler, Rosario. "'¿Opinión pública' frente a 'opinión publicada'? 1898: la cuestión cubana." *Revista de Indias*, 1998, vol. LVIII, No. 212, pp. 255-76.

Sexton, Jay. *Empire and Nation in Nineteenth-Century America*. New York: Hill and Wang, 2011.

Smith, Rogers M. "The Bitter Roots of Puerto Rican Citizenship," in Burnett, Christina Duffy & Marshall, Burke (eds.). *Foreign in a Domestic Sense. Puerto Rico, American Expansion, and the Constitution*. Durham and London: Duke University Press, 2001, pp. 373-88.

Stucki, Andreas. *Las guerras de Cuba. Violencia y campos de concentración (1868-1898)*. Madrid: La Esfera de los Libros, 2017 *(or. Aufstand un Zwangsumsiedlung. Die Kubanischen Unabhängigkeitskriege (1868-1898)*. Hamburg: Hamburger Edition, 2012).

Termes, Josep. *Anarquismo y sindicalismo en España (1864-1881)*. Barcelona: Crítica, 2000 (first published in 1965).

Thomas, Evan. *The War Lovers. Roosevelt, Loge, Hearst, and the Rush to Empire, 1898*. New York, Boston and London: Little, Brown and Company, 2010.

Thomas, Hugh. *Cuba. La lucha por la libertad*. Barcelona: Debolsillo, 2011 (first published as *Cuba. The Pursuit of Freedom*. London: Pan Macmillan, 1971).

Thompson, E. P. *The Making of the English Working Class*. London: Penguin, 1980 (first published in 1963).

Togores Sánchez, Luis E. "Antecedentes y causas de la revuelta tagala de 1896-1897," in Diego García, Emilio de & Ramos, Demetrio (dir.). *Cuba, Puerto Rico y Filipinas en la perspectiva del 98*. Madrid: Editorial Complutense, 1997, pp. 127-46.

Togores Sánchez, Luis E. "El asedio de Manila (mayo-agosto 1898). 'Diario de los sucesos ocurridos durante la guerra de España con los Estados Unidos, 1898'." *Revista de Indias*, 1998, vol. LVIII, No. 213, pp. 449-98.

Togores Sánchez, Luis E. "La última frontera: el establecimiento de la soberanía española en el país moro," in Elizalde, María Dolores, Fradera, Josep Maria & Alonso, Luis. *Imperios y Naciones en el Pacífico*, vol. II. Madrid: CSIC, 2001, pp. 675–98.

Tone, John Lawrence. *War and Genocide in Cuba, 1895–1898*. Chapel Hill: The University of North Carolina Press, 2006.

Trask, David F. *The War with Spain in 1898*. New York: Macmillan Publishing Co., 1981.

Trías Monge, José. *Puerto Rico. The Trials of the Oldest Colony in the World*. New Haven and London: Yale University Press, 1997.

Tuñón de Lara, Manuel. *Estudios sobre el siglo XIX español*. Madrid: Siglo XXI de España Editores, 1971.

Tuñón de Lara, Manuel. "Nacionalismos y la lucha de clases en la España contemporánea." *Iglesia viva: revista de pensamiento cristiano*, 1981, No. 95–96, pp. 429–46.

Tusell Gómez, Javier. "Maura: una propuesta para la solución del problema de Cuba," in Cervera Pery, José Ramón et al. *La presencia militar española en Cuba (1865–1905)*. Madrid: Ministerio de Defensa / Instituto Español de Estudios Estratégicos, 1995, pp. 111–24.

Uralde Cancio, Marilú. *Voluntarios de Cuba española (1850–1868)*. Havana: Editorial de Ciencias Sociales, 2011.

Velázquez Díaz, Mayela. "El legado social hispano en Guantánamo: el Casino Español," in Azcona Pastor, José Manuel & Escalona Chadez, Israel (dir.). *Cuba y España. Procesos migratorios e impronta perdurable (siglos XIX y XX)*. Madrid: Dykinson, 2014, pp. 144–61.

Vicens Vives, Jaume. *Industrials i Polítics (segle XIX)*. Barcelona: Ediciones Vicens Vives, 1991 (first published in 1958).

Vilar, María José. "Un cartagenero para Ultramar: Miguel Tacón y el modelo autoritario de la transición del Antiguo Régimen al liberalismo en Cuba (1834–1838)." *Anales de Historia Contemporánea*, 2000, No. 16, pp. 239–78.

Villares, Ramón & Moreno Luzón, Javier. *Restauración y dictadura*. Fontana, Josep & Villares, Ramón (Dir.). *Historia de España*, vol. VII. Barcelona and Madrid: Crítica/Marcial Pons, 2009.

Winock, Michel. *Histoire de l'extrême droite en France*. Paris: Seuil, 1994.

Yllán Calderón, Esperanza. "Un proyecto de cesión a Francia de las islas Filipinas (1839)," in Jover Zamora, José María (dir.). *El siglo XIX en España: doce estudios*. Barcelona: Editorial Planeta, 1974, pp. 253–83.

Zozaya Montes, María. "El origen dieciochesco de los casinos españoles y su raíz italiana," in Núñez Roldán, Francisco (ed.). *Ocio y vida cotidiana en el mundo hispánico moderno*. Seville: Universidad de Sevilla, 2007, pp. 617–30.

Index

Abárzuza, Buenaventura 167
Abreu, Tomás 31
Acosta, José Julián 81
Acosta y Albear, Francisco de 61, 71
African War 29–34, 37–9, 41, 136. *See also* Morocco
Agüero, Joaquín de 13
Aguilera, Francisco Vicente 49
Aguinaldo, Emilio 194, 199, 202
Alarcón, Pedro Antonio de 33
Albacete, Salvador 101
Aldama, Miguel de 10, 52
alfonsinos 88, 93–4
Alfonso XIII
    Battalion 182
    Infantry Regiment 151
    ship 158
Alonso, Felipe 60
Alphonse, Prince (Alphonse XII) 26–7, 39, 87–8, 90, 94, 98
Álvarez Chacón, Julio 135
Álvarez de la Campa, Alonso 59–60
Álvarez, Francisco 146, 153
Álvarez Pérez, J. 62
Álvarez, Segundo 135
Amadeus I 70, 77, 82
Amblard, Arturo 173, 177
American Civil War 9, 43, 45, 178
Antilles 44. *See also* Spanish power
    counterrevolution 45–9
    electoral system 110
    end of the Spanish Empire 214
    integristas vs reformists 45
    protectionist policy 23
    Sagasta's policy 169
    Santo Domingo's sovereignty 35–6
    slavery in 7–8, 44
    Spanish Army 17
    suicidal policy 119
    ties with Spain 44–5
    United States' interest in 27, 38
Anyera clan 29

Apezteguía, Julio de 109
Aponte, Cristiano 113
Arango, Augusto 57
Argentina 2, 65, 88, 128
Argüelles, Ramón de 159
Ariza, Juan de 88, 90
Armenteros, José Isidoro 13
Arredondo y Olea, Martín 33
Arrillaga Roqué, Juan 114
Artilleros Voluntarios Distinguidos de Línea 2
Asensio Pérez, Antonio 212
Ateneo de Manila 194
Autonomist Party (Cuba) 109, 118, 170, 173
Autonomist Party (Puerto Rico) 111, 114–15, 169
auxiliary forces 1–3, 37, 78–9, 125, 133, 156, 179, 188, 199
Ayacucho, Battle of 3
Azcárraga Palmero, Marcelo 138

Bacardí, Facundo 19
Báez, Buenaventura 35–6
Bakunin, Mikhail 69
Balaguer, Víctor 65, 117, 192
Balbás Capó, Vicente 185, 208, 213
Baldrich, Gabriel 79, 82–3
Ballesteros, Norberto 65
Barros, Manuel 65
Batallón de Voluntarios Distinguidos del Comercio 3
Batista, Fulgencio 213–14
Batrell Oviedo, Ricardo 153
Becerra, Manuel 116–17
Berber clans 29, 33, 136–7
Betances, Ramón Emeterio 41, 167, 182
Bismarck, Otto von 192
Black *mambí* uprising 213
Blanco, Julián 115
Blanco, Ramón 98–9, 168–73, 176–7, 195–7, 204, 210, 212

Bolívar, Simón 2, 62
Bourbon dynasty 2, 44, 88
Bravo, Juan 212
Bravo, Sixto 210
British Empire 13
    abolition of slavery 8
Bronze Titan. *See* Maceo, Antonio
Buffalo Bill 176
bullfighting 32
Burguete, Ricardo 161

Caballero de Rodas, Antonio 56, 73
Caja de Ahorros 15
Calderón y Pontisi, Ricardo 173
Calhoun, John C. 8
Calleja, Emilio 142, 145–6, 147
Calvo, Manuel 89
Camps y Feliu, Francisco 74
Cañameras y Ferrer, Jaime 128
Candelaria Combat 156–7
Cánovas del Castillo, Antonio 94–6, 98, 119, 147, 151, 155, 157, 167, 169–70
Carbó, Buenaventura 57
Carlist War
    First 10, 17, 50
    Third 98–9, 128, 158–9
Carrera, Santiago 171
Casinos Españoles 56, 65, 88–90, 110
Cassola, Manuel 118
Castañón, Gonzalo 48, 58–60, 62, 64
Castelló Anglada, Melitón 210
Castelví, Guillermo 212
Castillejos, Battle of 31
Catalonia
    economic policy 96
    industrial bourgeoisie unrest 23
    textile industry 87, 92
    Volunteers 18–19, 177
Ceballos, Francisco 56, 69
Celis Aguilera, José 117
Celso Barbosa, José 169
Cepeda, Francisco 111, 114
Cervera Baviera, Julio 188
Cervera, Pascual 179, 186
Céspedes, Carlos Manuel de 31, 49, 58
Ceuta 29–32, 136
Chincha Islands War 30
Círculo de Hacendados 6, 103
círculos hispano-ultramarinos 88, 91–6

Cirujeda, Francisco 163
Civil Guard 13, 22, 50, 72, 79, 84, 98, 112–13, 126, 141, 172, 183–4, 195, 200
Cleveland, Grover 166
Club de La Habana 10–11
Cochinchina Campaign 30
Cody, William F. *See* Buffalo Bill
Colomé, Juan Atilano 54
Coloured Disciplined Militias 77
Compañía de Patriotas Voluntarios Distinguidos del Sr. D. Fernando VII 3
Compañía Trasatlántica Española 92
Compromise of 1850 9, 16
Conservative Party 95, 117, 172
constitucionales 170
Corujo, José Ignacio 80
Council of Sequestered Goods (*Consejo de Bienes Embargados*) 54
creoles
    conspiracy against Spain 41
    Disciplined Militias 79
    exclusion from military 12
    liberal regime's distrust 5–7
    military defense of Cuba 23–4
    new reality, after the war 208
    peninsulares 2
    situation of Volunteers after war 208, 211
    social promotion 2–3
    Villanueva Theatre 52
    Volunteers 17, 32
Crombet, Francisco Adolfo "Flor" 147
Crown of Castile 1, 7
Cuba. *See also* Havana
    absence of party politics 31
    against annexation 15–22
    Autonomist Party 109
    Black *mambí* uprising 213
    Café del Louvre 52, 60
    campana de la tea, or torch campaign 155
    civil war 73–6, 209
    Conservative National Committee 72
    Constitutional Union Party 108–9, 116, 118, 120, 131, 159, 169–72
    Council of Sequestered Goods 75
    Cuba Española 171

decree of January 12, 1869 54
defensive system 22
1895 war 144–7
elite autonomy 3–7, 52, 55
end of Spanish sovereignty 205–6
Grito de Yara 44, 82
integristas 45, 49
international dimension 22–3
lack of banking system 6
La Escepción 48
La Voz de Cuba 49–50
legal member of the Spanish Nation 7
Liberal Party 108–9
Milicias Disciplinadas
 (Disciplined Militias) 1
nationalists 209
Noble Neighbors 11–14
peninsulares 100, 102, 104–5
political restructuring 107–21
pro-independence movement 108
reaction against annexation 15–22
reconstruction 97–105
revolutionary government 49–61, 203
slave revolt in 1843–4 8
slave trade 6, 8
social hierarchy of whites 18–19
Spanish Antillean politics 3–4
sugar aristocracy 4–6
Ten Years' War 73, 95, 109, 115, 118, 120, 123, 128, 137–8, 144–5, 147, 151–2, 157–9
three wars for independence 204
US interest in 4, 7, 22
Volunteers 22–8, 40, 47–9, 207–8
war in 44, 46, 63, 95, 144–7, 166, 168, 206
working-class *peninsulares* 46
Cuban Revolutionary Party 139, 144, 182

Dabán, Antonio 182–4
Dabán, Luis 125–6
Despujols, Eulogio 124
Diario de la Marina 15, 47
Díaz, Policarpo 114
Díaz Quintero, Francisco 63–4
Díez, Vicente 212
Disciplined Militias 1–3, 13, 24, 50, 77, 79–81, 214

Domínguez, Julio A. 212
Dominic Order 194
Duarte, Juan Pablo 34
Dulce, Domingo 38–9, 51, 52–3, 55–7, 81, 83, 89, 130, 172, 195
Dupuy de Lôme, Enrique 166

Echagüe, Rafael de 30
Echevarría, Policarpo 112
Ejército Libertador 153, 160–1, 163, 170–1, 180, 204
Elcano, Juan Sebastián de 191
El Correo Español 64–5
Elices Montes, Ramón 136
El Monje 175
Enrile y Hernán, Joaquín 79, 83
Escario García, Federico 178, 181
Espartero, Baldomero 22
Esquembre, Francisco 63
Estévanez, Nicolás 30
Estévez y Romero, Luis de 117
Europe 31, 69, 108, 165, 167
 parliamentary system 108
 use of armed civilians 1

Fabié, Antonio María 133
Fanelli, Giuseppe 69
Fashoda Incident 143
Feast of Corpus Christi 167
Ferdinand VII 3, 15, 62
Feria, Augusto 171
Fernández, José Ramón 40–1, 81–2, 109
Fernandina, Count of 12
Fernando Poo 54
Ferrer de Couto, José 73
Ferrer Torralba, Cástulo 101
Ferrer y Robert, Antonio 67–8, 101
Figuerola, Laureano 87, 92
First World War 214
Fontán, Ventura 181
Fournier, Enrique 209
Franco-Prussian War 125
French Army of Napoleon 152
French invasion of 1808 23

Galán, Lino 162–3
Galarza, Vicente 109
Gándara y Navarro, José de la 38
García, Calixto 50, 97, 165, 170, 179, 181

García de Paredes, José 113
García de Polavieja, Camilo 99–101, 103–5, 131, 137–8, 142, 197–8
García, Manuel 139–40
García Oña, Ricardo 72
Gener Batet, José 48, 59–60, 63
German U-boats 213
Gibert, José 69
Ginovés del Espinar, Felipe 55–6
Gómez, Máximo 75, 78, 97, 144–5, 147–8, 150, 160, 163–4, 170, 176
Gómez Núñez, Severo 180
Gómez Pulido, Ramón 79, 83
Gómez, Victoriano 171
González-Abreu, Pedro Nolasco 18
González Bobés, Eduardo 132
González Carvajal, Leopoldo 131
González Estéfani, Joaquín 55
González Parrado, Julián 168
Grave de Peralta, Julio 74, 75
guajiros 140, 150, 159–60, 162
Güell y Ferrer, Juan 92
Guerrilla del Casino Español 178, 196, 201
Guerrilla de San Rafael 196, 201
guerrilleros 162–3, 209
Guerrita de los Independientes de Color 213
Guinea, Gulf of 12, 54, 123
Gutiérrez de la Concha, José 4, 13–17, 20–4, 27, 140

Habsburgs 1, 29
Haiti's independence in 1804 35
Havana
    Casino Español 55, 88–90, 93, 192
    Cigar Selector's Protection Society 68
    electoral census 110
    habaneros 175
    laborante 174
    Labor Movement 67–71
    press freedom 172
    public order 53
    Shopkeepers Union (*Centro de Dependientes*) 67
    social and labor situation 68, 129–30, 146
    Tercios de Voluntarios y Bomberos Movilizados 164
    Tobacco Central Guild (*Gremio Central de Tabaco de La Habana*) 68

violence 52–61, 108
Volunteers 57, 61, 65–6, 76, 81, 118, 130–4, 148–9, 151–3, 159, 173–5, 177–81, 204–5, 212
Hearst, William Randolph 165
Hernández, Isidoro 62
Hernández, José del Carmen 171
Hernández y Mancebo, José Joaquín 207
Hostos, Eugenio María de 182
Humara, Remigio 156

Ibáñez, Francisco F. 72, 102–3
Indian Wars 178
Inspección de Montes 104
integristas
    and *alfonsinos* 94
    armed wing 45, 51
    casinos 56, 89
    Círculo de Hacendados 6
    clash with Cubans 52
    creation of militia 11–13
    in Cuba 45, 49, 63, 66, 71, 76–7, 79, 90–1, 93–6, 130–1, 145, 158, 169–71, 173–5, 177
    murder of Castañón 59, 61
    in Philippines 197
    position 5
    preference on captain general's power 7
    in Pureto Rico 45–6, 81–5, 110–12, 114–15, 125
    slave trade 14
    supporting Spanish 5–7, 11–13, 104, 107, 109–10, 212
    tense atmosphere 52–5
    voting rights 116–20
    working class 129
International Workingmen's Association (IWA) 69
Invading Army (*Ejército Invasor*) 155–6
Invasion of the West (*Invasión a Occidente*) 154–5
Isabella II 30, 43, 88
Izquierdo Villavicencio, Manuel 12

jíbaros 185
Jiménez Castellanos, Adolfo 205
Jovellar, Joaquín 77
Juliá Palmeta, Francisco 80

Junta Cubana 10
Junta de Defensa 177–8
Juntas de Socorro 104

Kansas-Nebraska Act of 1854 16
Katipunan 194–5

Labra, Rafael María de 117–18
Lachambre, José 145
La Escalera conspiracy 13
La Gloriosa (The Glorious revolution). *See* September 1868 revolution
Larrea y Lisa, Francisco 188
Larrínaga, Jacinto 12
Las Glorias del Voluntario 62
Laws of the Indies or *Leyes de Indias* 7
Lawton, Henry Ware 181
Lee, John Fitzhugh 171, 174
León, Saturnino 171
Lersundi, Francisco 50–1, 71
Liberal Party 82, 108–9, 111, 115, 117, 119, 145, 169
Liberal Union
　cabinet of 1860 43
　series of reforms 43–4
Liceo Artístico y Literario 15
Little War 100–1, 127, 168
Lodge, Henry Cabot 166
López, Antonio 92, 192
López de Ayala, Adelardo 45, 53, 87, 94
López de Ayala, Ramón 60
López del Campo, Aurelio 76
López de Legazpi, Miguel 191
López, Narciso 10–13, 16–17, 22
López Roberts, Dionisio 54
Lostau, Baldomero 93
Loynaz del Castillo, Enrique 155

Maceo, Antonio 97–8, 139, 144–5, 147–8, 150, 154–6, 161
Machicote, Juan Bautista 82, 93
Maciá y Doménech, Narciso 164, 205, 208
Maeztu, Ramiro de 129
Magellan, Ferdinand 191
Mahan, Alfred T. 166
Malo Parra, Juan 212
Mal Tiempo, Battle of 149
mambí army 63, 75, 148–50, 153–6, 162, 164, 169–71, 174, 179–80

Mangual, Cleto 113
Manifest Destiny 166
Manifesto of Montecristi 144
Manila 1, 30, 33, 144
　Volunteers 191–8, 200–3
Manzanedo, Marquis of 92
Margallo's War 137, 152
Maria Christina of the Two Sicilies (Queen Regent) 147, 151, 168, 171
Marín, Sabas 130, 140, 184
Martí, José 58, 139, 144–5, 147–8, 150
Martínez de Campos, Arsenio 94, 97–8, 137, 147–9, 151–5, 157–8, 212
Martínez Illescas, Rafael 187
Martínez, Jacinto María (bishop of Havana) 12, 51, 57
Martínez Nubla, Elías 212
Martínez Plowes, Juan 79, 84
Martínez, Saturnino 68
Maseda, Enrique 149
Masó, Bartolomé 146
Mason, Roberto 181
Masó Parra, Juan 171, 212
Mateo, Juan 212
Mattei Lluveras, Antonio 184
Maura, Antonio 119–21, 145
Maza, Cayetano de La 146
McKinley, William 166–7, 176, 185
Melilla 29, 32, 136–7, 147, 152
Méndez Benegasi, Francisco 71
Méndez Capote, Domingo 171
Méndez Rey, Eustasio 142
Menéndez Acebal, Alejandro 134
Merchán, Rafael María 50
Merritt, Wesley 201
mesnadas 1
Messina, Félix María de 40, 42
Mexico 9, 16, 22, 30, 32, 88
Mexico City 3, 11, 56
Meza, Juan de 104
Midley, S. D. 181
Miles, Nelson A. 186–7
Milicias de Color (Coloured Militias) 13
Milicias Honradas (Honorable Militias) 2
Milicia Voluntaria de Nobles Vecinos (Volunteer Militia of Noble Neighbors) 12
Miró Argenter, José 156
Moderate Party 14, 39, 43, 87

Moncada, Guillermón 145
Monroe Doctrine 10, 38
Moors 1, 30
Morales, José María 18
Moré, José Eugenio 18–19, 102, 109, 118, 131
Moreno Bueso, José 178, 196
Moreno, Carlos 178
Moreno, Francisco 130–1
Moreno Solano, Fernando C. 66
Moret Law 91
Moret, Segismundo 91
Morocco 29–33, 37–40, 43, 49, 99
   economic compensation and trade rights to Spain 32
   military campaigns 123, 128, 136–7
   volunteers 30–4
Muhammad V, Sultan 32
Munné, José 96

Nápoles Fajardo, Antonio José 75
National League (*Liga Nacional*) 93–4
National Production Promotion (*Fomento de la Producción Nacional*) 92
Nebraska-Kansas Act (1854) 9, 16
New Spain 1, 3–4, 192
Noble Neighbors 11–14

O'Donnell, Leopoldo 11, 22–4, 29–30, 32
O'Higgins, Bernardo 2
Olano y Caballero, José 56
Olavarrieta, Ventura 64
Olney, Richard 166
Opportunist Party 208
Oriente
   Autonomist Party 118
   Compañía Voluntarios Veteranos Reserva de Holguín 70
   garrisons 71
   rebel army 50, 74, 78–9, 97, 99–100, 154
   sugar mills 102
   Volunteers 72, 103, 117
   war 53, 57, 131, 140, 144, 147–51, 165, 170, 177–80
Ortega, Ricardo 2–3, 203
Ostend Manifesto 16
Otero y Pimentel, Luis 66, 170
Ottomans 22
Our Lady of El Cobre 27

Padial y Vizcarrondo, Luis 41–2
Palacios y González, Romualdo 110–11, 113–14
Palomino, Joaquín de 63
Pando, Luis Manuel 74, 118, 168, 177
Panic of 1866 43
Partido de los Independientes de Color 213
Peace Tree (*Árbol de la Paz*) 181
Peláez, Antonio 55
peninsulares
   anarchist ideals 129–33
   in Cuba 17–20, 24–5, 32, 46–51, 53, 60, 62, 65, 67–9, 73–5, 77, 80, 91, 95, 100–2, 174, 206–9, 211
   Cuban domination 6, 24
   discontented youth 151–2
   elite's role (Cuba) 3
   immigration 105
   Los Mojados was planning to kill 112
   Los Secos to kill 113
   Military Service Law of 1885 127–9
   in Philippines 196–8, 207–11
   position in Spanish monarchy 2
   in Puerto Rico 40–2, 80–1, 84, 183–5, 188–9, 207–11
   representation in New Spain 3
   role in Spanish Empire 2–7, 12, 87, 104
Pérez, Higinio 209
Pérez Morís, José 82
Peru 3, 30, 32
Pezuela, Juan de la 14
Philip II 191
Philip IV 29
Philip V 1
Philippines. *See also* Manila
   Casino Español 195–7
   Christianization 191, 194–5
   dissolution of the Volunteers 203
   end of Spanish sovereignty 205–6
   ethnicities 193
   geographical position 192
   Grito de Balintawak 191
   Ilustrados 193–4
   Liga Filipina 194
   Macabebes 203, 210
   nationalism 193–4
   Philippine-American War 210
   rebel commanders 199
   revolutionary government 203

uprisings 196–7, 200
Volunteers in 191–203, 208
Pieltain, Cándido 70
Pierce, Franklin 16
Pinar del Río Battalion 13
Pintó, Ramón 15, 20
  affair 22–3
Plan de La Fernandina 145
Polk, James K. 10
Porset, Adolfo 172
Pozos Dulces, Count of 54
Prim, Juan 30–1, 43–4, 51, 57–8, 89–90
Primo de Rivera, Fernando 198–200
Primo de Rivera y Sobremonte, Rafael 79, 85
Progressive Biennium (1854–6) 43
Provincial Militias 1–2
Puerto Príncipe Volunteers 12–13, 27, 57–8, 71, 76–7, 99, 102–3, 107, 131, 141, 160, 210
Puerto Rico. *See also* San Juan
  abolition of slavery 83
  Americanization of 214
  Autonomist Party 110–15
  Betances and Belvis manifesto 41
  Conservative Party 82, 108
  Disciplined Militias 80–1
  end of Spanish sovereignty 205–6
  Grito de Lares 44, 79
  integristas 45–6
  jíbaros uprising 41
  legal member of the Spanish Nation 7
  Liberal Party 82, 111
  libreta 80
  National Guard of the United States 214
  Paris negotiation 203
  peninsulares 40–2
  political restructuring 107–21
  Provincial Council (*Diputación Provincial*) 82
  Reformist Liberal Party 108
  Santo Domingo war 40
  Spanish-American war 209
  US military occupation 143, 182–9, 208, 214
  Volunteers in 40–2, 79–85, 117, 127, 187–8, 207–8, 212
  war in 182–9
  wave of reprisals 209

Puig y Pí, Pedro 80, 187
Pulido, Mamerto 54
Pulitzer, Joseph 165
Pyrenees War 34

Quesada, Feliciano 171
Quitman, John A. 16

Ramos Izquierdo, Luis 212
Ramos Izquierdo, Manuel 18
Rebellion Cantonal 77
reglamento 24–5, 53, 81, 85, 104, 125–6, 137–8, 141, 150, 199
Retana, Wenceslao Emilio 197
Revista de Puerto Rico 114
Ribero Lemoyne, Felipe 37
Ribó Palandaries, José Joaquín 65
Riego, Rafael de 62
Rigal, Segundo 54
Rivero Méndez, Ángel 185, 187–8
Rizal, José 194, 197
  El filibusterismo 194
  execution 198
  Noli me tangere 194
Rodríguez Arias, Alejandro 105, 141
Rodríguez, Gerónimo 141
Rodríguez y Pérez, Pascual 59
Rojas Paúl, Juan Pablo 184
Roloff, Carlos 161
Romero, Jiménez, Enrique 64–5
Roncali, Federico 11–12
Roosevelt, Theodore 166, 176
Rosado y Brincau, Rafael 125
Ros de Olano, Antonio 30
Rubiales, Luis 71
Ruiz Belvis, Segundo 41
Ruiz y López, Francisco Matías 64
Ruiz Zorrilla, Manuel 94

Sagasta, Práxedes Mateo 110, 119, 131, 168
Sainz, Rufino 88
Saladrigas, Carlos 109
Salamanca y Negrete, Manuel 105, 131, 139
Salmerón y Alonso, Francisco 64
Samá, Salvador 18
Sampson, William T. 179, 185–6
San Esteban de Cañongo, Count of 12, 18

San Juan 30, 40–1, 100, 112
  British attack 80
  Casino Español 90, 93
  Volunteers 82–3, 124–6, 17, 183–8
San Martín, José de 2
Sans, Jaume 180
Santana, Pedro 35–6
Santiago de Cuba, Battle of 201
Santiago, Florencio 187
Santo Domingo 98–9, 123, 128
  Dominican ruling class 35–6
  Hispaniola war 38
  reasons for war in 1861 34
  Restoration War 34–40, 99, 158
  Spanish power 34–40
  Volunteer Battalion 40
Sanz, José Laureano 79, 81, 92
Sartorius brothers 145
Second World War 213
September 1868 revolution 43, 47–8, 65–6, 77, 85
  integrismo 47
  unstable regime 44
  Volunteers 46–7
Serrano, Francisco 36, 38, 44, 94
Seven Years' War 1, 13
Sexenio Democrático 44
Sexenio Revolucionario 44, 87
Shafter, William R. 179–81
Sitges 19, 68, 101, 140
Sociedad de Socorros Mutuos de Cocheros Blancos (insurance company) 132
Soler y Morell, Juan Antonio 204–5
Soler y Pla, Santiago 90
Sorní y Grau, José Cristóbal 84
Soto Villanueva, Julio 183–4
Spanish Abolitionist Society 81, 114
Spanish Independence war (1808–14) 2, 7
Spanish power
  anticolonial wars 143
  Bailén victory 2
  bankruptcy 23
  decline in Europe 1
  Disaster of 1898 143
  end of sovereignty 208–9, 214
  French invasion 2
  labor violent strikes against 23
  liberal regime 5–7
  military institution 1

peninsulares, role 2–7, 12
political tradition. 7
proclamation of the Republic 77
revolutionary crisis 43–5
slave trade 5, 9
U.S. military action 172–6, 180–1, 185, 199–200, 203, 209, 211–12
voting rights 109
war against the Moors 30
Spanish textile industry 43
Spanish Unconditional Party 112–14, 117, 124, 126, 183, 187, 213
Suárez Vigil, Miguel 63

Tacón, Miguel 3, 6–7, 24
Tacón Theatre 17, 32
Tamayo, Esteban 146
Tellería, Antonio C. 88
Tirailleurs Volunteers Battalion 208
Toral, José 177, 179–81, 200, 202
Toraya, Juan 88
Torres-Pardo, Rafael 93
Torre y Ormaza, Simón de la 79
Torriente, Cosme de la 31
Trafalgar, Battle of 25
Treaty of Peace 206
Triay, José E. 61–2
Trocadero, Battle of 15
Trusteeship Law (*Ley del Patronato*) 96

Ubarri, Pablo 109, 124–5, 136
United States
  Bleeding Kansas 9
  Cuban annexation 8–11
  war against Spain 172–6, 180–1, 185, 199–200, 203, 209, 211–12
  against Weyler 165–82
Urquía, Juan de 212
USS *Maine* 175–6

Vandama y Calderón, Eugenio 118, 134–5, 138
Vara de Rey, Joaquín 178
Velázquez de Cuéllar, Diego 181
Venezuela 2, 6, 9–10, 62, 184
Vila, Baudilio 39
Villate, Blas 56, 59, 65, 89
Vizcarrondo, Julio 81, 114
Vizcaya (cruiser) 175

Voluntarios Distinguidos Ligeros de Cazadores 2
Voluntarios Macheteros 185
Voluntarios Tiradores 2
Volunteers. *See also specific entries*
　after the war 207–14
　Black 33
　Chapelgorris del Cerro 129
　in the *Consejo* 54
　Constancy Medal (*Medalla a la Constancia*) 124
　disappearance 207–8
　dismantling 203–6
　fight against banditry 138–42
　forcible mobilization 76–9
　insurrection 149–58
　Integridad Nacional 46
　Labor Movement and 67–70
　last years 143–4
　military concept 123–9, 213
　Military Service Law of 1885 127–9
　mobilization 70–3, 76–9, 147–9
　Morocco 30–4
　national integrity 107–21
　politically charged background 214
　in Puerto Rico 40–2, 79–85, 124–5
　reform projects 133–7
　reglamento 53, 137–8
　as Royal Decree November 7, 1878 123
　Santo Domingo 35–40
　social unrest 129–33
　spectacular growth 30–1
　war propaganda 61–6
　working class 48–9, 52, 67, 69–70, 130, 132

Wad Ras, Battle of 32, 162
Weyler y Nicolau, Valeriano 154, 157–60, 162–5, 168, 170, 172
　reconcentración 160–2
Wheeler, Joseph 181
Woodford, Stewart L. 167
Wood, Leonard 205
World War I. *See* First World War
World War II. *See* Second World war

yanquis 176, 178, 182

Zanjón Pact (*Pacto del Zanjón*) 95, 97, 102, 123, 127, 140
Zenea, Juan Clemente 57–8
Zulueta y Amondo, Julián 3, 6, 26, 47, 51, 89

Plate 1 Havana Volunteers. *La Ilustración de Madrid*, May 27, 1870, p. 8.

Plate 2 Havana Volunteers. *La Ilustración de Madrid*, May 27, 1870, p. 9.

EXMO. SR D. JULIAN ZULUETA,

Coronel del 2º Batallon de Voluntarios de la Habana.

Plate 3 Julián de Zulueta, one of Cuba's biggest landowners and slaveholders, as colonel of the 2nd Volunteer Battalion of Havana. José Joaquín Ribó, *Historia de los Voluntarios Cubanos*, vol. I, 1872, p. 622.

El Sr. D. José Gener, Capitan de la 6.ª Comp.ª del 6.º Batallon de Voluntarios de la Habana.

Plate 4 Captain José Gener Batet, owner of the cigar brand "La Escepción", one of the responsibles of the murder of the eight medicine students on November 27, 1871. El Moro Muza, July 31, 1870, p. 1.

Plate 5 Castillo de la Real Fuerza, in Havana, former seat of Cuba's Volunteer Subinspector General's Office. Taken by the author in 2015.

Plate 6 Monument to the eight medicine students murdered on November 27, 1871, Havana, unveiled in 1890. Taken by the author in 2015.

Plate 7 Officers of the 3rd Company, 1st Volunteer Battalion of Cárdenas (Matanzas), 1895. National Library of Spain, Sig. 17-174-62.

Plate 8 Cuban Volunteers who fought on April 23, 1896 against a party of 400 rebels in Socarrás. Published by the magazine La Caricatura, Havana, on July 9, 1896. Spain, Ministry of Defence, AGMM, Iconography, Sig. F-05939.

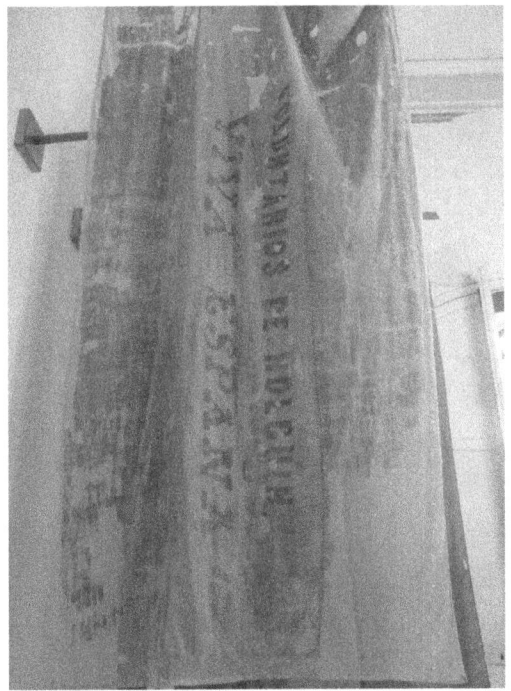

Plate 9 Patriotic Flag of the Volunteers Battalion of Holguín (Oriente). Museum of the City. Palace of the Captains Generals, Havana. Taken by the author in 2015.

Plate 10 Volunteers of Dimas changing the guard at the Tejar Fort. Published by *La Caricatura*, Havana, on July 30, 1896. Signed by José Gómez de la Carrera on July 18, 1896. Spain, Ministry of Defence, AGMM, Iconography, Sig. F-05953.

Plate 11 Staff of the Volunteer Battalion of Puerto Rico No. 1. Ángel Rivero Méndez, *Crónica de la Guerra Hispanoamericana en Puerto Rico*, 1922, p. 449.

Plate 12 3rd Company, Loyal Volunteers' Battalion of Manila, taken by G. Sternberg, 1896. Spain, Ministry of Defence, AGMM, Iconography, Sig. F-09200.

Plate 13 Officers of the Loyal Volunteers' Battalion of Manila taken by G. Sternberg, 1896. Spain, Ministry of Defence, AGMM, Iconography, Sig. F-09196.

Plate 14 A Group of Macabebe Volunteers arriving to the port of Barcelona aboard the steamship *Alicante* on June 8, 1900. *La Ilustración Artística*, June 18, 1900, p. 402.

www.ingramcontent.com/pod-product-compliance
Lightning Source LLC
Chambersburg PA
CBHW062130300426
44115CB00012BA/1868